MICROECONOMICS

MICROECONOMICS

Avi J. Cohen
York University
University of Toronto

Pearson Canada Inc., 26 Prince Andrew Place, North York, Ontario M3C 2H4.

9780134821283

1   18

Library and Archives Canada Cataloguing in Publication

Cohen, Avi J., author

    Microeconomics / Avi J. Cohen (York University, University of Toronto).

ISBN 978-0-13-482128-3 (spiral bound)

    1. Microeconomics—Textbooks. 2. Textbooks. I. Title.

HB172.C57 2018   338.5   C2018-901509-8

Contents

Pearson FlexText

Essential Employability Skills

Top skills employers seek:

Success in any sector is dependent upon more than core academic knowledge or technical and occupational skills. Employers need critical thinkers, problem solvers, and leaders to tackle the challenges of today's workplace. Employees with successful career paths learn to communicate effectively, engage appropriately with others, and be self-reliant. Effective career readiness and employability strategies develop the whole learner and incorporate personal and social capabilities; critical thinking and problem-solving skills; and academic and occupational knowledge.

That is what Pearson FlexText is all about.

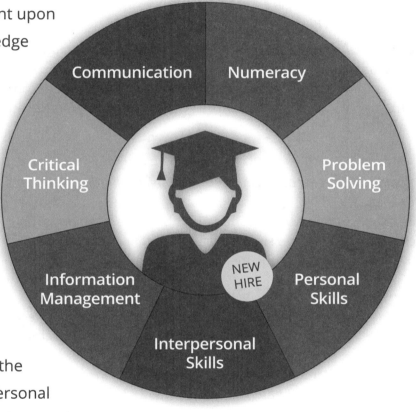

Pearson FlexText helps bridge the skills gap and helps students and instructors make the most of valuable face-to-face class time.

We created this resource to help students achieve academic success while also developing the key skills that hiring managers value in candidates.

Communication Skills

Defining skill areas: reading, writing, speaking, listening, presenting, and visual literacy

Students may not be developing their reading skills because they do not have access to course materials – either by choice or by circumstance. FlexTexts are affordable and accessible. FlexTexts include learning objectives and chapter summaries in combination with concise discussions of key topics to support reading comprehension, and provide individual and group activities that afford students the opportunity to practice their writing and communication skills.

Numeracy Skills

Defining skill areas: understanding and applying mathematical concepts and reasoning, analyzing and using mathematical data, and conceptualizing

This FlexText is designed to be an in-class activity workbook, one that allows faculty to provide instructional support to students as they apply mathematical and statistical analysis across a range of activities.

Critical Thinking & Problem-Solving Skills

Defining skill areas: analyzing, synthesizing, evaluating, decision making, creativity, and innovative thinking

The exercises and activities found in this FlexText are not simply factual, recall, or "skill and drill" activities. They engage students at different levels of Bloom's Taxonomy to help students develop critical thinking and problem-solving skills.

Information Management Skills

Defining skill areas: gathering and managing information, selecting and using appropriate tools and technology for a task or project, computer literacy, and internet skills

Not all of the exercises in a FlexText are pen-and-paper activities. Many require students to engage with online information and assets to help them investigate how to analyze and solve an array of problems and challenges.

Interpersonal Skills

Defining skill areas: teamwork, relationship management, conflict resolution, leadership, and networking

FlexText is designed to be brought into class. It can help to facilitate group work and collaborative problem solving, and activities can be implemented in ways that help students to develop their interpersonal skills.

Personal Skills

Defining skill areas: managing self, managing change, being flexible and adaptable, engaging in reflexive practice, and demonstrating personal responsibility

Making the decision to purchase course materials and actively engage with course content is one of the first steps toward demonstrating personal responsibility for success in school. The page layout of a FlexText also encourages note taking and promotes the development of strong study skills.

1 Scarcity, Opportunity Cost, Trade, and Models

LEARNING OBJECTIVES

L01 Explain scarcity and describe why you must make smart choices among your wants.

L02 Define and describe opportunity cost, the most important concept in economics.

L03 Describe how comparative advantage, specialization, and trade make us all better off.

L04 Explain how models like the circular flow model make smart choices easier.

L05 Differentiate microeconomic and macroeconomic choices, and explain the Three Keys model for smart choices.

LEARN...

What do you want out of life? Riches? Love? Adventure? To make the world a better place? Happiness? Children? A long and healthy life? All of the above?

Many people believe economics is just about money and business, but economics can help you get what you want out of life. The Nobel Prize–winning author George Bernard Shaw said "Economy is the art of making the most of life." Economics is about getting the most for your money, but it is also about making smart choices generally. If you learn a little economics, it will help you make the most of your life, whatever you are after. That knowledge will help you better understand the world around you and the choices you face as a citizen.

You don't need to be trained as an economist to lead a productive and satisfying life. But if you can learn *to think like an economist*, you can get more out of whatever life you choose to lead, and the world will be better for it.

This chapter introduces the most important economic concepts — scarcity, opportunity cost, and comparative advantage. Because of scarcity, choices involve a trade-off, leading to the concept of opportunity cost — the single most important concept in all of economics. Incentives are also crucial for understanding choices. Opportunity cost and comparative advantage are key to understanding why specialization and voluntary trade make us all better off. The most basic choice is producing for yourself or specializing, trading in markets, and depending on others. We will use a simple example to explain the argument behind all cases for freer trade.

Thinking like an economist means building models. Your first model, the circular flow model, reduces the complexity of the economy to three sets of players — households, businesses, and governments — who interact in markets. Models are the mental equivalent of controlled experiments in a laboratory. The positive/normative distinction is also part of thinking like an economist, as is the difference between microeconomics and macroeconomics.

Scarcity and Choice

 L01 Explain scarcity and describe why you must make smart choices among your wants.

Can you afford to buy everything you want? If not, every dollar you spend involves a choice. If you buy the Nintendo Switch, you might not be able to afford your English textbook. If you treat your friends to a movie, you might have to work an extra shift at your job or give up your weekend camping trip.

It would be great to have enough money to buy everything you want, but it would not eliminate the need to make smart choices. Imagine winning the biggest lottery in the world. You can buy whatever you want for yourself, your family, and your friends. But you still have only 80-some years on this planet (if you are lucky and healthy), only 24 hours in a day, and a limited amount of energy. Do you want to spend the week boarding in Whistler or surfing in Australia? Do you want to spend time raising your kids or exploring the world? Will you go to that third party on New Year's Eve or give in to sleep? Do you want to spend money on yourself, or set up a charitable foundation to help others? Bill Gates, one of the richest people on Earth, has chosen to set up the Bill and Melinda Gates Foundation. With billions of dollars in assets, the Foundation still receives more requests for worthy causes than it has dollars. How does it choose which requests to fund?

Economists call this inability to satisfy all of our wants the problem of **scarcity**. Scarcity arises from our limited money, time, and energy. All mortals, even billionaires, face the problem of scarcity. We all have to make choices about what we will get and what we will give up. Businesses with limited capital must choose between spending more on research or on marketing. Governments must make similar choices in facing the problem of scarcity. Spending more on colleges and universities leaves less to spend on health care. Or if governments try to spend more on all social programs, the higher taxes to pay for them mean less take-home pay for all of us.

Because none of us — individuals, businesses, governments — can ever satisfy all of our wants, smart choices are essential to making the most of our lives. **Economics** is about how individuals, businesses, and governments make the best possible choices to get what they want, and how those choices interact in markets.

 # Practice...

1. Which statement about scarcity is *true*?

   a. Scarcity is only a problem for underdeveloped countries.

   b. Scarcity is only a problem for idealistic people.

   c. Every person faces scarcity.

   d. All of the above are true.

2. The problem of scarcity

   a. would disappear if we did not have to make choices.

   b. arises because of limited money, time, and energy.

   c. arises because limited human expectations cannot be satisfied with available knowledge.

   d. arises because of limited money, time, and memory.

 # Practice...

3. You can't get everything you want because you are limited by
   a. time.
   b. money.
   c. energy.
   d. all of the above. *(circled)*

4. The main implication of scarcity in economics is that people must
   a. make choices. *(circled)*
   b. be selfish.
   c. be unhappy.
   d. like money.

5. The problem of scarcity exists
   a. only when people are unemployed.
   b. only in economies with incentives.
   c. only in economies without incentives.
   d. in all economies. *(circled)*

Apply...

1. Olga chooses to live at home rather than move into residence during her first year of college.
   She often brags about the fact that she saves a lot of money by living at home.
   Provide some examples of what Olga may have given up by choosing to live at home.

   university experiences on Residence, learning about idependence, time because of transit

2. Social activists argue that materialism is one of the biggest problems with society: If we all wanted less, instead of always wanting more, there would be plenty to go around for everyone. Do you agree with this statement? Why or why not?

Opportunity Cost

L02 Define and describe opportunity cost, the most important concept in economics.

Scarcity means you must choose. If you want the most out of what limited money and time you have, you need to make smart choices. A choice is a fork in the road. You have to compare the alternatives — where does each path take you — and then pick one. You make a smart choice by weighing benefits and costs.

Choices Are Trade-Offs

What are you going to do with the next hour? Since you are reading this, you are considering studying as one choice. If you were out far too late last night, or up taking care of a crying baby, sleep might be your alternative choice. If those are your top choices, let's compare benefits of the two paths from this fork. For studying, the benefits are higher marks on your next test, learning something, and perhaps enjoying reading this chapter. For sleep, the benefits are being more alert, more productive, less grumpy, and perhaps avoiding the pain of reading this chapter.

If you choose the studying path, what is the cost of your decision? It is the hour of sleep you give up (with the benefits of rest). And if you choose sleep, the cost is the studying you give up (leading to lower marks).

- A choice is a trade-off — you give up one thing to get something else.

- The **opportunity cost** of any choice is the cost of the best alternative given up.

- Opportunity cost is the most important concept for making smart choices.

Opportunity Cost Beats Money Cost

Opportunity cost is more important than money cost. Suppose you win a free trip to Bermuda that has to be taken the first week in December. What is the money cost of the trip? Zero — it's free. But imagine you have a business client who can meet to sign a million-dollar contract only during the first week in December. What is the opportunity cost of your "free" trip to Bermuda? $1 million. A smart decision to take or not take the trip depends on opportunity cost, not money cost.

All choices are forks in the road, and the cost of any path taken is the value of the best path you must give up. Because of scarcity, every choice involves a trade-off — to get something, you must give up something else. To make a smart choice, the value of what you get must be greater than the value of what you give up. The benefits of a smart choice must outweigh the opportunity costs.

Incentives Work   Since smart choices compare costs and benefits, your decisions will change with changes in costs or benefits. We all respond to **incentives** — rewards and penalties for choices. You are more likely to choose a path that leads to a reward, and avoid one with a penalty. A change in incentives causes a change in choices. If your business deal is worth only $100 instead of $1 million, you might take the trip to Bermuda. If you were up most of last night, you are more likely to sleep than to study. If you have a test tomorrow instead of next week, you are more likely to study than to sleep.

To make the most out of life and make smart decisions, you must always ask the questions, "What is the opportunity cost of my choice?" and "Do the additional benefits outweigh the opportunity costs?"

 # Practice...

6. In deciding whether to study or sleep for the next hour, you should consider all of the following *except*

   a. how much tuition you paid.

   b. how tired you are.

   c. how productive you will be in that hour.

   d. how much value you place on sleeping in that hour.

7. If business starts booming and companies compete to hire workers, the

   a. opportunity cost of upgrading to a college diploma increases.

   b. opportunity cost of upgrading to a college diploma decreases.

   c. incentive to drop out of college decreases.

   d. choice about going to college does not change as long as tuition does not change.

8. The opportunity cost of attending college

   a. is less than the money cost.

   b. depends only on what you could earn by working full-time.

   c. includes the income you could have earned working full-time.

   d. depends on the benefits of going to college.

9. In making a smart choice,

   a. the value of what you give up must be greater than the value of what you get.

   b. the value of what you get must be greater than the value of what you give up.

   c. if the value of what you give up is greater that the value of what you get, you should lower the value of what you give up.

   d. if the value of what you give up is greater that the value of what you get, you should raise the value of what you get.

10. Ayesha missed her shift at the restaurant to go to a soccer game. She paid $30 for the ticket, $20 for parking, and spent $10 on popcorn. If she had worked her shift, Ayesha would have earned $100. Her opportunity cost of attending the game is

    a. $60.

    b. $100.

    c. $150.

    d. $160.

 Apply...

3. Seat belts save lives. Suppose that a city doubles the penalty for being caught driving without a seat belt to try to increase seat belt use among drivers.

   a. Use the concepts of incentives and opportunity cost to explain how this policy will influence driver behaviour.

   Since gov't incentives were introduced, the OC of driving w/o a seat belt has risen. Therefore, more people will drive with a seatbelt on.

   b. Suppose the city evaluates the results of the policy and finds that the number of traffic deaths actually *increased* after the policy was introduced. Can you think of a reason for this result?

   Seatbelts kill.

4. Ashley, Doug, and Mei-Lin are planning to travel from Halifax to Sydney. The trip takes one hour by airplane and five hours by train. The air fare is $100 and train fare is $60. They all have to take time off from work while travelling. Ashley earns $5 per hour in her job, Doug $10 per hour, and Mei-Lin $12 per hour.

   Use the table below to calculate the opportunity cost of air and train travel for each person. Assuming they all make smart choices as economizers, how should each of them travel to Sydney?

Traveller	Train	Plane	
Ashley			
a. Fare	$ 60	$ 100	Train
b. Opportunity cost of travel time at $5/hr	$ 25	$ 5	
Total Cost	$ 85	$ 105	
Doug			
a. Fare	$ 60	$ 100	Either
b. Opportunity cost of travel time at $10/hr	$ 50	$ 10	
Total Cost	$ 110	$ 110	
Mei-Lin			
a. Fare	$ 60	$ 100	Plane
b. Opportunity cost of travel time at $12/hr	$ 60	$ 12	
Total Cost	$ 120	$ 112	

 **Apply...**

5. Vladimir loves riding the bumper cars at the amusement park, but he loves the experience a little less with each additional ride. In estimating the benefit he receives from the rides, Vladimir would be willing to pay $10 for his first ride, $7 for his second ride, and $4 for his third ride. Rides actually cost $5 each for as many rides as Vladimir wants to take. This information is summarized in the table below.

Ride	1st	2nd	3rd
Additional benefit ($)	10	7	4
Additional cost ($)	5	5	5

21
15

a. If Vladimir chooses by comparing total benefit and total cost, how many rides will he take?

He would take 2 rides because his benefit at the third ride is now lower than the cost of the third ride

b. If Vladimir chooses by comparing additional benefits and additional costs for each ride, how many rides will he take?

c. Is Vladimir better off by comparing total benefits and costs, or by comparing additional benefits and costs? Explain your answer behind Vladimir's smart choice.

Gains from Trade

 Describe how comparative advantage, specialization, and trade make us all better off.

Our standard of living is much higher than it was hundreds of years ago. Trade is the key to making all of us better off. Any time two people make a voluntary trade, each person feels that what they get is of greater value than what they give up. If there weren't mutual benefits, the trade wouldn't happen.

Opportunity cost is the key to the mutual benefits from trade. Here's a simple example. Jill and Marie are each self-sufficient pioneers producing food and shelter. Each grows her own wheat to make bread, and chops her own wood for fire and shelter. Figures 1 and 2 show the different possible combinations of bread and wood each can produce in a month.

Figure 1   Jill's Production Possibilities

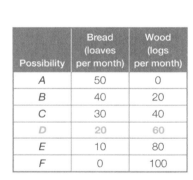

Possibility	Bread (loaves per month)	Wood (logs per month)
A	50	0
B	40	20
C	30	40
D	20	60
E	10	80
F	0	100

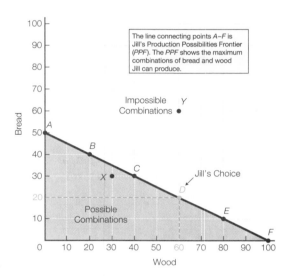

Figure 2   Marie's Production Possibilities

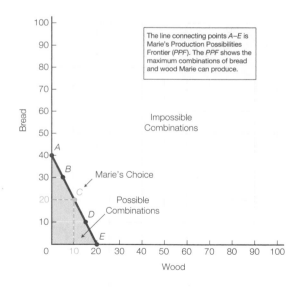

Possibility	Bread (loaves per month)	Wood (logs per month)
A	40	0
B	30	5
C	20	10
D	10	15
E	0	20

Because Jill and Marie are each self-sufficient, that means each can only consume what she produces herself. Jill chooses point *D* on her *PPF*, and Marie chooses point *C* on her *PPF*.

Production Possibilities Frontier

Each black line in the graphs is a **production possibilities frontier** —
PPF for short.

- A *PPF* shows the maximum combinations of products or services
  that can be produced with existing inputs.
- A *PPF* is the boundary between possible and impossible combinations
  of outputs.
- Points on the *PPF* are preferred to points inside the *PPF* because people
  prefer more to less.

Can Jill and Marie Make a Deal?

Can trade make both Jill and Marie better off? It doesn't look promising,
especially for Jill. Jill is a better bread maker than Marie and a better wood
chopper. Jill has an **absolute advantage** — the ability to produce at a lower
absolute cost than another producer — over Marie in both bread production
and wood production. Jill is more productive as a bread maker and as a wood
chopper.

   If you are not keen on history, then in place of Jill and Marie, think of China
and Canada. If China can produce everything at lower cost than Canada, can
there be mutually beneficial gains from trade for both countries? What's the
benefit for China? Won't all Canadians end up unemployed?

Comparative Advantage

Mutually beneficial gains from trade do not depend on absolute advantage,
they depend on **comparative advantage** — the ability to produce a product or
service at a lower *opportunity cost* than another producer.

   To calculate opportunity costs along any *PPF*, compare two adjacent possible
combinations, and use the formula

$$\text{Opportunity cost} = \frac{\text{Give Up}}{\text{Get}}$$

   Figure 3 shows the opportunity cost calculations for Jill and Marie.
Opportunity cost is measured in term of what you must give up of the other
product.

Figure 3   Opportunity Costs for Jill and Marie

	Opportunity Cost of 1 Additional	
	Loaf of Bread	Log of Wood
Jill	Gives up 2 logs of wood	Gives up ½ loaf of bread
Marie	Gives up ½ log of wood	Gives up 2 loaves of bread
Comparative Advantage	Marie has comparative advantage (lower opportunity cost) in bread-making	Jill has comparative advantage (lower opportunity cost) in wood-chopping

   Since comparative advantage is defined as lowest opportunity cost (not
lowest absolute cost), you can see that Marie has a comparative advantage in
bread-making, while Jill has a comparative advantage in wood-chopping.

   HINT: Whenever you are trying to figure out comparative advantage, always
create a table like Figure 3, with the two traders in the rows, and the two
products in the columns.

Mutually Beneficial Gains from Trade

There are mutually beneficial gains from trade if people/countries specialize in producing the product in which they have a comparative advantage, and trade for the other product. According to comparative advantage, Jill should specialize in only chopping wood, and Marie should specialize in only making bread. Jill produces 100 logs of wood and no bread, and Marie produces 40 loaves of bread and no wood. They then trade 20 logs of wood for 20 loaves of bread along the blue Trade Lines below. Figure 4 tells the story of Jill and Marie's specialization and trade.

Figure 4   Mutually Beneficial Gains from Trade

Jill specializes in producing only wood, moving from point *D* to point *F* on her *PPF*. She then trades 20 logs of wood to Marie for 20 loaves of bread, moving from point *F* to point *F'* along the trade line. Jill can now consume 80 logs of wood and 20 loaves of bread, a combination that was impossible before trade.

Marie specializes in producing only bread, moving from point *C* to point *A* on her *PPF*. She then trades 20 loaves of bread to Jill for 20 logs of wood, moving from point *A* to point *A'* along the trade line. Marie can now consume 20 logs of wood and 20 loaves of bread, a combination that was impossible before trade.

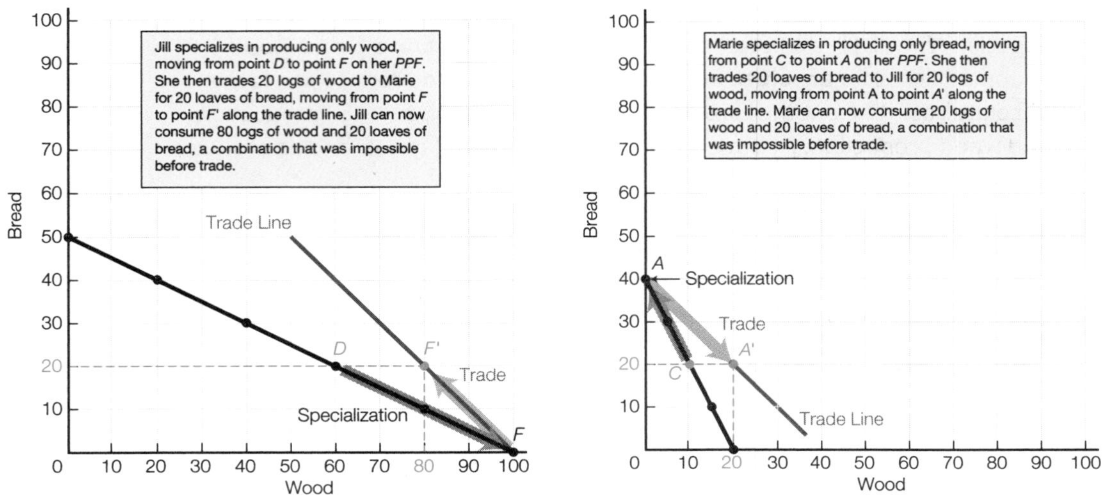

a) Jill's Gains from Trade

b) Marie's Gains from Trade

Achieving the Impossible

After trading, Jill and Marie are both better off than when they were each self-sufficient. Each can consume a combination of wood and bread — outside her *PPF* — that was impossible before trade. Voluntary trade is *not* a zero-sum game, where one person's gain is the other's loss. Both traders gain.

These gains from trade happen without anyone working harder, without any improvement in technology, and without new inputs.

There are gains for both Jill and Marie, even though Jill has an absolute advantage in producing everything at lower cost. Differences in opportunity costs — comparative advantage — are the key to mutually beneficial gains from trade. The trade can be between individuals, or between countries. That is why China trades with Canada, even though China can produce most things more cheaply than Canada can. There are still differences in comparative advantage based on opportunity costs.

All arguments you will ever hear in favour of freer trade are based on comparative advantage, which is based on the most important concept in economics — opportunity cost.

 **Practice...**

11. Mutually beneficial gains from trade come from
    a. absolute advantage.
    b. comparative advantage.
    c. self-sufficiency.
    d. China.

12. The simplest way to calculate opportunity cost is
    a. $\dfrac{\text{Give Up}}{\text{Get}}$
    b. $\dfrac{\text{Get}}{\text{Give Up}}$
    c. Give Up − Get
    d. Get − Give Up

13. In one hour, Chloe can bake 24 cookies or 12 muffins. Zabeen can bake 6 cookies or 2 muffins. For mutually beneficial trade, Chloe should bake
    a. cookies because she has a comparative advantage.
    b. cookies because she has an absolute advantage.
    c. muffins because she has a comparative advantage.
    d. muffins because she has an absolute advantage.

14. On a graph of a production possibilities frontier (*PPF*), impossible combinations of outputs are represented by
    a. the slope of the *PPF*.
    b. points inside the *PPF*.
    c. points on the *PPF*.
    d. points outside the *PPF*.

15. If Ying can increase production of houses without decreasing production of any other product, then Ying
    a. is producing inside his production possibilities frontier.
    b. is producing on his production possibilities frontier.
    c. is producing outside his production possibilities frontier.
    d. must prefer houses to any other product.

(handwritten top margin)

Tova	wid	wog		wd	wog	Ron
	0	15		0	10	
OC wid = 5/10 = 1/2 +10	10	10) -5		5	5	
	20	5)		10	0	
	30	0				

Apply...

6. Tova and Ron are the only two remaining inhabitants of the planet Melmac. They spend their 30-hour days producing widgets and woggles, the only two products needed for happiness on Melmac. It takes Tova 1 hour to produce a widget and 2 hours to produce a woggle, while Ron takes 3 hours to produce a widget and 3 hours to produce a woggle.

   a. For a 30-hour day, draw an individual *PPF* for Tova, then for Ron.

Tova

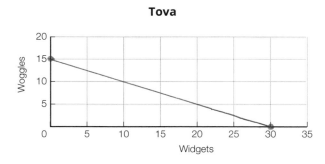

Ron

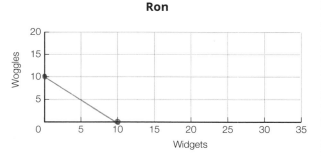

   b. To start, Tova and Ron are each self-sufficient. Define self-sufficiency. Explain what the individual *consumption possibilities* are for Tova, then for Ron.

   _____

   _____

   _____

   c. Who has an absolute advantage in the production of widgets? of woggles? Explain your answers.

   Tova for both. In 30 hours, she can make the most of both

   _____

   d. Who has a comparative advantage in the production of widgets? of woggles? Explain your answers.

   wid   wog

   Tova

   Ron

   _____

   e. Tova and Ron each specialize in producing only the product in which she or he has a comparative advantage. One spends 30 hours producing widgets, the other spends 30 hours producing woggles. What will be the total production of widgets and woggles?

   _____

   _____

   _____

 Apply…

f. Tova and Ron exchange 7 widgets for 5 woggles. On your *PPF* diagrams in 6a, plot the new point of Tova's consumption, then of Ron's consumption. Explain how these points illustrate gains from trade.

_____

_____

_____

_____

7. The best auto mechanic in town (who charges $120/hour) is also a better typist than her office manager (who earns $20/hour). The mechanic decides to do her own typing. Is this a smart choice for her to make? Explain your answer. [*Hint:* Fill in the table. The best alternative employment for the office manager is another office job that also pays $20/hour.]

	O.C. of 1 Additonal Hour of	
	Mechanic Services	**Typing**
Mechanic		
Office Manager		
Comparative Advantage		

_____

_____

_____

_____

_____

_____

8. Classroom Game — Is Trade Mutually Beneficial?

Before game starts, Instructor asks class, "Why do people trade?" Trade includes trading money for a product or service. Write answers on the board.

Every student should bring to class one or more small items they no longer want, or small candies.

Instructor gives students the opportunity to trade. No one is required to trade. Allow 5–10 minutes for trades. Students may trade more than once. At the end of trading, here are discussion questions for the Instructor to ask.

a. How many students made a trade?

b. For anyone who made at least one trade, "Why did you decide to trade?"

c. Of those who made trades, how many feel better off as a result of the trade(s)?

d. If anyone who trades says she or he is not better off, please explain why.

e. Why did some students decide not to trade?

f. Did the trading results support or disprove the reasons on the board about "Why do people trade?"

g. What conclusions can you draw from this game?

Thinking Like an Economist

 Explain how models like the circular flow model make smart choices easier.

Economists think like map-makers. To plan a trip across Canada, you could look at a satellite photo that captures every aspect of Canada that can be seen from space. But the photo doesn't show details that are important for your trip — roads, railways, or ferry services. A map is much more useful than the photo because it focuses your attention on the information that is most relevant for your task, and leaves all other information in the background.

Learning to think like an economist allows the key "roads" to making smart choices stand out. This kind of thinking makes it easier to make decisions and understand the complex world around you.

Let's apply this way of thinking to the definition of economics: Economics is about how individuals, businesses, and governments make the best possible choices to get what they want, and about how those choices interact in markets. Another famous definition of economics by Alfred Marshall, a legendary professor at the University of Cambridge, is "Economics is the study of mankind in the ordinary business of life."

Circular Flow Model

The maps that economists use are called economic models. A **model** is a simplified representation of the real world, focusing attention on what's important for understanding a specific idea or concept.

Figure 5   The Circular Flow of Economic Life

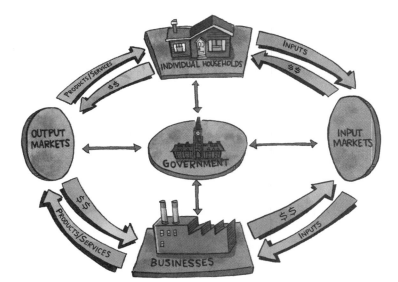

Figure 5 is an economic model called the *circular flow of economic life*. It shows the simplest big picture of how to think about economic choices. All the complexity of the Canadian economy is reduced to three sets of players: households, businesses, and governments. Individuals in households ultimately own all of the **inputs** of an economy — the productive resources used to produce products and services. The four types of inputs are labour (the ability to work), natural resources, capital equipment, and entrepreneurial ability. Even the assets of the largest corporations, such as Imperial Oil or Ford, are ultimately owned by individual shareholders.

Households and businesses interact in two sets of markets:

- In input markets, businesses buy the inputs they need to produce products and services; households are sellers.

- In output markets, businesses sell their products and services; households are buyers.

- Governments set the rules of the game and can choose to interact, or not, in any aspect of the economy.

- As part of the rules of the game, governments enforce **property rights** — legally enforceable guarantees of ownership of physical, financial, and intellectual property.

Models as the Economist's Laboratory

A good economic model helps you make smart choices, or helps you better understand or predict the facts of the world around you. To test models against the facts, economists do what natural scientists do. We assume that "other things are unchanged," to remove the influence of the factors left out of the simplified model. Here is a natural science example.

The law of gravity predicts that, all other factors unchanged, objects fall at the same rate regardless of their mass. If we drop a bowling ball and a feather from a tall building, and find the bowling ball hits the ground first, does that disprove the law of gravity? No, because we are not controlling for air resistance, which changes the path of the feather more than the bowling ball. To accurately test the law of gravity, we must perform the same experiment in a laboratory vacuum, so that we eliminate, or control for, the influence of air resistance as an "other factor." We need to keep all other factors unchanged.

Economists have it much tougher than scientists. We can't pause everything in the world while focusing only on the factors we are interested in. Instead, we have to use economic models to isolate the factors we think are important. Economic models focus attention on what is important by assuming that all other things not in the model are unchanged. Thinking like an economist and using economic models is the mental equivalent of the controlled experiments of the laboratory.

John Maynard Keynes once said, "Economics is a science of thinking in terms of models, joined to the art of choosing models which are relevant to the contemporary world."

Positive and Normative Statements

In trying to explain the facts of the world, economists, like other scientists, distinguish facts from opinions.

Positive statements are about what is; they can be evaluated as true or false by checking the facts.

Normative statements involve value judgments or opinions, and cannot be factually checked, tested, or shown to be true or false. A normative statement is based on personal values, which differ among individuals.

Practice...

16. All of the following are inputs *except*

    a. capital equipment.

    b. natural resources.

    c. governments.

    d. labour.

17. The players in the circular flow model include

    a. businesses, governments, inputs.

    b. households, businesses, governments.

    c. governments, input markets, output markets.

    d. governments, markets, countries.

18. In the circular flow model,

    a. businesses ultimately own all inputs of an economy.

    b. businesses are sellers and households are buyers in input markets.

    c. households are sellers and businesses are buyers in output markets.

    d. governments set the rules of the game.

19. A good economic model

    a. is easier to test than experiments in a laboratory.

    b. helps you understand or predict the economic world around you.

    c. includes as much information as possible.

    d. changes many factors at the same time.

20. Which statement is normative?

    a. You should call your mother every week.

    b. Drinking 14 beers in one hour will probably make you sick.

    c. Men live longer than women.

    d. Women live longer than men.

Apply...

9. If you are trying to decide whether to buy a car, what are the most important factors to focus on when making your decision? What are some of the factors that you ignore, or leave out of your decision? Explain how your thinking resembles an economic model.

    _____

    _____

    _____

    _____

    _____

    _____

    _____

    _____

Apply...

10. Answer these questions about the circular flow model.

   a. In input markets, who are the sellers and who are the buyers? Start at the top of the circular flow model and explain the process of selling and buying in input markets.

   _____

   _____

   _____

   _____

   _____

   b. In output markets, who are the sellers and who are the buyers? Start at the bottom and explain the process of selling and buying in output markets.

   _____

   _____

   _____

   _____

   _____

   c. When one "trip" around the circle has ended,
      i. what have households received?
      ii. what do business end up with?
      iii. how do these end points set up the next "trip" around the circular flow?

   _____

   _____

   _____

   _____

   _____

   d. Governments enforce property rights as one of the "rules of the game." What happens to incentives to trade if there are no property rights? Illustrate your answer by picking any exchange/trade and describe what might happen without property rights.

   _____

   _____

   _____

   _____

   _____

   _____

to be continued

Apply...

continued

11. Identify each statement below as either positive or normative. If it is positive, rewrite it so that it becomes normative. If it is normative, rewrite it so that it becomes positive. For each positive statement, explain how you might test to see if it is true (matches the facts) or false.

a. A government tax on cigarettes will reduce sales of cigarettes.

_____

_____

_____

b. The Government of Canada should raise taxes to reduce the deficit.

_____

_____

_____

c. Imports from China are eliminating jobs in Canada.

_____

_____

_____

d. Governments should impose rent controls to create more affordable housing.

_____

_____

Models for Microeconomics and Macroeconomics

 Differentiate microeconomic and macroeconomic choices, and explain the Three Keys model for smart choices.

The economic way of thinking, while always concerned with smart choices and their interactions in markets, can be applied on different scales to understand microeconomics and macroeconomics.

Microeconomics **Microeconomics** analyzes the choices made by individuals in households, individual businesses, and governments, and how those choices interact in markets. Microeconomic choices for individuals include whether to go to college or to get a job, whether to be self-sufficient or to specialize and trade, whether to take out a bank loan or to run up a credit card balance, and whether to get married or to stay single. Microeconomic choices for businesses include what product to produce, how much to spend on research and development of new products, which technology to use, which marketing strategy to use, and whether to outsource manufacturing to China or produce in Canada. Microeconomic choices for governments focus on individual industries. For example, should the government step in and regulate the mobile phone industry or let competition determine the winners and losers? How would a carbon tax affect car sales?

Macroeconomics   When we step back from individual details and look at the big picture, we are taking a "macro" view. **Macroeconomics** analyzes the performance of the whole Canadian (or any country's) economy and the global economy, the combined outcomes of all individual microeconomic choices. Macroeconomics focuses on overall outcomes of market interactions, including Canadian unemployment, inflation rates, government deficits and surpluses, interest rates set by the Bank of Canada, the value of the Canadian dollar, and international trade. Macroeconomics also examines the policy choices governments make that affect the whole economy — for example, whether to play an active economic role by spending and taxing (more likely for New Democrats or Liberals) or to leave the economy alone (more likely for Conservatives), whether to raise or lower taxes, whether to raise or lower interest rates, and whether to defend the value of the Canadian dollar or let it be determined by economic forces.

Microeconomics looks at the individual trees, while macroeconomics looks at the forest.

Three Keys Model for Smart Choices

Whether you are studying microeconomics or macroeconomics, all smart choices begin with microeconomic choices. Figure 6 shows a second economic model to guide smart microeconomic choices. This model doesn't look like a traditional map (no cities or roads), but it works like all maps and models do — focusing your attention on the information that is most useful for making a smart choice, and leaving other information in the background.

Figure 6   The Three Keys Model

- Key 1 is most important. Compare additional benefits and additional opportunity costs. This is the principle behind all microeconomic decisions.
- Keys 2 and 3 simply provide more of the details behind Key 1.

- Economists use the word "marginal" instead of "additional," so you can also read Key 2 as "Count only **marginal benefits** — additional benefits from your next choice — and **marginal opportunity costs** — additional opportunity costs from your next choice." Thinking like an economist means thinking at the margin.

- Key 3 details the costs to include, which people often miss.

- **Implicit costs** are the opportunity costs of investing your own money or time.

- **Negative externalities** are costs that affect others who are external to a choice or trade.

- **Positive externalities** are benefits that affect others who are external to a choice or trade.

If you are studying microeconomics, you will learn more about the details in The Three Keys model. The Three Keys, together with the circular flow model, will also guide your macroeconomic choices and understanding of the economy.

Practice...

21. Microeconomics focuses on
    a. smart choices, while macroeconomics focuses on voluntary trade.
    b. the choices of individual economic players, while macroeconomics focuses on performance of the whole economy.
    c. performance of the whole economy, while macroeconomics focuses on the choices of individual economic players.
    d. opportunity costs, while macroeconomics focuses on negative and positive externalities.

22. Which headline is about macroeconomics?
    a. "Consumers switch from minivans to hybrids"
    b. "Amazon fights a tax on e-commerce"
    c. "Japan's economy is still in recession"
    d. "Farmers stop using pesticides"

23. Viki paid $12 to see the new *Star Trek* movie. Once inside, she must decide whether or not to buy popcorn for $4. Buying the popcorn is a smart choice if Vicki gets benefits of at least
    a. $4.
    b. $8.
    c. $12.
    d. $16.

24. Before starring in *Iron Man,* Robert Downey Jr. had acted in many movies with first-weekend box office revenues averaging $5 million. *Iron Man* earned $102 million in its first weekend. The success of *Iron Man* _____ the opportunity cost of hiring Robert Downey Jr. and _____ the marginal benefit to movie producers of hiring him.
    a. decreases; increases
    b. decreases; decreases
    c. increases; decreases
    d. increases; increases

25. To make a smart economic choice, consider all of the following *except*
    a. past costs and benefits.
    b. external costs and benefits.
    c. additional costs and additional benefits.
    d. implicit costs.

 **Apply...**

12. List the Three Keys to smart choices, and highlight the most important words in each key.

_____
_____
_____
_____
_____

13. Highway 407 ETR in Toronto is a toll road that uses transponders to keep track of how many kilometres you drive on it, and then sends you a monthly bill. Highway 401 runs parallel to Highway 407 and is free. Why do drivers voluntarily pay the tolls? (Use opportunity cost in your answer.) Suppose the government could calculate the cost per kilometre of the pollution damage from your driving, and send you a similar monthly bill. How might that additional cost affect your decision to drive?

_____
_____
_____
_____
_____
_____

14. The questions below are about differences between microeconomics and macroeconomics.

   a. Fill in the blanks.

   _____ analyzes the performance of the whole Canadian economy

   and the global economy, the combined outcomes of all individual microeconomic choices.

   _____ analyzes the choices made by individuals in households,

   individual businesses, and governments, and how those choices interact in markets.

   b. For each of the following media headlines, circle whether it is about microeconomics, macroeconomics, or if you are unsure which. Give a one-sentence explanation of your answer.

      i. "Will Mobile Phone Rates Fall as Shaw Buys Wind Mobile?"

      Micro / Macro / Unsure

_____
_____
_____

to be continued

continued

ii.   "Beyond Pricing Startup Helps AirBnB Homeowners Boost Revenues from Their Rentals"

Micro / Macro / Unsure

_____

_____

_____

iii.   "Loonie Takes Biggest Tumble in 3 Months after Bank of Canada Cuts Outlook for Growth"

Micro / Macro / Unsure

_____

_____

_____

iv.   "Why Pricing Traffic Congestion Is Critical to Beating It"

Micro / Macro / Unsure

_____

_____

_____

v.   "Government Deficit Fighting Not as Important as Investing in Infrastructure"

Micro / Macro / Unsure

_____

_____

_____

vi.   "Inflation Has Not Yet Followed Lower Unemployment in America"

Micro / Macro / Unsure

_____

_____

_____

vii. "Higher Alberta Minimum Wage Benefits Both Workers and Employers"

Micro / Macro / Unsure

_____

_____

KNOW...

Summary of Learning Objectives

1. Because of the problem of **scarcity,** you can never satisfy all of your wants. Making the most out of your life requires smart choices about what to go after, and what to give up.

2. Opportunity cost is the most important concept both in economics and for making smart choices in life. The **opportunity cost** of any choice is the cost of the best alternative given up.

3. Opportunity cost and comparative advantage are key to understanding why specializing and trading make us all better off. There are mutually beneficial gains from trade if each producer specializes in producing the product for which they have a **comparative advantage** — the ability to produce at a lower *opportunity cost* than another producer.

4. The circular flow **model,** like all economic models, focuses attention on what's important for understanding and shows how smart choices by households, businesses, and governments interact in input markets and output markets. Economists distinguish **positive statements** (about what is; can be evaluated as true or false by checking the facts) from **normative statements** (based on value judgments about what you believe should be; cannot be tested or evaluated as true or false by checking the facts).

5. The Three Keys model summarizes the core of microeconomics, providing the basis for smart choices in all areas of life. **Microeconomics** analyzes choices that individuals in households, individual businesses, and governments make, and how those choices interact in markets. **Macroeconomics** analyzes the performance of the whole Canadian (or any country's) economy and the global economy, the combined outcomes of all individual microeconomic choices.

Key Terms

absolute advantage: the ability to produce a product or service at a lower absolute cost than another producer

comparative advantage: the ability to produce a product or service at lower opportunity cost than another producer

economics: how individuals, businesses, and governments make the best possible choices to get what they want, and how those choices interact in markets

externalities: costs or benefits that affect others external to a choice or a trade

implicit costs: hidden opportunity costs of what a business owner could earn elsewhere with time and money invested

incentives: rewards and penalties for choices

inputs: productive resources — labour, natural resources, capital equipment, and entrepreneurial ability — used to produce products and services

macroeconomics: analyzes performance of the whole Canadian (or any country's) economy and the global economy, the combined outcomes of all individual microeconomic choices

marginal benefits: the additional benefit from a choice, changing with circumstances

marginal opportunity cost: additional opportunity costs from the next choice

microeconomics: analyzes choices that individuals in households, individual businesses, and governments make, and how those choices interact in markets

model: a simplified representation of the real world, focusing attention on what's important for understanding

negative externalities: costs to society from your private choice that affect others, but that you do not pay

normative statements: based on value judgments about what you believe should be; cannot be tested or evaluated as true or false by checking the facts

opportunity cost: cost of best alternative given up

positive externalities: benefits to society from your private choice that affect others, but that others do not pay you for

positive statements: about what is; can be evaluated as true or false by checking the facts

production possibilities frontier (*PPF*): maximum combinations of products or services that can be produced with existing inputs

property rights: legally enforceable guarantees of ownership of physical, financial, and intellectual property

scarcity: the problem that arises because we all have limited money, time, and energy

Answers to Practice

1. **c** We all have limited money, time, and energy.
2. **b** Definition.
3. **d** All limited for all people.
4. **a** Because we can't have everything we want, we must choose.
5. **d** Scarcity is a universal problem.
6. **a** Paid tuition is the same for either choice.
7. **a** Going to college means giving up a good job with a higher wage.
8. **c** Opportunity cost includes income given up and money paid for tuition.
9. **b** Additional benefits of what you get must be greater than opportunity costs of what you give up.
10. **d** Money costs ($30+$20+$10) you could have spent on something else, plus income given up ($100).
11. **b** Differences in opportunity costs are key to gains from trade.
12. **a** See formula.
13. **c** Chloe's opportunity cost of muffins (2 cookies per muffin) is lower than Zabeen's (3 cookies per muffin).

14. **d** *PPF* represents maximum possible combinations.

15. **a** With unused inputs inside *PPF*, you can increase output without opportunity cost by using unemployed inputs.

16 **c** Governments set the rules of the game — are not inputs to production.

17. **b** These players interact in input and output markets.

18. **d** Other answers would be correct if switch businesses and households.

19. **b** Good models select information to include, change one factor at a time, and are hard to test because many factors change simultaneously in the real world.

20. **a** Notice the word *should*. Other statements can be shown to be true or false.

21. **b** Definition.

22. **c** About a country's economic performance.

23. **a** Compare only additional benefits from eating popcorn to additional cost of $4.

24. **d** Because moviegoers will pay more to see Downey, movie producers will pay more to hire him.

25. **a** All other costs and benefits are part of the Three Keys.

2 Demanders and Suppliers

LEARNING OBJECTIVES

L01 Explain why smart choices depend on marginal benefits, not total benefits, and on marginal costs, not total costs.

L02 Explain the law of demand, and describe the roles of substitutes and of willingness and ability to pay.

L03 Explain the difference between a change in quantity demanded and a change in demand, and list five factors that change demand.

L04 Explain the law of supply and describe the roles of higher profits and higher marginal opportunity costs of production.

L05 Explain the difference between a change in quantity supplied and a change in supply, and list six factors that can change supply.

LEARN...

In the circular flow model, governments set the rules of the game, but individuals (in households) and businesses make most of the choices. Individuals and businesses play roles both as demanders and as suppliers. In input markets, individuals are suppliers (of inputs labour, capital , land and entrepreneurship) and businesses are demanders. In output markets, businesses are suppliers (of products and services) and individuals, acting as consumers, are demanders.

In this chapter, you will learn what's behind our choices to demand or buy, and our choices to supply or sell. When things change — prices, incomes, technologies — you will also learn to analyze how choices change. What effect does advertising have on demand? Why are businesses using robots to replace human workers?

We choose among alternatives, or substitutes. Consumers choose between different phone plans, eating out or cooking at home, or getting to school by bike or transit. Businesses choose between producing different products, using different technologies, or deciding how many workers to hire.

All demand and supply decisions are based on Key 1 — choose (to demand or to supply) only when additional benefits are greater than additional opportunity costs. Smart demand and supply decisions are also made at the margin using Key 2 — count only additional benefits and additional costs.

You will learn all of the reasons behind consumers' willingness and ability to pay for products, and behind businesses' willingness to supply products to earn profits. The next chapter combines these reasons, putting together demand and supply to explain how prices and quantities are determined in markets.

Marginal Benefits and Marginal Opportunity Costs

 Explain why smart choices depend on marginal benefits, not total benefits, and on marginal costs, not total costs.

Marginal Benefits Change with Circumstances

As a consumer, the additional benefits or satisfaction you expect to get from a product or service depend on the circumstances.

Marginal Benefits Decrease with Quantity   You just finished an intense workout at the gym and desperately want something to drink. Your buddy, who is always trying to make a buck, says, "I have a 6-pack of Gatorade. How much will you pay for a bottle?" The first Gatorade after a workout is very satisfying — it has a high marginal benefit, and you would be willing to pay a lot (while wondering if this guy is really a buddy). The second Gatorade is less satisfying, and a third might make you sick.

- **Marginal benefit** is key to how much you are willing to pay.
- Decreasing marginal benefit means decreasing willingness to pay for additional quantities of the same product or service.

The Diamond-Water Paradox   A focus on marginal benefit helps make sense of the following paradox. What's more valuable in providing benefits or satisfaction — diamonds or water? Water is essential for survival, while diamonds are unnecessary. Why do diamonds cost far more than water? You solve the paradox by distinguishing marginal benefit from total benefit. You would die without water, so you are willing to pay everything you can for the first drink. But when water is abundant, what are you willing to pay, at the margin, for your next drink today? Not much. Marginal benefit is low, though the total benefit of all water consumed (including the first, life-saving drink) is high.

Diamonds won't keep you alive, but they are scarce, and desirable for that reason. What would you pay for your first diamond? A lot. Marginal benefit is high. Because diamonds are scarce, there aren't many out there, so total benefit is low.

- Willingness to pay depends on marginal benefit, not total benefit, so people are generally willing to pay more for a diamond (high marginal benefit) than for a glass of water (low marginal benefit).

Marginal Costs Change with Circumstances

For businesses, the additional cost of producing a product or service depends on the circumstances. Let's look at a business: Paola's Parlour for Piercing and Nails. With the labour and equipment in her shop, Paola can do piercings or paint fingernails. Her workers are equally skilled at piercing, but their fingernail skills differ from expert to beginner. Figure 1 shows the different combinations of fingernail sets and piercings that Paola's Parlour can produce in a day.

Figure 1   Paola's Parlour Production Possibilities Frontier (*PPF*)

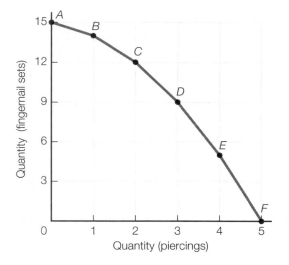

Combination	Fingernails (full sets)	Piercings (full body)
A	15	0
B	14	1
C	12	2
D	9	3
E	5	4
F	0	5

Marginal Costs Increase with Quantity   Look what happens if Paola wants to increase her production of piercings from 0 (combination *A*), to 1, to 2, . . . up to 5 (combination *F*). To get more piercings, Paola gives up doing nailsets. Remember,

$$\text{Opportunity cost} \ = \ \frac{\text{Give Up}}{\text{Get}}$$

Figure 2 shows, in the last column, the marginal opportunity costs to Paola of producing more piercings.

Figure 2   Paola's Parlour Marginal Opportunity Costs

Combination	Fingernails (full sets)	Piercings (full body)	Marginal Opportunity Cost of Producing More Piercings (fingernail sets given up)
A	15	0	$\frac{(15-14)}{1} = 1$
B	14	1	$\frac{(14-12)}{1} = 2$
C	12	2	$\frac{(12-9)}{1} = 3$
D	9	3	$\frac{(9-5)}{1} = 4$
E	5	4	$\frac{(5-0)}{1} = 5$
F	0	5	

As Paola increases her quantity supplied of piercings, her marginal opportunity costs increase, from 1 fingernail set given up for the first piercing to 5 fingernail sets given up for the fifth piercing. These increasing marginal opportunity costs (**marginal costs** for short) arise because Paola's staff are not equally good at painting. As Paola reduces fingernail output to produce the first piercing, which worker will she switch first? Remember all are equally good at piercing. She will switch the least productive fingernail painter. Her given-up, or forgone, fingernail production is small (1 set). To increase piercing production more, she has to switch more productive fingernail painters. Increasing marginal costs arise because inputs are not equally productive in all activities.

HINT: Why is the shape of Paola's *PPF* curved, while the *PPF*s for Jill and Marie in Chapter 1 are straight lines? As Jill (or Marie) switches between combinations of bread and wood, her marginal opportunity costs do not change because Jill's (or Marie's) skills do not change. She just changes the time spent on each task.

- When inputs are *not* equally productive in all activities, marginal opportunity costs increase with increases in quantity supplied.

- When inputs are equally productive in all activities, marginal opportunity costs are constant.

To be willing to supply more piercings, Paola's business needs a higher price to cover increasing marginal costs.

 # Practice...

1. All-you-can-eat buffet restaurants charge a fixed fee for eating. With each plate that Anna eats, she experiences
   a. decreasing marginal costs.
   b. increasing marginal costs.
   c. decreasing marginal benefits.
   d. increasing marginal benefits.

2. Thinking like economists, a dating couple should break up when
   a. total benefits of dating are greater than the total costs.
   b. total costs of dating are greater than the total benefits.
   c. marginal benefits of dating are greater than the marginal costs.
   d. marginal costs of dating are greater than the marginal benefits.

3. The price of diamonds is higher than the price of water because
   a. marginal benefits from diamonds are relatively high.
   b. marginal benefits from water are relatively high.
   c. total benefits from diamonds are relatively high.
   d. total benefits from water are relatively low.

4. If all inputs for a business are *not* equally productive in all activities, the opportunity cost of increasing output is
   a. decreasing.
   b. increasing.
   c. constant.
   d. high.

5. When all inputs for a business are equally productive in all activities, as the business increases output, marginal costs
   a. increase.
   b. decrease.
   c. are constant.
   d. are zero.

Apply...

1. You and your entrepreneurial buddy have a concession stand on the beach. It is a hot, sunny, crowded day, and you are selling a few $5 collapsible umbrellas as sun shades. The skies suddenly darken, rain begins to pour, and your buddy quickly switches the umbrella price sign to $10. Will you sell more or fewer umbrellas? Explain your thinking, and include the concept of marginal benefit in analyzing a customer's decision.

   _____

   _____

   _____

   _____

   _____

2. Employees do not like working long weekdays and on weekends, so employers offer higher wages for the extra time in the form of "overtime pay," which could be up to three times the regular wage. Use the concept of increasing opportunity cost to explain why it is important for businesses to offer overtime pay.

   _____

   _____

   _____

   _____

   _____

3. Suppose that an economy has the *PPF* in this table:

   a. Plot these possibilities on the graph, label the points, and draw the *PPF.*

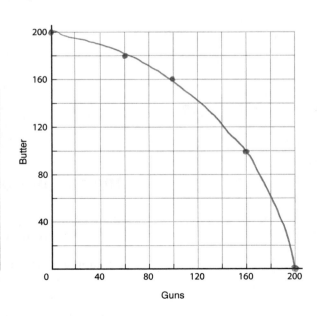

	Production Possibilities	
Possibility	**Maximum Units of Butter per Week**	**Maximum Units of Guns per Week**
A	200	0
B	180	60
C	160	100
D	100	160
E	0	200

to be continued

Apply...

continued

b. If the economy moves from possibility *C* to possibility *D*, what is the opportunity cost, in units of butter, of one gun?

$OC = 1 \, gun = \frac{100}{160} = \frac{10}{16} = \frac{5}{8} \, butter$

c. If the economy moves from possibility *D* to possibility *E*, what is the opportunity cost, in units of butter, of one gun?

$OC = 1 \, gun = \frac{0}{200} = 0 \, butters$

d. In general, what happens to the opportunity cost of guns as the output of guns increases? In general, what happens to the opportunity cost of butter as the output of butter increases? What do these results imply about inputs to production?

e. Instead of the possibilities given, suppose the *PPF* is a straight line joining points *A* and *E*. What does that imply about opportunity costs and inputs?

The Law of Demand

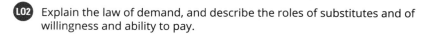 Explain the law of demand, and describe the roles of substitutes and of willingness and ability to pay.

Demand describes consumers' willingness and ability to pay for a product or service. Demand is not just what consumers want. Your must put your money (or time) where your mouth is in order to demand a product or service.

Demand depends on

- how badly you want a product.
- how much you are willing and able to give up for it.

How Badly Do You Want It?

Economists describe all of your wants — and how intense each want is — as your **preferences**.

- The more intense your preference is for a product or service, the more you are willing to pay, because you expect a high benefit from satisfying that want.

- For all products or services, even those satisfying intense wants, there are decreasing marginal benefits for additional units consumed.

What Will You Give Up?

No matter how much you want something, your demand for it also depends on how much you are willing and able to give up for it. Notice I used the words *give up* instead of *pay* for it. For most products we want, we pay with money. But to satisfy many other wants, we have to give up our time or effort. Spending time studying means not seeing friends, not playing with your kids, or working less at your job. In comparing additional benefits and additional costs, cost always means *opportunity cost* — what you are willing to give up.

Substitutes   How much you are willing to give up depends on wants or preferences, but also on what your alternative choices are. **Substitutes** are products or services used in place of each other to satisfy the same want. The more substitutes there are, the less you are willing to pay for a product. If bottled water is available, how much will you pay for a Gatorade? The ability to listen to free music affects your willingness to pay for music.

Income   How much you are willing or able to give up also depends on what you can afford. Are you able to pay the price of the product you want? Can you afford to take the time to relax when you have a test tomorrow?

Demand is not just what consumers want. Your must put your money (or time) where your mouth is in order to demand a product or service.

Market Demand

For each individual, **quantity demanded** is the amount you actually plan to buy at a given price, taking into account everything that affects your willingness and ability to pay.

Market demand is the sum of the demands of all individuals willing and able to buy a particular product or service. In general, consumers buy a smaller quantity at higher prices because

- consumers switch to cheaper substitutes.

- fewer people can afford to buy.

This inverse relationship (when one goes up, the other goes down) between price and quantity demanded is so universal that economists call it the **law of demand**: If the price of a product or service rises, the quantity demanded of the product or service decreases. If the price falls, the quantity demanded increases. The law of demand works as long as other influences on demand besides price do not change.

Figure 3 on the next page illustrates the inverse relation between price and quantity demanded for the market demand for water.

Figure 3   Market Demand for Water

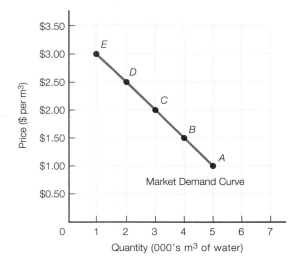

Row	Price ($ per m³)	Quantity Demanded (000's of m³ per month)
A	$1.00	5
B	$1.50	4
C	$2.00	3
D	$2.50	2
E	$3.00	1

The **demand curve** shows the relationship between price and quantity demanded when all other influences on demand besides price do not change.

Two Ways to Read a Demand Curve

The demand curve is a simple yet powerful tool summarizing the two forces that determine quantity demanded — the switch to substitutes, and willingness and ability to pay. Because there are two forces, Figure 4 shows two ways to "read" a demand curve. Both readings are correct, but each highlights a different force.

Figure 4   Two Ways to Read a Demand Curve

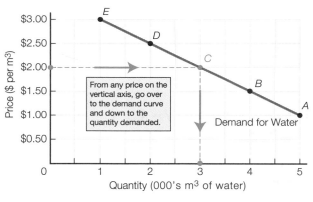

a) Reading the Demand Curve
as a Demand Curve

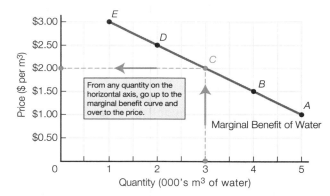

b) Reading the Demand Curve
as a Marginal Benefit Curve

- To read as a demand curve — start at any price and go over and down to the quantity demanded. The demand curve shows, for any price, what will be the quantity demanded.

- To read as a marginal benefit curve — start at any quantity and go up and over to the price. The marginal benefit curve shows, for any quantity, the maximum price people are willing and able to pay for that last unit available. Increasing quantities have decreasing marginal benefits.

Both readings are movements along an unchanged demand curve. The law of demand works as long as other influences on demand besides price do not change.

Practice...

6. Your preferences measure
   a. the availability of substitutes.
   b. how limited your time is.
   c. the price of a product.
   d. how badly you want something.

7. Costs are
   a. the dollar price you pay.
   b. whatever you are willing to give up.
   c. the answer to the question "What do you want?"
   d. whatever you are willing to get.

8. When the price of a product rises,
   a. consumers look for more expensive substitutes.
   b. quantity demanded increases.
   c. consumers look for cheaper substitutes.
   d. consumers use more of the product.

9. A sociology class is a substitute for an economics class if
   a. attending the two classes has the same opportunity cost.
   b. the two classes satisfy the same want.
   c. both classes are at the same time.
   d. both classes are taught by the same instructor.

10. Which statement about demand is *true*?
   a. Demand describes a consumer's desire for a particular product or service.
   b. You have a demand for music when you download it for free.
   c. Your concerns about the environment affect your demand for cars.
   d. All of the above are true.

Apply...

4. What is the difference between wants and demands?

_____

_____

_____

_____

_____

to be continued

Apply...

continued

5. You have tickets for a concert tonight that you have been looking forward to. Your mother, who is helping you pay your tuition, phones and says that it's very important to her that you come to Grandma's birthday party tonight. Using the law of demand, explain your decision — the concert or Grandma's party? [*HINT*: Think about opportunity cost.]

 Whoops

_____

_____

_____

6. Classroom Game — Auction Demonstrating the Law of Demand
    The best way to introduce the law of demand is to hold a real auction in class. The Instructor brings something students like (a Coke on a Pepsi-only campus, cookies, ...) and starts playing promoter, selling a wonderful (ice-cold Coke! Cookies made with real ginger!) product.

    The rules of the game are:

    • Instructor puts prices on the board, starting at $0, and asks students who are willing and able to pay that price to raise their hands. Instructor writes that quantity next to the price.

    • Raise price in 50–cent increments, but jump to larger increments if that seems to work better.

    • Students must pay with cash (no debit or VISA) and the highest bidder must buy the product.

    Instructor questions after the auction ends:

    a. What is the relation between price and quantity demanded on the board?

    b. What factors went into your decisions, at each price, to raise your hand or not?

    c. At what price did quantity demanded decrease the most?
        What is it about that particular price that caused such a large decrease?

    d. What conclusion can you draw about the important forces behind the law of demand?

Changes in Demand — Moving the Margins

L03 Explain the difference between a change in quantity demanded and a change in demand, and list five factors that change demand.

Quantity Demanded versus Demand

Demand summarizes all influences on a consumer's choice. Your demand for any product or service reflects your willingness and ability to pay. Willingness to pay depends on your preferences, what substitutes are available, and marginal benefit. Ability to pay depends on your income. As long as these factors (and a few more) do not change, the law of demand holds true: If the price of a product or service rises, the quantity demanded decreases.

But when change happens, economists distinguish between two kinds of change shown in Figure 5:

- If the price of a product or service changes, that affects *quantity demanded*.
  This is represented graphically by a movement along an unchanged demand curve.

- If anything else changes, that affects *demand*.
  This is represented graphically by a shift of the entire demand curve.

Figure 5   Change in Quantity Demanded versus a Change in Demand

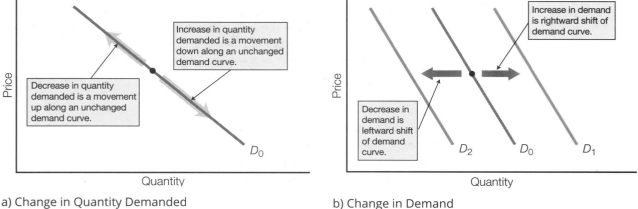

a) Change in Quantity Demanded

b) Change in Demand

Quantity demanded is a much more limited term than *demand*. Only a change in price changes *quantity demanded*. A change in any other influence on consumer choice changes *demand*.

Five Ways to Change Demand and Shift the Demand Curve

There are five important factors that can change market demand — the willingness and ability to pay for a product or service. They are

- Preferences
- Prices of related products
- Income
- Expected future prices
- Number of consumers

Preferences   Businesses advertise to try and get you to want their product, to persuade you that you need what they sell. An economist describes advertising as an attempt to increase your preferences for a product or service. Successful advertising increases your *willingness* to pay.

Any increase in consumers' willingness and ability to pay is called an **increase in demand** — a rightward shift of the demand curve. Any decrease in consumers' willingness and ability to pay is called a **decrease in demand** — a leftward shift of the demand curve.

Prices of Related Products   Many products (or services) you buy are related. Changes in the price of a different, related product affect your demand for the original product. There are two main types of related products — substitutes and complements.

Substitutes are products or services that can be used in place of each other to satisfy the same want. Headphones and earbuds are substitutes for listening to music. A rise in the price of a substitute (headphones) increases demand for the other product (earbuds).

Complements are products (or services) that are used together to satisfy the same want. Cars and gasoline are complements for driving. A fall in the price of a complement (cars) increases demand for the other product (gasoline).

Income Having more money, or more income, increases your *ability* to pay. For most products and services, an increase in income increases demand (demand curve shifts rightward) and a decrease in income decreases demand. Economists call these products and services **normal goods**.

Not all products are normal goods. If you have been a poor student living on Kraft Dinner, you may never want to eat it again once you can afford real food. Economists call products and services for which an increase in income *decreases* demand **inferior goods** — products and services that you buy less of when your income increases. A decrease in income increases demand for inferior goods.

Expected Future Prices A fall in the expected future price of a product (or service) decreases demand today — today's demand curve for that product shifts leftward. An expected future price rise increases demand today — today's demand curve shifts rightward.

Number of Consumers An increase in the number of consumers increases demand — the market demand curve shifts rightward. A decrease in the number of consumers decreases demand — the market demand curve shifts leftward.

Figure 6 summarizes the differences between the law of demand (focusing on quantity demanded and movements along the demand curve) and the factors that change demand (and shift the demand curve).

Figure 6   Law of Demand and Changes in Demand

The Law of Demand *The quantity demanded of a product or service*	
Decreases if:	*Increases if:*
• price of the product or service rises	• price of the product or service falls

Changes in Demand *The demand for a product or service*	
Decreases if:	*Increases if:*
• preferences decrease	• preferences increase
• price of a substitute falls	• price of a substitute rises
• price of a complement rises	• price of a complement falls
• income decreases (normal good)	• income increases (normal good)
• income increases (inferior good)	• income decreases (inferior good)
• expected future price falls	• expected future price rises
• number of consumers decreases	• number of consumers increases

Why Bother Distinguishing between Quantity Demanded and Demand?

Between 2010 and 2012, gas prices in Canada rose from about $1 to $1.40 per litre. But the quantity of gasoline drivers bought actually *increased*. Does that disprove the "law of demand"? If nothing else changed during those years except the price of gasoline, the answer would be yes. The law of demand states that if the price of a product rises, the quantity demanded decreases, *as long as other factors besides price do not change*. But many things besides price also changed, including the number of drivers and cars. The increase in the number of drivers increased demand for gasoline. The effect of the increase in demand outweighed the price effect of the decrease in quantity demanded.

The distinction between quantity demanded and demand is the economist's equivalent of a controlled experiment. The law of demand holds constant all factors other than the price of the product to isolate the effect of a change in price on quantity demanded. When other factors change, we will use the shifts of the demand curve to analyze the effect of those factors.

 # Practice...

11. Demand

    a. increases with a rise in price.

    b. is the same as quantity demanded.

    c. changes with income. ✓

    d. decreases with a rise in price.

12. Some sales managers are talking about business. Which quotation refers to a change in *quantity demanded*?

    a. "Since our competitors raised their prices, our sales have tripled."

    b. "Because it's been such a warm winter, our sales of wool scarves are down from last year."

    c. "The Green movement has made our biodegradable products best-sellers."

    d. "We decided to cut our prices, and there was a big increase in our sales."

13. Which could cause a leftward shift of the demand curve for a product?

    a. increase in income

    b. decrease in income

    c. decrease in the price of a substitute

    d. all of the above

14. If the price of cars rises, the demand for tires

    a. increases.

    b. decreases.

    c. stays the same.

    d. depends on the price of tires.

15. If Kraft Dinner is an inferior good, a rise in the price of Kraft Dinner

    a. decreases the quantity demanded of Kraft Dinner.

    b. increases the quantity demanded of Kraft Dinner

    c. decreases demand for Kraft Dinner.

    d. increases demand for Kraft Dinner.

Apply...

7. The questions below are about the market for fidget spinners. The numbers in columns 1 and 2 of the table show the original market demand.

Price	Quantity Demanded	
	Original D_0	New D_1
$1	500	600
$2	400	500
$3	300	400
$4	200	300
$5	100	200

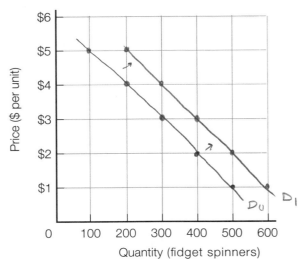

a. On the graph above, plot the points from the table and draw the original market demand curve. Label it D_0.

b. One year later, columns 1 and 3 show the new market demand. On the same graph, plot the new points and draw the new market demand curve. Label it D_1.

c. Describe this change by using some of the words — increase; decrease; demand; quantity demanded.

_____

_____

d. List changes in at least six factors that could explain the shift of the market demand curve from D_0 to D_1.

_____

_____

_____

_____

_____

_____

e. Reading D_0 and D_1 as marginal benefit curves, explain what changed for the 400th fidget spinner.

_____

_____

_____

_____

 Apply...

8. There are some "status goods," like Rolex watches, that people want to own because they are expensive. In contradiction to the law of demand, if Rolex watches were less expensive, fewer "status-seeking" consumers would demand them. Reconcile status products with the law of demand. How does the existence of cheap "knock-off" imitations of Rolex watches fit with the law of demand?

_____

_____

_____

_____

_____

9. Roses sell for about $40 a bouquet most of the year, and at that price, worldwide sales are 6 million bouquets per month. Every February, the price of roses doubles to $80 a bouquet, but the quantity of roses demanded and sold also increases, to 24 million bouquets per month. The cost of producing roses doesn't change throughout the year. Does this violate the law of demand? Explain your answer.

_____

_____

_____

_____

_____

_____

The Law of Supply

 L04 Explain the law of supply and describe the roles of higher profits and higher marginal opportunity costs of production.

Demand is not just what you want. It is your willingness and ability to pay for a product or service. Similarly, supply is not just offering things for sale. **Supply** is the overall willingness of businesses (or individuals) to sell a particular product or service because the price covers all opportunity costs of production.

Market Supply

Quantity supplied is a more limited concept than supply. It is the amount you actually plan to supply at a given price, taking into account everything that affects your willingness to supply.

Market supply is the sum of the supplies of all businesses willing to produce a particular product or service. In general, businesses supply a larger quantity at higher prices. Rising prices create two incentives for increased quantity supplied:

- higher profits.
- the need to cover higher marginal opportunity costs of production.

This positive relationship between price and quantity supplied (both go up together) is so universal that economists call it the **law of supply**: If the price of a product or service rises, the quantity supplied increases. If the price falls, the quantity supplied decreases. The law of supply works as long as other factors besides price do not change.

Figure 7 illustrates the positive relation between price and quantity supplied for the market supply of piercings.

Figure 7   Market Supply of Piercings

Row	Price (marginal opportunity cost or minimum willing to accept per piercings)	Quantity Supplied (piercings)
A	$ 20	100
B	$ 40	200
C	$ 60	300
D	$ 80	400
E	$100	500

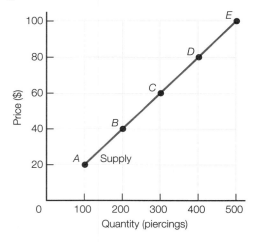

The **supply curve** shows the relationship between price and quantity supplied when all other influences on supply besides price do not change.

Two Ways to Read a Supply Curve

The supply curve is a simple yet powerful tool summarizing the two forces that determine quantity supplied — the desire for higher profits and the need to cover increasing marginal opportunity costs of production. Because there are two forces, Figure 8 shows two ways to "read" a supply curve. Both readings are correct, but each highlights a different force.

Figure 8   Two Ways to Read a Supply Curve

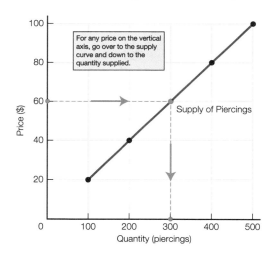

a) Reading the Supply Curve
    as a Supply Curve

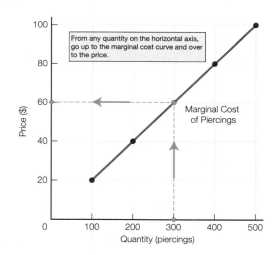

b) Reading the Supply Curve
    as a Marginal Cost Curve

- To read as a supply curve — start at any price and go over and down to the quantity supplied. The supply curve shows, for any price, what will be the quantity supplied.

- To read as a marginal cost curve — start at any quantity and go up and over to the price. The marginal cost curve shows, for any quantity, the minimum price businesses will accept that covers all marginal opportunity costs of production.

Both readings are movements along an unchanged supply curve. The law of supply works as long as other influences on supply besides price do not change.

Practice...

16. When prices rise, individuals and businesses devote more of their time and resources to producing or supplying because

    a.) of the desire for profits.

    b. higher profits usually mean higher costs.

    c. of the desire for higher prices.

    d. of higher demand.

17. As the price of a product or service *rises*,

    a. supply increases.

    b. quantity demanded increases.

    c. demand increases.

    d.) quantity supplied increases.

18. Market supply is the

    a. sum of the minimum prices that each business is willing to accept for each quantity.

    b.) sum of the quantities supplied by all businesses at each price.

    c. maximum amount each business is willing to accept for each quantity.

    d. maximum price each business will charge for each quantity.

19. A market has 10 identical businesses. When the price is $50, one business's quantity supplied is 70 units and market supply is

    a.) 3500 units.

    b. 500 units.

    c.) 700 units.

    d.) 70 units.

20. When reading a supply curve as a marginal cost curve, each

    a. price tells you the quantity supplied at that price.

    b. price tells you the supply at that price.

    c. quantity tells you the maximum price business will charge for that unit.

    d.) quantity tells you the minimum price business will accept to supply that unit.

 **Apply...**

10. In the circular flow model, individuals in households are suppliers in input markets. The most common service we all supply is our labour — our ability to work. This question is about your labour supply choices.

   a. Key 1— Choose only when additional benefits are greater than additional opportunity costs — also applies to choices about how many hours to work. What are the additional benefits of working more hours? What are the additional opportunity costs?

   _____

   _____

   _____

   _____

   b. You normally work 10 hours a week at a part-time job paying $15 per hour, but your boss calls you in a panic and begs you to work as many hours next week as possible. The timing is terrible, as you have two tests, and your out-of-town best friend is coming soon for the only visit you will have in months. But the boss offers you double time of $30 per hour. What happens to the number of hours you choose to supply working? What non-work activities would you give up? [No right answers, just personal choices.]

   _____

   _____

   _____

   _____

   _____

   c. If the boss offers you triple time of $45 per hour, what happens to the number of hours you choose to supply working? What additional, different non-work activities would you give up?

   _____

   _____

   _____

   _____

   d. Generally, as the price paid for your labour rises, what happens to the quantity of hours you are willing to supply? As you give up alternative uses of your time, do you give up the most valuable activities first, or the least valuable activities? Do your answers show the pattern of increasing marginal opportunity cost that Paola's Piercing and Fingernail Parlour (LO1 of this chapter) experiences in increasing the quantity of piercings supplied? Explain.

   _____

   _____

   _____

   _____

   _____

   _____

Apply…

11. This question is about supply.

    a. State the Law of Supply. What are two reasons rising prices create incentives for increased quantity supplied?

    _____

    _____

    _____

    _____

    b. There are two ways to read a supply curve. Explain how to read a supply curve as a supply curve. Which reason behind the law of supply is associated with the supply curve reading?

    _____

    _____

    _____

    _____

    c. Explain how to read a supply curve as a marginal cost curve. Which reason behind the law of supply is associated with the marginal cost reading?

    _____

    _____

    _____

    _____

What Can Change Supply?

L05 Explain the difference between a change in quantity supplied and a change in supply, and list six factors that can change supply.

Quantity Supplied versus Supply

Supply summarizes all influences on business choices. Businesses' willingness to sell a particular product or service depends on profitability and marginal opportunity costs of production. But there are other factors that affect the willingness to produce a product or service. As long as those factors do not change, the law of supply holds true: If the price of a product or service rises, the quantity supplied increases.

But when change happens, economists distinguish between two kinds of change shown in Figure 9:

- If the price of a product or service changes, that affects *quantity supplied*. This is represented graphically by a movement along an unchanged supply curve.

- If anything else changes, that affects *supply*. This is represented graphically by a shift of the entire supply curve.

Figure 9   Changes in Quantity Supplied versus a Change in Supply

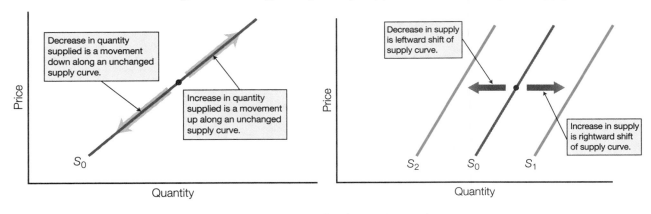

a) Change in Quantity Supplied   b) Change in Supply

Quantity supplied is a much more limited term than *supply*. Only a change in price changes *quantity supplied*. A change in any other influence on business choice changes *supply*.

Six Ways to Change Supply and Shift the Supply Curve

There are six important factors that can change market supply — business willingness to produce a product or service. They are

- Technology
- Environment
- Prices of inputs
- Prices of related products or services produced
- Expected future prices
- Number of businesses

Technology   A new technology increases productivity and decreases costs. At any price for a product, businesses supply a greater quantity because they make more profits. Or, for any quantity, marginal opportunity costs of production are lower, so businesses will accept a lower price for producing the same quantity.

Any increase in businesses' willingness to supply at any price is called an **increase in supply** — a rightward shift of the supply curve. Any decrease in businesses' willingness to supply is called a **decrease in supply** — a leftward shift of the supply curve.

Environment   Bad or good environmental changes — droughts, storms, earthquakes, global warming — can have an effect on supply. Droughts destroy crops, decreasing market supply and shifting the supply curve leftward. Good weather conditions produce bumper crops, increasing market supply and shifting the supply curve rightward.

Price of Inputs   If electricity prices fall, a business's energy costs fall. At any price for its products, a business earns higher profits and will supply more. Lower input prices increase market supply and shift the supply curve rightward.

Businesses must pay inputs a price that matches the best opportunity cost of the input owner. If wages are rising elsewhere, a business must raise wages to attract workers. Higher wages or other input prices means higher costs, and, at any price, lower profits. Market supply decreases. The supply curve shifts leftward.

Prices of Related Products and Services   Businesses can often use their inputs to produce more than one product or service. Paola's Parlour produces piercings and fingernail sets — those are related services because they use the same inputs. If the price of fingernail sets falls from $20 to $10 per set, Paola will shift inputs out of fingernails and into piercings, as relative profits are now higher in piercings. Lower prices for a related product or service increase the supply of the alternative product or service. The supply curve of the alternative (piercings) shifts rightward.

Expected Future Prices   A fall in the expected future price of a product or service increases supply today — today's supply curve for that product or service shifts rightward. An expected future price rise decreases supply today — today's supply curve shifts leftward.

Number of Businesses   An increase in the number of businesses increases market supply — the supply curve shifts rightward. A decrease in the number of businesses decreases market supply — the supply curve shifts leftward.

Figure 10 summarizes the differences between the law of supply (focusing on quantity supplied and movements along the supply curve) and the factors that change supply (and shift the supply curve).

Figure 10   Law of Supply and Changes in Supply

The Law of Supply *The quantity supplied of a product or service*	
Decreases if:	*Increases if:*
• price of the product or service falls	• price of the product or service rises

Changes in Supply *The supply for a product or service*	
Decreases if:	*Increases if:*
• _____	• technology improves
• environmental change harms production	• environment change helps production
• price of an input rises	• price of an input falls
• price of a related product or service rises	• price of a related product or service falls
• expected future price rises	• expected future price falls
• number of businesses decreases	• number of businesses increases

Why Bother Distinguishing between Quantity Supplied and Supply?

The average price of an ultrabook computer in Canada fell from around $2000 in 2010 to under $500 in 2016. But the quantity of ultrabook computers businesses sold increased. Does that disprove the "law of supply"? If nothing else changed during those years except the price of ultrabooks, the answer would be yes. The law of supply states that if the price of a product falls, the quantity supplied decreases, *as long as other factors besides price do not change.* But many things besides price also changed, including technological improvements in computer chips and falling input prices. Using the marginal cost reading of an increase in supply, at any quantity supplied, businesses were willing to accept a lower price because marginal opportunity costs of production were lower.

The effect of the increase in supply outweighed the price effect of the decrease in quantity supplied.

The distinction between quantity supplied and supply is the economist's equivalent of a controlled experiment. The law of supply holds constant all other factors than the price of the product to isolate the effect of a change in price on quantity supplied. When other factors change, we will use the shifts of the supply curve to analyze the effect of those factors.

 # Practice...

21. Which factor does *not* change supply?
    a. prices of inputs
    b. expected future prices
    c. price of the supplied product or service
    d. number of businesses

22. The supply of a product or service increases with a(n)
    a. improvement in technology producing it.
    b. rise in the price of a related product or service produced.
    c. rise in the price of an input.
    d. rise in the expected future price of the product or service.

23. The furniture industry switches to using particleboard (glued wood chips) rather than real wood, reducing costs. This
    a. decreases supply.
    b. increases supply.
    c. does not change furniture supply.
    d. effect on supply depends on demand.

24. Which factor changes supply?
    a. income
    b. environmental change
    c. number of consumers
    d. price of a complement

25. Popeye's Parlour supplies both piercing and tattoo services. Higher prices for piercings cause Popeye's
    a. quantity supplied of tattoos to increase.
    b. quantity supplied of tattoos to decrease.
    c. supply of tattoos to increase.
    d. supply of tattoos to decrease.

 **Apply…**

12. Watch the video (http://tinyurl.com/flextext-robots) about an army of noodle-shaving robots invading restaurants in China. Here are questions for discussion:
    - What created the incentive for the invention of the robots?
    - How do you represent the invention of the robots using a supply curve?
    - Explain two ways to read the supply curve for meals with noodles, comparing supply before and after the invention.
    - Will robots cause unemployment for workers?

13. You have two part-time jobs, babysitting and pizza delivery. After younger babysitters start working for less, babysitting clients pay only $10 instead of $15 per hour. What happens to your supply of hours for delivering pizzas? Explain.

    _____

    _____

    _____

    _____

14. Your friend Pablo opens up a tattoo parlour because he thinks body art is a profitable industry. He is trying to forecast how different factors in the industry would affect supply in the market for tattoos. He knows you are taking a course in economics and asks you to verify whether his predictions are true or false. Explain any false prediction.

    a. The entry of new businesses into the industry will increase supply.
    True / False

    b. An increase in the minimum wage will increase supply.
    True / False

    c. A rise in the price of piercings (a related service) will reduce supply of tattoos.
    True / False

    d. An improvement in tattoo technology will increase supply.
    True / False

    e. A rise in the price of tattoos will increase supply.
    True / False

KNOW...

Summary of Learning Objectives

1. Consumers' willingness to pay depends on **marginal benefits**, not total benefits. Marginal benefits change with circumstances. The price at which businesses are willing to supply depends on **marginal costs**. Marginal costs are ultimately **opportunity costs**, and change with circumstances.

2. The **demand curve** combines two forces that determine quantity demanded — switch to substitutes, and willingness and ability to pay. The **law of demand** is that as price rises, quantity demanded decreases. The demand curve can be read as a demand curve and as a marginal benefit curve.

3. **Quantity demanded** changes only with a change in price — a movement along an unchanged demand curve. All other influences on consumer demand change **demand**. An **increase in demand** shifts the demand curve rightward, a **decrease in demand** shifts the demand curve leftward. Five factors that change demand are preferences, prices of related products, income, expected future prices, and number of consumers.

4. The **supply curve** combines two forces that determine quantity supplied — the desire for more profits, and the need to cover increasing marginal opportunity costs of production. The **law of supply** is that as price rises, quantity supplied increases. The supply curve can be read as a supply curve and as a marginal cost curve.

5 **Quantity supplied** changes only with a change in price — a movement along an unchanged supply curve. All other influences on business willingness to produce change **supply**. An **increase in supply** shifts the supply curve rightward, a **decrease in supply** shifts the supply curve leftward. Six factors that change supply are technology, environment, prices of inputs, prices of related products or services produced, expected future prices, and number of businesses.

Key Terms

complements: products or services used together to satisfy the same want

decrease in demand: decrease in consumers' willingness and ability to pay; leftward shift of demand curve

decrease in supply: decrease in businesses' willingness to produce; leftward shift of supply curve

demand: consumers' willingness and ability to pay for a particular product or service

demand curve: shows the relationship between price and quantity demanded, other things remaining the same

increase in demand: increase in consumers' willingness and ability to pay; rightward shift of demand curve

increase in supply: increase in businesses' willingness to produce; rightward shift of supply curve

inferior goods: products or services you buy less of when your income increases

law of demand: if the price of a product or services rises, quantity demanded decreases, other things remaining the same

law of supply: if the price of a product or services rises, quantity supplied increases, other things remaining the same

marginal benefit: additional benefit from a choice, changing with circumstances

marginal cost: additional opportunity cost of increasing quantity supplied, changing with circumstances

market demand: sum of demands of all individuals willing and able to buy a particular product or service

market supply: sum of supplies of all businesses willing to produce a particular product or service

normal goods: products or services you buy more of when your income increases

opportunity cost: cost of best alternative given up

preferences: your wants and their intensities

quantity demanded: amount you actually plan to buy at a given price

quantity supplied: amount you actually plan to supply at a given price

substitutes: products or services used in place of each other to satisfy the same want

supply: businesses' willingness to produce a particular product or service because price covers all opportunity costs

supply curve: shows the relationship between price and quantity supplied, other things remaining the same

Answers to Practice

1. **c**   After paying fixed fee, marginal cost of each additional plate is constant and equals zero.

2. **d**   Reverse of Key 1 — don't choose when marginal costs are greater than marginal benefits.

3. **a**   Price depends on marginal benefits, not total benefits.

4. **b**   If all inputs are equally productive, marginal cost is constant.

5. **c**   As inputs switch between tasks, no changes in opportunity costs.

6. **d**   Intensities of your wants.

7. **b**   *Give up* includes money, time, and effort.

8. **c**   With switch to cheaper substitutes, quantity demanded decreases.

9. **b**   Definition of substitutes.

10. **c**   Demand requires you to be willing *and able* to pay. Concern about the environment probably decreases your willingness to buy (pay for) a car.

11. **c**   Other answers are about *quantity demanded*.

12. **d** Lowering prices moves along the demand curve. Other quotations are about changes in *demand* — shifts of the demand curve.

13. **d** **a** true for inferior goods; **b** true for normal goods.

14. **b** Cars and tires are complements.

15. **a** Price only affects quantity demanded. Change in income changes demand.

16. **a** Businesses want higher profits. High prices don't mean high profits if costs are also high.

17. **d** Rising prices increase quantity supplied, not supply, and decrease quantity demanded, not demand.

18. **b** Definition. Supply curve shows *minimum* prices businesses willing to accept.

19. **c** Adding 70 units for each of 10 businesses gives a quantity supplied of 700 units at the $50 price.

20. **d** Starting at a quantity, read a marginal cost curve up and over.

21. **c** Price changes quantity supplied.

22. **a** Only **a** shifts supply curve rightward. Other answers shift supply curve leftward.

23. **b** Rightward shift of supply curve.

24. **b** Other factors change demand.

25. **d** Piercings and tattoos are products related in production.

3

The Demand and Supply Model

LEARNING OBJECTIVES

L01 Describe what markets do and explain how shortages and surpluses affect market prices.

L02 Summarize how equilibrium prices match quantity demanded and quantity supplied and illustrate Adam Smith's concept of the invisible hand.

L03 Use the demand and supply model to predict how a change in demand or a change in supply affects equilibrium prices and quantities.

L04 Predict how combined changes in demand and supply affect equilibrium prices and quantities, and describe the modelling technique of comparative statics.

L05 Demonstrate the efficiency of markets using the concepts of consumer surplus and producer surplus.

LEARN ...

Have you ever organized a milestone birthday party (20th, 50th, 80th?) and felt like it was a miracle everything worked out? There are so many details to coordinate — who's helping with the food, who's decorating the cake, who's tending bar, and what about toilet paper? Now imagine organizing one day in the life of Toronto. Think about the millions of consumers who each make hundreds of decisions about what to eat or which headphones to buy. Think about the thousands of businesses that decide what to produce, where to find inputs, who to hire. Somehow, businesses produce just about everything consumers want to buy — for a price. With no one in charge, it seems miraculous. How are all those billions of decisions coordinated so that you (and everyone else) can find the food you want for breakfast, the headphones you want at the electronics store, let alone water, jobs, gas, and places to live?

If all that doesn't seem enough of a miracle, consider that the coordination problem is a fast-moving target. Mexican food becomes fashionable, condos replace houses, new immigrants arrive with different tastes — and yet businesses adjust, and we all continue to find the changing items we look for.

Markets and prices are the keys to these apparent miracles. As consumers, we each make smart choices in our own interests. Businesses make smart choices in pursuit of profits. Markets, when they work well, create incentives that coordinate the right products and services being produced in the right quantities and at the right locations to satisfy our wants.

You will use the demand and supply model to understand how markets form prices. Those prices provide signals and incentives coordinating the choices of consumers and businesses. Whether you are trying to understand the decisions in a market economy, or just trying to get ahead in life, the demand and supply model is a powerful tool to help you make smart choices.

Price Signals from Combining Demand and Supply

 Describe what markets do and explain how shortages and surpluses affect market prices.

Markets Mix Competition and Cooperation

A **market** is not a place or a thing: It's a process — the interactions between buyers and sellers. Markets exist wherever there is a process of competing bids (from buyers or demanders) and offers (from sellers or suppliers). All markets contain a negotiation between a buyer and a seller that results in an exchange.

Markets are an unlikely mix of competition and cooperation. Buyers compete against each other trying to get the same product. Sellers compete with other sellers for customers by offering a lower price or higher quality.

When there is a voluntary exchange between a buyer and a seller, both sides cooperate and end up better off. A buyer only demands a product if the marginal benefit is at least as great as the price — the buyer's marginal opportunity cost. A seller only supplies a product if the price covers at least the marginal opportunity cost. "Better off" doesn't require the buyer to get the lowest price, or the seller to get the highest price. Any price for a product that is lower than the marginal benefit of the buyer and higher than the marginal opportunity cost of the seller benefits both buyers and sellers.

Where Do Prices Come From?

Prices are the outcome of a market process of competing bids and offers. But why do most stores sell Gatorade for $3 a bottle, or doughnuts for 99 cents? Where do these prices come from? Why do prices settle at particular numbers? The economist's answer to these questions is that prices come from the interaction of demand and supply in markets with appropriate property rights.

Paradoxically, the best way to understand why prices settle at particular numbers is to look at what happens in markets when prices have *not* settled. Figure 1 combines the market demand and supply curves for piercings.

Figure 1   Market Demand and Supply for Piercings

Price	Quantity Demanded	Quantity Supplied	Shortage (−) or Surplus (+)
$ 20	1200	200	−1000
$ 40	900	400	−500
$ 60	600	600	0
$ 80	300	800	+500
$100	0	1000	+1000

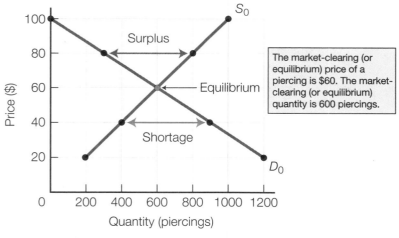

We know from the law of demand that consumers prefer lower prices, and we know from the law of supply that businesses prefer higher prices. How do prices get set in a way that combines these opposite goals?

Shortages and Frustrated Buyers   In Figure 1, what if the market price of piercings were $40? Consumers want to buy 900 piercings, but Paola and other piercing parlours are only willing to supply 400 piercings. There are 500 frustrated buyers (900 – 400 = 500) who are willing and able to pay $40 but can't get a parlour to do the piercing. This is a **shortage**, where quantity demanded exceeds quantity supplied. In markets with shortages, or **excess demand**, consumers experience long lineups and out-of-stock items at stores. Businesses experience products flying off the shelves. On the graph, the horizontal distance between the supply and demand curves at the price of $40 represents that shortage of 500 piercings. This is the red arrow labelled *shortage*.

Shortages encourage competition among buyers. The consumers who most want the piercing will be willing to pay a bit more than $40, rather than being left with nothing. Shortages create pressure for prices to rise. Rising prices then provide signals and incentives for businesses to increase quantity supplied, and for consumers to decrease quantity demanded, eliminating the shortage.

Surpluses and Frustrated Sellers   Instead of $40, what if the market price of piercings were $80 in Figure 1? Consumers want to buy only 300 piercings, but piercing parlours are eagerly willing to supply 800 piercings. There are 500 unsold piercings (800 – 300 = 500) and frustrated sellers. This is a **surplus**, where quantity supplied exceeds quantity demanded. In markets with surpluses, or **excess supply**, businesses experience underemployed inputs and unsold products. Those consumers willing and able to buy at the higher price experience their choice of where to buy and sellers who are eager to please. On the graph, the horizontal distance between the demand and supply curves at the price of $80 represents that surplus of 500 piercings. This is the blue arrow labelled *surplus*.

Surpluses encourage competition among sellers. The businesses that are most efficient or desperate for sales will cut their prices rather than be faced with idle workers and no revenues. Surpluses create pressure for prices to fall. Falling prices then provide signals and incentives for businesses to decrease quantity supplied, and for consumers to increase quantity demanded, eliminating the surplus.

Self-Interest at Work

What is remarkable about all of these price and quantity adjustments is that no consumer or business needs to know anything about anyone's personal wants or production capabilities. Prices serve as signals to buyers and sellers, and all anyone has to do is consider his or her own self-interest. As long as there is an imbalance between quantity demanded and quantity supplied, prices adjust and send signals for consumers and businesses to change their smart choices. As a byproduct of all these self-interested individual decisions made by complete strangers, markets provide the products and services we want.

Practice...

1. The place where buyers and sellers meet is called a(n)

   a. store.

   b. economy.

   c. market.

   d. party.

2. Voluntary exchange happens in a market when the

   a. price is less than the marginal opportunity cost of the seller.

   b. price equals or exceeds the marginal opportunity cost of the buyer.

   c. marginal benefit for the buyer is less than the price.

   d. marginal benefit for the buyer exceeds the price.

3. If a market is not at the market-clearing price,

   a. prices adjust.

   b. prices send signals for consumers and businesses to change their smart choices.

   c. quantities adjust.

   d. all of the above.

4. When the price is too high we see

   a. surpluses.

   b. frustrated buyers.

   c. excess demand.

   d. empty store shelves.

5. A shortage is the amount by which quantity

   a. supplied exceeds quantity demanded.

   b. demanded exceeds quantity supplied.

   c. supplied exceeds the equilibrium quantity.

   d. demanded exceeds the equilibrium quantity.

 **Apply…**

1. You are negotiating over the price of a new car with a car dealer. Explain how this process contains both cooperation and competition.

    _____

    _____

    _____

    _____

2. Apu wants to set the market-clearing equilibrium price, so he surveys all three families on his street to determine how many cappuccinos per day they are willing to buy at different prices. He gives them four price options. Their answers are summarized on the following table.

    a. What is the market quantity demanded for each price? Fill in the grey boxes.

Price per Iced Capuccino	Flanders Family Quantity Demanded	Van Houten Family Quantity Demanded	Simpson Family Quantity Demanded	Market Quantity Demanded
$1	2	5	5	
$2	1	3	4	
$3	0	1	3	
$4	0	0	2	

    Apu also estimates his costs and determines how many iced cappuccinos he is willing to sell. Apu's supply is summarized in the following table:

Price per Iced Capuccino	Apu's Quantity Supplied
$1	7
$2	8
$3	9
$4	10

    b. What is the market-clearing, or equilibrium, price? Explain.

    _____

    _____

    _____

    c. If Apu sets the price higher than the equilibrium price,

        i.   will there be a shortage or surplus in the market?

        ii. will there be pressure for the price to rise or fall? Explain.

    _____

    _____

    _____

    _____

to be continued

Apply...

continued

d. If Apu sets the price lower than the equilibrium price,

   i. will there be a shortage or surplus in the market?

   ii. will there be pressure for the price to rise or fall? Explain.

3. Most provincial parks charge a fixed price for a camping permit, and allow you to reserve specific campsites in advance. By the time the summer holiday weekends arrive, all the permits are usually taken. There is excess demand but no price adjustment. Suggest a pricing system for provincial parks that allows them to take advantage of the higher demand for campsites on holiday weekends. Your system should explain who is competing and who is cooperating.

Equilibrium Prices and Adam Smith's Invisible Hand

L02 Summarize how equilibrium prices match quantity demanded and quantity supplied and illustrate Adam Smith's concept of the invisible hand.

The price that coordinates quantity demanded and quantity supplied is so important that economists have two names for it.

Market-Clearing Price

Market-clearing price is one name for the price that equalizes quantity demanded and quantity supplied. At the market-clearing price, there are no frustrated buyers or sellers. There is a match for every buyer and seller. All go home happy. Everyone who volunteers to exchange $60 for a piercing in Figure 1 (consumers buying and businesses selling) is better off, or they wouldn't have bought and sold.

Equilibrium Price

The second name is the **equilibrium price**. *Equilibrium* is a term from physics that means a balance of forces resulting in an unchanging outcome. The equilibrium price exactly balances forces of competition and cooperation to coordinate the smart choices of consumers and businesses. At the equilibrium price, there is no tendency for change, and no incentives for anyone — consumers or businesses — to change their own self-interested, smart decisions. Everyone has done the best they can in exchanging, given the wants and resources they started with.

The Invisible Hand

The fact that consumers find businesses have produced just about everything they want to buy, with no one in charge, and that billions of decisions get coordinated is due to the interaction of demand and supply in markets with appropriate property rights. The law of demand is shorthand for the smart choices of consumers. The law of supply is shorthand for the smart choices of businesses. Equilibrium prices and quantities result when smart choices are coordinated. The forces of competition are balanced with the forces of cooperation. Price signals in markets create incentives so that while each person acts only in her own self-interest, the unintended consequence is the coordinated production of all the products and services we want.

Perhaps the most famous phrase in economics that describes this outcome is Adam Smith's *invisible hand* in his 1776 book, *The Wealth of Nations*:

> When an individual makes choices, "he intends only his own gain, and he is in this . . . led by an invisible hand to promote an end which was no part of his intention. . . . By pursuing his own interest he frequently promotes that of the society more effectually than when he really intends to promote it."

The miracle is that markets channel self-interest as though "by an invisible hand" so that society produces the products and services we want, without the government doing anything beyond setting the rules of the game.

 # Practice...

6. A price at which there are no shortages and no surpluses is a
    a. maximum price.
    b. minimum price.
    c. affordable price.
    d. market-clearing price.

7. Surpluses are eliminated by
    a. allowing prices to rise.
    b. allowing prices to fall.
    c. increasing quantity supplied.
    d. decreasing quantity demanded.

8. Market-clearing prices
    a. are set by the visible hand of government.
    b. scare away all consumers from the market.
    c. scare away all businesses from the market.
    d. balance the forces of competition and cooperation.

9. In equilibrium,
    a. the price consumers are wiling to pay equals the price suppliers are willing to accept.
    b. consumers would like to buy more at the current price.
    c. producers would like to sell more at the current price.
    d. the force of cooperation is stronger than the force of competition.

10. Price signals in markets
    a. require detailed information about preference and costs.
    b. coordinate the preferences of government officials.
    c. create incentives for producers to produce the products and services consumers want.
    d. lead consumers to favour the public interest rather than their private interests.

 **Apply...**

4. In an attempt to promote the social good of energy conservation, Toronto Hydro introduced the Peaksaver Program. Participating households received a $25 reward for allowing a "peaksaver" switch to be installed on their central air conditioners, which briefly turns off the air conditioner during peak demand times on hot summer days. Do you think the program would work without the $25 reward? Why or why not?

_____

_____

_____

_____

_____

5. The table below shows the market for robotic rubber ducks.

Price	Quantity Demanded	Quantity Supplied
$40	500	300
$50	450	350
$60	400	400
$70	350	450
$80	300	500

a. If the price of a duck is $40, is there a shortage or a surplus? Of how many ducks? Explain who is frustrated, and how the forces of competition will change the smart choices of demanders and of suppliers.

_____

_____

_____

_____

_____

b. If the price of a duck is $70, is there a shortage or a surplus? Of how many ducks? Explain who is frustrated, and how the forces of competition will change the smart choices of demander and of suppliers.

_____

_____

_____

_____

_____

 # Apply...

   c. What is the equilibrium price? What is the equilibrium quantity?

_____

_____

_____

_____

6. Explain the idea of Adam Smith's *invisible hand*. Your explanation should illustrate the balance between the forces of competition and cooperation at equilibrium prices.

_____

_____

_____

_____

_____

_____

What Happens to Equilibrium Prices and Quantities When Demand or Supply Change?

L03 Use the demand and supply model to predict how a change in demand or a change in supply affects equilibrium prices and quantities.

Even if markets settle at equilibrium prices and temporarily succeed in coordinating the plans of consumers and businesses, what happens when something changes? Will markets still be efficient?

Believe it or not, all stories so far about shortages, surpluses, mutually beneficial trades, and adjusting prices and quantities actually had very limited change. Yes, prices and quantities and smart decisions changed, but in the background I was holding constant the five major influences on demand and the six major influences on supply.

A demand curve isolates the relationship between price and quantity demanded by holding constant all other influences on consumers' choices — preferences, prices of related products, income, expected future prices, and number of consumers.

A supply curve isolates the relationship between price and quantity supplied by holding constant all other influences on businesses' choices — technology, environment, input prices, prices of related products produced, expected future prices, and number of businesses.

Instead of slogging through changes in each of the 11 influences, I have grouped them together — increases and decreases in demand, and increases and decreases in supply. Let's look at how these changes affect equilibrium prices and quantities. The starting point for each change is the equilibrium in the piercing market in Figure 1 on page 54.

Increases in Demand

Figure 2 shows an increase in demand.

Figure 2   Increase in Demand

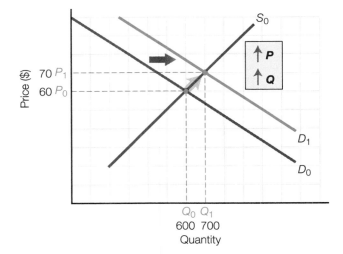

	Quantity Demanded		Quantity Supplied
Price	Original (D_0)	New (D_1)	(S_0)
$40	900 $\rightarrow$	1150	400
$50	750 $\rightarrow$	900	500
$60	600 $\rightarrow$	850	600
$70	450 $\rightarrow$	700	700
$80	300 $\rightarrow$	550	800

The demand curve shifts rightward from D_0 to D_1. At every price, the new quantity demanded is 250 piercings *more* than the original quantity. At the original price of $60, there is now a shortage. Competition between consumers drives up the price, increasing the quantity supplied (a movement up along the unchanged supply curve). The equilibrium price rises ($\uparrow P$) from $60 to $70 and the equilibrium quantity increases ($\uparrow Q$) from 600 to 700. At the new equilibrium price, quantity demanded once again equals quantity supplied.

Decreases in Demand

Figure 3 shows a decrease in demand.

Figure 3   Decrease in Demand

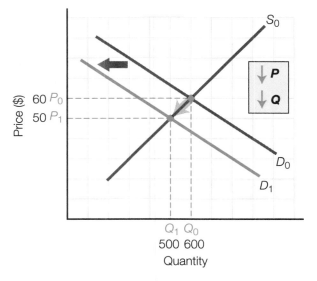

	Quantity Demanded		Quantity Supplied
Price	Original (D_0)	New (D_1)	(S_0)
$40	900 $\rightarrow$	650	400
$50	750 $\rightarrow$	500	500
$60	600 $\rightarrow$	350	600
$70	450 $\rightarrow$	200	700
$80	300 $\rightarrow$	50	800

The demand curve shifts leftward from D_0 to D_1. At every price, the new quantity demanded is 250 piercings *less* than the original quantity. At the original price of $60, there is now a surplus. Competition between businesses for scarce customers drives down the price, decreasing the quantity supplied (a movement down along the unchanged supply curve). The equilibrium price falls ($\downarrow P$) from $60 to $50 and the equilibrium quantity decreases ($\downarrow Q$) from 600 to 500. At the new equilibrium price, quantity demanded once again equals quantity supplied.

Increases in Supply

Figure 4 shows an increase in supply.

Figure 4   Increase in Supply

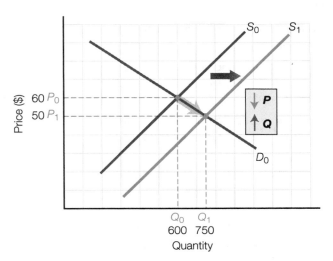

Price	Quantity Demanded (D_0)	Quantity Supplied	
		Original (S_0)	New (S_1)
$40	900	400 → 650	
$50	750	500 → 750	
$60	600	600 → 850	
$70	450	700 → 950	
$80	300	800 →1050	

The supply curve shifts rightward from S_0 to S_1. At every price, the new quantity supplied is 250 piercings *more* than the original quantity. At the original price of $60, there is now a surplus. Competition between businesses for scarce customers drives down the price, increasing the quantity demanded (a movement down along the unchanged demand curve). The equilibrium price falls ($\downarrow P$) from $60 to $50 and the equilibrium quantity increases ($\uparrow Q$) from 600 to 750. At the new equilibrium price, quantity demanded once again equals quantity supplied.

Decreases in Supply

Figure 5 shows a decrease in supply.

Figure 5   Decrease in Supply

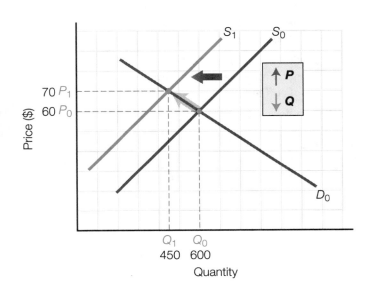

Price	Quantity Demanded (D_0)	Quantity Supplied	
		Original (S_0)	New (S_1)
$40	900	400 → 150	
$50	750	500 → 250	
$60	600	600 → 350	
$70	450	700 → 450	
$80	300	800 → 550	

The supply curve shifts leftward from S_0 to S_1. At every price, the new quantity supplied is 250 piercings *less* than the original quantity. At the original price of $60, there is now a shortage. Competition between consumers drives up the price, decreasing the quantity demanded (a movement up along the unchanged demand curve). The equilibrium price rises ($\uparrow P$) from $60 to $70 and the equilibrium quantity decreases ($\downarrow Q$) from 600 to 450. At the new equilibrium price, quantity demanded once again equals quantity supplied.

 # Practice...

11. Coffee is a normal good. A decrease in income
    a. increases the price of coffee and increases the quantity demanded of coffee.
    b. increases the price of coffee and increases the quantity supplied of coffee.
    c. decreases the price of coffee and decreases the quantity demanded of coffee.
    d. decreases the price of coffee and decreases the quantity supplied of coffee.

12. An increase in the price of Pepsi (a substitute for coffee)
    a. increases the price of coffee and increases the quantity demanded of coffee.
    b. increases the price of coffee and increases the quantity supplied of coffee.
    c. decreases the price of coffee and decreases the quantity demanded of coffee.
    d. decreases the price of coffee and decreases the quantity supplied of coffee.

13. Farmland can be used to produce either cattle or corn. If demand for cattle increases,
    a. demand for corn increases.
    b. supply of corn increases.
    c. demand for corn decreases.
    d. supply of corn decreases.

14. The equilibrium price falls when supply
    a. increases or demand decreases.
    b. decreases or demand increases.
    c. increases or demand increases.
    d. decreases or demand decreases.

15. If bus fares fall but fewer people are riding the bus, it is likely that
    a. supply decreased.
    b. supply increased.
    c. demand decreased.
    d. demand increased.

 **Apply…**

7. Watch the SourceFed video (http://tinyurl.com/FlexText-bacon) containing two separate explanations for rising bacon prices. Here are questions for discussion:

    • Draw a demand and supply diagram representing the initial equilibrium in the pork/bacon market.

    • Using your diagram, how would you model the most important explanation for rising bacon prices? What is the most important factor that changes either the demand or supply curve?

    • Draw another diagram, and model the other explanation [*HINT: Epic Mealtime*] for rising bacon prices. What is the most important factor that changes either the demand or supply curve?

      Instructor — you can do this exercise for the class as a whole, or break the students into small groups and have each group work out the analysis and report back.

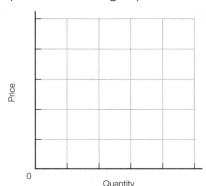 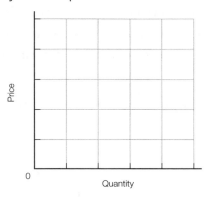

8. A tax on crude oil raises the cost of the most important input used to produce gasoline. A supporter of the tax claims that it will not raise the price of gasoline using the following argument. "While the price of gasoline may rise initially, that price increase will cause the demand for gasoline to decrease, which will push the price back down." What is wrong with this argument?

    _____

    _____

    _____

    _____

    _____

to be continued

Apply...

continued

9. The market for wine in Canada is initially in equilibrium. Beer is a close substitute for wine; cheese and wine are complements. Use demand and supply models to analyze the effect of each of the following (separate) events on the equilibrium price and quantity in the Canadian wine market. Assume that all other factors remain unchanged except for the event listed. For each of these five events, explain what happens to the equilibrium price (rises, falls, remains the same, or unable to predict) and the equilibrium quantity (increases, decreases, remains the same, or unable to predict).

    a. The income of consumers increases (wine is a normal good).

    b. Early frost destroys a large part of the world grape crop.

    c. A new churning invention reduces the cost of producing cheese.

    d. A new fermentation invention reduces the cost of producing wine.

    e. A new government study links wine drinking and increased heart disease.

    [Use the graphs below to draw your five models of the wine market.]

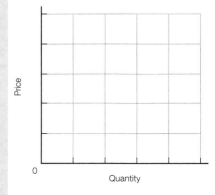
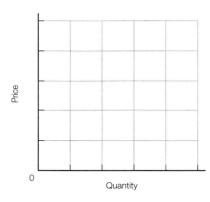
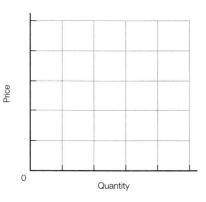

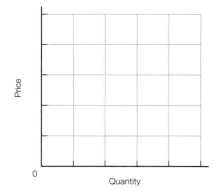
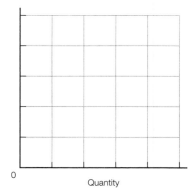

Predicting the Effects of Combined Changes in Demand and Supply

 L04 Predict how combined changes in demand and supply affect equilibrium prices and quantities, and describe the modelling technique of comparative statics.

Once you allow both demand and supply to change at the same time, the effects on the equilibrium price and quantity are a bit more complicated. Figure 6 shows those combined effects. P_0 and Q_0 are the original price and quantity before the changes. P_1 and Q_1 are the new equilibrium price and quantity after the changes in both demand and supply.

In all combinations of changes in both demand and supply, we can still predict the effect on *either* the equilibrium price or the equilibrium quantity. But there is not enough information to predict the effects on *both* price and quantity.

Figure 6   The Effects of Combined Changes in Demand and Supply

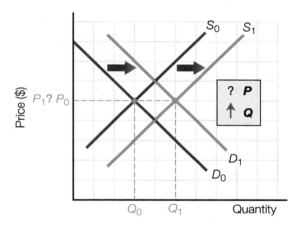

a)   Increase in Both Demand and Supply

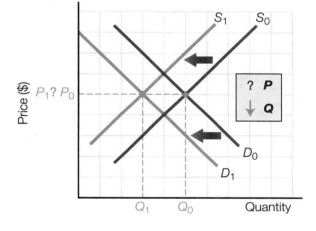

b)   Decrease in Both Demand and Supply

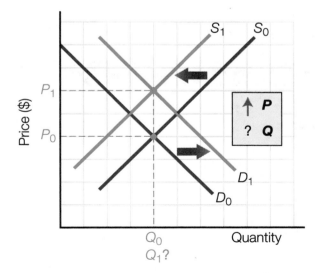

c)   Increase in Demand and Decrease in Supply

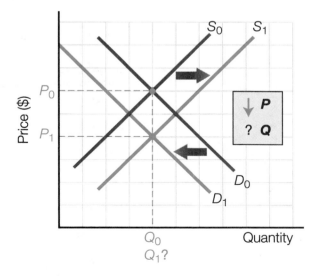

d)   Decrease in Demand and Increase in Supply

Economists Do It with Models

All of these simple demand and supply graphs are models. They focus our attention on the reasons why mutually beneficial trades happen in a market, and select just enough information to predict where equilibrium prices and quantities will end up. As well, the models tell us when we do not have enough information to make predictions.

In the real world, all eleven factors that influence consumers' and businesses' choices are changing constantly. Demand and supply graphs are like controlled laboratory experiments. They hold all influences constant except one (or two), so we can see the effect of that influence alone.

Start in Equilibrium When I draw demand and supply curves that intersect at price P_0 and quantity Q_0, I am holding constant all eleven factors that can shift the demand or supply curves and influence consumers' and businesses' choices. At the original equilibrium outcome, there is no tendency for change. This is our starting point.

One Change at a Time In each "thought experiment" in Figures 2 – 5, I change one factor that affects demand or supply, while continuing to hold all other influences constant. The results of these controlled thought experiments are the new equilibrium outcomes of price P_1 and quantity Q_1. At the new equilibrium outcome, once again there is no further tendency for change. Even in Figure 6, when two factors change, we are still comparing an original equilibrium outcome with a second equilibrium outcome, while continuing to hold all other influences constant.

This simplified way of using a model to isolate the impact of one (or two) factors in the economy is called **comparative statics** — the comparison of two equilibrium outcomes. Static means unchanging. Each equilibrium is static — there is no tendency for change. We start with one equilibrium outcome, change a single factor that affects demand or supply, and then compare it to the new equilibrium outcome. This simplified comparison allows us to predict changes in price and quantity, despite all of the complexities in the real world.

My favourite saying for this way of thinking is "Economists do it with models." Figure 7 summarizes all possible effects of changes in demand and supply.

Figure 7   Effects of Changes in Demand or Supply

Change	Shifts of Curves	Effect on Equilibrium Price	Effect on Equilibrium Quantity
Increase in Demand	Demand shifts rightward	↑	↑
Decrease in Demand	Demand shifts leftward	↓	↓
Increase in Supply	Supply shifts rightward	↓	↑
Decrease in Supply	Supply shifts leftward	↑	↓
Increase in Demand and Increase in Supply	Demand shifts rightward; Supply shifts rightward	Need exact numbers to predict outcome	↑
Decrease in Demand and Decrease in Supply	Demand shifts leftward; Supply shifts leftward	Need exact numbers to predict outcome	↓
Increase in Demand and Decrease in Supply	Demand shifts rightward; Supply shifts leftward	↑	Need exact numbers to predict outcome
Decrease in Demand and Increase in Supply	Demand shifts leftward; Supply shifts rightward	↓	Need exact numbers to predict outcome

Practice...

16. Which will cause prices to fall?
    a. demand increases and supply decreases
    b. demand increases and supply increases
    c. demand decreases and supply decreases
    d. demand decreases and supply increases

17. If demand increases and supply decreases, this leads to
    a. higher prices.
    b. lower prices.
    c. chaos.
    d. a shortage in the market.

18. A technological improvement lowers the cost of producing coffee. At the same time, preferences for coffee decrease. The *equilibrium quantity* of coffee
    a. increases.
    b. decreases.
    c. remains the same.
    d. increases or decreases, depending on the relative shifts of demand and supply curves.

19. If both demand and supply increase, the equilibrium price
    a. rises and the equilibrium quantity increases.
    b. falls and the equilibrium quantity increases.
    c. could rise or fall, and the equilibrium quantity increases.
    d. could rise or fall, and the equilibrium quantity decreases.

20. If the equilibrium price of boots falls, either the demand for boots
    a. decreased or the supply of boots decreased, or both.
    b. increased or the supply of boots increased, or both.
    c. decreased or the supply of boots increased, or both.
    d. increased or the supply of boots decreased, or both.

Apply...

10. Predicting changes in equilibrium prices and quantities is harder when both demand and supply change at the same time. You run a halal butcher shop in Ottawa and expect an increase in the number of Muslims in Ottawa who prefer halal meat. Rents for retail space are also falling all over town. Predict what will happen to the equilibrium price for halal meat. Predict what will happen to the equilibrium quantity. Explain your predictions.

_____

_____

_____

_____

_____

_____

_____

11. The market for coffee is originally in equilibrium with demand curve D_0, supply curve S_0, equilibrium price P_0 and equilibrium quantity Q_0. On the graph, draw and label the original equilibrium.

Two events happen at the same time. There is a rise in wages of coffee pickers and a rise in the price of tea (a substitute for coffee).

a. On the graph, draw any shift(s) in the demand and supply curves. Label any shifted demand curve as D_1 and any shifted supply curve as S_1. Label the new equilibrium price as P_1 and the new equilibrium quantity as Q_1.

Based on your demand and supply model, predict what happens to the equilibrium price and to the equilibrium quantity.

_____

_____

_____

b. What is the name of the modelling technique for making your predictions? Explain this technique in words.

_____

_____

_____

_____

Apply...

12. Over the past year, the equilibrium price of beachballs fell from $8 to $4, but the equilibrium quantity of beachballs sold in the market increased from 100 to 150. This kind of observation seems to disprove the law of supply.

    a. State the law of supply.

    _____

    _____

    _____

    b. To save the law of supply for beachballs, give an example of a change in one factor behind either the supply or the demand curve that could explain how a price fall could be followed by an increase in the quantity sold. Identify both the factor and the direction of change.

    _____

    _____

    _____

    c. Draw a simple demand and supply graph that shows the original equilibrium price and quantity for beachballs, the change caused by your example in part b, and the new equilibrium price and quantity.

    Use the numbers above in the question to label the coordinates of the original equilibrium price and quantity, and the coordinates of the new equilibrium price and quantity.

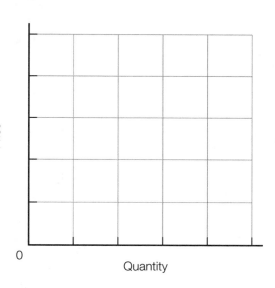

    d. Circle the correct answers. What happened in the beachball market was *caused by*

    a(n)   increase / decrease
    in   demand / quantity demanded / supply / quantity supplied

        resulting in

    a(n)   increase / decrease
    in   demand / quantity demanded / supply / quantity supplied.

Consumer Surplus, Producer Surplus, and Efficiency

 Demonstrate the efficiency of markets using the concepts of consumer surplus and producer surplus.

The demand and supply model allows us to predict changes in prices and quantities. We can also read demand and supply curves as marginal benefit and marginal cost curves. Focusing on marginal benefits and marginal costs allows us to measure the efficiency of market outcomes.

Consumer Surplus

Any market demand curve is also a marginal benefit curve. Figure 8 reproduces the demand curve from Figure 1 and labels it also as a marginal benefit (*MB*) curve.

Figure 8   Marginal Benefit and Consumer Surplus

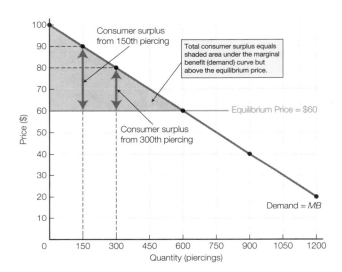

A *market* demand curve combines the willingness and ability to pay of *all* consumers in this market. Some consumers, with a high willingness and ability to pay, are located up at the top left of the demand curve. Others, with less willingness and ability to pay, are located further down along the demand curve.

To read the demand curve as a marginal benefit curve, start with a quantity and go up and over to see the maximum price someone is willing and able to pay. For the 150th piercing, someone is willing and able to pay $90. For the 300th piercing, someone is willing and able to pay $80.

At the equilibrium price in the market, everyone pays $60 for each piercing. But for each of the first 599 piercings, someone was willing and able to pay more. On the graph, that extra benefit is the vertical distance between the marginal benefit curve and the market price. Economists call this extra benefit **consumer surplus** — the difference between the amount a consumer is willing and able to pay, and the price actually paid. If we combine the consumer surplus for every piercing sold, the consumer surplus equals the green shaded area under the marginal benefit (demand) curve, but above the market price.

Producer Surplus

Any market supply curve is also a marginal cost curve. Figure 9 reproduces the supply curve from Figure 1 and labels it also as a marginal cost (*MC*) curve.

Figure 9   Marginal Cost and Producer Surplus

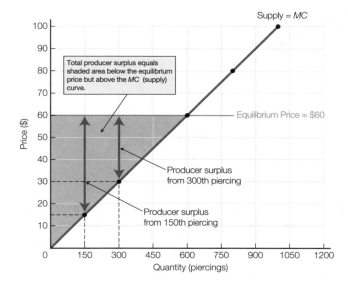

A *market* supply curve combines the supply decisions of *all* businesses in a market — the minimum prices businesses are willing to accept in order to supply piercings, covering all marginal opportunity costs of production. Businesses with low marginal opportunity costs are located down at the bottom of the supply curve. Others, with higher marginal opportunity costs, are located further up the supply curve.

To read the supply curve as a marginal cost curve, start with a quantity and go up and over to see the minimum price a business is willing to accept for producing that unit. For the 150th piercing, some business is willing to accept $15. For the 300th piercing, some business is willing to accept $30.

At the equilibrium price in the market, every business receives $60 for each piercing. But for each of the first 599 piercings, some business was willing to accept less. On the graph, that extra revenue above marginal cost is the vertical distance between the marginal cost curve and the market price. Economists call this extra benefit **producer surplus** — the difference between the amount a producer is willing to accept, and the price actually received. If we combine the producer surplus for every piercing sold, the producer surplus equals the blue shaded area below the market price but above the marginal cost (supply) curve.

Economic Efficiency

When Adam Smith's *invisible hand* works well, markets produce the products and services that consumers want, at competitive prices that are profitable for businesses, and everyone is happy. But happiness is relative. How do we know there isn't a better outcome out there? Consumer surplus and producer surplus are useful measures for comparing outcomes.

Figure 10, on the next page, combines the demand (marginal benefit) and the supply (marginal cost) curves from Figures 8 and 9.

Figure 10   Maximum Total Surplus

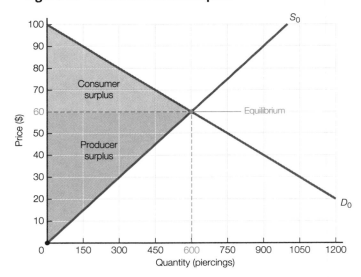

Combining the green area of consumer surplus with the blue area of producer surplus — the total shaded area — gives us the **total surplus**. The quantity that results in the "best" outcome is the quantity with the largest total surplus.

For every unit up to the 600th piercing, marginal benefit is greater than marginal cost. For each unit, there is some consumer willing and able to pay a price greater than the minimum price some producer needs to receive to be willing to supply it. At a price of \$60, consumers and businesses both benefit from every unit produced. This is an **efficient market outcome**. Consumers buy only products and services where marginal benefit is greater than price. These products and services are produced at the lowest costs, and price just covers all opportunity costs of production. This is the outcome where the demand (marginal benefit) and supply (marginal cost) curves intersect.

Inefficient Outcomes

The only way to know if an efficient outcome is "best" is to compare it with other outcomes and to measure the total surplus. Figure 11 shows examples of inefficient outcomes that are not "best" and that have lower total surplus.

Figure 11   Inefficient Outcomes

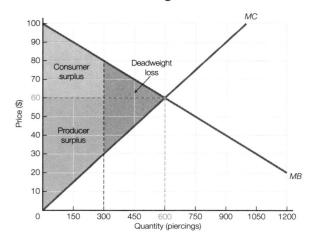

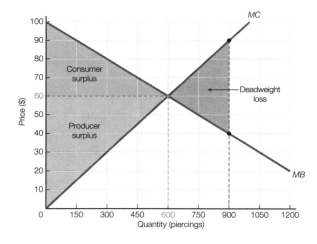

a) Inefficiency of Producing Too Little

b) Inefficiency of Producing Too Much

If output stopped at 300 units (graph a), the total area of consumer surplus (green) plus producer surplus (blue) is less than the total surplus for 600 units in Figure 10. The difference between the two areas of total surplus is the grey triangle labelled **deadweight loss**. The output of 300 units is inefficient because there are mutually beneficial trades that do not happen. Producing and selling all piercings between 300 and 600 would make consumers and producers better off because marginal benefits are greater than marginal costs.

If output continued beyond 600 to 900 units (graph b), there is a different deadweight loss from producing too much. For each unit beyond 600, marginal cost is greater than marginal benefit. This deadweight loss must be subtracted from the green consumer and blue producer surplus areas to calculate the total surplus for 900 units.

 Practice...

21. Consumer surplus is the
    a. difference between the amount a consumer is willing to accept and the price actually received.
    b. difference between the amount a consumer is willing and able to pay and the price actually paid.
    c. difference between the amount a consumer is willing and able to pay and the amount a producer is willing to accept.
    d. area under the marginal benefit curve.

22. Producer surplus is the area
    a. under the marginal benefit curve but above the marginal cost curve.
    b. under the marginal benefit curve but above the market price.
    c. below the market price but above the marginal cost curve.
    d. above the marginal cost curve.

23. For any quantity produced up to the efficient quantity, total surplus is the
    a. deadweight loss.
    b. area under the marginal benefit curve but above the market price.
    c. area above the marginal benefit curve but below the market price.
    d. area under the marginal benefit curve but above the marginal cost curve

24. If the quantity produced is more than the efficient market outcome,
    a. deadweight loss is eliminated.
    b. total surplus is greater than total surplus for the efficient market outcome.
    c. marginal cost is greater than marginal benefit.
    d. marginal benefit is greater than marginal cost.

25. In an efficient market outcome,
    a. products and services are produced at lowest cost.
    b. total surplus is the lowest.
    c. consumers buy only products and services where marginal benefit is less than price.
    d. deadweight loss is the highest.

Apply...

13. In the market for e-readers, at the prices of $40, $60, $80, $100, and $120, the following quantities are demanded: 2000, 1600, 1200, 800, and 600 units. The quantities supplied at those prices are: 400, 800, 1200, 1600, and 2000 units. Draw a graph of this market. For the 800th unit, what is the consumer surplus; what is the producer surplus?

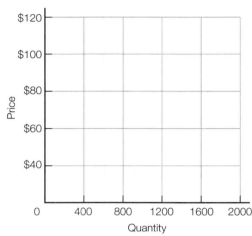

14. The figure shows the market for slugs. Note that the demand curve is also a marginal benefit curve, and the supply curve is also a marginal cost curve.

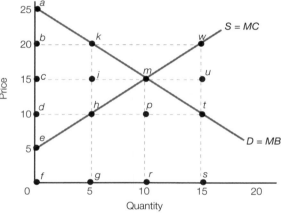

a. If the slugs market is efficient, describe the area of consumer surplus (use the labels of points around the edges of the area, e.g., area *abk*). Define consumer surplus without referring to an area.

_____

_____

_____

_____

b. If the slugs market is efficient, describe the area of producer surplus (use the labels of points around the edges of the area, e.g., area *abk*). Define producer surplus without referring to an area.

_____

_____

_____

c. If output is at *Q* = 5, describe the area of deadweight loss. Define deadweight loss.

_____

_____

_____

_____

Apply...

d. If output stops at $Q = 5$, use the marginal benefit and marginal cost curves to describe the inefficiency that exists for a quantity like $Q = 6$.

_____

_____

_____

15. The figure shows the market for champagne. Note that the demand curve is also a marginal benefit curve, and the supply curve is also a marginal cost curve.

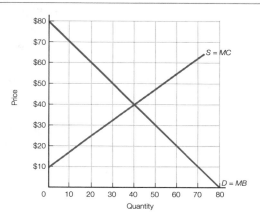

a. The champagne market is in equilibrium. Calculate the consumer surplus. Calculate the producer surplus. What is the total surplus?

_____

_____

_____

_____

b. What is the condition for an efficient market outcome?

_____

_____

_____

c. Suppose now that that there is overproduction in the champagne market and output is 60 bottles. Calculate the deadweight loss. What is the total surplus?

_____

_____

_____

_____

d. How does total surplus compare to the answer in part a? Is the output of 60 bottles efficient?

_____

_____

_____

_____

KNOW...

Summary of Learning Objectives

1. **Markets** connect competition between buyers, competition between sellers, and cooperation between buyers and sellers. When there are **shortages**, competition between buyers drives prices up. When there are **surpluses**, competition between sellers drives prices down.

2. **Equilibrium prices** (or **market-clearing prices**) balance quantity demanded and quantity supplied, coordinating the smart choices of consumers and businesses. Price signals in markets create incentives, so that while each person acts only in her own self-interest, Adam Smith's invisible hand of competition produces the miracle of the ever-changing production of products and services we most want.

3. The demand and supply model allows us to predict the effects on equilibrium prices and quantities of a change in any of the five factors influencing demand or the six factors influencing supply.

4. For combined changes in demand and supply, we can predict the effect on *either* the equilibrium price or the equilibrium quantity. But there is not enough information to predict the effects on *both* price and quantity. All predictions of the demand and supply model use the technique of **comparative statics** to simulate a controlled laboratory experiment — comparing two equilibrium outcomes to isolate the effect of changing one (or two) factors at a time.

5. The concepts of **consumer surplus** and **producer surplus** are based on reading demand and supply curves as marginal benefit and marginal cost curves. An efficient market outcome has the largest **total surplus** — the sum of consumer surplus and producer surplus. Prices just cover all marginal opportunity costs of production, and consumers' marginal benefit equals businesses' marginal cost. An inefficient outcome has **deadweight loss**.

Key Terms

comparative statics: comparing two equilibrium outcomes to isolate the effect of changing one factor at a time

consumer surplus: the difference between the amount a consumer is willing and able to pay, and the price actually paid

deadweight loss: decrease in total surplus compared to an economically efficient outcome

efficient market outcome: consumers buy only products and services where marginal benefit is greater than marginal cost; products and services produced at lowest cost, with price just covering all opportunity costs of production

equilibrium price: the price that equalizes quantity demanded and quantity supplied, balancing the forces of competition and cooperation, so that there is no tendency for change

excess demand (shortage): quantity demanded exceeds quantity supplied

excess supply (surplus): quantity supplied exceeds quantity demanded

market: the interaction between buyers and sellers

market-clearing price: the price that equalizes quantity demanded and quantity supplied

producer surplus: the difference between the amount a producer is willing to accept, and the price actually received

shortage (excess demand): quantity demanded exceeds quantity supplied

surplus (excess supply): quantity supplied exceeds quantity demanded

total surplus: consumer surplus plus producer surplus

Answers to Practice

1. **c** Definition.
2. **d** Price must cover marginal opportunity cost of seller and be less than marginal benefit for buyer.
3. **d** When prices change, so do smart choices and quantities.
4. **a** Excess supply and frustrated sellers.
5. **b** Horizontal distance between demand and supply curves at that price.
6. **d** Equilibrium price.
7. **b** Excess supply leads to price-cutting competition among sellers.
8. **d** Equilibrium is a balance of forces.
9. **a** No one wants to buy or sell more.
10. **c** Prices guide the *invisible hand*.
11. **d** Demand shifts leftward and fall in price moves down along unchanged supply curve.
12. **b** Demand shifts rightward and rise in price moves up along unchanged supply curve.
13. **d** Rise in cattle prices causes farmers to shift land from corn to cattle.
14. **a** Draw rightward shift of supply or leftward shift of demand.
15. **c** Leftward shift of demand causes fall in price and decrease in equilibrium quantity.
16. **d** Draw leftward shift of demand and rightward shift of supply.
17. **a** Draw rightward shift of demand and leftward shift of supply.
18. **d** Supply shifts rightward, demand shifts leftward, price definitely falls.
19. **c** See Figure 6a on page 67.
20. **c**   Leftward shift of demand or rightward shift of supply.
21. **b** Area under the marginal benefit curve and above the (market) price actually paid.
22. **c** Difference between the minimum price willing to accept and price actually received, for all units.
23. **d** Consumer surplus plus producer surplus.
24. **c** For any quantity greater than the equilibrium quantity, read up to the marginal cost and marginal benefit curves.
25. **a** Total surplus is highest, and consumers buy when MB > price.

4 Elasticity

LEARNING OBJECTIVES

L01 Define and calculate elasticity of demand, and explain three factors that determine it.

L02 Explain how the relationship between elasticity of demand and total revenue determines business pricing strategies.

L03 Explain elasticity of supply and how it helps businesses avoid disappointed customers.

L04 Define cross elasticity and income elasticity of demand, and explain how they measure substitutes and complements, normal and inferior goods, and necessities and luxuries.

L05 Use elasticity to explain who pays sales taxes and government tax choices.

LEARN...

Don't you love a good sale — 40 percent off, 70 percent off? Most consumers do. But do businesses love a good sale? Profit-seeking businesses would rather charge higher prices for what they sell. But to get consumers to buy, businesses must pick price points that match the market's — all consumers' — willingness and ability to pay. Higher prices might not always be best for business. Why do businesses have 70-percent-off sales, voluntarily lowering prices and bringing in less per unit?

I'm sure you have heard the answer to this question: "They'll make it up on volume!" Lower prices mean lower profit margins per unit, but a greater quantity sold. How do businesses decide whether it's a smart choice to set a higher price or a lower price?

In this chapter you will learn about elasticity, which is the most important tool used by anyone working in marketing or sales. Elasticity also helps explain supply shortages, why movie theatres won't let you bring in your own snacks, why governments tax alcohol and cigarettes, and who pays the HST. You may think you know who pays the tax, but I bet you'll be surprised by the answer.

Next to opportunity cost, elasticity is probably the most helpful concept for making smart choices by businesses and governments.

Price Elasticity of Demand

 Define and calculate elasticity of demand, and explain three factors that determine it.

We know from the law of demand that (all other things unchanged) a rise in price decreases quantity demanded, and a fall in price (sale's on!) increases quantity demanded (more volume). A smart business pricing decision depends on *by how much* quantity demanded changes when price changes. This *responsiveness* of quantity demanded to a change in price is related to just how badly consumers want the product or service — how much more or less people will buy as the price falls or rises.

The tool that businesses use to measure consumer responsiveness and make pricing decisions is called the **price elasticity of demand** or, more simply, elasticity. **Elasticity** measures by how much quantity demanded responds to a change in price.

Measuring Responsiveness

Elasticity is all about responsiveness. When you pull on an elastic, *by how much* does it stretch or respond? When the price of a product changes, price elasticity of demand measures by how much quantity demanded responds.

Inelastic Demand   A diabetic has a high willingness to pay for insulin. What happens to the quantity of insulin demanded when the price rises? If the price rises enough, quantity demanded may decrease slightly as the poorest diabetics perhaps try to get by with a little less per dose. But in the market for insulin, there is very little response of quantity demanded to a rise in price. The demand for insulin is **inelastic**.

Look at the steeply sloped market demand curve for insulin in Figure 1a. Even a large rise in price, from P_0 to P_1, causes only a small decrease in the quantity demanded for insulin, from Q_0 to Q_1. The demand for a product or service is inelastic if there is a small response in quantity demanded when its price rises.

Figure 1   Inelastic and Elastic Demand

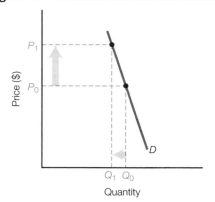

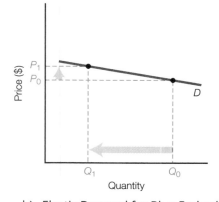

a) Inelastic Demand for Insulin

b) Elastic Demand for Blue Earbuds

Elastic Demand   What about the market demand for blue earbuds? If the price of blue earbuds rises, what happens? Most consumers consider black or white earbuds to be identical substitutes, and aren't willing to pay extra for blue. Consumers switch to non-blue earbuds, so the quantity demanded of blue earbuds decreases drastically. There is a large response of quantity demanded to a rise in price. The demand for blue earbuds is **elastic**. The market demand curve for blue earbuds in Figure 1b is very flat. Just a small rise in price, from P_0 to P_1, causes a large decrease in quantity demanded, from Q_0 to Q_1.

Calculating Elasticity of Demand

Businesses use this simple formula to calculate elasticity.

$$\text{Price elasticity of demand} = \frac{\text{Percentage change in quantity demanded}}{\text{Percentage change in price}}$$

The formula assumes that all of the other five factors that can affect demand are unchanged, so this is like a controlled experiment measuring just the relationship (in the law of demand) between quantity demanded and price.

Let's substitute some numbers into the formula. For insulin, if a 10-percent rise in price causes a 2-percent decrease in quantity demanded, the calculation is

$$\text{Price elasticity of demand for insulin} = \frac{2 \text{ percent}}{10 \text{ percent}} = 0.2$$

The answer, 0.2, is less than 1. Any elasticity value less than 1 is considered to be inelastic. Technically, the correct answer is – 0.2. However, economists ignore the negative sign in calculating price elasticity of demand.

For blue earbuds, if a 10-percent rise in price causes a 50-percent decrease in quantity demanded, the calculation is

Any elasticity value greater than 1 is considered to be elastic.

$$\text{Price elasticity of demand for blue earbuds} = \frac{50 \text{ percent}}{10 \text{ percent}} = 5$$

When elasticity equals 1, economists say that demand is "unit elastic." The percentage change in quantity equals the percentage change in price. The key thing to remember about elasticity of demand is if it is less than 1 it is inelastic, and if it is greater than 1 it is elastic.

Perfect Elasticities   Two extreme cases never observed in the real world may still help you better understand elasticity. The most extreme inelastic demand is elasticity equal to zero. The vertical demand curve in Figure 2a on the next page has zero elasticity. There is no change in quantity demanded no matter what the change in price. This is called **perfectly inelastic demand**. The most extreme elastic demand is elasticity equal to infinity. The horizontal demand curve in Figure 2b has infinite elasticity. There is near infinite response in the quantity demanded to the slightest change in price. This is called **perfectly elastic demand**.

Figure 2   Extreme Elasticities of Demand

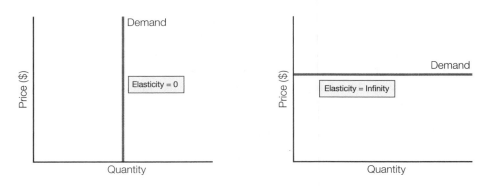

a) Perfectly Inelastic Demand   b) Perfect Elastic Demand

Elasticity is about responsiveness. Perfectly inelastic demand has zero responsiveness. Insulin and addictive drugs probably come closest to perfectly inelastic demand. When there are no substitutes for a product or service, the elasticity of demand approaches zero.

For perfectly elastic demand, even the smallest change in price produces a huge — almost infinite — response in quantity demanded. The example of blue earbuds comes close to having infinite elasticity. A tiny rise in the price of blue earbuds causes the quantity demanded to collapse toward zero. As the substitutes available for a product or service get better, the elasticity of demand gets larger. The elasticity of demand for perfect substitutes approaches infinity.

Midpoint Formula for Measuring Elasticity of Demand   This simple formula allows you to calculate the elasticity of a demand curve between any two points like (Q_0, P_0) and (Q_1, P_1) on any demand curve. It is all you need to use for analyzing most business pricing decisions.

$$\text{Price elasticity of demand} = \frac{\text{Percentage change in quantity demanded}}{\text{Percentage change in price}}$$

But the simplification hides a problem. Suppose the price of a pair of earbuds in Figure 1b on page 82 rises from \$10 to \$11 — a 10% change (\$1 divided by \$10 equals 10%). But if we reverse the story and have the price fall from \$11 to \$10, then the change is only 9.1% (\$1 divided by \$11 equals 9.1%). Since we are calculating elasticity between two points on the demand curve, it makes no sense to have a different number just because we describe the change as a rise rather than a fall in price.

To more accurately measure the elasticity between two points on a demand curve and overcome the price-change problem, economists use the *average* of the two prices and the *average* of the two quantities demanded. The more accurate formula for price elasticity of demand is called the midpoint formula.

$$\frac{\dfrac{Q_1 - Q_0}{\left(\dfrac{Q_1 + Q_0}{2}\right)}}{\dfrac{P_1 - P_0}{\left(\dfrac{P_1 + P_0}{2}\right)}}$$

Change in quantity demanded
Average quantity demanded between two points
Change in price
Average price between two points

Starting at the top, $(Q_1 - Q_0)$ is the change in quantity demanded. And $(Q_1 + Q_0) \div 2$ is the average quantity demanded between the two points on the demand curve. The change in quantity demanded divided by the average change in quantity demanded gives us the percentage change in quantity demanded. *This is the same as in the numerator of the simple formula.*

On the bottom half of the midpoint formula, $(P_1 - P_0)$ is the change in price. And $(P_1 + P_0) \div 2$ is the average price between the two points on the demand curve. The change in price divided by the average change in price gives us the percentage change in price. *This is the same as in the denominator of the simple formula.*

By using *average* quantity demanded and *average* price, the midpoint formula gives the same answer whether you calculate for a price rise (where P_1 is greater than P_0) or a price fall (where P_1 is less than P_0). Because economists don't use negative numbers for elasticity of demand, you can ignore any minus signs in the final answer.

Factors Determining Elasticity

Three main factors influence price elasticity of demand: available substitutes, time to adjust, and proportion of income spent on a product or service.

Available Substitutes   When something becomes more expensive, people economize on its use and look for substitutes. The more substitutes there are, the easier it is to switch away from a product or service whose price rises, and the more elastic is demand.

There is a connection between whether substitutes are available and whether a product or service is a *necessity* or a *luxury.* Necessities like insulin for diabetics, or heat in the winter, usually have few substitutes and are necessary for your well-being. As price rises for a necessity, consumers still buy it. Most necessities have inelastic demand. Luxuries, like good restaurants or Caribbean vacations, are not essential for your well-being and usually have many substitutes. Because you don't need a luxury product or service, when its price rises you may not buy at all or you may switch to one of the many available substitutes. Luxuries have more elastic demand.

Time to Adjust   When prices rise, it often takes time to adjust and to find substitutes. If gasoline prices rise and you have to drive to work, you can't do much initially to decrease your quantity of gasoline demanded — you can cut back on pleasure driving and errands. With more time though, you could arrange a car pool, and with much more time, you might buy a hybrid car or move closer to work. Time allows consumers to find substitutes. The longer the time to adjust to a price rise, the more elastic demand becomes.

Proportion of Income Spent   Suppose the price of salt increases by 100%, from $1 per kilo to $2 per kilo. By how much will you reduce your quantity demanded of salt? Not much. What if the price of a car increases by 100%, from $20 000 to $40 000? The quantity demanded of cars will collapse. A key difference between the examples is the proportion of income spent on the product. We spend a tiny fraction of our income on salt, so a big percentage price rise doesn't increase our total spending much. But buying a car is one of the largest purchases you will make: A big percentage price rise makes it unaffordable. The greater the proportion of income spent on a product, the more elastic demand becomes.

Practice...

1. The fact that butter and margarine are close substitutes makes
   a. demand for butter more elastic.
   b. demand for butter more inelastic.
   c. butter an inferior good.
   d. margarine an inferior good.

2. If the price elasticity of demand is 2, a 1 percent fall in price will
   a. double the quantity demanded.
   b. decrease the quantity demanded by half.
   c. increase the quantity demanded by 2 percent.
   d. decrease the quantity demanded by 2 percent.

3. Two points on the demand curve for volleyballs are

Price	Quantity Demanded
$19	55
$21	45

   What is the midpoint elasticity of demand between these two points?
   a. 2.5
   b. 2.0
   c. 0.5
   d. 0.4

4. A vertical demand curve has a price elasticity of
   a. zero.
   b. greater than zero but less than one.
   c. greater than one.
   d. infinity.

5. Price elasticity of demand will be larger,
   a. the shorter the time to adjust.
   b. the greater the proportion of income spent on the product.
   c. the harder it is to find good substitutes.
   d. when all of the above are true.

 **Apply...**

1. A jewellery store cuts its prices on watches by 20 percent, and its quantity sold increases by 40 percent. Calculate the price elasticity of demand for watches. Is it elastic or inelastic?

   _____

   _____

   _____

   _____

   _____

2. If a union leader claims that "higher wages increase living standards without causing unemployment," what is she assuming about the elasticity of demand for labour?

   _____

   _____

   _____

   _____

3. In the women's clothing market, which is likely to be more inelastic, demand for the latest fashions or demand for clothing in general? If you were the marketing manager of a women's clothing chain, use your answer to explain why store managers should, or should not, exclude the latest arrivals in their next sale.

   _____

   _____

   _____

   _____

Elasticity and Total Revenue

 Explain how the relationship between elasticity of demand and total revenue determines business pricing strategies.

If your business holds a 70-percent-off sale, customers will be happy, but will the business be better off? Whether a business will be better off from raising prices or cutting prices depends on the elasticity of demand for its product or service. Elasticity of demand is the most important concept for determining if lower prices will lead your business to take in more or less money.

Total Revenue

"Better off," in this chapter, means your business will bring in more money. Total revenue is all of the money received from sales, and equal to price per unit (P) multiplied by the quantity sold (Q).

Total revenue $= P \times Q$

There is a simple relationship between elasticity and total revenue. When a business cuts prices for its product or service,

- if demand is elastic, the percentage increase in quantity is greater than the percentage decrease in price, so total revenue ($P \times Q$) increases.
- if demand is inelastic, the percentage increase in quantity is less than the percentage decrease in price, so total revenue ($P \times Q$) decreases.
- if demand is unit elastic, the percentage increase in quantity equals the percentage decrease in price, so total revenue ($P \times Q$) remains the same.

Figure 3 summarizes the relationship between elasticity and total revenue for a price cut.

Figure 3   Elasticity and Total Revenue

When Demand Is:		Price Cut Causes:
Elastic (> 1)	% change in Q > % change in P	Increased total revenue
Inelastic (< 1)	% change in Q < % change in P	Decreased total revenue
Unit Elastic (= 1)	% change in Q = % change in P	Unchanged total revenue

Price Cuts Are Smart When Facing Elastic Demand

A price cut is a smart decision when your business faces elastic demand. You receive a lower price on each unit sold, but you do make it up on volume! The percentage increase in quantity outweighs the percentage decrease in price, so total revenue increases.

If you are selling blue earbuds, consumers' demand for your product is elastic, which means that if they don't get a low price, they are very willing and able to shop elsewhere because good substitutes are available. When you cut the price of blue earbuds even a little, you attract all of the bargain hunters. Your total revenue increases because the large increase in quantity outweighs the small decrease in price.

Price Rises Are Smart When Facing Inelastic Demand

The smart decision when your business faces inelastic demand is to raise prices. You receive a higher price on each unit sold, and while you lose some sales, the percentage increase in price is greater than the percentage decrease in quantity, so total revenue increases.

If you are selling insulin, consumers' demand is inelastic, which means that they will not easily shop elsewhere because there are no good substitutes. When you raise the price of insulin, you don't lose many customers. Your total revenue increases because the percentage increase in price outweighs the small percentage decrease in quantity.

Calculating Elasticity and Total Revenue

Even if you were not looking forward to using the midpoint formula for price elasticity of demand (is there anybody who was looking forward to it?), I hope to convince you that a detailed numerical example is worth a few minutes of your time.

Elasticity along a Straight Line Demand Curve   Figure 4 shows calculations for midpoint elasticity and total revenue for points *A – F* along a straight line demand curve (Figure 5 on the next page).

Figure 4   Midpoint Elasticity and Total Revenue Calculations

Point	Price ($)	Quantity Demanded	Elasticity	Total Revenue ($)
A	50	0	$\dfrac{(15-0)}{(15+0)/2} = 9$	0
B	40	15	$\dfrac{(40-50)}{(40+50)/2} = 2.33$	600
C	30	30	$\dfrac{(45-30)}{(45+30)/2} = 1$	900
D	20	45	$\dfrac{(20-30)}{(20+30)/2} = 0.43$	900
E	10	60	$\dfrac{(75-60)}{(75+60)/2} = 0.11$	600
F	0	75	$\dfrac{(0-10)}{(0+10)/2}$	0

Columns 2 and 3 give the price (*P*) and quantity (*Q*) coordinates for each point on the demand curve. That is all you need to calculate elasticity using the midpoint formula.

Column 4 shows the elasticity between each set of points. For example, the elasticity between points *A* and *B* is 9, between points *B* and *C* is 2.33, and so on. Because elasticity is calculated *between* two points, the numbers for elasticity appear *halfway* between the rows for the two points. (See why it is called the midpoint formula?) Column 4 has detailed calculations between 3 of the 5 sets of points: *A* to *B*, *C* to *D*, and *E* to *F*. For now, ignore the last column of Total Revenue.

As you look at the other elasticity calculations, notice that elasticity changes between different points along the straight line demand curve, from 9 to 2.33 to 1 to 0.43 to 0.11. Between *A* and *B* and between *B* and *C* demand is elastic (greater than 1). Between *C* and *D* demand is unit elastic (equal to 1). Between *D* and *E* and between *E* and *F* demand is inelastic (less than 1).

Along a straight line, slope is constant — it does not change. In contrast, elasticity changes along a straight line demand curve. *Elasticity is not the same as slope.* That is why it is techincally incorrect to describe an entire demand curve as elastic or inelastic.

Calculating Total Revenue The last column in Figure 4 on the previous page shows total revenue for each point on the demand curve. Total revenue is price times quantity. For point *A*, total revenue is $50 × 0 = $0. For point *B*, total revenue is $40 × 15 = $600. To understand the pattern of total revenue and its connection to elasticity, look at Figure 5.

Figure 5a shows the different values for elasticity along the different parts of the demand curve. The top part of the demand curve is elastic, the middle part is unit elastic, and the lower part is inelastic.

Now look at the graph of total revenue in Figure 5b. The horizontal axis measures quantity, the same as the horizontal axis of Figure 5a. The vertical axis measures total revenue, $P \times Q$. Calculating total revenue for every quantity between 0 and 75 gives a symmetrical, mountain-shaped curve. As quantity increases, total revenue rises, reaches a peak, and then falls.

Figure 5   Elasticity and Total Revenue

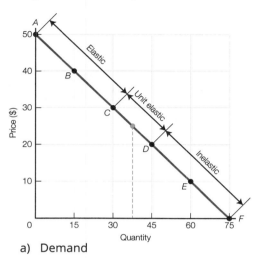

a) Demand

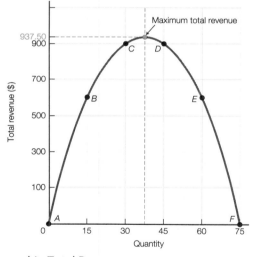

b) Total Revenue

Price Cuts and Total Revenue Start at point *A* on the demand curve (corresponding to zero quantity and zero total revenue on the total revenue curve in Figure 5b). Price cuts move us down along the demand curve. What happens to total revenue? As price falls along the elastic part of the demand curve, from points *A* to *B* to *C*, total revenue on the bottom graph increases from 0 to $600 to $900. Halfway between points *C* and *D*, at a quantity of 37.5 and a price of $25, total revenue reaches a maximum of $937.50. Looking between points *C* and *D*, where demand is unit elastic, as price falls from $30 to $20, total revenue stays constant at $900. Finally, between points *D* and *E* and *F*, as price falls and we move further down along the inelastic part of the demand curve, total revenue decreases from $900 to $600 to $0.

The combination of the top demand graph (with the different elasticities) and the bottom total revenue graph tells the story behind business pricing strategies. If your business is facing elastic demand along the upper portion of the demand curve, cutting your price increases total revenue, and moves you up the total revenue mountain (which is smart). If your business is facing inelastic demand along the lower portion of the demand curve, cutting your price decreases total revenue, and moves you down the other side of the total revenue mountain (which is not smart).

 # Practice...

6. A fall in tuition fees decreases a college's total revenue if the price elasticity of demand for college education is

   a. negative.

   b. greater than zero but less than one.

   c. equal to one.

   d. greater than one.

7. If the Jets cut ticket prices and total revenue does not change, the price elasticity of demand for tickets is

   a. zero.

   b. greater than zero but less than one.

   c. equal to one.

   d. greater than one.

8. Lady Gaga (LG) and Tony Bennet (TB) record an album together. LG thinks they would be better off raising the price of their album, while TB claims they would be better off lowering the price. Which statement about the price elasticity of demand for albums is *true*?

   a. LG thinks it equals zero, and TB thinks it equals 1.

   b. LG thinks it is price elastic, and TB thinks it is price inelastic.

   c. LG thinks it equals 1, and TB thinks it equals zero.

   d. LG thinks it is price inelastic, and TB thinks it is price elastic.

9. A new technology lowers the cost of printers. If the demand for printers is price inelastic, printer sales

   a. decrease and total revenue increases.

   b. decrease and total revenue decreases.

   c. increase and total revenue increases.

   d. increase and total revenue decreases.

10. Business people talk about price elasticity of demand without using the actual words. Which statement is about *elastic* demand?

   a. "Most of my customers are bargain hunters. Since I set my prices just a few cents below my competitors', sales are booming."

   b. "With the recent economic recovery, people have more income to spend and sales are booming, even at the same prices as before."

   c. "A price cut won't help me. It won't increase sales, and I'll just get less money for each unit that I was selling before."

   d. "I don't think a price cut will make any difference to my bottom line."

Apply...

4. The express train from Toronto's Pearson Airport to the downtown Union subway station has been controversial since it starting running in 2015. Metrolinx, which runs the trains, was hoping for 7000 riders a month, but found only about 2000 riders a month were willing to pay the $27.50 one-way fare.

    In 2017, Metrolinx cut the price of riding the train, and according to media reports, half the price bought the Union–Pearson express train twice the riders. [Half the price is a 50% cut; twice the riders is a 100% increase.]

    a. State the simple general formula for the price elasticity of demand.

    b. Based on the media reports, use the formula to calculate the express train's price elasticity of demand.

    c. Before the fare cut, Metrolinx's worry was that the express train was not earning enough revenue.

        Based on your calculation above, the fare cut has (circle the correct answer)

        increased / decreased / kept constant

        total revenue.

5. Use the midpoint formula for price elasticity of demand on page 84 to explain why elasticity is not the same as slope.

6. Concession stands at movie theatres charge high prices for popcorn, drinks, and other refreshments. This pricing strategy increases total revenue. What does that imply about the price elasticity of demand for refreshments in movie theatres? What theatre policy helps make this demand elastic or inelastic?

Price Elasticity of Supply

 L03 Explain elasticity of supply and how it helps businesses avoid disappointed customers.

We know from the law of supply that (all other things unchanged), a rise in price causes an increase in quantity supplied. A smart business supply decision depends on *by how much* you increase quantity supplied when the price rises. By how much will you increase your work hours in response to your boss's higher wage offer? What determines by how much Paola's Parlour increases her quantity supplied of piercings as the price of piercings rises?

The law of supply tells us that price and quantity supplied increase together and decrease together. We will look at the question: What changes more, the price or the quantity supplied? This responsiveness of quantity supplied to a change in price is related to self-interest and the desire for profits, but mostly it has to do with how easy or costly it is to increase production.

Responsiveness   Price elasticity of demand measures the responsiveness of the quantity demanded by consumers to a change in price. **Elasticity of supply** measures *by how much* the quantity supplied by businesses responds to a change in price.

Just like for demand, the quantity supplied can be inelastic (unresponsive to a change in price) or elastic (very responsive). Let's look at some examples.

Consider an industry like gold mining. When the world price of gold rises, what happens to the quantity of gold supplied? Not much, and certainly not quickly. Gold is hard to find, and opening new gold mines is very expensive and takes years, even decades. The supply of new gold nuggets is inelastic, because quantity supplied is relatively unresponsive to even large rises in price. For **inelastic supply**, there is a small response in quantity supplied when the price rises.

Toward the other extreme, the supply of snow-shovelling services in most Canadian towns is relatively elastic. If the price offered rises even a bit, there is a willing supply of kids with shovels who don't have many other equally well-paying chances to work. And for anyone with a truck, it's not difficult or expensive to attach a plow and clear driveways in your spare time before or after your regular job. Even a small rise in price causes a large increase in the quantity supplied of shovelling services, so supply is elastic. For **elastic supply**, there is a large response in quantity supplied when the price rises.

Perfect Elasticities of Supply   Figure 6 shows the extreme cases of elasticity of supply, which are similar to the extreme cases of elasticity of demand.

Figure 6   Extreme Elasticities of Supply

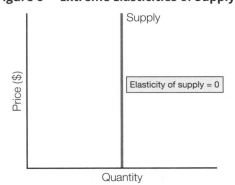

a) Perfectly Inelastic Supply

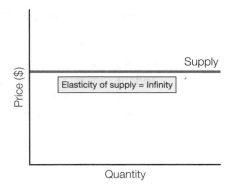

b) Perfect Elastic Supply

The most extreme inelastic supply is elasticity of supply equal to zero. The vertical supply curve in Figure 6a on the previous page has zero elasticity of supply. Quantity supplied is totally unresponsive to any percentage change in price. This is called **perfectly inelastic supply**.

The most extreme elastic supply is elasticity of supply equal to infinity. The horizontal supply curve in Figure 6b has infinite elasticity of supply. This is the snow-shovelling example. If there were millions of kids desperate for even a penny more, a tiny increase in the price for snow-shovelling services would cause the percentage increase in quantity supplied to explode. Responsiveness is huge, approaching infinity. This is called **perfectly elastic supply**.

Measuring Business Responsiveness

The simple formula for calculating elasticity of supply is

$$\text{Elasticity of supply} = \frac{\text{Percentage change in quantity supplied}}{\text{Percentage change in price}}$$

This is a controlled experiment measuring just the relationship between quantity supplied and price.

- If the percentage change in quantity supplied is less than the percentage change in price, elasticity of supply is less than 1 and is inelastic. Quantity supplied is relatively unresponsive to a change in price.

- If the percentage change in quantity supplied is greater than the percentage change in price, elasticity of supply is greater than 1 and is elastic. Quantity supplied is relatively responsive to a change in price.

Midpoint Formula for Measuring Elasticity of Supply The midpoint formula for calculating elasticity of supply is similar to the midpoint formula for elasticity of demand on page 84. The only difference is that Q_0, Q_1, P_0, and P_1 refer to points on a supply curve instead of on a demand curve.

$$\cfrac{\cfrac{Q_1 - Q_0}{\left(\cfrac{Q_1 + Q_0}{2}\right)}}{\cfrac{P_1 - P_0}{\left(\cfrac{P_1 + P_0}{2}\right)}}$$

- $Q_1 - Q_0$ ← Change in quantity supplied
- $\left(\dfrac{Q_1 + Q_0}{2}\right)$ ← Average quantity supplied between two points
- $P_1 - P_0$ ← Change in price
- $\left(\dfrac{P_1 + P_0}{2}\right)$ ← Average price between two points

Factors Determining Elasticity of Supply

What causes supply to be inelastic for some individuals and businesses and elastic for others? Two important causes are the availability of additional inputs and the time it takes to produce the product or service.

If Paola's Parlour can easily hire more employees and buy more studs, all at the same prices, then her supply of piercings will be elastic. Even a small percentage rise in the price of piercings will cause her to increase her quantity supplied because her profits will increase. But if, as she tries to increase her quantity supplied, she faces higher opportunity costs and has to pay more for her inputs, it will take a bigger percentage rise in the price of piercings to get her to provide even a small increase in quantity. In that case, her supply is inelastic.

Availability of Inputs The availability of inputs also helps explain the difference between supply elasticities for gold mining and snow shovelling. It is difficult to find new inputs for mining (gold deposits and gold mines), while it is easy to attract new workers to snow shovelling. Easy availability of new inputs makes for more elastic supply, while difficult and costly availability of new inputs makes for more inelastic supply.

Time To see the importance of time, compare Paola's supply of piercings with supply in the gold-mining industry. When the price of piercings rises, Paola can quickly adjust her quantity supplied. When gold prices rise, it can take years or even decades for the quantity supplied to adjust. Industries with quick time to production tend to have more elastic supply. Industries with slow time to production tend to have more inelastic supply.

Why Do We Care about Elasticity of Supply?

In 2007, the Alberta housing market was booming. Oil revenues were raising incomes for everyone in the industry and beyond, and new workers were moving into the province to take well-paying jobs. New-home builders were expanding the quantity supplied of housing as fast as they could, but ended up disappointing many customers when they couldn't deliver the quantities at the prices promised.

It is never good business to promise more than you can profitably deliver, and understanding elasticity of supply is important for avoiding broken promises. Shortages and higher wages in the building trades limited the profitable availability of inputs. Housing construction, although not as time-consuming as mining, does take time to adjust to new price conditions. A smart entrepreneur can't change these business conditions, but he or she can use elasticity of supply to more accurately predict outputs and prices, and avoid disappointing customers.

It is always a smart business decision to pay no more for an input than you have to. An employer, desperate to get more hours out of his staff during a holiday season, might offer double-time wages, when time-and-a-half would have attracted the necessary increase in quantity supplied of labour. Knowing about elasticity of supply enables smart, informed choices, and can only help a business's bottom line.

Practice...

11. The statement "Even after the reward was doubled, nobody volunteered for the mission" is an example of
    a. the law of supply.
    b. elastic supply.
    c. inelastic supply.
    d. inelastic demand.

12. There is a high elasticity of supply for a business
    a. in a small town with no available workers.
    b. in a large town with many available workers.
    c. with workers who are lazy and unwilling to work additional hours.
    d. with workers who threaten to quit if their hours are reduced.

13. Since real trees take a very long time to grow, this year's supply of real Christmas trees is
    a. low.
    b. high.
    c. elastic.
    d. inelastic.

14. Mike's Mystery Meats cut prices just a little, and sales exploded. Mike couldn't keep up with demand, and had to turn away customers. Mike's
    a. demand is inelastic and supply is inelastic.
    b. demand is elastic and supply is elastic.
    c. demand is elastic and supply is inelastic.
    d. demand is inelastic and supply is elastic.

15. The size of *both* the elasticity of demand and the elasticity of supply depend on
    a. the time to adjust to a price change.
    b. the proportion of income spent on a product or service.
    c. the availability of inputs.
    d. the availability of substitutes for consumers.

 Apply...

7. An unexpected October heat wave makes consumers desperate to buy more air conditioners, but suppliers have none in stock. What factors might affect how quickly suppliers can restock their shelves? What does this have to do with the price elasticity of supply?

_____

_____

_____

_____

_____

_____

8. If your boss offers you a 20-percent raise, and in response you work 10-percent more hours, how would you describe your price elasticity of labour supply? Are these smart choices for both of you? Explain your answer.

_____

_____

_____

_____

_____

_____

_____

9. Your business is about to launch an advertising campaign, announcing your new low prices. You hope the ads will bring in many more customers. Explain why you need to be concerned about your elasticity of supply.

_____

_____

_____

_____

_____

_____

More Elasticities of Demand

 Define cross elasticity and income elasticity of demand, and explain how they measure substitutes and complements, normal and inferior goods, and necessities and luxuries.

Elasticity is all about measuring responsiveness — *by how much* quantity (demanded or supplied) responds to a change in price. Measurement of real events connects our simplified economic models of demand and supply to the real world. By comparing the models with measured facts, we can evaluate how well the models work to help us understand and predict what is going on out there.

Instead of measuring by how much quantity demanded or supplied responds to a change in its price, we can also look at how quantity demanded responds to changes in other variables — changes in the prices of related products and changes in income. In this section, we'll look at other elasticities that allow us to measure some familiar economic concepts like substitutes, complements, necessities, and luxuries. The sizes of these elasticity measures have practical implications for business decisions.

Cross Elasticity of Demand

Remember the important distinction between a change in quantity demanded and a change in demand? (If not, do a quick review on page 37.) The quantity demanded of a product or service changes with a change in its price, while changes in any of the other factors affect demand. One of the factors held constant for the law of demand is the price of related products and services — substitutes and complements.

The **cross elasticity of demand** connects two *different* products or services. It measures the responsiveness of the demand for one product or service to a change in the price of another — a substitute or complement — other things unchanged. This is the simple formula for calculating the cross elasticity of demand:

$$\text{Cross elasticity of demand} = \frac{\text{Percentage change in quantity demanded}}{\text{Percentage change in price of a substitute or complement}}$$

The cross elasticity of demand can be a positive number or a negative number. We can't avoid negative numbers this time because this elasticity measure provides information about the direction, as well as size, of a response. The cross elasticity of demand is positive for a substitute and negative for a complement. To better understand why, we'll focus first on the direction of the response and then on the size.

Substitutes Consider how people clean their sidewalks: either spraying them with a hose or sweeping them with a broom. Water, sprayed with a hose, is a substitute for brooms. Dustpans, for collecting the dirt and leaves, are a complement for brooms.

When the price of water rises, people economize on their use of water for cleaning and substitute brooms. The demand for brooms increases — the demand curve for brooms shifts rightward.

A rise in the price of water increases the demand for brooms. A fall in the price of water decreases the demand for brooms. The price of water (denominator) and the quantity demanded of brooms (numerator) both change in the same direction. The cross elasticity of demand for substitutes is a positive number.

Complements   What happens to the demand for brooms when the price of dustpans rises? The combined cost of using a broom with a dustpan is now higher, so people economize on their use of both brooms and dustpans. The demand for brooms decreases — the demand curve for brooms shifts leftward.

A rise in the price of dustpans decreases the demand for brooms. A fall in the price of dustpans increases the demand for brooms. The price of dustpans (denominator) and the demand for brooms (numerator) change in opposite directions. The cross elasticity of demand for complements is a negative number.

By How Much?   Calculating the cross elasticity of demand using the simple formula gives you a sign — positive or negative — that tells you if you are analyzing substitutes or complements. The calculation also gives a number — the size of the cross elasticity of demand.

What does a number like + 3.0 mean for cross elasticity of demand compared to a number like + 0.5? Large numbers mean large shifts. Small numbers mean small shifts. Positive numbers mean the demand curve shifts rightward. Negative numbers mean the demand curve shifts leftward.

The more perfect the substitutes or complements, the bigger the number for cross elasticity of demand. An example of almost perfect substitutes is blue and black earbuds. Water and brooms are probably not as good substitutes for each other, so the number for their cross elasticity of demand is smaller. Perfect complements are products or services that are always used together. An example of perfect complements is left and right shoes. (Imagine if you had to buy left shoes separately from right shoes!) Whenever you buy one, you also buy the other. French fries and gravy are not such close complements. Many would rather eat their fries with ketchup or vinegar or just salt, so their cross elasticity of demand will be smaller.

Measuring the cross elasticity of demand gives more precise information about the size of shifts of demand curves. When both demand and supply shift together, the models in Chapter 3 cannot predict what happens to the equilibrium price (when demand and supply both increase or decrease) or to the equilibrium quantity (when demand and supply change in opposite directions). The outcomes depend on how large or small the shifts of the demand and supply curves are. The cross elasticity of demand provides that shift size information and improves our understanding of how markets work.

Cross elasticity of demand also provides practical information for businesses. If you are selling cars and gasoline prices rise, cross elasticity gives you an idea of the (negative) impact on your car sales.

Income Elasticity of Demand

Income is another factor that changes demand and shifts the demand curve.

The **income elasticity of demand** measures the responsiveness of the demand for a product or service to a change in income, other things unchanged. This is the simple formula for calculating the income elasticity of demand:

$$\text{Income elasticity of demand} = \frac{\text{Percentage change in quantity demanded}}{\text{Percentage change in income}}$$

Income elasticity of demand can also be a positive or negative number — positive for a normal good and negative for an inferior good. Again, let's focus first on the direction of the response and then on the size.

Normal Goods   Airline travel is a normal good. An increase in income, all other things unchanged, increases the demand for airline travel. With more income, you are more likely to fly than to travel by car or train. The demand curve for airline travel shifts rightward.

Income elasticity of demand for normal goods is a positive number. Income and demand both change in the same direction. An increase in income increases the demand for airline travel, while a decrease in income decreases the demand for airline travel.

Inferior Goods   Kraft Dinner (KD) is an inferior good. Many people eat KD because they can't afford the food they really want. When income increases, people can better afford higher-priced foods and restaurant meals, so the demand for KD decreases. The demand curve shifts leftward.

Income elasticity of demand for inferior goods is a negative number. Income and demand change in opposite directions. An increase in income decreases the demand for KD while a decrease in income increases the demand for KD.

Necessities and Luxuries   Necessities and luxuries tend to have different *price* elasticities of demand because of different availability of substitutes. Whether a normal good is a necessity or a luxury is shown by the size of the number for *income* elasticity of demand.

Necessities tend to have **income inelastic demand** — income elasticities of demand less than one (but greater than zero). The percentage change in quantity demanded is less than the percentage change in income. Products with income inelastic demand include beer, furniture, and salt. When your income goes up, you buy more, but not much more, of products and services with income inelastic demand.

Luxuries tend to have **income elastic demand** — income elasticities of demand greater than one. The percentage change in quantity demanded is greater than the percentage change in income. Examples of income elastic demand include airline travel, jewellery, and movies. When your income goes up, you buy a lot more of products and services with income elastic demand.

For businesses, it is useful to know whether your product's income elasticity of demand is negative (an inferior good), positive but less than one (a necessity), or positive and greater than one (a luxury). If the economy is going into a recession and incomes are falling, you can predict increases in demand and sales for KD, large decreases in demand for luxury items, and more modest decreases in demand for necessities. Your plans for future supply will be more accurate with good information about income elasticity of demand.

Quick Guide to Elasticity Measures

Figure 7 is a good study device for reviewing all elasticity concepts.

Figure 7   Measures of Elasticity

Price Elasticity of Demand			
Simple Formula	Description	Measures	Necessities or Luxuries
Percentage change in quantity demanded / Percentage change in price	Perfectly Inelastic	Zero	
	Inelastic	Greater than zero, but less than 1	Necessities
	Unit Elastic	1	
	Elastic	Greater than 1	Luxuries
	Perfectly Elastic	Infinity	

Elasticity of Supply			
Simple Formula	Description	Measures	
Percentage change in quantity supplied / Percentage change in price	Perfectly Inelastic	Zero	
	Inelastic	Greater than zero, but less than 1	
	Unit Elastic	1	
	Elastic	Greater than 1	
	Perfectly Elastic	Infinity	

Cross Elasticity of Demand			
Simple Formula	Description	Measures	
Percentage change in quantity demanded / Percentage change in price of a substitute or complement	Substitutes	Positive	
	Complements	Negative	

Income Elasticity of Demand			
Simple Formula	Description	Measures	Necessities or Luxuries
Percentage change in quantity demanded / Percentage change in income	Normal Good	Positive	
	Inferior Good	Negative	
	Income Inelastic Demand	Positive and less than 1	Necessities
	Income Elastic Demand	Positive and greater than 1	Luxuries

Practice...

16. The cross elasticity of the demand for white tennis balls with respect to the price of yellow tennis balls is probably

    a. negative and high.

    b. negative and low.

    c. positive and high.

    d. positive and low.

17. The cross elasticity of demand between any two products is defined as the percentage change in the

    a. price of a product divided by the percentage change in the price of a substitute or complement.

    b. price elasticity of demand for one product divided by the percentage change in the price elasticity of demand for a substitute or complement.

    c. quantity demanded of a product divided by the percentage change in income.

    d. quantity demanded of one product divided by the percentage change in the price of a substitute or complement.

18. If a 10-percent increase in income causes a 5-percent increase in quantity demanded, what is the income elasticity of demand?

    a. 0.5

    b. – 0.5

    c. 2.0

    d. – 2.0

19. If a 4-percent decrease in income causes a 2-percent decrease in the consumption of pencils, then

    a. the income elasticity of pencils is negative.

    b. pencils are a necessity and a normal good.

    c. pencils are a luxury and a normal good.

    d. pencils are an inferior good.

20. Luxuries tend to have income elasticities of demand that are

    a. greater than one.

    b. greater than zero but less than one.

    c. positive.

    d. negative.

 **Apply...**

10. Suppose you lose your job and start receiving employment insurance. You income falls by 60 percent.

    a. Your spending on grits increases by 20 percent. What kind of a good are grits (normal, inferior, necessity, luxury)? Show any calculations that support your answer.

    _____

    _____

    _____

    _____

    b. Your spending on clothes decreases by 40 percent. What kind of a good are clothes (normal, inferior, necessity, luxury)? Show any calculations that support your answer.

    _____

    _____

    _____

    _____

11. What do you think the number would be for the cross-elasticity of demand of two products that seem totally unrelated to each other (positive or negative, size)? Explain your answer.

    _____

    _____

    _____

    _____

    _____

    _____

12. Evidence suggests that babies are a normal good for lower income earners and an inferior good for higher income earners. Use the income elasticity of demand to explain what this means, using the definitions of "normal" and "inferior" goods.

    _____

    _____

    _____

    _____

    _____

    _____

Tax Incidence and Government Tax Choices

L05 Use elasticity to explain who pays sales taxes and government tax choices

In Canada, the federal government sales tax is called the Goods and Services Tax (GST), and in many provinces it is combined with provincial sales taxes as the Harmonized Sales Tax (HST). Sales taxes are charged as a percentage of the price of what you buy. Canadian consumers love to complain about having to pay high sales taxes. But do consumers pay the tax? And how do governments decide which products and services to tax? Elasticity helps answer those questions.

Tax Incidence

The question of who pays the tax is called tax incidence. **Tax incidence** is the division of a tax between buyers and sellers, and depends on the elasticities of demand and supply.

Let's use a simple example where instead of a percentage, the tax is a fixed dollar amount of $20 per unit. The math is simpler that way. Many actual sales taxes, like those on cigarettes and gasoline, are a fixed dollar amount.

Figure 8 shows the (made-up) market for exercycles (exercise bicycles). The market is initially in equilibrium at the intersection of the demand (*D*) and supply (*S*) curves. The equilibrium price is $200 per exercycle and the equilibrium quantity is 50.

Figure 8   A Sales Tax on Businesses

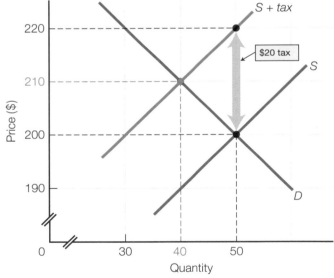

The government decides to place a $20 tax on every exercycle sold. Governments collect sales taxes monthly from the sellers — the exercycle businesses have to send in $20 for each unit they sell. The tax increases the sellers' costs by $20 per exercycle, just as if input prices went up by $20 per unit. The tax shifts the supply curve leftward to the supply curve labelled *S + tax*.

This graph makes more sense when you read the supply curve up and over as a marginal cost curve, because the tax shifts the supply curve up by a distance equal to the amount of the tax. The pink vertical arrow indicates the $20 tax. For the 50th exercycle, going up to the original supply curve and over to the price axis shows a marginal cost of $200. Going up from the 50th exercycle to the new *S + tax* curve and over shows a marginal cost of $220. Sellers now have to pay the original $200 marginal costs per exercycle plus the $20 tax.

The sellers pay the tax to the government, but your receipt for exercycles shows the $20 tax that you, as the buyer, pay. So who is paying the tax?

The answer, in this case, is that the buyer and the seller each pay part of the tax. After the tax, the new equilibrium price is $210, so buyers are paying $10 more per exercycle. The sellers are receiving that extra $10 per exercycle, but then pay $20 per exercycle to the government. So the sellers are also paying $10 per exercycle. The tax incidence of the $20 per exercycle tax is split evenly between buyers and sellers.

Taxes are not always split evenly between buyers and sellers. The division depends on elasticities of demand and supply. Once again, the extreme values of elasticity give the clearest insight into how elasticity affects tax incidence.

Tax Incidence with Extreme Demand Elasticities   Figure 9 shows who pays the sales tax when demand is perfectly inelastic and perfectly elastic.

Figure 9   Tax Incidence with Extreme Demand Elasticities

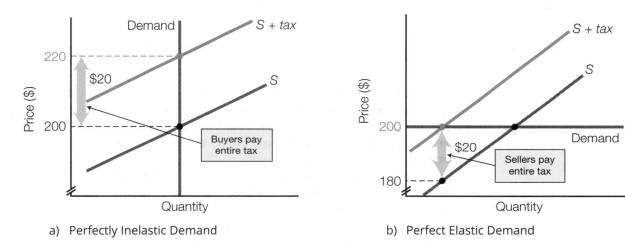

a) Perfectly Inelastic Demand

b) Perfect Elastic Demand

When demand is perfectly inelastic — Figure 9a — the supply curve shifts up by the $20 amount of the tax. Perfectly inelastic demand means buyers will pay any price for the product and not decrease quantity demanded. The equilibrium price rises by the full amount of the tax, from $200 to $220. Buyers pay the entire tax.

When demand is perfectly elastic — Figure 9b — the supply curve again shifts up by the amount of the tax of $20. But with perfectly elastic demand, buyers are not willing to pay even a penny more for the exercycles. The equilibrium price remains at $200, and sellers have to absorb the entire $20 tax. Sellers receive $200 per unit from buyers, but have to send the government $20 for each exercycle, ending up with $180.

These extreme demand elasticities almost never happen in the real world. But they provide the basis for general rules about tax incidence that apply to all real-world situations:

- The more inelastic demand is, the more buyers pay of a tax.

- The more elastic demand is, the more sellers pay of a tax.

Tax Incidence with Extreme Supply Elasticities Figure 10 shows who pays the sales tax when supply is perfectly inelastic and perfectly elastic.

Figure 10 Tax Incidence with Extreme Supply Elasticities

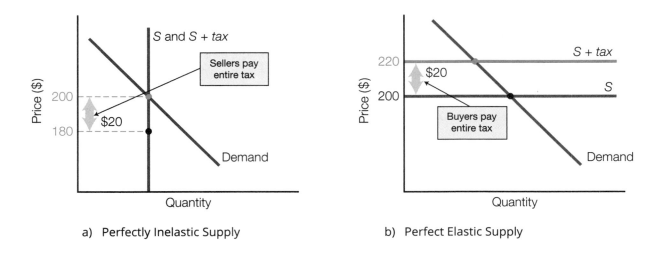

a) Perfectly Inelastic Supply

b) Perfect Elastic Supply

When supply is perfectly inelastic — Figure 10a — the tax does not shift the supply curve. Suppliers will accept any price for the given quantity. The equilibrium price remains at $200, and sellers absorb the entire $20 tax. Sellers receive $200 per exercycle from buyers, but have to send the government $20 per sale, ending up with $180.

When supply is perfectly elastic — Figure 10b — the supply curve shifts up by the $20 amount of the tax. The equilibrium price rises from $200 to $220, so buyers pay the entire tax.

Like the extreme demand elasticities, the extreme supply elasticities provide the basis for general rules about tax incidence:

- The more inelastic supply is, the more sellers pay of a tax.

- The more elastic supply is, the more buyers pay of a tax.

Figure 11 summarizes the general rules about tax incidence.

Figure 11 Elasticity and Tax Incidence

When Demand Is	Tax Incidence
Perfectly inelastic	Buyers pay all of a tax
Inelastic	Buyers pay more of a tax
Elastic	Sellers pay more of a tax
Perfectly elastic	Sellers pay all of a tax
When Supply Is	Tax Incidence
Perfectly inelastic	Sellers pay all of a tax
Inelastic	Sellers pay more of a tax
Elastic	Buyers pay more of a tax
Perfectly elastic	Buyers pay all of a tax

What's in Taxes for Government?

No matter who pays the tax, the tax money goes to the government. Figure 12 shows how governments estimate the tax revenues they collect from a sales tax.

Figure 12 Tax Revenues

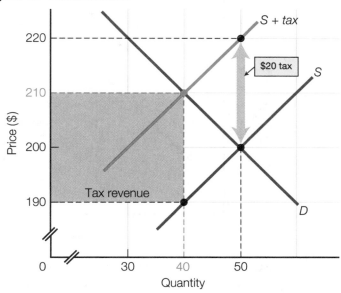

The shaded blue rectangle represents the revenue from the $20 per unit sales tax on exercycles. The height of the rectangle is the $20 tax per unit, and the width is the quantity, or number of units sold: 40 exercycles. The tax revenue formula is

tax per unit × units sold

or

$20 × 40 = $800.

Tax revenue depends on the elasticities of demand and supply. In general, the more inelastic demand and supply are, the greater the tax revenue for government. Why? Sales taxes decrease supply and therefore decrease the equilibrium quantity in a market. Elasticities determine *by how much* quantity decreases because of the tax. The more inelastic demand and supply are, the smaller the decreases in quantity, keeping the tax revenue larger.

For this reason, governments try to tax products and services with inelastic demands or supplies. Commonly taxed products like alcohol, cigarettes, and gasoline all have inelastic demands. While there are many reasons why governments choose to tax specific products and services, smart government choices for sales tax revenue depend on elasticities.

Elasticity is a concept that can be stretched (that's economist humour) to measure the responsiveness of quantity demanded to changes in other variables besides price — changes in the prices of related products and changes in income. These elasticity measures help connect simple demand and supply models to real-world concepts like substitutes, complements, necessities, and luxuries, and help governments make smart tax policy choices.

Your opportunity cost of using elasticity concepts is doing a little math, but your benefit is a better understanding of how markets work and by how much consumers and businesses respond to changes in incentives, whether in the form of prices, incomes, or taxes.

Practice...

21. The tax incidence on buyers is greater the more

    1   elastic demand is.

    2   inelastic demand is.

    3   elastic supply is.

    4   inelastic supply is.

    a.   2 and 3

    b.   1 and 3

    c.   2 and 4

    d.   1 and 4

22. If the price of a product is not affected by a sales tax,

    a.   supply is perfectly elastic.

    b.   demand is perfectly elastic.

    c.   elasticity of supply is greater than elasticity of demand.

    d.   demand is perfectly inelastic.

23. If the equilibrium quantity sold of a product is not affected by a sales tax,

    a.   elasticity of demand is greater than elasticity of supply.

    b.   supply is perfectly elastic.

    c.   supply is perfectly inelastic.

    d.   demand is perfectly elastic.

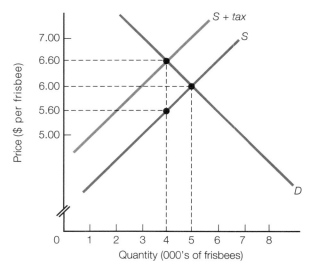

24. The graph above shows the market for frisbees before and after a government tax. On each frisbee, the seller's share of the tax is

    a. $5.60.

    b. $1.00

    c. $0.60

    d. $0.40

25. Revenue collected by government from a sales tax is greater the more

    1   elastic demand is.

    2   inelastic demand is.

    3   elastic supply is.

    4   inelastic supply is.

    a.   1 and 4

    b.   2 and 4

    c.   1 and 3

    d.   2 and 3

Apply...

13. The Ministry of Treasury wants to put a $0.15-per-unit excise (sales) tax on one of two products — comic books or dog biscuits. As a summer student at the Ministry, you are given an assignment by the Director of Taxes, Dr. More. You must choose the product that meets two objectives: (1) It will yield the greatest tax revenue and (2) the major incidence of the tax will fall on consumers (buyers). Ministry researchers have estimated the supply and demand curves (without the tax) for each market. The comic-book market is shown in the first graph and the dog-biscuit market in the second graph.

a. Shift the appropriate curve to reflect the tax and draw it on the graph. Label the curve either "*S + tax*" or "*D + tax*." Identify the new equilibrium price and quantity. Compare the total expenditure in the original and new equilibriums.

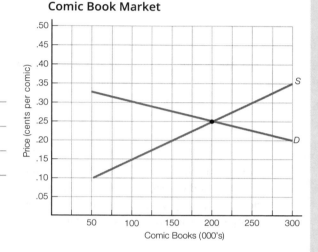

_____

_____

_____

_____

b. Calculate the total tax revenue collected, and indicate it as an area on the graph.

_____

_____

c. How much of the tax is paid by consumers? by sellers?

_____

_____

Now perform the same analysis on the dog biscuit market.

d. Shift the appropriate curve to reflect the tax and draw it on the dog biscuit graph. Label the curve either "*S + tax*" or "*D + tax*." Identify the new equilibrium price and quantity. Compare the total expenditure in the original and new equilibriums.

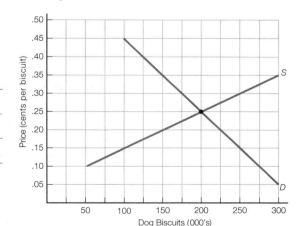

_____

_____

_____

_____

Apply...

   e. Calculate the total tax revenue collected and indicate it as an area on the graph.

       _____

       _____

   f. How much of the tax is paid by consumers? by sellers?

       _____

       _____

   g. What is your recommendation to Dr. More? Explain.

       _____

       _____

       _____

14. Governments use sales taxes both to collect revenue and to change behaviour. If cigarette taxes are intended to discourage smoking rather than raise revenue, what elasticities of supply and demand for cigarettes will help governments achieve this policy objective? How do those elasticities compare to the elasticities that give government the most tax revenue?

       _____

       _____

       _____

       _____

       _____

KNOW...

Learning Objectives

1. **Elasticity** measures how responsive quantity demanded is to a change in price, and depends on available substitutes, time to adjust, and the proportion of income spent on the product.

2. Elasticity determines business pricing strategies to earn maximum total revenue — cut prices when there is **elastic demand** and raise prices when there is **inelastic demand**.

3. **Elasticity of supply** measures the responsiveness of quantity supplied to a change in price, and depends on the difficulty, expense, and time involved in increasing production.

4. Other elasticity concepts measure the responsiveness of quantity demanded to changes in prices of related products and income. **Cross elasticity of demand** is positive for substitutes and negative for complements. **Income elasticity of demand** is positive for normal goods, negative for inferior goods, and can distinguish necessities (**income inelastic demand** positive and less than 1) and luxuries (**income elastic demand** positive and greater than 1).

5. **Tax incidence** — the division of a sales tax between buyers and sellers — depends on elasticities of demand and supply. Buyers pay more of a tax the more inelastic demand is and the more elastic supply is. Sellers pay more of a tax the more elastic demand is and the more inelastic supply is. The more inelastic demand and supply are, the greater the tax revenue for government. For maximum revenue, governments try to tax products and services with inelastic demands and supplies.

Key Terms

cross elasticity of demand: measures the responsiveness of the demand for a product or service to a change in the price of a substitute or complement

elastic demand: large response in quantity demanded when price rises

elastic supply: large response in quantity supplied when price rises

elasticity (price elasticity of demand): measures by how much quantity demanded responds to a change in price

elasticity of supply: measures by how much quantity supplied responds to a change in price

income elastic demand: for normal goods that are luxuries, the percentage change in quantity is greater than the percentage change in income

income elasticity of demand: measures the responsiveness of the demand for a product or service to a change in income

income inelastic demand: for normal goods that are necessities, the percentage change in quantity is less than the percentage change in income

inelastic demand: small response in quantity demanded when price rises

inelastic supply: small response in quantity supplied when price rises

perfectly elastic demand: price elasticity of demand equals infinity; quantity demanded has an infinite response to a change in price

perfectly elastic supply: price elasticity of supply equals infinity; quantity supplied has an infinite response to a change in price

perfectly inelastic demand: price elasticity of demand equals zero; quantity demanded does not respond to a change in price

perfectly inelastic supply: price elasticity of supply equals zero; quantity supplied does not respond to a change in price

price elasticity of demand (elasticity): measures by how much quantity demanded responds to a change in price

tax incidence: the division of a tax between buyers and sellers

Answers to Practice

1. **a** Better substitutes mean more elastic demand.

2. **c** Use simple formula. Price and quantity demanded are inversely related.

3. **b** Use midpoint formula. Percentage change in quantity = 20%. Percentage change in price = 10%.

4. **a** No (zero) change in quantity demanded no matter what the change in price.

5. **b** Also longer time to adjust and easier to find substitutes.

6. **b** Fall in price decreases total revenue for inelastic demand.

7. **c** Unit elastic demand.

8. **d** Raising price increases total revenue for inelastic demand. Lowering price increases total revenue for elastic demand. But LG and TB probably should stick to singing and forget about economics.

9. **d** Supply shifts rightward. Equilibrium quantity increases and price falls. With inelastic demand, total revenue decreases.

10. **a** Small fall in prices causes large increase in quantity demanded. For elastic demand, quantity demanded has large response to change in price.

11. **c** Large rise in price produces no change in quantity supplied.

12. **b** More available inputs.

13. **d** Longer production times mean more inelastic supply.

14. **c** Elastic demand because large response of quantity demanded to small fall in price. Mike can't respond with increased quantity supplied fast enough, so inelastic supply.

15. **a** **b** and **d** apply only to demand, while **c** applies only to supply.

16. **c** Almost perfect substitutes.

17. **d** Definition. Measures responsiveness of the demand for one product (quantity) to a change in the price of another (substitute or complement).

18. **a** Use simple formula. Positive for normal goods.

19. **b** Income elasticity of demand for pencils = + 0.5.

20. **a** Positive because normal goods. Necessities have income elasticities of demand between zero and one.

21. **a** See Figure 11 on page 106.

22. **b** Sellers pay entire tax because buyers will not pay more.

23. **c** Sellers will accept any price to supply given quantity.

24. **d** Tax is $1.00, price rises by 60 cents from $6.00 to $6.60, so buyers pay 60 cents and sellers pay remaining 40 cents.

25. **b** The more inelastic demand and supply are, the smaller the decreases in quantity, keeping the tax revenue larger.

5 Government Policy Choices: Efficiency and Equity

LEARNING OBJECTIVES

L01 Explain how government-fixed prices cause quantities to adjust and market coordination to fail.

L02 Describe price ceilings and explain the unintended consequences of government rent-control policies.

L03 Describe price floors and explain the unintended consequences of government minimum wage laws.

L04 Explain government policy trade-offs between efficient and equitable outcomes, and two different concepts of equity.

LEARN...

Every time gas prices jump by 20 cents per litre, the complaints begin — oil companies are price gouging, gas taxes should be lowered, governments should do something. When drivers (who are also voters) complain about prices, politicians notice. Parliament holds hearings, and sometimes — as with Canada's New Energy Program in 1974 — governments actually fix gas prices, making it illegal for suppliers to charge higher prices. The pattern is similar when tenants (voters) complain that rents are too high, or workers (voters) complain that wages are too low. Governments respond with rent-control policies or minimum wage laws.

When high (or low) prices cause voters pain, governments are tempted to fix prices. Despite good intentions, the consequences are usually not what governments intended. Prices are signals that coordinate the smart decisions of consumers and businesses. Fixed prices cripple the flow of information and the incentives that make markets effective at producing what we want. In this chapter, we look at what happens when prices can't adjust.

Government policy choices, like consumer and business choices, involve trade-offs. When governments act to correct problems of affordability and fairness that markets create, there are often better solutions than fixed prices. But sometimes governments might still make smart policy choices that give up the market's benefits of flexible prices in order to promote more equitable outcomes.

Unintended Consequences of Government Policies

 Explain how government-fixed prices cause quantities to adjust and market coordination to fail.

When governments fix prices, markets try to coordinate those policy choices with consumer and business choices. The coordinated outcomes are often not what policymakers intended. But we can still use the Three Keys model, comparing marginal benefits and marginal costs, to judge if government policies are smart choices.

Shortages When Prices Fixed Below Equilibrium

Suppose gas regularly sells for $1 per litre. That is an equilibrium price, matching the quantity of gas demanded and quantity of gas supplied at 85 million litres per month. Then a Middle East conflict destroys some oil refineries, and supply decreases.

The graph in Figure 1 shows the unchanged market demand (D_0), the original market supply (S_0), and the new market supply for gasoline (S_1) after supply decreases. The table shows, for every price, the quantities behind the demand curve D_0 (column 2) and the new market supply curve S_1 (column 3). The last column shows, for every price, the difference between quantity demanded and quantity supplied.

Figure 1   Gasoline Market with Shortage

Price per Litre	Quantity Demanded (millions of litres per month)	Quantity Supplied (millions of litres per month)	Shortage (−) or Surplus (+) (millions of litres per month)
$0.80	95	35	−60
$1.00	**85**	**55**	**−30**
$1.20	75	75	0
$1.40	65	95	+30
$1.60	55	115	+60

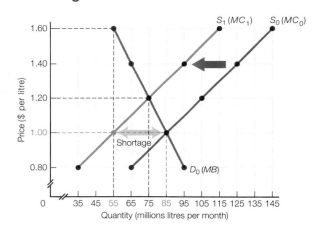

Prices Adjust After supply shifts leftward from S_0 to S_1, if the price remains at $1 per litre there is a shortage. The quantity demanded (85 million litres per month) is unchanged. But at the price of $1 per litre, gasoline suppliers will only supply 55 million litres per month. There is a shortage of 30 million litres per month, indicated by the pink horizontal arrow on the graph.

So begins the classic Chapter 3 shortage story. Consumers compete against each other for the now hard-to-find gasoline, and bid up prices. Gasoline suppliers respond to the rising prices by supplying increased quantities. Rising prices also decrease quantity demanded, as consumers substitute away from more expensive gas, which fewer can afford. With flexible prices, adjustments continue until the price reaches the new equilibrium price of $1.20 per litre. At that market-clearing price, the shortage is eliminated and the quantity of gas demanded again matches the quantity supplied (75 million litres per month). This is how well-functioning markets coordinate smart choices for consumers and businesses.

Quantities Adjust What if the government, facing an election and worried about driver/voter complaints, passes a law making it illegal for anyone to sell gasoline for more than $1 per litre? Governments can fix prices, but they can't force businesses to produce if that price is not profitable.

The fixed-price story does not have a happy ending. At $1 per litre, suppliers are only willing to supply 55 million litres per month. Now that prices can't adjust, buyers will be frustrated. If you read the demand curve as a marginal benefit curve (up and over), the 55 millionth litre of gas is worth $1.60 to some consumer drivers. Drivers will try hard to find gasoline; available gasoline is worth much more to them than the fixed $1 price. Consumers lucky enough to get gas either spend hours driving around looking for stations with supplies, wait in long line-ups, or bribe gas station owners to supply them first. Most give up some driving — there is a shortage of 30 million litres per month. *Quantities adjust.*

Fixing prices does not change the voluntary quality of market exchanges. Businesses supply only if price covers all opportunity costs of production. Consumers demand only if they are willing and able to pay that price. For any price, set by the market or by governments, businesses can reduce output, shut down factories, or move inputs elsewhere. Consumers can reduce their purchases, keep their wallets shut, or buy something else. There are always substitutes.

Governments can legally fix prices, but consumers and businesses will *adjust quantities* to make their respective smart choices at the fixed price. The smart choices of consumers and of businesses are not coordinated when prices can't adjust. Both groups are unhappy, which is not what the policymakers intended.

Surpluses When Prices Fixed Above Equilibrium

When price is set too high, there is a surplus. Figure 2 repeats the information for the gasoline market in Figure 1 after supply decreases.

Figure 2   Gasoline Market with Surplus

Price per Litre	Quantity Demanded (millions of litres per month)	Quantity Supplied (millions of litres per month)	Shortage (−) or Surplus (+) (millions of litres per month)
$0.80	95	35	− 60
$1.00	**85**	**55**	**− 30**
$1.20	75	75	0
$1.40	65	95	+ 30
$1.60	55	115	+ 60

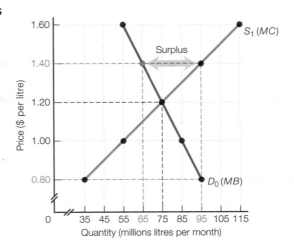

Prices Adjust Suppose the price of gas is $1.40 per litre, above the equilibrium price. Suppliers are happy to supply 95 million litres per month, but consumers demand only 65 million litres. There is a monthly surplus of 30 million litres of gasoline, indicated by the blue horizontal arrow on the graph.

Businesses compete for hard-to-find customers, and cut prices. Falling prices increase quantity demanded as consumers buy more of the now-cheaper gas. Suppliers respond to the falling prices by decreasing quantities supplied. With flexible prices, adjustments continue until the price reaches the equilibrium price of $1.20 per litre. The surplus is eliminated and the quantity of gas demanded again matches the quantity supplied (75 million litres per month).

Quantities Adjust   What if government fixed an above-equilibrium price of $1.40 per litre? If you read the demand curve as a marginal benefit curve, the 95 millionth litre that suppliers would like to sell is worth only $0.80 to some consumers. Consumers won't pay $1.40 for a litre of gas that has a benefit of only $0.80. For all litres greater than 65 million, marginal benefit is less than the cost of $1.40. Without price cuts, consumers will buy only 65 million litres. The surplus of 30 million litres sits in storage tanks. Businesses reduce the quantity of gasoline produced in future months, until the unsold surplus gasoline finally is sold. *Quantities adjust.*

The smart choices of consumers and the smart choices of businesses are not coordinated when prices can't adjust. Businesses are willing to supply more gasoline, but are frustrated because they cannot sell it. And in a voluntary market system, neither businesses nor governments can force consumers to buy more at the higher price.

Fixed Prices Prevent Markets from Functioning Well

When governments fix prices, either below or above the equilibrium price, the smart choices of consumers and businesses are not coordinated. The only way shortages or surpluses disappear is by quantities adjusting to whichever is less — to quantity supplied (with a shortage), or to quantity demanded (with a surplus).

 Practice...

1. When prices are fixed below equilibrium,
   a. there is a decrease in demand.
   b. quantity demanded is greater than quantity supplied.
   c. there is an increase in supply.
   d. quantity supplied is greater than quantity demanded.

2. When prices are fixed above equilibrium,
   a. sellers are frustrated.
   b. there are shortages.
   c. quantity demanded is greater than quantity supplied.
   d. buyers are frustrated.

3. When prices are fixed below equilibrium, all of the following happen *except*
   a. shortages.
   b. frustrated buyers.
   c. quantity adjustments.
   d. surpluses.

Practice...

4. A price ceiling set by government above the equilibrium price results in

    a. surpluses.

    b. shortages.

    c. the equilibrium price.

    d. an increase in supply.

5. When governments set a price that is not an equilibrium price, the quantity actually sold

    a. is determined by the quantity supplied.

    b. is determined by whichever is more, quantity supplied or quantity demanded.

    c. is determined by whichever is less, quantity supplied or quantity demanded.

    d. cannot be determined without knowing if there is a shortage or a surplus.

Apply...

1. If government makes it illegal for businesses to lower their prices, and there is a surplus of products and services in the market, explain how consumers and businesses will react.

    _____

    _____

    _____

    _____

2. When the government fixes prices below equilibrium, quantity supplied does not equal quantity demanded. Explain why quantity adjusts to whichever is less — quantity supplied or quantity demanded — instead of to whichever is more.

    _____

    _____

    _____

    _____

3. You own a flower shop and usually sell roses for $25 a dozen. In the month before Valentine's Day, your suppliers charge you a higher price for roses. A politician, who has many romantics in his riding, gets Parliament to pass a private member's bill making it illegal to charge more than $25 for a dozen roses. Other flower prices are not fixed. What will be your smart business choice for Valentine's Day?

    _____

    _____

    _____

    _____

    _____

Price Ceilings and Rent Controls

 Describe price ceilings and explain the unintended consequences of government rent-control policies.

Not many citizens feel good seeing people sleeping out on the streets on a freezing winter night. Homelessness and a lack of affordable housing are serious problems in most big Canadian cities. To help solve these problems, compassionate and well-intentioned individuals, charitable organizations, and religious groups often ask governments to do something by controlling rents. **Rent controls** are a form of price fixing (rents are the monthly "price" of apartments). Governments set a maximum rent (called a **price ceiling**) that limits how high rents can be raised, while allowing rents to be flexible downward.

Governments introduce rent-control policies in response to concerns of many groups. Rent controls obviously benefit renters, but also appeal to citizens who believe government should help those who are less fortunate, simply because it is the ethical thing to do. Religious groups also believe in helping the poor. Social activists argue that in a relatively wealthy and enlightened society like Canada, governments should ensure that essential services — affordable housing, education, health care — are available to all citizens. These services are too important, they argue, to be left to impersonal, profit-oriented markets to provide.

Benefits and Costs of Rent-Control Policies

Like any choice, a government policy choice to do something about homelessness must weigh benefits and costs.

Benefits   What are the perceived benefits of rent controls? A political benefit to governments (not to renters) is that the government does not have to spend any money (building shelters or affordable apartments), yet voters see that the government is doing something to help.

For those who can find apartments, rent controls reduce the amount of money they pay for housing, leaving more money for food, clothing, and other necessities. Some citizens and politicians who believe in the "Robin Hood principle" — named after the famous character from medieval folklore who robbed the rich and gave to the poor — see rent controls as a way of redistributing income from (relatively) rich landlords to (relatively) poor tenants.

Costs   Every choice has an opportunity cost. What costs should be compared to benefits in deciding if rent controls are a smart policy choice for helping the homeless?

Rent controls have some undesirable and unintended consequences. Like any fixed price, rent controls cripple the coordinating forces of well-functioning markets. Rent ceilings set below the equilibrium, market-clearing rent create a classic shortage. (A rent ceiling above the equilibrium rent is irrelevant. When apartments are readily available for $1500 per month, a law preventing rents from rising above $1600 has no effect.)

Figure 3   Market for Two-Bedroom Apartments

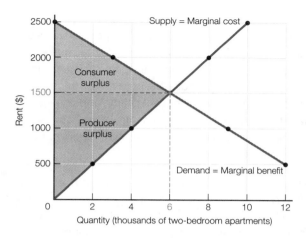

a)   Market for Two-Bedroom Apartments

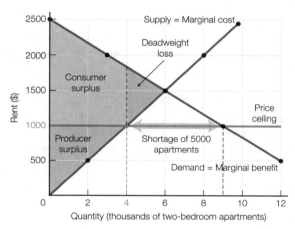

b)   Market for Two-Bedroom Apartments
     with Rent Controls

Figure 3 shows a market for two-bedroom apartments without rent controls (Figure 3a) and with rent controls (Figure 3b). Let's focus first on the prices (rents) and quantities. In Figure 3a, the equilibrium rent is $1500, and the equilibrium quantity is 6000 apartments.

With a price ceiling for rents set at $1000 in Figure 3b, landlords only supply 4000 apartments. The quantity of housing supplied is less than the 6000 apartments supplied at the equilibrium rent. Those who find apartments are better off, but there are *fewer apartments available*. Quantities adjust. With a shortage of 5000 apartments, consumers who can no longer find apartments are frustrated and worse off.

Inefficiency of Rent Controls

The marginal benefit and marginal cost reading of the demand and supply curves in Figure 3 allows us to compare the efficiency of the equilibrium outcome with the rent-controlled outcome. Recall from Chapter 3 that total surplus (consumer surplus plus producer surplus) is at a maximum for an efficient market outcome. All mutually beneficial trades happen, and marginal benefit equals marginal cost for the last (6000th) apartment rented in Figure 3a.

Because rent controls restrict the supply of housing, consumer surplus (green), producer surplus (blue), and total surplus in Figure 3b are less than for the efficient market outcome in Figure 3a. The grey area of deadweight loss in Figure 3b represents mutually beneficial trades between consumers and landlords that don't happen with rent controls. With marginal benefits greater than marginal costs between 4000 and 6000 apartments, each of those additional 2000 apartments would make both consumers and landlords better off. But quantity supplied stops at 4000 apartments, where the marginal benefit of the 4000th apartment is far greater than the marginal cost. There are consumers willing and able to pay more than $1000 if only they could find an apartment.

Unintended Consequences of Rent Controls

Reducing Supply   While governments can fix rents, they cannot force landlords to supply apartments if the rent does not cover all opportunity costs of supplying apartments. At the controlled rents, some landlords may make more money by turning their building into condominiums, again reducing the supply of apartments. A homeowner who rents out a basement apartment in her house may decide it's not worth it at the lower rent ceiling and convert that space back to her own family's use. Smart choices change with changes in prices. With more time to adjust to the lower rent ceiling, fewer apartment buildings may be built (still more condos instead).

Landlord Power   With tenants competing for scarce apartments and willing to pay more than the controlled rent, landlords have the bargaining power. Landlords may allow the physical condition of their properties to deteriorate, since they can be sure of finding tenants. Spending less on maintenance improves their profits in the short run. Landlords may also charge a potential tenant "key money," which is a polite term for a bribe, in exchange for giving that tenant (as opposed to the many other willing tenants) the key to the scarce apartment. Landlords can more easily discriminate against renting to tenants they don't like, both for legitimate reasons (are college students more likely to do property damage?) and illegitimate reasons (on the basis of race or religion).

Subsidizing the Rich   A final unintended consequence is that rent controls also subsidize the (relatively) rich! Rent controls apply to all apartments, not just apartments rented by those who have difficulty affording housing. High-income tenants, who are both willing and able to pay more for their apartments, pay only the controlled rent.

Alternatives to Rent Controls

Are rent-control policies a smart choice for governments trying to ensure more affordable housing? Almost every economist out there would give a strong *no* for an answer. Rent controls, like any fixed price, sacrifice the flexibility and advantages of well-functioning markets to produce the products and services we want and direct them to those most willing and able to pay. While intended to improve the supply of affordable housing, rent controls have many drawbacks, including the unintended results of reducing the quantity of apartments on the market, and subsidizing housing for those who can afford it.

If, as a society, we want to help the homeless or create more affordable housing, better choices are available. Alternative policies include providing low-income consumers with government subsidies that could be applied to any housing they might find in the market. Or governments can build affordable housing and make sure it is available only to those who need it the most. While every government policy choice has opportunity costs (will government employees do a better job of running a housing development than a private business?), these policies allow markets to flexibly coordinate the smart decisions of consumers and business, and result in more rental units, without subsidizing well-off tenants who do not need support.

There is a bigger policy question behind rent controls. Should governments make policy choices based on ethical concerns, even if those choices limit the ability of markets to function well? We will address that important question at the end of this chapter.

Practice...

6. Government rent ceilings

   a. keep rents below equilibrium rents.

   b. keep rents above equilibrium rents.

   c. keep rents equal to equilibrium rents.

   d. increase the quantity of rental housing.

7. Rent ceilings

   a. reduce the quantity of private rental construction.

   b. reduce the quantity of existing rental units.

   c. lower the quality of existing rental units.

   d. do all of the above.

8. Eliminating rent controls should lead landlords to create additional rental apartments. The increase in apartments is *largest* when

   a. supply is inelastic.

   b. supply is elastic.

   c. demand is inelastic.

   d. demand is elastic.

9. Some provinces relaxed rent controls by permitting landlords to charge market rents when the current tenants move out. This gives

   a. tenants an incentive to stay in their apartments.

   b. landlords an incentive to let the quality of existing apartments deteriorate.

   c. governments an incentive to pass anti-eviction laws so that landlords can only remove current tenants with just cause.

   d. all of the above.

10. Government housing subsidies are a better policy alternative to rent controls because

   a. housing subsidies provide income for governments.

   b. housing subsidies are less expensive than rent controls.

   c. market-clearing prices coordinate the choices of landlords and renters.

   d. rents stay above equilibrium rents.

Apply...

Use this graph of a market for apartments to answer questions 4 and 5.

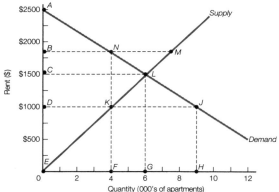

4. Fill in the blanks. In the market for apartments without rent controls:

   a. the equilibrium rent is _____ and the equilibrium quantity of apartments rented is _____.

   b. consumer surplus is area _____ [list the edges of the area — for example, *AEL*].

   c. producer surplus is area _____ [list the edges of the area — for example, *AEL*].

   d. total surplus is area _____ [list the edges of the area — for example, *AEL*].

5. Fill in the blanks. If the government sets a rent ceiling of $1000 in the market for apartments:

   a. the rent is _____ and the quantity of apartments rented is _____.

   b. consumer surplus is area _____ .

   c. producer surplus is area _____ .

   d. the deadweight loss of the rent-controlled outcome is area _____ .

   e. the difference between the quantity demanded and the quantity supplied of apartments

      is a (circle the correct answers)

      surplus / shortage

      of   *KJ / FG / GH / KJ* apartments.

6. Many people argue that education, like housing, is an essential service that should be affordable — perhaps even free — for all citizens. Zero tuition is a price ceiling in the market for education. Describe a set of policies that accomplishes the goal of education affordability for all, but avoids the problems of price controls that you have just learned about.

   _____

   _____

   _____

   _____

   _____

   _____

Price Floors and Minimum Wages

 Describe price floors and explain the unintended consequences of government minimum wage laws.

Minimum wage laws arose in the early 1900s in Canada to protect the less fortunate and most vulnerable members of society. 2018 hourly minimum wages in Canada range from $11.00 in Newfoundland to $11.35 in British Columbia, $13.60 in Alberta and $14.00 in Ontario. Further increases are scheduled in many provinces for 2018. There is a vigorous debate in Canada about the pros and cons of an increased minimum wage for helping the working poor.

   A minimum wage is a fixed price for businesses hiring unskilled labour. It fixes a price floor, making it illegal for a business to hire anyone for a wage less than the minimum.

Benefits and Costs of Minimum Wage Laws

There are both benefits and costs to minimum wage laws.

Labour Markets Are Input Markets

Before looking at the benefits and costs of setting minimum wages in the labour market, I want to re-orient you with the circular-flow model from Chapter 1 (Figure 5, page 14), reproduced here. Households and businesses interact in two sets of markets — input markets (on the right), where businesses buy the inputs they need from households to produce products and services, and output markets (on the left), where businesses sell their products and services to households.

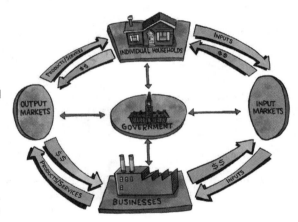

   Labour markets have an important difference from housing or gasoline markets. Housing and gasoline are outputs, so businesses are the sellers and suppliers and households are the buyers and demanders. Labour is an input, so the roles are reversed. Households are the sellers and suppliers, and businesses are the buyers and demanders. Governments set the rules of the game and, in this chapter, choose to interact in both output markets (rent ceilings) and input markets (minimum wages).

Benefits   What are the benefits of minimum wages? Like rent controls, a political benefit is that the government does not have to spend any money, yet voters perceive that the government is helping the working poor. More importantly, those workers who keep their jobs after the minimum wage is raised are better off. They get a raise.

Costs   What are the costs to weigh against the benefits to decide if minimum wage laws are a smart policy choice? Figure 4 on the next page shows an unskilled labour market without and with a minimum wage. The equilibrium, market-clearing wage in Figure 4a is $9 per hour, and the equilibrium quantity is 34 000 hours of labour.

Figure 4   Market for Unskilled Labour

Wage ($ per hour)	Quantity Demanded (thousands of hours per year)	Quantity Supplied (thousands of hours per year)	Shortage (–) or Surplus (+) (thousands of hours per year)
$11	30 000	38 000	+ 8000
$10	32 000	36 000	+ 4000
$ 9	34 000	34 000	0
$ 8	36 000	32 000	– 4000
$ 7	38 000	30 000	– 8000

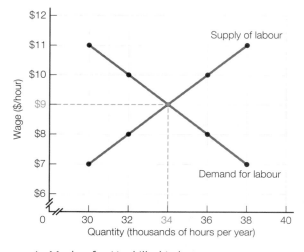

a)   Market for Unskilled Labour

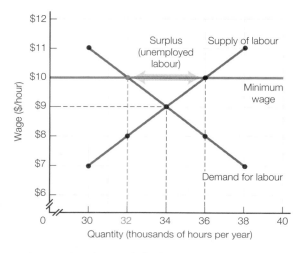

b)   Market for Unskilled Labour with a Minimum Wage

At a minimum wage of $10 per hour in Figure 4b, businesses demand, or hire, only 32 000 hours of unskilled labour. Workers supply 36 000 hours. The extra 4000 hours of labour is a *surplus* in the labour market. If prices could adjust, competition between workers looking for jobs would put downward pressure until the wage fell to the equilibrium wage and the quantity of labour hired increased to the equilibrium quantity of 34 000 hours. But the price is fixed at the minimum wage. When prices can't adjust, quantities will.

Unintended Consequences of Minimum Wages

At the fixed minimum wage, the quantity of labour demanded is less than at the equilibrium wage. When any input to production becomes more expensive, businesses reduce the input — hiring fewer workers and searching for cheaper substitutes. If wages for janitors rise, businesses may switch from paper towels in washrooms to air dryers so they need fewer janitors. Businesses buying labour (in input markets) act like any smart consumer buying products and services (in output markets) — when the price rises, the quantity demanded decreases and the search is on for cheaper substitutes.

Unemployment   When the government raises wages to the minimum legal wage, workers who are still hired at the new $10 minimum wage are better off, but there will be fewer jobs available. Quantities adjust.

At a minimum wage above the equilibrium wage, there is a surplus of workers willing to work. The quantity of labour supplied is greater than the quantity demanded by employers. Workers who can no longer find jobs spend more time and resources job searching, and are worse off. Statistics Canada defines workers actively seeking work but who cannot find jobs as "unemployed." Raising the minimum wage tends to increase unemployment. While governments can fix minimum wages, they cannot force employers to hire workers.

Inefficiency   Minimum wage laws create inefficiency in the labour market, much like rent controls create inefficiency in the housing market. Reading the demand and supply curves in Figure 4 as marginal benefit and marginal cost curves shows the inefficiency. On your own, identify the areas of consumer surplus, producer surplus, and deadweight loss in a labour market without (Figure 4a) and with (Figure 4b) a minimum wage. If you shade those areas, consumer surplus, producer surplus, and total surplus in Figure 4b are less than the efficient labour market outcome in Figure 4a.

Weighing the Benefits and Costs of Minimum Wages

So, are minimum wage laws a smart policy choice for governments trying to help the working poor? Many economists would say no, but not as strongly as to rent controls. Workers who get or keep jobs at the higher minimum wage are better off. On the other hand, like any fixed price, minimum wages sacrifice the flexibility and advantages of well-functioning markets in coordinating the smart choices of consumers and workers and businesses. Minimum wages cause some unemployment because, when prices are fixed, quantities adjust.

How many workers lose their jobs when minimum wages rise? Economists call this an empirical question — the answer comes from real-world data. Those data are inconclusive. In some cases where minimum wages were introduced or increased, there were significant job losses. In others, there was not much change in employment among unskilled workers.

Elasticity of Demand for Unskilled Labour   The number of jobs lost when the minimum wage increases depends on the *elasticity of demand* for labour. When demand for unskilled labour is inelastic and businesses have few substitutes, a rise in the wage produces only a small response in decreased quantity demanded. The case is stronger for a minimum wage. But if demand for labour is elastic and businesses can easily substitute machines for people, a rise in the minimum wage produces a large decrease in the quantity of labour demanded. The minimum wage policy is less beneficial. Elasticity is important not just for businesses deciding on sale prices, but also for social activists making the case for a minimum wage and for governments making smart policy choices.

Whatever the data show, a full answer to the question, "Do minimum wages help the working poor?" requires us to compare gains from workers who remain employed with higher incomes and the lost income of workers who lose their jobs.

Alternatives to Minimum Wage Laws

Most economists believe there are better policy choices to help the working poor — choices that do not sacrifice a market's flexibility to coordinate smart decisions of consumers, workers, and businesses. Governments can provide training to unskilled workers so they become eligible for higher-paying jobs, or give direct wage supplements to raise their standard of living without risking higher unemployment. Like all choices, these policy alternatives have opportunity costs — they are more expensive than minimum wages in helping the working poor, so governments must decide where the money will come from.

Practice...

11. Statistics Canada defines someone as *unemployed* if he is

    a. actively seeking work but unable to find a job.

    b. injured and unable to work.

    c. a full-time student.

    d. serving time in jail.

12. A new minimum wage law most *hurts* the working poor when

    a. demand for unskilled labour is inelastic.

    b. gains from workers who remain employed are greater than the lost income of workers who lose their jobs.

    c. businesses have many substitutes for unskilled labour.

    d. all of the above are true.

Use this graph to answer questions 13 and 14.

13. If a minimum wage is set at $9, what is the quantity of unemployment?

    a. 50

    b. 40

    c. 20

    d. 0

14. If a minimum wage is set at $18, what is the quantity of unemployment?

    a. 50

    b. 40

    c. 10

    d. 0

15. Raising the minimum wage results in large job losses if

    a. labour supply is elastic.

    b. labour demand is inelastic.

    c. it is difficult for businesses to find substitutes for workers.

    d. businesses can easily substitute robots for workers.

 **Apply...**

7. The daily demand for and supply of unskilled labour are given in the table below.

Daily Unskilled Labour Market		
Wage Rate per hour	Quantity Labour Demanded (hours)	Quantity Labour Supplied (hours)
$ 6	1000	400
$ 8	800	500
$ 10	600	600
$ 12	400	700
$ 14	200	800

a. Fill in the blanks. The equilibrium wage rate is $ _____ per hour, and the quantity of labour hired

is _____ hours.

b. Fill in the blank. Suppose the government imposes a minimum wage of $12 per hour.

Unemployment in the labour market is _____ hours.

c. Labourers who keep their jobs and now earn a higher wage are clearly better off as a result of the minimum wage. But labourers who lose their jobs (because businesses demand less labour at higher wages) are worse off. One way to measure the net impact of a minimum wage law is to compare the total income earned by labourers before the minimum wage, and the total income earned by labourers after the minimum wage.

    i.   Before the minimum wage, what is the total daily income earned by labourers ?

    _____

    _____

    _____

    ii. After the minimum wage, what is the total daily income earned by labourers ?

    _____

    _____

    _____

d. Circle the correct answer. Comparing your answers in part **c**, the new minimum wage has made labourers

    Better Off / Worse Off / No Different

e. Based on your answers in parts **c** and **d**, is there anything you can say about the price elasticity of demand for labour? Explain your answer.

    _____

    _____

    _____

to be continued

 **Apply...**

continued

8. Some argue that an increase in the minimum wage, because it affects all employers equally, will *not* increase unemployment. The Canadian Centre for Policy Alternatives argues that "in the real world it doesn't work out that way." The dry-cleaning industry, with many low-wage workers, is an example: "You raise the minimum wage and the cost of dry cleaning will go up slightly. But all of the dry cleaning companies across Ontario are going to have their cost structures changing in exactly the same way. And the last time I checked, people don't take their laundry to Buffalo to get it cleaned."

   a. What is the simplest way for businesses to adjust to the rising costs, assuming that the economy is doing well and individuals are not cutting back on their spending on laundry?

   _____

   _____

   _____

   _____

   _____

   b. Some businesses may not be able to afford to pay their workers the new minimum wage. List other solutions (besides simply laying off current workers) that the laundry business could consider in response to a rising minimum wage.

   _____

   _____

   _____

   _____

9. A new government policy is being considered to raise the minimum wage. If you were a lobbyist supporting this policy, what arguments would you make? What data would you include? If you were a lobbyist for business and against this policy, what arguments would you make? What data would you provide to support your position?

   _____

   _____

   _____

   _____

   _____

   _____

   _____

   _____

   _____

   _____

   _____

Trade-Offs between Efficiency and Equity

 Explain government policy trade-offs between efficient and equitable outcomes, and two different concepts of equity.

As an economist, I believe that when prices and quantities are allowed to adjust, well-functioning markets create incentives that balance the forces of competition (between consumers and between businesses) and the forces of cooperation (voluntary, mutually beneficial exchanges). When each consumer and business makes smart choices based only on self-interest, the coordinated result is the output of all the products and services we value most.

An appreciation for what markets can do does *not* translate into the conclusion that "Governments should always keep their hands off markets." Allowing markets to operate without government interaction is a choice, and every choice has an opportunity cost. I also believe, like some social activists, religious groups, and other economists, that the opportunity cost of allowing markets to work well is sometimes unfairness or inequality.

Let me explain. There are many hard-core (and long-suffering) Maple Leafs fans. Joe (not his real name) watches every hockey game on TV and attends games at the Air Canada Centre when someone gives him a ticket he usually can't afford. If the Leafs ever make it to the seventh game of the Stanley Cup finals, there is no one more desperate, more willing, or more deserving to see the game. But poor Joe (literally and figuratively) won't be there. Tickets will go to the highest bidders, including corporate executives who will write them off as business expenses.

Efficient Market Outcomes

To say markets produce the products and services we value the most means that outputs go to those most *willing and able to pay*. Joe is willing, but he is not able, so he gets no ticket. Something about this outcome does not seem fair. Economists use the word efficient to describe the outcome of a well-functioning market. But an *efficient* market outcome (Chapter 3, pp. 73–74) may not be fair or equitable.

The dictionary definition of efficient is "acting or producing effectively with a minimum of waste, expense, or unnecessary effort." When markets work well, businesses compete with each other, and successful, profitable businesses use inputs in the lowest cost combinations and produce products and services that consumers demand. Businesses voluntarily produce the quantities that consumers are willing and able to buy, and prices just cover all opportunity costs of production, including a normal profit.

Consumers compete with each other for the outputs of businesses, which go to those most willing and able to pay. Consumers voluntarily buy the quantities that businesses have produced. Because consumers buy only when marginal benefit is greater than the equilibrium price (marginal cost), they get the most "bang per buck," spending their income to get maximum possible satisfaction from every dollar. This coordination of smart choices by both businesses and consumers is an efficient market outcome. Total surplus, the sum of consumer surplus and producer surplus, is at a maximum.

Who Is Excluded from Efficient Market Outcomes?

Consumers who do not buy at equilibrium prices fall into two categories. The first doesn't find the product or service worth the price (marginal benefit is less than price) even though she can afford it. There are always substitutes.

The second simply can't afford it, even though he wants it and finds the marginal benefit greater than the price. Joe, dejectedly watching the Stanley Cup on TV at home, is part of the second category.

Joe's misfortune is not a life-shattering tragedy. But what if, instead of the market for hockey tickets, we are talking about markets for what many consider to be essential services like housing, education, or health care? Are the benefits of an efficient market worth the sacrifice that might have to be made in terms of unfairness or inequality?

Let's look at the trade-offs between efficiency and equity in the market for health care.

Health Care   Federal and provincial governments set the prices paid to the doctors, nurses, and hospitals who supply health-care services. The Canadian government guarantees free access to most health-care services to all permanent residents and citizens, paying for those services through tax revenues. Governments fix the price of each health-care service (how much a doctor gets paid for an office visit, how much a hospital gets paid for providing a bed with nursing services, and so on), but governments cannot force doctors or nurses to work or force hospitals to admit patients. Each health-care practitioner can choose the quantity of services to provide at the fixed price. Some choose not to supply services in Canada at all, going instead to work in the United States, where prices are higher. There are alternatives for suppliers as well as for consumers.

Many dedicated and talented health-care workers work hard to provide fine medical care. But have you ever waited to get an appointment with a medical specialist in Canada? Do you know someone who is on a waiting list for a CAT scan or a surgical procedure? Of course the answer to these questions is "yes." When prices can't adjust, quantities will, and waiting lists are the most visible form of a quantity adjustment.

At the fixed price to consumers of zero, and a government-set price to health-care suppliers, it is no surprise that the quantity demanded of medical services is far greater than the quantity supplied. As with any shortage, the market produces only the quantity that suppliers are willing to provide, and frustrated consumers demanding medical care end up on waiting lists. This is inefficiency in the health-care system in Canada.

Is Inefficient Health Care All Bad?   Does an inefficient market for health care mean that Canadian governments have made a not-smart policy choice? Not necessarily.

Consider the alternative of allowing a private market for health-care services, where consumers pay the bills; doctors, nurses, and hospitals set prices; and governments just set the rules of the game and enforce property rights. The United States health-care system has many of these qualities. With shortages, prices rise, quantities demanded decrease, quantities supplied increase, and waiting lists disappear. The fortunate people who receive health-care services are those most willing and able to pay. Anyone not able to afford the equilibrium price does not receive medical care. They are in the same category as Joe. But since these consumers include families desperate for life-saving surgeries who simply cannot afford to pay, their tragedies are real. There are about 30 million people in the United States who do not have health-care benefits from an insurance policy, which means they must pay all their medical bills themselves.

A switch in Canada to a private market in health-care services would add flexibility and incentives, and end waiting lists. Doctors, nurses, and health-care services would flow to where they are most valued, which means to those consumers most willing and able to pay. Some doctors would return to Canada from the United States. Market-driven health care would likely be more efficient, but the "haves" will get excellent care, and the "have-nots" may get no care at all. A private-market outcome may be efficient, but at the cost of being less equitable. The Canadian-style outcome is more equitable, but at the cost of being less efficient.

In making these comparisons between health care in Canada and the United States, I am leaving out many details of both systems. The Canadian system has some market-based incentives and flexibility, and the U.S. system has some role for government through the Medicare and Medicaid programs. Private insurance companies also set many prices and limit quantities of services. As you learned in Chapter 1, a useful model must leave out less important details to focus attention on the most important information. I believe my simplifications help to show the key issue — the trade-off between efficiency and equity.

Equal Outcomes or Equal Opportunities?

Consider these government policy choices. *Should* the government implement rent controls to help the homeless? *Should* the government pass minimum wage laws to help the working poor? *Should* the government push a health-care system that emphasizes equity over efficiency (Canadian style), or one that emphasizes efficiency over equity (U.S. style)? All these policy choices involve trade-offs between efficiency and equity. Your answer to these questions, or any politician's answer, depends on the *relative value* placed on efficiency versus equity. The word *should* is the sign of a **normative statement** — based on value judgments about what you believe should be. Normative statements, unlike **positive statements**, cannot be tested or evaluated as true or false by checking the facts.

In choosing between efficiency and equity, we must be careful about what those words mean. Economists agree on the definition of an efficient market outcome. But there is far less agreement — among economists or citizens — on what equity means. The two most common definitions of *equity* emphasize equal outcomes or equal opportunities.

Equal Outcomes   When everyone ends up with the same result, that is an equal outcome. The outcomes can be children getting identical slices of birthday cake, individuals earning the same income, citizens each getting one vote, or everyone getting access to the same level of health-care services. The end result is the same for all.

Equal Opportunities   An alternative definition of equity emphasizes starting conditions instead of end results. A game — including the "game of life" — is equitable if everyone has equal opportunities at the start. The same rules apply to everyone. No one has any unfair advantages. With equal opportunities, each individual can end up with a different-sized piece of cake, a different income, or different health-care services, based on her choices, effort, and luck. There will be winners and losers, but there is equity in the form of equal opportunities.

The Politics of Equity   How do definitions of efficiency and equity matter for policy choices? Politicians will compete for your vote by proposing policies that they hope you agree with. The choices below about minimum wage laws also apply to rent controls and health-care policies.

A conservative politician on the right of the political spectrum might oppose minimum wage laws because she believes the efficiency of markets is most important for generating the economic prosperity that will ultimately help people who are poor. She also might believe that markets are already equitable because they provide everyone with *equal opportunities*. She fully expects that each person's income and accomplishments in life will differ with differences in talents, initiative, and luck.

A left-leaning politician might favour minimum wage laws because he believes equity is more important than efficiency. He would accept some inefficiency and less economic prosperity for all if it improves the *equality of incomes*. He does not believe that poor children have the same opportunities as rich children.

You cannot decide that one politician is wrong and the other right just on the basis of facts. You can decide which politician's values best match your own values.

 **Practice...**

16. In markets without any government interaction, who gets an apartment is decided by who is most

    a. willing to pay.

    b. able to pay.

    c. willing and able to pay.

    d. willing and able to dance.

17. An efficient market outcome does all of the following *except*

    a. coordinate smart choices of businesses and consumers.

    b. exclude those unwilling to pay but able to pay.

    c. deliver output to those most willing and able to pay.

    d. deliver output to those willing to pay but unable to pay.

18. Market-driven health care generally

    a. has few waiting lists.

    b. is more efficient than equitable health care.

    c. provides little care to those who cannot afford it.

    d. does all of the above.

19. Which statement is *normative*?

    a. Health care in America is less expensive than in Canada.

    b. Health care should be free to the poor.

    c. People who see their doctor at least once a year live longer.

    d. Health care costs more than dental care.

20. A right-leaning politician probably

    a. is more concerned with efficiency than with equity.

    b. is right-handed.

    c. thinks equality of outcomes is more important than equality of opportunities.

    d. does not think like an economist.

 **Apply...**

10. If you had to choose between a health-care system run by the market or run by government, which would you prefer? Explain the reasoning behind your choice. What changes in your life might make you change your choice?

   _____

   _____

   _____

   _____

   _____

   _____

   _____

   _____

   _____

   _____

   _____

11. Arguments often end with someone saying, "Everyone is entitled to an opinion." Does that mean that all opinions are equally valid? (The positive/normative distinction can help answer this question.)

   _____

   _____

   _____

   _____

   _____

   _____

   _____

   _____

12. Pick a political party in Canada. Based on the policy statements on the party's website, how would you describe its positions on issues of efficiency versus equity?

   _____

   _____

   _____

   _____

   _____

   _____

   _____

   _____

KNOW...

Learning Objectives

1. When governments fix prices, the smart choices of consumers and businesses are not coordinated. Quantities adjust to whichever is less — quantity supplied or quantity demanded.

2. **Rent controls** — a **price ceiling** — fix rents below equilibrium, market-clearing levels, and quantity adjustments have the unintended consequences of apartment shortages, landlord power, and subsidies to tenants able to pay. Alternatives to rent controls that keep the flexibility of well-functioning markets include government subsidies to the poor and government-supplied housing.

3. **Minimum wage laws — a price floor** — fix wages above equilibrium, market-clearing levels, and quantity adjustments have the unintended consequence of more unemployment and inefficiency. When the demand for unskilled labour is inelastic and businesses have few substitutes, a rise in the minimum wage benefits the working poor. When the demand for unskilled labour is elastic and businesses can easily substitute machines for people, a rise in the minimum wage hurts the working poor. Alternatives to minimum wages that keep the flexibility of well-functioning markets include training programs to help unskilled workers get higher-paying jobs and wage supplements.

4. Well-functioning markets are efficient, but not always equitable. Governments may smartly choose polices that create more equitable outcomes, even though the trade-off is less efficiency. Two different **normative** concepts of equity are equal outcomes — often emphasized by the political left — and equal opportunities — often emphasized by the political right.

Key Terms

minimum wage laws (example of **price floor**): minimum price set by government making it illegal to pay a lower price

normative statements: based on value judgments about what you believe should be; cannot be tested or evaluated as true or false by checking the facts

positive statements: about what is; can be evaluated as true or false by checking the facts

price ceiling (or **rent controls**): maximum price set by government, making it illegal to charge a higher price

price floor (or **minimum wage laws**): minimum price set by government, making it illegal to pay a lower price

rent controls (example of **price ceiling**): maximum price set by government, making it illegal to charge a higher price

Answers to Practice

1. **b** Price below the equilibrium price creates shortage with quantity demanded greater than quantity supplied.

2. **a** There is a surplus, with quantity supplied greater than quantity demanded. Sellers cannot sell all of the quantity they are willing to supply.

3. **d** There are shortages, frustrated buyers, and quantity sold adjusts to quantity supplied.

4. **c** There is a surplus at a price above equilibrium. Competition between sellers will cause prices to fall back to equilibrium. A price ceiling prevents rising prices, but prices can still fall.

5. **c** For a shortage, quantity supplied is less than quantity demanded. For a surplus, quantity demanded is less than quantity supplied.

6. **a** Rent controls are only effective if the ceiling is set below the equilibrium, market-clearing price.

7. **d** Create incentives to reduce quantity and quality of rental units.

8. **b** Elastic supply means even a small increase in price causes a large response in increased quantity supplied. Elasticity of demand is not relevant for the quantities supplied.

9. **d** All unintended consequences of the law.

10. **c** Subsidies are more expensive for governments than rent controls, but preserve the flexibility of prices and market coordination.

11. **a** Definition of unemployment. Others are classified as "not in the labour force."

12. **c** Hurts most when there are many substitutes, elastic demand for labour, and losses outweigh gains.

13. **d** Minimum wage is a price floor, but wages can legally rise to equilibrium wage of $12.

14. **b** Difference between quantity of labour supplied (50) and quantity of labour demanded (10).

15. **d** Large job losses also if labour demand elastic. Labour supply elasticity not relevant for business hiring decisions.

16. **c** Willingness or intensity of need alone is not enough.

17. **d** Those unable to pay are excluded. People who choose not to pay (but are able to pay) also do not participate as buyers in a market.

18. **d** Efficient but inequitable in excluding those unable to pay.

19. **b** Notice the word *should*. Other statements are positive — can be evaluated as true or false by checking the facts.

20. **a** Values efficiency more than equity, and thinks equality of opportunities is more important than equality of outcomes.

6 Consumer Model Basics: Utility behind Demand

LEARNING OBJECTIVES

L01 Explain the connection between total utility and marginal utility, and show how diminishing marginal utility explains the law of demand and the downward-sloping demand curve.

L02 Explain how consumers maximize total utility by equalizing the marginal utility per dollar spent on all products and services.

L03 Use the distinction between total utility and marginal utility to explain the diamond-water paradox and the measurement of consumer surplus.

LEARN ...

Thinking like an economist means using models — simplified representations of the real world that hold other things unchanged to focus attention on what's important. Economic models are the mental equivalent of laboratory controlled experiments.

Talking like an economist means using the terms *utility* and *utility maximizing*. Jeremy Bentham (1748 – 1832) first described the concept of utility in his 1789 book, *Introduction to the Principles of Morals and Legislation*. According to Bentham, "By utility is meant that property in any object . . . to produce benefit, advantage, pleasure, good, or happiness" to an individual. Economists adopted the term from Bentham. Utility is the same as what we have called the *benefit* or *satisfaction* individuals get from consuming a product or service — from drinking water or a Gatorade, using headphones, getting a piercing. . . .

Bentham also originated the ethical theory of Utilitarianism, which states that the best choices *maximize utility*. Utility maximizing applies to individual choices, as well as to society's choices. For any individual choice, how do we get the most benefit or satisfaction while minimizing the pain or cost? Key 1 of the Three Keys model — Choose only when additional benefits are greater than additional opportunity costs — has its origins in Utilitarianism.

Bentham's goal for society was "the greatest happiness for the greatest number." Maximizing utility for society means adding up all benefits or satisfactions and subtracting all pains or costs. The concepts of consumer surplus and total surplus are social measures of utility maximization. My favourite phrase for utility maximizing is *getting the most bang for your buck*. The *bang* is the benefit/satisfaction/utility and the *buck* (a slang term for a dollar) is the pain/cost you must pay.

This chapter takes much of what you already know about smart choices, about demand, and about social measures of efficiency like consumer surplus, and translates it into the language of utility. Utility is another way of understanding the law of demand, and how consumers facing the problem of scarcity make smart choices among different products and services.

Demand, Total Utility, and Marginal Utility

 Explain the connection between total utility and marginal utility, and show how diminishing marginal utility explains the law of demand and the downward-sloping demand curve.

Let's review what you already know about demand and then translate it into the language of utility.

Demand describes consumers' willingness and ability to pay for a particular product or service. Demand depends on

- how badly you want a product.

- how much you are willing and able to give up for it.

Your **preferences** describe your wants and their intensities. The more intense your preference is for a product, the more you are willing to pay, because you expect a high benefit from satisfying that want. Utility measures the intensity of your wants. **Utility** is a measure of the benefit or satisfaction from consuming a product or service. There are two measures of utility — total utility and marginal utility.

Total Utility and Marginal Utility

Total utility is the sum of the marginal utilities of all units, measuring the total benefit or satisfaction from all units consumed of a product or service. **Marginal utility** measures the *additional* benefit or satisfaction from consuming an *additional* unit and changes with circumstances. Economists measure benefit with an imaginary unit called a *util*. Figure 1 gives a numerical example of the utility you might get from drinking Gatorade.

Figure 1   Total Utility and Marginal Utility from Bottles of Gatorade

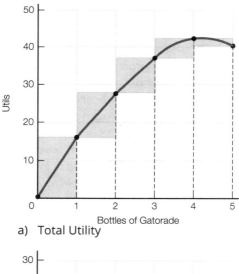

a) Total Utility

b) Marginal Utility

Bottles of Gatorade Consumed	Total Utility (utils)	Marginal Utility (utils)
0	0	
		16
1	16	
		12
2	28	
		8
3	36	
		6
4	42	
		−2
5	40	

Diminishing Marginal Utility   Look first at the table of numbers. The first bottle of Gatorade you drink gives 16 utils of benefit. As the only bottle so far, your total utility is 16 utils. A second bottle adds 12 utils of benefit, increasing your total utility to 28 utils. A third bottle adds even fewer utils of benefit — 8 utils — bringing your total utility from all three bottles to 36 utils. A fourth bottle adds only 6 utils of benefit, while a fifth bottle starts to make you feel sick — it actually decreases total utility by 2 utils.

You saw this pattern of decreasing numbers for marginal utility in Chapter 2, where we called it *decreasing marginal benefit*. In the language of utility, it is called **diminishing marginal utility**. As you consume more of a product or service, marginal utility eventually decreases. Marginal utility is the *change in total utility* as you consume more Gatorade. Because marginal utility is the change in total utility in moving between 0 and 1 bottle, between 1 and 2 bottles, etc., it is listed halfway between the total utility numbers.

Graphing Utility   The graphs in Figure 1 plot the numbers in the table. Figure 1a shows the total utility from 1, 2, 3, 4, and 5 bottles of Gatorade. Because total utility is the benefit from all bottles consumed, the numbers for total utility appear directly above the number of bottles. For example, 1 bottle gives 16 utils of benefit, so 16 utils is plotted directly above 1 bottle. Total utility generally increases as the quantity consumed increases. (The only exception is the extreme case where marginal utility is negative and totally utility decreases, as in the increase from 4 to 5 bottles.)

Figure 1b shows the marginal utility of the 1st, 2nd, 3rd, 4th, and 5th bottles of Gatorade. Because marginal utility measures the *change* in total utility as you drink more bottles, marginal utility appears *halfway* between bottles. For example, the marginal utility added in going from 1 bottle to 2 bottles — 12 utils — is plotted halfway between 1 and 2 bottles.

The shaded rectangles on the total utility graph in Figure 1a represent the marginal utilities of each additional bottle. For example, the height of the second rectangle between 1 and 2 bottles measures the marginal utility — 12 utils — of drinking the 2nd bottle. Those marginal utility rectangles and numbers transfer to Figure 1b.

Marginal Utility Changes with Circumstances   The additional benefit you get from a bottle of Gatorade changes with circumstances. After an intense workout at the gym, a first bottle has high marginal utility, and you are willing to pay a lot. After drinking that bottle, a second bottle has less marginal utility, and you are not willing to pay as much. And if you haven't been to the gym at all, or aren't thirsty, or hate the taste, a first bottle of Gatorade may have no marginal utility. Your willingness to pay for a product or service does not depend on total utility. It depends on marginal utility, which changes with circumstances.

Demand Curve Is a Marginal Utility Curve

Diminishing marginal utility gives another explanation for the **law of demand**. If the price of a product or service rises, the quantity demanded decreases, other things remaining the same. The demand curve shows the relationship between price and quantity demanded when all other influences on demand besides price do not change.

Figure 4b on page 34 in Chapter 2 shows how to read the demand curve as a marginal benefit curve. Translated into the language of utility, Figure 2 shows the demand curve for water as a marginal utility curve.

Figure 2   Reading the Demand Curve as a Marginal Utility Curve

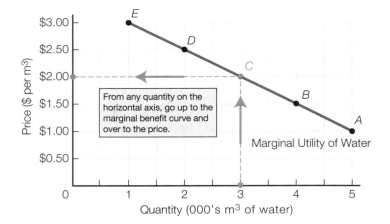

To read the demand curve as a marginal utility curve, start at any quantity and go up and over to the price. The marginal utility curve shows, for any quantity, the maximum price people are willing and able to pay for that last unit available. To find the maximum price, people are willing and able to pay for the 3000th cubic metre of water, trace a line up to the marginal utility curve and over to the $2 price. Increasing quantities have decreasing marginal utility. Willingness to pay depends on marginal utility. Ability to pay depends on income, which will we add to the explanation in the next section.

Practice...

1. Total utility is always

   a. increasing when marginal utility is positive.

   b. decreasing when marginal utility is positive.

   c. greater than marginal utility.

   d. less than marginal utility.

2. Because of diminishing marginal utility, as you consume more of a product, total utility

   a. decreases at an increasing rate.

   b. decreases at a decreasing rate.

   c. increases at an increasing rate.

   d. increases at a decreasing rate.

3. Total utility equals the

   a. area below the demand curve but above the market price.

   b. sum of the marginal utilities of each unit consumed.

   c. marginal utility of the last unit divided by price.

   d. marginal utility of the last unit multiplied by price.

4. You read a

   a. demand curve as the minimum price people are willing and able to pay.

   b. demand curve as a total utility curve.

   c. marginal utility curve from quantity up and over to price.

   d. marginal utility curve over from price and down to quantity.

5. Look at the market for water in the graph below.

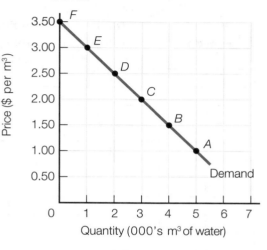

   At point *A*, the

   a. minimum price people are willing and able to pay for all 5000 cubic metres of water is $1.

   b. maximum price people are willing and able to pay for all 5000 cubic metres of water is $1.

   c. minimum price people are willing and able to pay for the 5000th cubic metre of water is $1.

   d. maximum price people are willing and able to pay for the 5000th cubic metre of water is $1.

Apply...

1. The table below give Ally's utility from consuming popcorn and candy bars.

Ally's Utility from Popcorn			Ally's Utility from Candy Bars		
Bags of Popcorn	Total Utility (utils)	Marginal Utility (utils)	Number of Candy Bars	Total Utility (utils)	Marginal Utility (utils)
0	0		0	0	
1			1	14	
		16			
2	36		2	26	
					10
3	50		3		
4			4	44	
		10			7
5	72		5		
6	80		6	57	

   a. Fill in the grey boxes in the table of Ally's utility from popcorn.

   b. Fill in the grey boxes in the table of Ally's utility from candy bars.

You will use this information later in Apply question 5.

2. What is the economist's definition for preferences? for demand? What is the difference between preferences and demand?

_____

_____

_____

_____

_____

3. You go to an all-you-can-eat restaurant, and pay the $30 fixed price to get in. Once you sit down, you must order one dish at a time. What determines how many dishes you continue to order? What does *not* influence your choice of ordering additional dishes? Explain if the concept of demand or of diminishing marginal utility is more important for explaining when you stop eating.

_____

_____

_____

_____

_____

_____

Rule for Maximum Total Utility

 L02 Explain how consumers maximize total utility by equalizing the marginal utility per dollar spent on all products and services.

The model of consumer choice, like all models, starts with some simplifications, and holds other things unchanged.

All consumers face the problem of scarcity. We all have unlimited wants, but limited time, energy, and money. To get the most out of our limited resources, we have to make smart choices. In the model of consumer choice,

- getting "the most" means trying to *maximize total utility*.

- "limited resources" simply means a fixed, unchanged amount of money to spend.

- prices are set in the market — individual consumers cannot change the prices of the products and services they buy.

- choice is limited to two products.

With a limited amount of money, facing market-set prices, how do consumers make smart choices that maximize total utility?

Choose until Marginal Utility per Dollar Spent Is Equal

Let's take a simplified example. Alexa has $10 to spend, and only two products to spend it on. Gatorade costs $1 per bottle, and Green Detox costs $2 per bottle. In Figure 3, columns 2 and 5 show Alexa's marginal utility for each bottle consumed. Those numbers reflect Alexa's personal preferences. Columns 3 and 6 take those marginal utility numbers and divide by the price of the product. Since Gatorade costs $1 per bottle, the marginal utility of each bottle, and the marginal utility divided by $1, are equal. For Green Detox, which costs $2 per bottle, the marginal utility per dollar is half the marginal utility alone.

Figure 3   Alexa's Preferences and Marginal Utility per Dollar Spent

Gatorade: Price = $1 per bottle			Green Detox: Price = $2 per bottle		
Bottle of Gatorade	Marginal Utility (utils)	Marginal Utility per $ (utils)	Bottle of Green Detox	Marginal Utility (utils)	Marginal Utility per $ (utils)
1st	16	16	1st	30	15
2nd	12	12	2nd	20	10
3rd	8	8	3rd	12	6
4th	6	6	4th	4	2
5th	–2	–2	5th	2	1

Unlike Figure 1 on page 138, Figure 3 is missing numbers for total utility. I hope you are also wondering, since the consumer's goal is to maximize *total* utility, why does this table have only *marginal* utility numbers? It is because marginal utility is the key for making a smart choice about total utility.

Here is the rule for maximum total utility.

Continue buying the product with the largest marginal utility per dollar
until all money is spent and
marginal utility per dollar is equal for all products.

The larger the value of marginal utility per dollar spent, the greater is the bang per buck. To understand why this rule maximizes total utility, let's apply it to the numbers in Figure 3 on the previous page and go through Alexa's choices of Gatorade or Green Detox, bottle by bottle.

Alexa's Bottle-by-Bottle Choices   What will Alexa buy first with her $10, a bottle of Gatorade or of Green Detox? Marginal utility per dollar spent is larger for Gatorade (16) than for Green Detox (15), so the rule says buy Gatorade. With the $9 she has left, what does Alexa buy next? A second bottle of Gatorade has a marginal utility per dollar of 12, but if she buys her first bottle of Green Detox, its marginal utility per dollar is 15. Alexa buys the Green Detox. With the $7 she has left, Alexa can next buy either her second bottle of Gatorade (12) or her second bottle of Green Detox (10). She buys the Gatorade. From her remaining $6 she next buys her second bottle of Green Detox, because its marginal utility per dollar (10) is larger than for her third bottle of Gatorade (8). Alexa's next choice is between a third bottle of Gatorade (8) and a third bottle of Green Detox (6). She buys her third bottle of Gatorade and is down to $3. A fourth bottle of Gatorade or a third bottle of Green Detox give the same marginal utility per dollar (6), so it doesn't matter which she buys. If she buys the Green Detox first, she has $1 left to buy her fourth bottle of Gatorade (6). If instead she buys the Gatorade first, she has $2 left to buy the third bottle of Green Detox (6).

After all of these choices, Alexa spends her $10 to buy 4 bottles of Gatorade and 3 bottles of Green Detox. At the end, the marginal utility per dollar spent is equal (6) for the two products. According to the rule, that should give maximum total utility. How do we know if it did?

Maximum Total Utility?   We can find Alexa's total utility by adding up the marginal utility for all of her bottles. That sum is 42 for the four Gatorade bottles (16 + 12 + 8 + 6 = 42) and 62 (30 + 20 + 12 = 62) for the three Green Detox bottles. To find total utility, we add the marginal utility for each bottle, *not* marginal utility per dollar spent. Her total utility is 104 utils (42 + 62 = 104).

To prove that this is her maximum total utility, you must calculate her total utility for other combinations of Gatorade and Green Detox bottles that she could buy with $10. To save you the trouble, here are other combinations that spend the same $10. Total utility for 2 Gatorade and 4 Green Detox is 94 utils. Total utility for 0 Gatorade and 5 Green Detox is 68 utils. Alexa's smart choice combining 4 Gatorade and 3 Green Detox has maximum total utility, and the marginal utility per dollar spent is the same for both products.

The Logic behind the Rule for Maximum Utility

The rule for maximum total utility is

Continue buying the product with the largest marginal utility per dollar
until all money is spent and
marginal utility per dollar is equal for all products.

If Alexa, or any consumer, has made a smart choice, the marginal utility per dollar spent is equal for all products. If we express the rule as an equation, for all products *A*, *B*, *C*, . . . *Z*, there is maximum total utility when

$$\frac{MU_A}{P_A} = \frac{MU_B}{P_B} = \ldots = \frac{MU_Z}{P_Z}$$

where MU_A is the marginal utility of product *A*, and P_A is the price of product *A*.

Consumer Equilibrium This outcome of smart choices, where the marginal utility per dollar spent is equal for all products, is called **consumer equilibrium**. The consumer is getting the most out of limited resources, and is maximizing total utility. Equilibrium means there is no tendency for change.

To understand the logic of why this equation must be true if the consumer has reached maximum total utility, let's look at what happens if it is *not* true.

Let's return to the simple model with just two products, *A* and *B*. You have made choices so that

$$\frac{MU_A}{P_A} > \frac{MU_B}{P_B}$$

The marginal utility per dollar spent on product *A* is greater than the marginal utility per dollar spent on product *B*. You are getting more bang per buck from *A* than from *B*. That means if you change your choices to buy a little more of *A*, and a little less of *B*, you will be better off. This is not an equilibrium because you have an incentive to change. Your total utility increases because the additional utility you get from more *A* is greater than the utility lost by giving up some *B*. This is Key 1 — Choose only when additional benefits are greater than additional opportunity costs. The gain in bang-per-buck from *A* is greater than the opportunity cost — the loss in bang-per-buck from *B*.

What happens as you buy more product *A* and less product *B*? The concept of diminishing marginal utility tells us that consuming more of *A* decreases the marginal utility from additional units of *A*. Consuming less of *B* increases the marginal utility of *B* because you are going back to earlier units with higher marginal utility.

What happens to the fractions MU_A/P_A and MU_B/P_B? Prices do not change — prices are set by the market. But the fraction MU_A/P_A gets smaller, and the fraction MU_B/P_B gets larger. As long as there is a difference in the value of the two fractions, the incentive for change continues, and you can increase total utility by buying more *A* and less *B*. The incentive for change ends only when the fractions are equal.

$$\frac{MU_A}{P_A} = \frac{MU_B}{P_B}$$

There is no way to get more bang per buck, and total utility is at a maximum.

The switch to more of product *A* and less of product *B* causes the fraction on the left to get smaller, and the fraction on the right to get larger. Only when you, or Alexa, reach the total utility-maximizing combination are the fractions equal, and the incentive to switch stops.

(Apply question 4 will ask you to explain the reverse story of what happens when $MU_A/P_A < MU_B/P_B$.)

The rule for maximum total utility is a combination of Keys 1 and 2:

- Choose only when additional benefit is greater than additional *opportunity cost*.

- Count only *additional* benefits and *additional* opportunity costs.

The rule gives the consumer the most bang per buck, focusing on *marginal utility per dollar spent*.

Deriving the Demand Curve from the Model of Consumer Choice

The model of consumer choice gives another explanation for the downward-sloping demand curve, based on consumers' utility-maximizing decisions.

Other Things Remaining the Same   A demand curve, for an individual or a market, shows for any price what the quantity demanded will be. The law of demand states that if the price of a product or service rises, quantity demanded decreases, other things remaining the same. *Other things remaining the same* is an important phrase. By holding constant all other influences on demand — consumers' willingness and ability to pay for a particular product or service — the demand curve isolates the effect on quantity demanded of only one variable — the price of the product. Only a change in price affects quantity demanded. A change in any other influence on demand shifts the demand curve.

When Alexa maximizes her total utility in choosing between Gatorade and Green Detox bottles, we already have one point on her demand curve for Gatorade. We are about to find a second point, and connecting those two points allows us to draw her demand curve. Let me explain.

When the price of Gatorade is $1 per bottle, Alexa chooses to buy 4 bottles of Gatorade. That combination of price ($1) and quantity demanded (4 bottles) is the result after holding constant all other influences that might affect Alexa's willingness and ability to pay. Alexa's *willingness* to pay is set by her preferences, and those preferences are reflected in her numbers for the utility she gets from different bottles of Gatorade (and Green Detox). Alexa's *ability* to pay is set by the $10 budget she has, which does not change.

Changing Only the Price of Gatorade   Figure 4 reproduces all of that information, with only one change. The price of Gatorade rises to $2 per bottle. What happens to Alexa's utility-maximizing choice?

Figure 4   Alexa's Utility Maximizing Choice after the Price of Gatorade Rises

Gatorade: Price = $2 per bottle			Green Detox: Price = $2 per bottle		
Bottle of Gatorade	Marginal Utility (utils)	Marginal Utility per $ (utils)	Bottle of Green Detox	Marginal Utility (utils)	Marginal Utility per $ (utils)
1st	16	8	1st	30	15
2nd	12	6	2nd	20	10
3rd	8	4	3rd	12	6
4th	6	3	4th	4	2
5th	−2	−1	5th	2	1

The only difference between Figure 4 and Figure 3 is in the third column for *Marginal Utility per $* for Gatorade. Now that Gatorade costs $2 per bottle instead of $1, the unchanged marginal utility numbers for Gatorade are divided by $2. Alexa again applies the rule for maximum total utility.

Continue buying the product with the largest marginal utility per dollar until all money is spent and marginal utility per dollar is equal for all products.

Alexa's Bottle-by-Bottle Choices Alexa first buys a bottle of Green Detox, because its marginal utility per dollar (15) is larger than for the 1st bottle of Gatorade (8). She buys a 2nd bottle of Green Detox with a marginal utility per dollar of (10). With the $6 she has left, what does Alexa buy next? A third bottle of Green Detox has a marginal utility per dollar of 6, but if she buys her first bottle of Gatorade, its marginal utility per dollar is 8. Alexa buys the Gatorade, and is down to $4. A second bottle of Gatorade or a third bottle of Green Detox give the same marginal utility per dollar (6), so it doesn't matter which she buys. If she buys the Gatorade first, she has $2 left to buy her third bottle of Green Detox (6). If instead she buys the Green Detox first, she has $2 left to buy the second bottle of Gatorade (6).

With unchanged preferences and an unchanged budget, Alexa's smart choice that maximizes total utility is now 2 bottles of Gatorade and 3 of Green Detox. Total utility is 90, the sum of 28 utils from two Gatorade bottles (16 + 12 = 28) and 62 utils (30 + 20 + 12 = 62) from three Green Detox bottles. You can calculate total utility for other combinations of Gatorade and Green Detox bottles that cost $10 to show that Alexa's combination of 2 Gatorade and 3 Green Detox bottles has maximum total utility.

After the rise in the price of Gatorade, Alexa's $10 budget doesn't buy as much as it did before, so she has fewer bottles in total and a lower total utility (90 utils instead of 104 utils). We also have a second point on Alexa's demand curve for Gatorade. With a price of $2 per bottle, Alexa's quantity demanded is 2 bottles of Gatorade.

Figure 5 plots the two combinations of price and quantity demanded that result from Alexa's utility-maximizing smart choices. At a price of $1, Alexa buys 4 bottles of Gatorade. When the price rises to $2, Alexa buys 2 bottles.

Figure 5   Alexa's Demand Curve for Gatorade

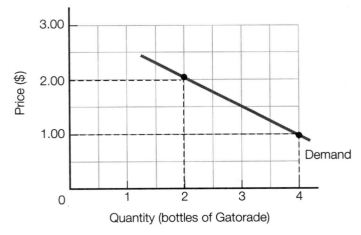

Practice...

6. Broomhilda is initially maximizing her total utility in consuming products *X* and *Y*. The price of *X* doubles, all other things unchanged. For Broomhilda to again maximize total utility, her quantity of *X* consumed must

   a. increase until the marginal utility of *X* doubles.

   b. decrease until the marginal utility of *X* doubles.

   c. decrease to half the initial quantity.

   d. decrease until the marginal utility of *X* decreases to half the initial level.

7. In consumer equilibrium,

   a. the marginal utility of each product is equal.

   b. the total utility from each product is equal.

   c. total utility is maximized.

   d. marginal utility is maximized.

8. Taylor is maximizing his utility in his consumption of Porsches and diamonds. If the marginal utility of his last purchased Porsche is twice the marginal utility of his last purchased diamond, then we know with certainty that

   a. the price of a Porsche is twice the price of a diamond.

   b. the price of a diamond is twice the price of a Porsche.

   c. Taylor buys twice as many Porsches as diamonds.

   d. Taylor buys twice as many diamonds as Porsches.

9. If Soula is maximizing her utility and two products have the same marginal utility, she

   a. buys only one.

   b. buys equal quantities of both.

   c. gets the same total utility from each.

   d. is willing to pay the same price for each.

10. The price of beer is twice the price of back bacon. At Bob's current quantities consumed, his marginal utility of back bacon is twice his marginal utility of beer. To maximize total utility, Bob must

   a. buy more beer and less back bacon.

   b. buy less beer and more back bacon.

   c. buy twice as much beer and one-half as much back bacon.

   d. not change his current quantities of beer and back bacon.

 **Apply...**

4. A consumer has made choices between products *A* and *B* so that $MU_A/P_A < MU_B/P_B$. The marginal utility per dollar spent on product *A* is less than the marginal utility per dollar spent on product *B*. Tell the story of the choices the consumer has an incentive to make to return to consumer equilibrium.

_____

_____

_____

_____

_____

_____

_____

5. This question is a continuation of Apply question 1 about Ally's choices between popcorn and candy bars.

   a. Suppose the price of a bag of popcorn is $1 and the price of a candy bar is $0.50. Based on the tables you filled in in Apply question 3, fill in the grey boxes in the table below for marginal utility per dollar spent for each product.

	Popcorn Price = $1		Candy Bar Price = $0.50
Bags of Popcorn	**Marginal Utility per $** (utils)	**Number of Candy Bars**	**Marginal Utility per $** (utils)
1st		1st	
2nd		2nd	
3rd		3rd	
4th		4th	
5th		5th	
6th		6th	

   b. Ally has $4 and spends it only on popcorn and candy bars. If she maximizes her utility, what quantities of popcorn and candy bars does she buy? Show that her choices meet the condition for consumer equilibrium.

_____

_____

_____

_____

_____

to be continued

continued

    c. What is Ally's total utility from the combination of popcorn and candy bars in part **b**? If, instead, Ally buys 3 bags of popcorn and 2 candy bars, explain why she would not be maximizing her total utility using numbers both for total utility and for marginal utility per dollar.

_____

_____

_____

_____

_____

_____

_____

_____

6. One more question about Ally's choices of popcorn and candy bars. Suppose Ally's preferences and her $4 budget remain unchanged, but the price of a candy bar doubles to $1.

    a. Fill in the grey boxes in the table below for marginal utility per dollar spent for each product.

	Popcorn Price = $1		Candy Bar Price = $1
Bags of Popcorn	**Marginal Utility per $** (utils)	**Number of Candy Bars**	**Marginal Utility per $** (utils)
1st		1st	
2nd		2nd	
3rd		3rd	
4th		4th	
5th		5th	
6th		6th	

    b. What utility-maximizing quantities of popcorn and candy bars does Ally now buy?

_____

_____

_____

_____

Apply...

c. Based on all of the information you have about Ally, draw her demand curve for candy bars.

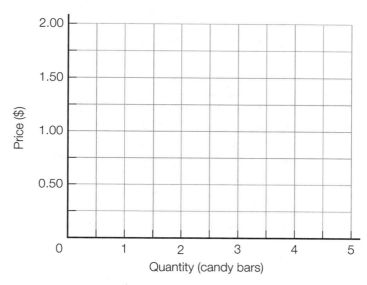

Total Utility, Marginal Utility, and Consumer Surplus

L03 Use the distinction between total utility and marginal utility to explain the diamond-water paradox and the measurement of consumer surplus.

In the model of consumer choice, consumers try to maximize total utility, but the key is to focus on marginal utility per dollar spent. The distinction between total utility and marginal utility provides richer explanations for other demand-related topics we have discussed previously — the diamond-water paradox and consumer surplus.

The Diamond-Water Paradox

We can easily translate the discussion of the diamond-water paradox in Chapter 2 into the language of utility. What's more valuable in providing utility — diamonds or water? Water is essential for survival, while diamonds are unnecessary. Why do diamonds cost far more than water? You solve the paradox by distinguishing marginal utility from total utility.

You would die without water, so you are willing to pay everything you can for the first drink, which has high marginal utility. But when water is abundant, what are you willing to pay, at the margin, for your next drink today? Not much. Marginal utility is low, though the total utility of all water consumed (including the first, life-saving drink) is high.

Diamonds won't keep you alive, but they are scarce, and desirable for that reason. What would you pay for your first diamond? A lot. Marginal utility is high. Because diamonds are scarce, there aren't many out there, so total utility from all diamonds consumed is low.

The rule for maximum total utility also applies to the choice between water and diamonds. In consumer equilibrium, the marginal utility per dollar spent must be equal for water and diamonds.

$$\frac{MU_{water} \text{ (low)}}{P_{water} \text{ (low)}} = \frac{MU_{diamonds} \text{ (high)}}{P_{diamonds} \text{ (high)}}$$

Although water has high total utility, because it is abundant its marginal utility and price are both low. Diamonds are scarce, so their marginal utility and price are both high. But the ratio of marginal utility to price can be equal for water and diamonds. For example, if water has a marginal utility of 2 utils and a price of $1 per bottle, the value of the ratio equals 2 (2 divided by $1). If diamonds have a marginal utility of 200 utils and a price of $100 per diamond, the value of the ratio also equals 2 (200 divided by $100). The rule of equal marginal utility per dollar spent still applies to products as different as water and diamonds.

Prices are proportional to *marginal utility*, not total utility.

Consumer Surplus

The distinction between total utility and marginal utility also appears in graphs of consumer surplus and total surplus. Because this chapter is about consumer choice, we will focus on consumer surplus.

Demand is about willingness and ability to pay, and the demand curve illustrates consumer surplus. **Consumer surplus** is the difference between the amount a consumer is *willing and able to pay*, and the price actually paid.

Figure 6a is a modification of the demand curve for piercing in Figure 8 on page 72. In the language of utility, it is the market marginal utility curve for piercings, adding together the individual demand (marginal utility) curves for all consumers. The marginal utility curve shows, for any quantity, the maximum price someone is willing and able to pay for that last unit. For example, for the 150th piercing, someone is willing and able to pay $90. For the 300th piercing, someone is willing and able to pay $80. Willingness to pay depends on marginal utility. Because of diminishing marginal utility, increasing quantities have decreasing marginal utility.

Adding up the vertical marginal utilities for each piercing between 1 and 600 gives the total utility from all 600 piercings. We did a similar addition for Alexa's choices of Gatorade and Green Detox in Figures 3 and 4. We added her marginal utilities for each bottle to get her total utility from all bottles. Even though total utility did not appear directly in Figures 3 and 4, we calculated it by adding up marginal utilities. Figure 6a shows directly the green area of total utility as the sum of all 600 piercings' vertical marginal utilities.

Figure 6b shows the consumer surplus in the piercing market. To measure consumer surplus, start with the area of total utility from all 600 piercings, then subtract the amount actually paid. The red shaded area represents the $3600 ($60 × 600 piercings) consumers paid for those 600 piercings. The remaining shaded green triangle represents the consumer surplus.

Figure 6   Total Utility, Marginal Utility, and Consumer Surplus

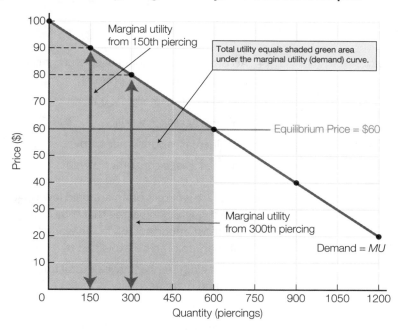

a)   Total Utility and Marginal Utility

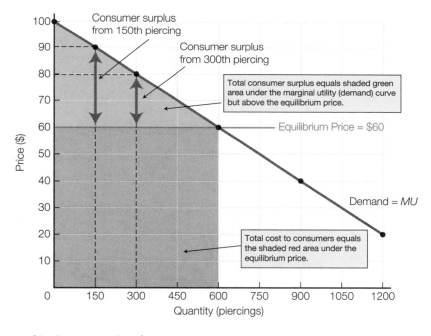

b)   Consumer Surplus

Consumer surplus graphically represents Bentham's goal for society of "the greatest happiness for the greatest number." Maximizing utility for society means adding up all benefits or satisfactions (total utility) and subtracting all pains or costs (amount paid). The most efficient and best outcome for consumers usually has the largest consumer surplus. Consumer surplus is a social measure of maximum total utility.

Practice...

11. The price of diamonds is higher than the price of water because

    a. total utility from diamonds is relatively high.

    b. total utility from water is relatively low.

    c. marginal utility from diamonds is relatively high.

    d. marginal utility from water is relatively high.

12. For any equilibrium quantity in a market, consumer surplus is the area

    a. under the demand curve but above the market price.

    b. under the demand curve.

    c. equal to the market price multiplied by the quantity.

    d. under the demand curve but above the supply curve.

13. For any equilibrium quantity in a market, total utility is the area

    a. under the demand curve but above the market price.

    b. under the demand curve.

    c. equal to the market price multiplied by the quantity.

    d. under the demand curve but above the supply curve.

14. According to the model of consumer choice, a rise in the price of a product

    a. decreases marginal utility.

    b. increases total utility.

    c. increases consumer surplus.

    d. decreases consumer surplus.

15. Childcare workers often are paid low wages even though many agree that they have "the most important job in the world." This paradox can be explained by

    a. the difference between total utility and marginal utility.

    b. an abundant supply of childcare workers.

    c. the low marginal utility of the last childcare worker hired.

    d. all of the above.

 **Apply…**

7. Explain how to resolve the diamond-water paradox using the condition for consumer equilibrium.

_____

_____

_____

_____

_____

_____

8. Use this graph of the market for water to answer the questions below.

   a. If the market price is $1.50, calculate and show the area of consumer surplus.

   _____

   _____

   _____

   _____

   _____

   _____

   b. If the market price is $1.50, how much do consumers pay for all of the water they buy?

   _____

   _____

   _____

   c. If the market price is $1.50, calculate and show the area of total utility.

   _____

   _____

   _____

   _____

9. Bentham's goal for society of "the greatest happiness for the greatest number" can be described in the language of utility. Explain how consumer surplus represents adding up all benefits or satisfactions (total utility) and subtracting all pains or costs (amount paid).

_____

_____

_____

_____

_____

KNOW...

Learning Objectives

1. **Total utility** is the sum of the marginal utilities of all units, measuring the total benefit or satisfaction from all units consumed of a product or service. **Marginal utility** measures the *additional* benefit or satisfaction from consuming an *additional* unit, and changes with circumstances. **Diminishing marginal utility** explains the **law of demand**.

2. The rule for maximum total utility is to continue buying the product with the largest marginal utility per dollar until all money is spent and marginal utility per dollar is equal for all products. The rule gives the consumer the most bang per buck, and focuses on marginal utility per dollar spent. The model of consumer choice gives another explanation for the downward-sloping demand curve by comparing **consumer equilibrium** before and after a change in price of only one product.

3. The distinction between total utility and marginal utility explains the diamond-water paradox and the measurement of consumer surplus. **Consumer surplus** — the difference between the amount a consumer is *willing and able to pay*, and the price actually paid — is a social measure of maximum total utility, the difference between the total utility and the total cost of a product.

Key Terms

consumer equilibrium: outcome that maximizes total utility and the marginal utility per dollar spent is equal for all products and services

consumer surplus: the difference between the amount a consumer is willing and able to pay, and the price actually paid

demand: consumers' willingness and ability to pay for a particular product or service

diminishing marginal utility: as you consume more of a product or service, marginal utility eventually decreases

marginal utility: additional benefits or satisfaction from consuming an additional unit of a product or service, changing with circumstances

preferences: your wants and their intensities

total utility: sum of the marginal utilities of all units; total benefits or satisfaction from all units consumed of a product or service

utility: measures the benefit or satisfaction from consuming a product or service

Answers to Practice

1. **a** Positive marginal utility adds to total utility. **c** false because for first unit, marginal utility = total utility.

2. **d** As each marginal utility you add is smaller, total utility increases, but not as quickly.

3. **b** Definition. The entire area below the demand curve.

4. **c** For any unit on the quantity axis, the marginal utility curve shows the maximum someone is willing and able to pay for that unit.

5. **d** Read demand curve up and over as a marginal utility curve, showing the maximum price willing and able to pay for that last unit.

6. **b** After the price of X doubles, the ratio MU_X/P_X is now less than MU_Y/P_Y. To equalize the ratios, Broomhilda must increase MU_X, which means consuming less of X, which increases its marginal utility.

7. **c** Maximum total utility with marginal utility per dollar spent equal for all products.

8. **a** Marginal utility divided by price must be equal for Porsches and diamonds, so if the marginal utility of a Porsche is twice that of a diamond, the price of a Porsche must also be twice the price of a diamond.

9. **d** Marginal utility determines willingness to pay. From the condition for consumer equilibrium, if marginal utilities are equal, prices are equal.

10. **b** To equalize marginal utility per dollar, Bob must increase his marginal utility from beer, which means buying less, and decrease his marginal utility from back bacon, which means buying more.

11. **c** Prices are proportional to marginal utility, not total utility.

12. **a** Definition.

13. **b** Sum of the marginal utilities for every unit.

14. **d** At higher price, area of consumer surplus is smaller. With decrease in quantity, marginal utility increases and total utility decreases.

15. **d** Same explanation as diamond-water paradox, where childcare workers are priced more like water than diamonds.

7 Producer Model Basics: Profits and Costs behind Supply

LEARNING OBJECTIVES

L01 Distinguish explicit costs from implicit costs, and describe how accounting profits miss implicit costs.

L02 Define normal profits and economic profits, and explain how they differ.

L03 Explain how economic profits signal smart business decisions to exit or enter an industry, while coordinating consumer and business choices.

L04 Distinguish short-run from long-run business decisions, and describe how short-run diminishing marginal productivity increases marginal costs and shapes the average total cost curve.

L05 Derive a business's long-run average cost curve from different short-run average total cost curves, and explain the differences among economies of scale, constant returns to scale, and diseconomies of scale.

LEARN...

Have you ever had a boss who acted like a little dictator? Have you ever fantasized about life without a boss and opening your own business? Your success in life will depend largely on how you spend your time and your money. Business success has a clear and simple measure — the bottom line, or the profits that remain once you subtract all costs from your revenues. But finding the bottom line and making smart business choices are not as simple as hiring an accountant to crunch the numbers.

It turns out that economists have something valuable to add to the accountant's calculation of profits. Our old friend *opportunity cost* is the hidden key to smart choices about spending your time and money, whether you are running your own business, working for others, or even investing your savings.

Economists also have something to add in identifying the costs behind business supply decisions. As any business owner will tell you, there are supply choices to be made in the short run, such as how many employees to hire, and different supply choices when there is more time to plan for the long run — build a bigger factory or expand into new markets.

The details in this chapter about profits and costs will help you make smart business choices of your own, as well as help you better understand how demand and supply direct markets to produce the products and services we value most.

Accounting Profits, Explicit Costs, and Implicit Costs

 Distinguish explicit costs from implicit costs, and describe how accounting profits miss implicit costs.

After suffering too many unkind bosses, Wahid listens to the entrepreneurial voice inside his head and decides to set up his own web design business. He has been saving for a while, and a small inheritance from his grandfather brings his total ($40 000) high enough to get started. Trying to make smart choices, he develops a business plan for Wahid's Web Wonders. Let's see what the plan looks like to an accountant.

Explicit Costs and Accounting Profits

Wahid's business plan for his first year appears in Figure 1. With the contacts from part-time web design jobs, he *expects* (this word will be important later on) to earn $60 000 in revenues in his first year.

Figure 1   Accountant's One-Year Business Plan for Wahid's Web Wonders

Total Expected Revenues			$60 000
Explicit Costs	Depreciation	$ 5 000	
	Rent	$14 000	
	Web Hosting	$ 3 000	
	Phone	$ 1 000	
	Advertising	$ 2 000	
Total Explicit Costs			$25 000
Accounting Profits			$35 000

Depreciation   To start his business, Wahid has to buy computer hardware and software that cost $20 000. He has to pay for that equipment all at once, which takes $20 000 of his $40 000 in savings. The equipment will last four years before it wears out. **Depreciation** is the decrease in value of equipment over time because of wear and tear and because it becomes obsolete.

When equipment lasts many years, Canada Revenue Agency (Canada's tax department) does not allow accountants to treat it all as a cost in the first year. Businesses must spread the cost over the lifetime of long-lasting equipment. If the equipment lasts four years, then the allowable depreciation cost is $5000 per year ($20 000 divided by four years).

Explicit Costs   Wahid finds an office to rent in the design district for $14 000 per year and has a web hosting package for $3000 per year. He estimates yearly phone expenses will be $1000 and advertising will cost $2000. These total costs (not counting depreciation) are $20 000 per year, which take the rest of Wahid's savings. These are explicit costs — costs a business pays directly. Accountants include depreciation as part of explicit costs, so adding the $5000 depreciation cost Wahid is allowed to count, explicit costs for Wahid's first year total $25 000.

Accounting Profits   To calculate accounting profits, accountants subtract explicit costs from revenues:

> Accounting Profits = Revenues − Explicit Costs (including depreciation)

So, for Wahid,

> Accounting Profits = $60 000 − $25 000 = $35 000

If things go according to plan, Wahid will end the first year with $35 000 in his pocket. Not bad for a first year in business. Or is it?

Your Time's Opportunity Cost

Accountants do not count the hidden opportunity costs of what a business owner could earn elsewhere with the time and money invested in the business. Economists call these hidden opportunity costs **implicit costs**.

The explicit, or out-of-pocket, cost of Wahid's time in his new business is zero — he is working for himself and not paying himself money. But in working for himself, he is giving up the best alternative use of his time. If the best job he could have (working for a boss) pays $38 000 per year, that is the implicit cost, or hidden opportunity cost, of Wahid's time invested in his own business.

Your Money's Opportunity Cost

If Wahid had to borrow money to start up the business, the interest he would pay to the bank would be an explicit cost to subtract from his revenues. But because Wahid did not borrow the $40 000 he invests in his business, the explicit cost of borrowing is zero — he is loaning the money to himself.

Nonetheless, by investing his money in his business, he is giving up the best alternative use of the money. Wahid could have put the money in the bank and earned interest for a year, or invested it elsewhere. The interest, or return on investing elsewhere, that Wahid gives up is the implicit cost — the hidden opportunity cost — of using his own money. He cannot use the same money in two different places at the same time.

Calculating the precise opportunity cost of investing your own money is tricky because returns from business investing are risky, while returns from the bank are guaranteed. Let me explain this unequal comparison of returns.

If you (or Wahid) invest $40 000 in a bank GIC (guaranteed investment certificate) that pays 5-percent interest, at the end of the year you get your $40 000 back and a guaranteed 5-percent return of $2000 ($40 000 × 0.05 = $2000) for a total of $42 000. You could instead invest $40 000 in your own business (or any other business), also with an expected return of 5 percent ($2000) if things go according to plan. But, if there is only an 80-percent chance that things will go well, which alternative would you choose? You probably would choose the safe 5-percent return from the bank instead of the risky 5-percent return from the business.

Risky Business   A more important question for calculating your money's opportunity cost is "What expected return would it take for you to go for the risky business investment?" You need to expect more than the safe 5 percent you get from the bank in order to compensate for the risk of the business investment. Your personal risk compensation depends on your personality and your assessment of just how risky the investment is.

If you are a gambler at heart, economists call you *risk-loving*. You might not require much risk compensation to go for the uncertain investment as long as the returns are just a bit higher than the guaranteed return. If you are more cautious, economists call you *risk-averse*. It would take a very high risk compensation to get you to go for the uncertain investment over the guaranteed bank investment.

Let's say you (and Wahid) believe an extra, expected 15-percent return would just compensate for the risk. You want an extra 15% risk premium, above the guaranteed 5%, to compensate for risk. Then you and Wahid would be equally pleased with the two paths: one with a guaranteed 5-percent return, the other with an expected 20-percent return.

In investing his own money, Wahid would be equally pleased with a guaranteed 5-percent return of $2000 on his initial investment of $40 000, or an expected 20-percent return of $8000. He would give up the guaranteed $2000 to try for an expected $8000 return, and he would give up the expected $8000 return in exchange for the guaranteed $2000. Either option measures the implicit cost — the hidden opportunity cost — of investing his $40 000.

Although Wahid's business plan *expects* (I told you this word would be important) revenues of $60 000 in the first year, the return is not guaranteed. So the number to use for the hidden opportunity cost of using and risking his own money is not the guaranteed bank return of 5 percent; it is the 20-percent expected return that adds a premium of 15 percent for risk compensation. The total expected return needs to be $8000 on his $40 000 risky investment ($40 000 × 0.20 = $8000).

Wahid's risk premium of 15 percent is personal to him. A different investor who is risk-loving would have a smaller risk premium. A more risk-averse investor would have a larger risk premium.

The next section looks at Wahid's "profits" once we consider implicit costs — the hidden opportunity costs — of investing his time and money.

Practice…

1. The decrease in the value of equipment over time because of wear and tear is

   a. deflation.

   b. depreciation.

   c. deduction.

   d. annualization.

2. Zabeen operates her own business and pays herself a salary of $20 000 per year. She refused a job that pays $30 000 per year. What is the opportunity cost of Zabeen's time in her business?

   a. $10 000

   b. $20 000

   c. $30 000

   d. $50 000

3. If you borrow money from the bank to start a business, the interest you pay the bank is

   a. an explicit cost.

   b. subtracted from revenues to calculate profits.

   c. included in calculating accounting profits.

   d. all of the above.

4. An economist considers someone who is a gambler and does not need much compensation to make an uncertain investment as

   a. risk-loving.

   b. risk-averse.

   c. crazy.

   d. all of the above.

5. The implicit costs of starting a business do *not* include

   a. compensation for business risk.

   b. forgone salary, when an entrepreneur quits a job to start the business.

   c. forgone rental income, when an entrepreneur evicts a tenant from his house to use the space for the business.

   d. depreciation.

 **Apply…**

1. Betty's Blogging is a small business and prepares the following plan about revenues and expenses in the first year:

   Expected revenue $50 000
   Cost of renting equipment $10 000
   Cost of web hosting $ 3 000
   Cost of phone and Internet $ 5 000
   Cost of advertising $ 2 000

   What are the explicit costs? What are the expected accounting profits for the year?

2. The current bank interest rate is 5 percent. You borrow $10 000 from the bank as well as invest $20 000 of your own money in a new business for a year. Detail the explicit costs and the implicit costs (hidden opportunity costs) for both amounts of money you are investing.

3. These questions are about attitudes towards risk.
   a. Explain the difference between a risk-loving person and a risk-averse person. Which type of person requires a higher risk premium when gambling or investing?

   b. If you take out a mortgage, you can choose a variable-rate mortgage or a fixed-rate mortgage. The interest rate on a variable-rate mortgage varies as market interest rates change. The interest rate on a fixed-rate mortgage is guaranteed to stay the same for the length of the mortgage. Historical data show that you almost always pay less interest on the full term of your mortgage if you choose a variable rate. Which type of person prefers a variable-rate mortgage over a fixed-rate mortgage, all other things being equal?

Normal Profits and Economic Profits

 Define normal profits and economic profits, and explain how they differ.

Accountants, economists, and ordinary people all think of profits as revenues minus costs. Profits are what's left over when all costs have been paid. And if costs are greater than revenues, there's a loss. But a more precise definition of profits and losses depends on what gets included in costs. And a precise definition is important for making smart business decisions.

Recall the accountant's definition of profits:

Accounting Profits = Revenues – Explicit Costs (including depreciation)

Economists have two more-precise definitions: normal profits and economic profits.

Normal Profits

Normal profits are compensation for the use of a business owner's time and money, the sum of implicit costs — the hidden opportunity costs. Normal profits are what a business owner must earn to do as well as he could have done in the best alternative uses of his time and money. In other words, normal profits are the average profits in other industries.

The *time component* of normal profits is the value of the best alternative use of the owner's time. For Wahid, that is the $38 000 he could have earned by using his time working for another company. The *money component* of normal profits is the best alternative return on investment, including risk compensation. For Wahid, that is the $8000 he expects on his $40 000 investment. So, normal profits for the first year of Wahid's Web Wonders business are $46 000 ($38 000 + $8000).

Economic Profits

The economist's definition of profits is "revenues minus *all opportunity costs*." Like accountants, economists subtract all explicit costs from revenues. These explicit, out-of-pocket costs are also opportunity costs. The best alternative use of the $25 000 Wahid spends on rent, phone expenses, and so on is still $25 000 worth of different business-related items he could have bought instead.

The key difference between economists and accountants is that economists also subtract implicit costs from revenues:

Economic Profits = Revenues – All Opportunity Costs

= Revenues – (Explicit Costs + Implicit Costs)

Since the sum of implicit costs is defined as normal profits, the definition of economic profits can also be written as

Economic Profits = Revenues – (Explicit Costs + Normal Profits)

Let me show you why the definition of economic profits matters for making smart business choices.

Figure 2 revisits Wahid's business plan as it would look to an economist.

Figure 2   Economist's One-Year Business Plan for Wahid

Total Expected Revenues			$60 000
Explicit Costs	Depreciation	$ 5 000	
	Rent	$14 000	
	Web Hosting	$ 3 000	
	Phone	$ 1 000	
	Advertising	$ 2 000	
Total Explicit Costs			$25 000
Accounting Profits			$35 000
Implicit Costs	Wahid's Time	$38 000	
	Wahid's Money	$ 8 000	
Total Implicit Costs			$46 000
Economic Profits			($11 000)*

*On business plans and balance sheets, losses are indicated with parentheses:
($11 000) is an eleven thousand dollar loss.

According to the economist's calculation, when you subtract all of Wahid's opportunity costs ($25 000 in explicit costs and $46 000 in implicit costs) from his expected revenues ($60 000), Wahid is suffering **economic losses** of $11 000. This means that Wahid is not covering all of his opportunity costs.

What Economists Find   Wahid's accounting profits are $35 000. But if, instead of working and investing in his business, he had worked elsewhere and invested his money either in the bank or in an investment equally as risky as his business, he would have earned between $40 000 (guaranteed) and $46 000 (expected). The amount of $35 000 in accounting profits might sound attractive, but it is not as good as Wahid's best alternative uses of his time and money.

Wahid has not made a smart choice (other than avoiding having a boss). He is worse off financially after a year of running his business than he would have been working and investing his money elsewhere.

To make a smart choice, Wahid must pay attention to Key 3 (which we haven't discussed until now) of the 3 Keys model: Be sure to count *all* additional benefits and costs, including *implicit costs* and *externalities*. Implicit costs are the difference between accounting profits and economic profits. (Externalities will appear in Chapter 12.)

IMPLICIT
COSTS &
EXTERNALITIES

Practice...

6. Normal profits include

   a. compensation for the use of a business owner's time and money.

   b. the sum of hidden opportunity costs.

   c. what a business owner could have earned elsewhere.

   d. all of the above.

7. Which is *not* another way of saying "hidden opportunity costs"?

   a. explicit costs

   b. implicit costs

   c. normal profits

   d. the sum of the opportunity costs of time and money

8. The difference between economists and accountants is that economists

   a. are smarter.

   b. are better looking.

   c. subtract implicit costs when calculating profits.

   d. add opportunity costs when calculating profits.

9. If your business earns accounting profits of $50 000 and has economic losses of $20 000, what are your implicit costs?

   a. $20 000

   b. $30 000

   c. $60 000

   d. $70 000

10. The definition of economic profits can also be written as

   a. Economic Profits = Revenues – (Explicit Costs + Normal Profits).

   b. Economic Profits = Revenues – (Explicit Costs + Implicit Costs).

   c. Economic Profits = Accounting Profits – Implicit Costs.

   d. all of the above.

 **Apply...**

4. Suppose Betty's Blogging business has the revenues and explicit costs in Apply question 1 on page 164. Betty's best alternative employment is working for $25 000 for a marketing company. Betty has to borrow $20 000 from the bank to start the business, at an interest rate of 10%. Betty wants her own business more than anything in the world, and is not looking for any risk compensation.

   a. Does this information change Betty's expected accounting profits? If so, what are they? What are Betty's implicit costs? What are Betty's expected economic profits?

   _____

   _____

   _____

   _____

   _____

   b. What would an economist recommend for Betty's Blogging business?

   _____

   _____

   _____

   _____

5. If your business earns accounting profits of $50 000 and economic profits of $20 000, what are your implicit costs?

   _____

   _____

   _____

   _____

   _____

   _____

6. You earn a good salary, but you hate your boss. You develop a plan to start your own business that projects economic profits of $5000 at the end of the first year. But just as you are about to go ahead with your new business, you are offered a job for $15 000 more than you were earning before. How does that change your projected economic profits? Would it change your decision to start your new business? Why or why not?

   _____

   _____

   _____

   _____

   _____

Economic Profits Direct the Invisible Hand

 Explain how economic profits signal smart business decisions to exit or enter an industry, while coordinating consumer and business choices.

Economic profits are the most important signal — the key bottom line — for judging smart business decisions. Accounting profits provide some useful information, but not enough. To illustrate, let's look at three alternative end-of-year scenarios for Wahid. While his business plan was based on expected revenues, what happens if his actual revenues turn out to be $60 000, $71 000, or $80 000? In each of the three scenarios, his explicit costs and implicit costs (normal profits) are the same as before (see Figure 2 on page 166).

In each of the three scenarios in Figure 3, Wahid has positive accounting profits, seeming to indicate that he is doing well. But the economic profit calculations tell a different story.

Figure 3   Alternative Revenue and Profit Scenario's for Wahid's Web Wonders

Scenario	One	Two	Three
Revenues	$ 60 000	$ 71 000	$ 80 000
Total Explicit Costs	$ 25 000	$ 25 000	$ 25 000
Implicit Costs	$ 46 000	$ 46 000	$ 46 000
Accounting Profits	$ 35 000	$ 46 000	$ 55 000
Economic Profits	($ 11 000)	$ 0	$ 9 000

In scenario one, with revenues of $60 000, Wahid's economic profits are negative — economic losses of $11 000. Wahid is kicking himself because he is worse off than if he had chosen the best alternative uses of his time and money — he is not even earning normal profits. His profits are less than average profits in other industries.

In scenario two, with revenues of $71 000, Wahid's economic profits are zero. That doesn't sound good, but it means that Wahid's revenues are just covering all of his opportunity costs of production (explicit costs and implicit costs). Wahid will be content. He did as well as he could have done with the best alternative uses of his time and money (and he was his own boss!). He is not kicking himself.

In scenario three, with revenues of $80 000, Wahid's economic profits are positive, $9000 *above normal profits*. Wahid is a happy web designer. Positive economic profits indicate he is doing better than the best alternative uses of his time and money. His profits are greater than average profits in other industries. Wahid has made a smart choice for his first year.

Wahid's smart choice combines Keys 1 and 3 of the Three Keys model. Key 1 says, "Choose only when additional benefits are greater than additional *opportunity costs*." Key 3 says, "Be sure to count *all* additional benefits and costs, *including implicit costs* and externalities." Additional benefits are Wahid's revenues. His business's additional opportunity costs include explicit costs and implicit costs. (Externalities, which are not important here, are discussed in Chapter 12.)

The combination of keys for business decisions can be written as "Choose only when revenues are greater than all opportunity costs," or, even more simply,

Choose only when economic profits are positive.

Economics Profits Signal the Way

Besides signalling smart business decisions, economic profits create incentives for businesses to supply the products and services that consumers demand.

In Chapter 3, we saw how markets coordinate the choices of consumers and businesses. Through the interaction of demand and supply, markets form equilibrium prices that signal smart choices.

In this chapter, we add economic profits to the description of the equilibrium price. For a business, changing prices affect both revenues (prices of products or services sold) and costs (prices of inputs bought). If well-run businesses simply focus on pursuing economic profits, they produce the products and services consumers want.

Just like traffic signals keep drivers moving smoothly to their different destinations quickly and safely, economic profits direct businesses to produce what consumers want. To see this more clearly, let's examine Wahid's three alternative scenarios for economic profits shown in Figure 3 on the previous page.

Scenario One   Economic losses are a red light to a business. Economics losses signal a business to direct its energy, talent, and money to a different industry where they will be more valued. For any business or industry, economic losses signal not-smart choices to avoid.

Scenario Two   With zero economic profits, a business is just covering all of its opportunity costs, including earning normal profits. This is a yellow light — proceed with caution. Profits for this business are the same as average profits on other roads, in other industries. Yellow is an "equilibrium" signal — no reason to change industries. Economists call this a business's **breakeven point**.

Scenario Three   Economic profits are a green light. The business has made a smart choice, and should consider investing more time and money in expanding. When outsiders see economic profits in a particular industry, they shift their time and money out of industries that are suffering economic losses or just breaking even, and into green-light industries.

Market Equilibrium

Economic profits and losses add another time dimension to the market price adjustments in Chapter 3.

Short-Run Market Equilibrium   If there are mismatches between quantity demanded and quantity supplied in a market, the resulting shortages or surpluses create pressure for prices to rise or fall. When prices adjust to the market-clearing equilibrium price, quantity demanded equals quantity supplied.

In **short-run market equilibrium**, quantity demanded equals quantity supplied, but economic losses or profits lead to changes in supply. The equilibrium price in Chapter 3 has no tendency for change *only if economic profits are zero.* Economic losses or economic profits signal additional adjustments in supply. With more time to adjust, business owners will follow the signals of economic losses and profits to move their abilities and money into different industries.

Economic Losses and Exit   When there are economic losses, prices do not cover all of the business's opportunity costs of production. Consumers don't value the product or service enough to pay the price that covers all business costs, including normal profits. Smart businesses get off that road, leave the industry, and move their time, money, and inputs elsewhere — to a promise of economic profits.

Figure 4a tells the story of economic losses and exit. The original demand and supply curves are D_0 and S_0. The short-run market equilibrium is at price P_S (the subscript S stands for *short-run*) and quantity Q_S. But at price P_S and quantity Q_S, businesses suffer economic losses. (The losses do not appear directly on the graph; they are a result of the combination of P_S, quantity Q_S, and costs.

Figure 4   Alternative Revenue and Profit Scenario's for Wahid's Web Wonders

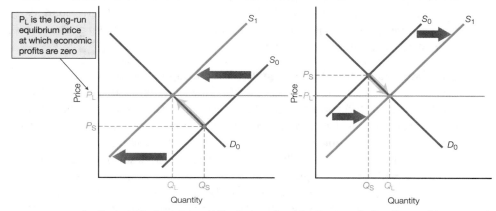

a) Economic Losses and Decreased Supply Lead to Long-Run Market Equilibrium

b) Economic Profits and Increased Supply Lead to Long-Run Market Equilibrium

When businesses exit the industry, supply decreases (Chapter 3). The supply curve shifts leftward toward S_1, which pushes prices up. The decrease in supply moves the market price up along the unchanged demand curve D_0. Businesses keep exiting, supply keeps decreasing, prices keep rising, and losses keep decreasing until the price rises to P_L (the subscript L stands for *long-run*) and the equilibrium quantity decreases to Q_L.

The yellow horizontal line at P_L represents the price at which economic profits are zero. At price P_L and quantity Q_L, revenues just cover all opportunity costs of production (including normal profits), and economic profits are zero.

Long-Run Market Equilibrium   When businesses are breaking even, and economic profits are zero, there is no strong incentive for any change. Businesses are doing as well as they could elsewhere. An industry is in **long-run market equilibrium** when quantity demanded equals quantity supplied, and businesses have zero economic profits. Business owners in this industry are not jumping for joy, but they are also not jumping out of windows because of financial ruin.

A long-run market equilibrium exists when all of the forces of demand and supply are in balance and economic profits are zero. The difference between short-run and long-run market equilibrium is the additional time it takes for supply changes to adjust economic profits or losses to zero.

In long-run market equilibrium, the price consumers are willing to pay just covers businesses' opportunity costs of production, including normal profits. Businesses are supplying the quantity of products or services that consumers are willing and able to buy at that price.

Economic Profits Signal a "Go"   The graph in Figure 4b on the previous page tells the story of economic profits and new business entry. The original demand and supply curves are D_0 and S_0. The short-run market equilibrium is at price P_S and quantity Q_S. But at price P_S and quantity Q_S, businesses are making economic profits. (The profits do not appear directly on the graph; they are a result of the combination of the price P_S, quantity Q_S, and costs.)

As new businesses enter the industry, supply increases. The supply curve shifts rightward toward S_1, which pushes prices down. The increase in supply moves the market price down along the unchanged demand curve D_0. But as long as economic profits remain, businesses keep entering, supply keeps increasing, prices keep falling, and profits keep decreasing until the price falls to P_L and the equilibrium quantity increases to Q_L. Supply stabilizes only once prices have fallen enough to just cover all opportunity costs of production, and economic profits fall to zero. At the long-run equilibrium price P_L and quantity Q_L, revenues just cover all opportunity costs of production (including normal profits), and economic profits are zero.

Economic Profits Are Supply Signals   On the supply side of markets, economic profits are the key signal directing the self-interest of businesses to produce the products and services that consumers want. Changes in economic profits trigger changes in supply, which change prices, moving an industry from a short-run market equilibrium to a long-run market equilibrium.

The long-run market equilibrium price is the price markets move toward. Economic profits are the signals for moving, and supply shifts are the mechanism for moving. By finding the real bottom line of economic profits, we reveal Adam Smith's invisible hand directing business owners' self-interest to produce the miracle of markets.

 Practice...

11. Businesses should enter an industry when
    a. economic profits are positive.
    b. additional benefits are greater than additional opportunity costs.
    c. revenues are greater than all opportunity costs.
    d. all of the above are true.

12. Which "signals the way" when making decisions to enter or exit an industry?
    a. revenues
    b. normal profits
    c. economic profits
    d. yield signs

13. When economic profits are zero, businesses are
    a. breaking even.
    b. not kicking themselves.
    c. likely to remain in the industry.
    d. all of the above.

14. When there are economic losses in an industry,
    a. price falls.
    b. supply decreases.
    c. quantity supplied decreases.
    d. demand decreases.

15. An industry is in short-run market equilibrium, and there are economic profits. What will *not* happen in the long run?
    a. equilibrium quantity decreases
    b. equilibrium price falls
    c. economic profits are zero
    d. normal profits are positive

Apply...

7. Explain how the rule "Choose only when additional benefits are greater than additional opportunity costs" is the same as "Choose when economic profits are positive."

_____

_____

_____

_____

_____

_____

8. What is the same about short-run market equilibrium and long-run market equilibrium? What is different?

_____

_____

_____

_____

_____

_____

_____

9. Businesses in the beachball market are currently earning zero economic profits. A heat wave strikes and demand for beachballs skyrockets, so a shortage develops, driving up beachball prices. Using economic profits as the key, use a demand-and-supply graph to explain all the choices that will be made before the beachball market once again returns to long-run market equilibrium with zero economic profits.

Price

0

Quantity

_____

_____

_____

_____

_____

_____

_____

_____

Short-Run Costs and Diminishing Marginal Productivity

 Distinguish short-run from long-run business decisions, and describe how short-run diminishing marginal productivity increases marginal costs and shapes the average total cost curve.

Smart business supply decisions depend on economics profits — revenues minus *all* opportunity costs of production, including explicit costs and implicit costs. This section moves the focus from implicit costs to explicit costs.

As you learned from the Chapter 2 example of Paola's Parlour for Piercing and Nails, businesses generally have increasing marginal costs. The supply curve for an individual business or for a market is upward sloping because rising prices create two incentives for increased quantity supplied: higher profits and the need to cover higher marginal costs of production. Marginal costs are the most important costs for smart profit decisions (Key 2 — Count only *additional* benefits and *additional* costs), but other costs also play a role. To begin a more complete explanation of what's behind the upward slope of producer supply curves, let's look more closely at explicit costs. The rest of the explanation must wait for Chapter 9 on Perfect Competition.

To start, we must distinguish short-run costs from long-run costs.

Short Run and Long Run in Microeconomics

A business's explicit costs for buying inputs to production depend on what control it has over changing inputs. Economists distinguish two microeconomic planning periods: the short run and the long run.

In economics, short run and long run do not refer to calendar time. The **short run** is a planning period during which some inputs are variable but at least one input is fixed (cannot be varied). The **long run** refers to a planning period long enough that all inputs can be varied.

Inputs that can vary in the short run include labour, energy, and raw materials. Inputs that are fixed in the short run but can vary in the long run include land, technology, factory buildings, capital, and management.

This section looks at short-run costs. The last section of the chapter looks at long-run costs.

Fixed Costs and Variable Costs

We will use the wheat industry to illustrate short-run costs. The wheat industry has many identical small sellers producing an identical product — bushels of wheat.

Wheat farmers, like most businesses, have fixed costs and variable costs. **Fixed costs** are for fixed inputs, and do not change with the quantity of output produced. Fixed costs for the wheat farmer include land costs, property taxes, and insurance. *To simplify the example, we are combining normal profits — compensation for a business owner's time and money — with fixed costs.*

Variable costs do change with output — they vary! Variable costs include the amount of water and fertilizer the farmer uses, and especially the number of labourers the farmer must hire to increase the quantity of wheat he grows. Adding together the fixed costs and the variable costs gives us **total cost**.

Total Cost = Total Fixed Costs (including normal profits) + Total Variable Costs

Diminishing Marginal Productivity

Let's use some easy, made-up numbers to illustrate these costs. To simplify even further, suppose that the farmer's only variable cost is what he pays for additional labourers.

Total Product and Marginal Product   Figure 5 shows what happens to the farmer's total output of wheat as he hires more labourers. Column 2 of the table lists the different number of labourers he could hire per year, from zero to five. Column 3 shows the total quantity of wheat produced per year when the labourers work with the fixed amount of land and other inputs. The total output that labourers produce when working with all fixed inputs is also called **total product.**

Figure 5   Total Product and Marginal Product

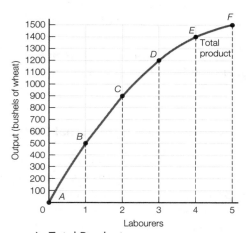

a) Total Product

Column				
1	2	3	4	5
Row	Labourers	Total Product (bushels of wheat)	Marginal Product (bushels of wheat)	Marginal Cost (of a bushel of wheat) (labour costs $1000 per year)
A	0	0		
			500	$ 2.00
B	1	500		
			400	$ 2.50
C	2	900		
			300	$ 3.33
D	3	1200		
			200	$ 5.00
E	4	1400		
			100	$10.00
F	5	1500		

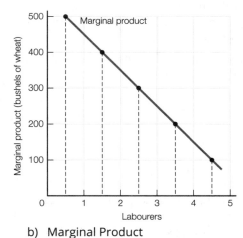

b) Marginal Product

Column 4 lists each labourer's **marginal product** — the *additional* output gained from adding one more labourer. Marginal product is calculated as the change in total product from adding one more labourer. As you might guess from Key 2 (count only *additional* benefits and *additional* costs), marginal product is more important than total product. Ignore the last column — marginal cost — for now.

Marginal Product Decreases   Marginal product is measured in bushels of wheat and decreases with each additional labourer. The first labourer hired increases total product from zero to 500 bushels of wheat. The marginal product of the first labourer is 500 bushels of wheat. Because marginal product is the *change* in total product, it is listed halfway between total products of zero and 500. The second labourer hired increases total product from 500 bushels to 900 bushels. Her marginal product is 400 bushels of wheat. The third labourer hired increases total product from 900 bushels to 1200 bushels, a marginal product of 300 bushels of wheat.

The numbers in the table in Figure 5 are shown in the graphs on the previous page. Figure 5a shows the total product produced by 1, 2, 3, 4, and 5 labourers. Because total product is the output of all labourers working with all fixed inputs, the numbers for total product appear directly above the total number of labourers. For example, 2 labourers produce an output of 900 bushels of wheat, so 900 bushels is plotted directly above 2 labourers.

Figure 5b shows the marginal product of the 1st, 2nd, 3rd, 4th, and 5th labourers. Because marginal product measures the *change* in total product as you add more labourers, marginal product appears halfway between labourers. For example, the marginal product in changing from 1 labourer to 2 labourers — 400 bushels — is plotted halfway between 1 and 2 labourers.

Looking at column 4 of the table or at Figure 5b, the marginal product of each additional labourer decreases. Marginal product decreases because of **diminishing marginal productivity**. With fixed amounts of land, tools, and other inputs, as you add more labourers, they have to share tools, and eventually may get in each others' way. Productivity diminishes. As you add more of a variable input to fixed inputs, the marginal product of the variable input eventually diminishes.

Measuring diminishing productivity and output in bushels of wheat or any product is a start, but businesses are interested in the bottom line of profits. To calculate profits, we have to turn these quantities of output into costs, and subtract costs from revenues.

From Diminishing Marginal Productivity to Increasing Marginal Costs

The marginal cost of an additional bushel of wheat depends on how much the farmer pays for each labourer. Marginal cost can be calculated as the additional opportunity cost of increasing quantity supplied, or as the change in total costs from producing an additional bushel of wheat. How much does each additional bushel of wheat cost the farmer as he increases output by hiring more labourers?

Increasing Marginal Costs Sticking with simple, made-up numbers, suppose each labourer can be hired for $1000 per year. The last column of the table in Figure 5 shows the farmer's marginal cost calculations.

The first labourer the farmer hires has a marginal product of 500 bushels of wheat. It costs the farmer $1000 for that labourer, so the marginal cost of each bushel the labourer produces is

$$\frac{\$1000}{500 \text{ bushels}} = \$2 \text{ per bushel of wheat}$$

This $2 is the *additional* cost the farmer must pay per bushel to increase output from zero to 500 bushels. The marginal cost of $2 per bushel does not include fixed costs, which we will get to soon.

To further increase output, the farmer must hire a second labourer for a year and pay an additional $1000. The second labourer produces only 400 additional bushels of wheat. The marginal cost of each bushel the second labourer produces is

$$\frac{\$1000}{400 \text{ bushels}} = \$2.50 \text{ per bushel of wheat}$$

For the 3rd, 4th, and 5th labourers, marginal costs per bushel continue to increase from $3.33 to $5.00 to $10.00.

As more labourers are hired and output increases, diminishing marginal productivity increases marginal costs.

Figure 6 graphs the quantity of output (on the horizontal axis) and the marginal cost (on the vertical axis) from the table of numbers in Figure 5. As with all marginal variables, marginal cost is plotted halfway between the relevant quantities of output. For example, marginal cost of $2 per bushel is plotted above 250 bushels, halfway between the zero bushels produced with no labour and the 500 bushels produced by the first labourer hired.

Figure 6   Increasing Marginal Cost

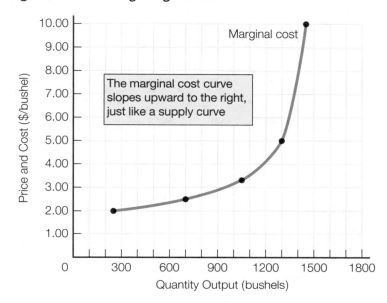

From Marginal Cost to Average Total Cost

To complete the picture of the farmer's costs, we add information about fixed costs. Let's say, for this example, total fixed costs (which include a payment for normal profits) are $1800.

Total Cost and Marginal Cost   The table in Figure 7 on the next page has the same columns as the table in Figure 5, except Figure 7 leaves out the marginal product column and adds cost columns. For each quantity of output in column 3, column 4 shows the total fixed cost (*TFC*). The $1800 is the same for every quantity of output, because fixed costs are fixed — they do not vary with output.

Column 5 shows the total variable cost (*TVC*) for hiring all labourers required to produce that quantity of output. A quantity of 900 bushels of output, for example, requires two labourers for a *TVC* of $2000.

Total cost (*TC*) in column 6 adds total fixed cost (*TFC*) and total variable cost (*TVC*).

The numbers in the marginal cost (*MC*) column are the same as in Figure 5 on page 175, but they are calculated in a different way. Figure 5 calculates marginal cost between rows by dividing an additional labourer's cost ($1000) by his or her marginal product measured in bushels of wheat. In Figure 7, marginal cost is also calculated between rows, but by taking the change in total cost and dividing by the change in quantity of output. For example, between Rows *A* and *B*, total cost changes by $1000 (from $1800 to $2800) and the quantity of output changes by 500 bushels (from zero to 500). $1000 divided by 500 bushels equals $2 per bushel.

Figure 7 Marginal Cost and Average Total Cost

				Column			
1	2	3	4	5	6	7	8
Row	Labourers	Output (Total Product bushels wheat)	TFC (Total Fixed Cost)	TVC (Total Variable Cost)	TC (Total Cost)	MC (Marginal Cost)	ATC (Average Total Cost)
A	0	0	$1800	0	$1800		– –
						$2.00	
B	1	500	$1800	$1000	$2800		$5.60
						$2.50	
C	2	900	$1800	$2000	$3800		$4.22
						$3.33	
D	3	1200	$1800	$3000	$4800		$4.00
						$5.00	
E	4	1400	$1800	$4000	$5800		$4.14
						$10.00	
F	5	1500	$1800	$5000	$6800		$4.53

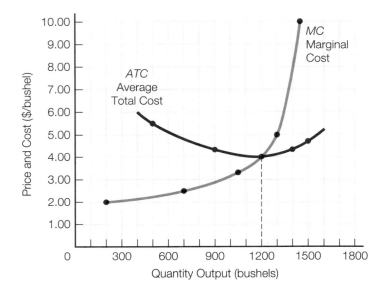

The two calculations give the same result because fixed costs do not change between rows *A* and *B*. The change in total cost ($1000) equals the additional labour cost ($1000) in Figure 5. And the change in output (500 bushels) between rows A and B equals the marginal product of the first labourer (500 bushels) in Figure 5.

Average Total Cost The last column (8) in Figure 7 shows the average total cost (*ATC*) of a bushel of wheat at each quantity of output. *ATC* is calculated for each row as total cost (*TC*) divided by quantity of output. For row *B*, the total cost (*TC*) is $2800 and the quantity of output is 500 bushels of wheat. So *ATC* equals $5.60 per bushel ($2800 divided by 500 bushels).

Marginal cost (*MC*) is the most important cost concept for business decisions, but average total cost (*ATC*) is a close second. All of the other cost concepts in Figure 7 are much less important and are shown mainly because they are necessary for calculating average total cost (*ATC*).

The graph in Figure 7 uses the numbers in the table to graph marginal cost and average total cost.

Marginal Cost and Average Total Cost   The average total cost curve has a U-shape. As output increases, ATC first decreases, reaches a minimum at 1200 bushels of output, and then increases. There is an important relationship between marginal cost and average total cost that explains the U-shape of the average total cost curve.

For any quantity between zero and 1200 bushels, marginal cost is less than average total cost — the marginal cost curve is below the average total cost curve. For any quantity greater than 1200 bushels, marginal cost is more than average total cost — the marginal cost curve is above the average total cost curve. The average total cost curve is decreasing for quantities up to 1200 bushels (downward sloping to the right), and increasing for quantities greater than 1200 bushels (upward sloping to the right). At the point where average total costs stop decreasing and start increasing, the average total cost curve is at its minimum — its lowest point — exactly at 1200 bushels of output. The marginal cost curve intersects the average total cost curve at the lowest point of the average total cost curve.

Marginal and Average Again   The relationship between marginal cost and average total cost is very similar to your average marks in a class. Suppose you have had three quizzes with scores of 4, 5, and 6 marks. You calculate your average mark by adding the scores and dividing by the number of quizzes — $(4 + 5 + 6) \div 3 = 15 \div 3 = 5$ marks.

You take an additional quiz (think additional = marginal) and do badly, getting only 1 mark. Because your additional quiz score is lower than your average, it pulls your average down. Your average is now 4 marks $(4 + 5 + 6 + 1) \div 4 = 16 \div 4 = 4$ marks. When marginal cost is less than average total cost, it pulls average total cost down. Like your marks, ATC is decreasing.

You take yet another quiz and get 19 marks. Good job! Your average is now 7 marks $(4 + 5 + 6 + 1 + 19) \div 5 = 35 \div 5 = 7$ marks. Because this additional (marginal) quiz score is higher than your average, it pulls your average up. When marginal cost is greater than average total cost, it pulls average total cost up. ATC is increasing.

Productivity and Cost Concepts Omitted from This Chapter

There are other productivity and cost concepts that your instructor and textbook may discuss, but that I have purposefully omitted for simplicity.

In Figure 5 on page 175, marginal productivity and the marginal product curve can initially increase before eventually decreasing. That does not change the definition of diminishing marginal productivity — when you add more of a variable input to fixed inputs, the marginal product of the variable input *eventually* diminishes. Figure 5 can also have an **average product** curve (total product divided by the number of labourers), also less important and omitted.

There are other average cost concepts we could calculate from the table in Figure 7. **Average fixed cost** is total fixed cost divided by quantity of output, while **average variable cost** is total variable cost divided by quantity of output. Each concept has an associated curve (average fixed cost curve and average variable cost curve) that could be added to Figure 7. There can also be an initial, downward-sloping range of the marginal cost curve.

I have purposefully omitted these less important concepts and curves to focus your attention on the most important short-run costs — marginal cost and average total cost. Many students find the complete graph of all four short-run cost curves (marginal cost, average total cost, average variable cost, average fixed cost) the most difficult graph in microeconomics, so I am trying to lessen the pain while improving your understanding.

Practice...

16. In the microeconomic short run,

    a. the planning period is one year or less.

    b. all inputs are variable.

    c. some inputs are variable and some inputs are fixed.

    d. all inputs are fixed.

17. Which combination will occur according to the concept of diminishing marginal productivity?

    1 Marginal productivity eventually increases.

    2 Marginal productivity eventually decreases.

    3 Marginal cost eventually increases.

    4 Marginal cost eventually decreases.

    a. 1 and 3

    b. 1 and 4

    c. 2 and 3

    d. 2 and 4

18. Which statement by a restaurant owner refers to diminishing marginal productivity?

    a. "The higher the quality of ingredients we use, the higher the cost of producing each meal."

    b. "We can increase the number of meals we serve by adding more kitchen staff, but each additional worker adds fewer meals than the previous worker because traffic in the kitchen gets worse."

    c. "We can serve the same number of meals with fewer kitchen staff, but we would have to buy more labour-saving kitchen equipment."

    d. "We can serve the same number of meals with less kitchen equipment, but we would have to hire more kitchen staff."

19. A business's fixed costs are $100. If total costs are $200 for one unit of output and $310 for two units, what is the marginal cost of the second unit?

    a. $100

    b. $110

    c. $200

    d. $210

20. If *ATC* is decreasing as output increases, *MC* must be

    a. less than *ATC*.

    b. equal to *ATC*.

    c. greater than *ATC*.

    d. decreasing.

 Apply…

10. For a fixed plant (land, factory, equipment), the table gives the total monthly output of golf carts that can be produced using varying quantities of labour.

    a. Complete the table for the marginal product of labour.

    b. On the graph, plot the points for marginal product (*MP*) and draw the marginal product curve. (Marginal product should be plotted halfway between the corresponding units of labour.) Explain what happens to the marginal product of labour as the quantity of labour increases. Where does diminishing marginal productivity begin?

Labourers (per month)	Output (units per month)	Marginal Product
0	0	
1	1	
2	3	
3	6	
4	13	
5	17	
6	20	
7	22	
8	23	

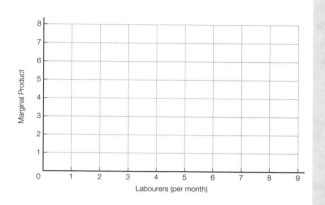

_____

_____

_____

_____

11. The table below shows the monthly short-run costs of golf cart production. The first two columns are the same as the table in Apply question 10. The cost of one labourer (the only variable input) is $2000 per month. Total fixed cost is $2000 per month.

L	Q	TFC ($)	TVC ($)	TC ($)	MC ($)	ATC ($)
0	0	2000				
1	1					
2	3					
3	6					
4	13					
5	17					
6	20					
7	22					
8	23					

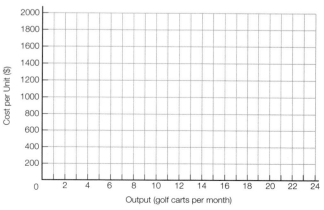

to be continued

Apply...

continued

a. Complete the table by calculating total fixed cost (*TFC*), total variable cost (*TVC*), total cost (*TC*), marginal cost (*MC*), and average total cost (*ATC*). Your completed table should look like the table in Figure 7 on page 178, with marginal cost entered between the rows.

b. On the graph, draw the *MC* and *ATC* curves. Be sure to plot *MC* between the corresponding units of output.

_____

_____

_____

_____

_____

12. These questions are about the relationship between marginal and average.

a. Why must the marginal cost curve intersect the average total cost curve at the minimum point of the average total cost curve?

_____

_____

_____

_____

_____

_____

_____

_____

b. Suppose the worst student at Hubertville High School transfers to Histrionic High School. Is it possible that the average grade point of the students at each school rises? Explain.

_____

_____

_____

_____

_____

_____

_____

_____

Long-Run Costs and Returns to Scale

 Derive a business's long-run average cost curve from different short-run average total cost curves, and explain the differences among economies of scale, constant returns to scale, and diseconomies of scale.

In the short run, some inputs are fixed. To increase output, businesses can only adjust the quantities of variable inputs. For each set of fixed inputs — fixed plant — the average total cost curve shows how a business's output and average costs change with changes in labour as the variable input.

In the long run, all inputs are variable. A business can change its plant size by buying new land, building a new factory, or changing its production technology. *Each change in plant size has a different average total cost curve.*

Long-Run Average Cost Curve

In the long run, a business can choose any of these many average total cost curves. How does it decide which size plant to build? The **long-run average cost curve** (*LRAC*) is a planning tool that shows the lowest average total cost for producing any quantity of output when the business has had time to change both its labour inputs and its plant size.

Figure 8 shows the connection between four possible short-run average total costs curves (*ATC*) and the long-run average cost curve. For any quantity of output on the horizontal axis, the long-run average cost curve consists of the lowest cost parts of each average total cost curve.

Figure 8   The Long-Run Average Cost Curve

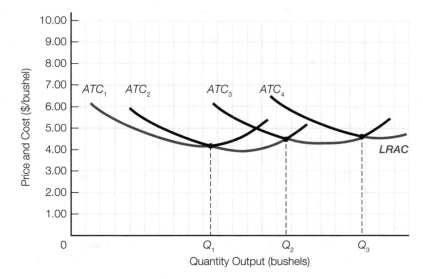

For any quantity up to Q_1 , the plant with ATC_1 is the lowest-cost way to produce. Between Q_1 and Q_2, the plant with ATC_2 is the lowest cost way to produce, between Q_2 and Q_3 it is ATC_3, and above Q_3 it is ATC_4. The long-run average cost curve is the darkened lowest-cost parts of the short-run average total cost curves.

Returns to Scale

The long-run average cost curve also illustrates the important concepts of returns to scale. Figure 9 on the next page shows the possible slopes along the long-run average cost curve *LRAC* when there are so many possible plant sizes that the scalloped curve in Figure 8 smooths out to the U-shaped curve.

Figure 9   Returns to Scale along a Long-Run Average Cost Curve

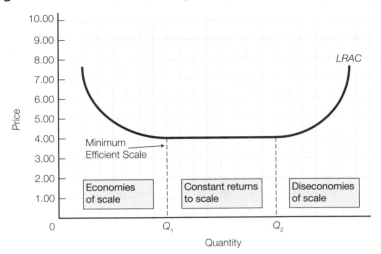

In the long run, when all inputs increase by the same percentage, increases in output can show three different returns to scale.

- **Economies of Scale** (also called **Increasing Returns to Scale**) — the percentage increase in a business's output is greater than the percentage increase in inputs. The long-run average cost curve slopes downward, with lower average costs at increased quantities of output.
- **Constant Returns to Scale** — the percentage increase in a business's output equals the percentage increase in inputs. The long-run average cost curve is horizontal, with constant average costs at increased quantities of output.
- **Diseconomies of Scale** (also called **Decreasing Returns to Scale**) — the percentage increase in a business's output is less than the percentage increase in inputs. The long-run average cost curve slopes upward, with higher average costs at increased quantities of output.

Figure 9 combines all three types of returns to scale on a single long-run average cost curve. But long-run average cost curves can also show only a single type of returns to scale.

- An always downward-sloping long-run average cost curve has only economies of scale (increasing returns to scale).
- A horizontal long-run average cost curve has only constant returns to scale.
- An always upward-sloping long-run average cost curve has only diseconomies of scale (decreasing returns to scale).
- The shape of an industry's long-run average cost curve depends on the specific technology and production conditions of that industry.

Regardless of the shape of any long-run average cost curve, the smallest quantity of output associated with the lowest cost is called the **minimum efficient scale**. In Figure 9, Q_1 is the minimum efficient scale.

Returns to Scale and Long-Run Costs   While diminishing marginal productivity is the key for understanding short-run costs and the shape of the average total cost curve, *returns to scale* are the key for understanding long-run costs and the shape of the long-run average cost curve. Returns to scale are the increase in output relative to the increase in inputs when *all* inputs increase by the same percentage.

Practice...

21. In the microeconomic long run,

    a. all inputs are variable.

    b. all inputs are fixed.

    c. only the plant size is fixed.

    d. businesses must reach diseconomies of scale.

22. The long-run average cost curve

    a. is a planning tool.

    b. shows the lowest-cost plant size for each quantity of output.

    c. consists of the parts of different short-run *ATC* curves where average total cost is lowest.

    d. is all of the above.

23. Constant returns to scale means that as all inputs are increased,

    a. total cost remains constant.

    b. long-run average cost remains constant.

    c. average total cost remains constant.

    d. larger businesses will have lower long-run costs.

24. if all inputs increase by 10 percent and output increases by less than 10 percent,

    a. average total cost is decreasing.

    b. average total cost is increasing.

    c. there are diseconomies of scale.

    d. there are economies of scale.

25. Minimum efficient scale is the smallest quantity of output where

    a. the *LRAC* curve reaches lowest cost.

    b. the *ATC* curve reaches lowest cost.

    c. economies of scale begin.

    d. diminishing marginal productivity begins.

Apply...

13. Suppose the long-run average cost curve for the energy storage battery industry is always downward sloping. If most businesses have relatively small plants, explain the competitive strategy of Elon Musk's Tesla Corporation, which produces batteries.

_____

_____

_____

_____

_____

14. What is the difference, if any, between diminishing marginal productivity and diseconomies of scale?

_____

_____

_____

_____

_____

_____

_____

KNOW...

Learning Objectives

1. **Accounting profits** equal revenues minus all **explicit costs**, including **depreciation**. But accounting profits miss implicit costs — the hidden opportunity costs — of a business owner's time and money.

2. Smart business decisions return at least **normal profits** — what a business owner could earn from the best alternative uses of her time and money. There are **economic profits** over and above normal profits, when revenues are greater than all opportunity costs of production, including explicit costs and implicit costs.

3. In **short-run market equilibrium**, quantity demanded equals quantity supplied, but economic profits or losses lead businesses to enter or exit an industry. Supply changes and prices adjust until the industry reaches **long-run market equilibrium**, with zero economic profits and no tendency for change. The simplest rule for smart business decisions is "Choose only when economic profits are positive." When businesses pursue economic profits, markets produce the products and services consumers want.

4. The two microeconomic planning periods are the **short run** (when some inputs are fixed and other inputs are variable) and the **long run** (when all inputs are variable). In the short run, because of **diminishing marginal productivity**, marginal costs increase as output increases, and the **average total cost** curve is U-shaped.

5. The **long-run average cost curve** (*LRAC*) is a planning tool for businesses thinking about varying all inputs and increasing plant size. The shape of the *LRAC* curve shows whether larger plants have cost advantages (downward-sloping **economies of scale**), constant costs (horizontal **constant returns to scale**), or cost disadvantages (upward-sloping **diseconomies of scale**).

Key Terms

accounting profits: revenues minus explicit costs (including depreciation)

average fixed cost: total fixed cost divided by quantity of output

average product: total product divided by the number of labourers

average total cost: total cost divided by quantity of output

average variable cost: total variable cost divided by quantity of output

breakeven point: business just earning normal profits — no economic profits, no economic losses

constant returns to scale: percentage increase in a business's output equals the percentage increase in inputs; constant long-run average costs

decreasing returns to scale (diseconomies of scale): percentage increase in a business's output is less than the percentage increase in inputs; increasing long-run average costs

depreciation: decrease in value of equipment over time because of wear and tear and because it becomes obsolete

diminishing marginal productivity: as you add more of a variable input to fixed inputs, the marginal product of the variable input eventually diminishes

diseconomies of scale (decreasing returns to scale): percentage increase in a business's output is less than the percentage increase in inputs; increasing long-run average costs

economic losses: negative economic profits

economic profits: revenues minus all opportunity costs (explicit costs plus implicit costs)

economies of scale (increasing returns to scale): percentage increase in a business's output is greater than the percentage increase in inputs; decreasing long-run average costs

explicit costs: costs a business pays directly

fixed costs: do not change with the quantity of output produced

implicit costs: hidden opportunity costs of what a business owner could earn elsewhere with time and money invested

increasing returns to scale (economies of scale): percentage increase in a business's output is greater than the percentage increase in inputs; decreasing long-run average costs

long run: in microeconomics, a planning period for businesses where the quantities of all inputs are variable

long-run average cost curve (*LRAC*)**:** shows the lowest average total cost for producing any quantity of output when all inputs can change

long-run market equilibrium: quantity demanded equals quantity supplied, economic profits are zero, no tendency for change

marginal product: additional output gained from adding one more unit of labour

minimum efficient scale: smallest quantity of output associated with lowest long-run average cost

normal profits: compensation for business owner's time and money; sum of implicit costs; what business owner must earn to do as well as best alternative use of time and money; average profits in other industries

short run: in microeconomics, a planning period for businesses where the quantities of some inputs are fixed, while the quantities of other inputs are variable

short-run market equilibrium: quantity demanded equals quantity supplied, but economic losses or profits lead to changes in supply

total cost: fixed costs plus variable costs

total product: total output that labourers produce when working with all fixed inputs

variable costs: change with changes in the quantity of output produced

Answers to Practice

1. **b** Definition.
2. **c** Best she could earn working somewhere else.
3. **d** Interest paid is an explicit cost that accountants subtract from revenues when calculating accounting profits.
4. **a** Definition of risk loving.
5. **d** Depreciation is an explicit cost.
6. **d** All implicit costs.
7. **a** Explicit costs, or out-of-pocket costs, are not hidden — the business pays them directly.
8. **c** Economic profits subtract implicit costs from accounting profits.
9. **d** If implicit costs are greater than accounting profits, economic profits are negative (economic losses).
10. **d** See definitions on page 165.
11. **d** All definitions of positive economic profits.
12. **c** Economic profit signals can be green (enter an industry), yellow (no change), or red (exit).

13. **d** Profits are the same as average profits in other industries. Businesses are just earning normal profits.

14. **b** Businesses exit the industry, so the market supply curve shifts leftward.

15. **a** Businesses enter, supply curve shift rightward, price falls, new equilibrium quantity increases. In long-run market equilibrium, economic profits are zero, which means businesses are just earning (positive) normal profits.

16. **c** The microeconomic short run is a planning period when at least one input is fixed, but other inputs are variable.

17. **c** Diminishing marginal productivity increases marginal costs.

18. **b** Marginal product (number of additional meals) of the variable input (workers) diminishes.

19. **b** Additional costs are ($310 – $200).

20. **a** *MC* is below *ATC* and is therefore pulling down *ATC*.

21. **a** Definition. In the long run there may be economies of scale, constant returns to scale, or diseconomies of scale.

22. **d** All are definitions of the *LRAC* curve.

23. **b** *LRAC* is horizontal. Total costs increase with output, but long-run average cost remains constant. Larger businesses have the same long-run costs as smaller businesses. *ATC* is a short-run concept.

24. **c** Definition. Since all inputs are variable in the long-run, **a** and **b** don't apply since they are short-run concepts.

25. **a** Definition. **b** and **d** are short-run concepts. **c** would be correct if it was where economies of scale end.

8 Market Structure and Pricing Power

LEARNING OBJECTIVES

L01 Use the distinction between price makers and price takers to describe differences between the market structures of monopoly, perfect competition, oligopoly, and monopolistic competition.

L02 Identify three main characteristics of market structure and explain their influence, with elasticity of demand, on a business's pricing power.

L03 Explain how businesses compete, and why the process of creative destruction improves productivity and living standards.

L04 Explain the roles of marginal revenue and marginal cost for smart business decisions about price and quantity, and state the rule that all price-taking and price-making businesses use to earn maximum profits in all market structures.

LEARN...

Do you prefer low or high prices? This is a trick question. If you answered "low prices," you were thinking as a consumer who buys Gatorade or headphones or doughnuts. If you answered "high prices," you were thinking as a business person who sells piercings, or web services, or your own hours of labour. In a market economy, we each play dual roles — as buyers (of the products and services we need) and as sellers (of inputs earning income).

As consumers or businesses, we rarely get to choose prices. Prices are determined through the interaction of demand and supply in markets. Prices settle somewhere between the maximum consumers are willing to pay (marginal benefit) and the minimum businesses are willing to accept (covering all marginal opportunity costs of production). Businesses generally seek higher prices, aiming for economic profits. Consumers seek lower prices that leave zero economic profits for businesses.

What determines exactly where market prices end up? Why are economic profits high in some markets and non-existent in others? The short answer is competition. This chapter explores how competition influences a business's power to price its products and services. That pricing power depends on what substitutes (competing products or services) are available to consumers and on the elasticity of demand.

Since we all sell something to earn income, whether as a business or a worker, knowing about competition helps you make smart choices in pricing your products and services, negotiating a salary, or competing with other sellers in your market.

Price Makers and Price Takers

 Use the distinction between price makers and price takers to describe differences between the market structures of monopoly, perfect competition, oligopoly, and monopolistic competition.

Think of yourself as a seller hoping to set high and profitable prices. Let's look at the competitive situations you might face, starting with the extremes of your best case and worst case. Then we'll look at the situations in between.

Monopoly

Here is an example of a seller's best case. It's Sunday night and your boss calls in a panic, begging you to work as many hours as possible next week. All your co-workers are sick and you are the only person who knows how to run the store. As the *only seller* of labour trained for that store, an economist would say you have a **monopoly**. The word monopoly comes from the Greek words "mono" (meaning "one") and "poly" (meaning "seller"). A monopoly is the only seller of a product or service — *no close substitutes are available.*

Price Maker   Instead of asking how many hours you will work at different wages, suppose your boss says, "I desperately need you to work 60 hours next week. I have no one else. Name your price." That power to set prices is called **market power**. A monopoly has maximum power to set prices. The only seller of a product or service that has no close substitutes is a **price maker**.

When Xerox Corporation developed the first photocopy machine in 1959, it had a monopoly. There were no other quick and inexpensive ways to copy a document. The only substitutes involved copying by hand, using carbon paper between two sheets of paper on a typewriter (when the typewriter keys pounded the first sheet, they also created a carbon copy on the paper behind), or going to a printing company. The original Xerox 914 machine leased for $95 per month (about $800 in today's dollars) and made enormous profits for Xerox. During the years before other photocopy machines appeared, Xerox earned profits at rates of 1000 percent — for every dollar Xerox spent, it got back $1000! Xerox was a highly profitable price maker with maximum pricing power.

Can't Force Buyers to Buy   While price makers have maximum power to set prices, their market power is still limited by what buyers are willing and able to pay. The law of demand always operates — higher prices mean lower quantity demanded. So the trade-off setting a higher price is lower sales. The price maker's goal is to find the price and quantity combination that yields the greatest profits. When your boss asks you to name your selling price for working, you could answer "one million dollars." It's a free country, and you can charge any price you want. But freedom exists for buyers, too — no one can be forced to buy. Your boss would likely laugh and close the store for the week because she would lose less by closing than by paying you $1 million. If Xerox set the price of its photocopiers much higher, customers might find it cheaper to go to printing companies or to pay for handwritten copies, or even to do without copies. The lower sales from higher prices might more than offset the higher price, so profits could be lower. Even monopoly price makers must live by the law of demand.

Inelastic Demand for Monopoly   The demand curve that a monopolist faces looks like Figure 1. The demand curve is steep and inelastic because there are no close substitutes. The law of demand applies — as the monopolist raises prices, quantity demanded decreases. When demand is inelastic, even a large percentage increase in price (from P_0 to P_1) causes only a small percentage decrease in quantity demanded (from Q_0 to Q_1). Because the increase in price is greater than the decrease in quantity demanded, higher prices increase total revenue (price × quantity) as long as demand is inelastic.

Figure 1   Monopoly's Inelastic Demand

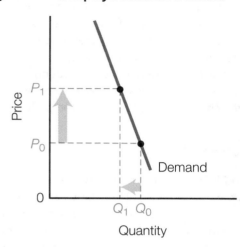

But if the price is set too high — $1 million — even a monopolist with maximum market power will have no buyers, no revenues, and no profits.

Perfect Competition

A small wheat farmer is a worst-case example of a seller's market power. Although the farmer is proud of the high-quality wheat he grows, thousands of other farmers in Canada and around the world are selling the identical product. Perfect substitutes for the farmer's wheat are instantly available.

Price Taker   If the market price of wheat is $4 per bushel, what chance does this farmer have of setting and getting a price higher than that? Even $4.01? The answer is zero. No buyer will pay even a penny more because he can easily get the identical product for $4. The farmer is a **price taker**, with no market power. This is a case of **perfect competition**, where many sellers produce identical products (perfect substitutes). Profits are limited to normal profits. The best this farmer, or any business in perfect competition, can hope for is to recover all of his opportunity costs of production, including normal profits. Economic profits are zero. This is the long-run market equilibrium scenario of Chapter 7. With no ability to raise prices, his only hope for economic profits is to produce at a lower cost than his competitors.

Demand Is Perfectly Elastic for Perfect Competition   A single small farmer or business in perfect competition faces a demand curve that looks like Figure 2. The demand curve is horizontal at the market price of $4 per bushel.

Figure 2   Perfectly Elastic Demand for Individual Business in Perfect Competition

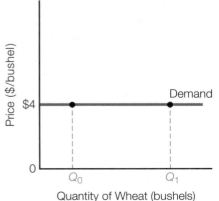

The bad news about being a small supplier in perfect competition is that you have no price-making power — you are a price taker. The good news is that no matter how much you supply (Q_0 or Q_1), the market will demand it. You will find buyers for any quantity you can produce, and you don't have to lower your price to sell more.

Because economic profits are zero, there is not much incentive to increase your capacity to produce output unless you can create a competitive advantage through lower costs, product differentiation, or innovation — strategies we will examine shortly.

Every business, or seller, dreams of being a price maker like a monopoly and dreads the prospect of perfect competition, where it is a passive price taker. Most business decisions are motivated by the desire for the economic profits and market power of a monopoly, yet the forces of competition are usually pushing businesses back toward their nightmare of perfect competition.

What factors common to all markets affect businesses' power to price? The answer is market structure — the characteristics that affect competition and a business's pricing power.

Oligopoly and Monopolistic Competition

If you think of monopoly as black and perfect competition as white, then most real-world market structures are in the many shades of grey between them. The markets in which you sell and buy as a business, worker, or consumer are almost all in between the extremes of monopoly and perfect competition. The most common market structures are oligopoly and monopolistic competition.

Oligopoly   An **oligopoly** is a market structure with a few big businesses that control most of the market. The word oligopoly again comes from the Greek — "oligos" ("few") and "poly" ("sellers"). The gaming hardware market is an oligopoly, with Microsoft, Sony, and Nintendo as the major sellers. Oligopolists are price makers, but don't have as much pricing power as a monopolist. Any time one of the major sellers changes its price, the others usually make a similar change. While there is product differentiation (playing with a Wii is different from playing on a PlayStation), the products are often fairly close substitutes — a characteristic closer to perfect competition. The cola market (Pepsi and Coke) is another example of an oligopoly. With available substitutes, demand is more elastic than for monopoly, but more inelastic than perfect competition.

Monopolistic Competition   **Monopolistic competition** is, by name, a mash-up of monopoly and perfect competition. Restaurants, piercing parlours, dry cleaners, and hair salons are all examples of monopolistic competition. Many small businesses are making similar but slightly differentiated products or services. The only hope for economic profits comes from the product differentiation that gives each business some slight pricing power, or from producing at lower cost. Businesses might differentiate their products or services to compete on quality, service, marketing, or price. Pricing power and elasticity of demand for monopolistic competition are closer to perfect competition than to monopoly.

Businesses in each market structure — monopoly, oligopoly, monopolistic competition, perfect competition — have different market power, ranging from the price-making power of monopoly to the passive price-taking of perfect competition. In the next sections you will learn more about market structure, other factors that determine market power, and how businesses use market power to compete.

Practice...

1. A monopolist
    a. is the only seller in a market.
    b. is a price maker.
    c. has no close substitute products or services.
    d. is all of the above.

2. The trade-off to setting a higher price is
    a. increased sales.
    b. decreased sales.
    c. increased revenues.
    d. nothing — there is no trade-off.

3. An individual business in perfect competition faces a demand curve that is
    a. perfectly inelastic.
    b. inelastic.
    c. elastic.
    d. perfectly elastic.

4. In perfect competition,
    a. every business produces a different product.
    b. a business has no incentive to keep costs low.
    c. a business can sell as much at it can produce, without lowering price.
    d. a business must lower its price to sell more.

5. Which market structure does *not* have pricing power?
    a. perfect competition
    b. monopolistic competition
    c. oligopoly
    d. monopoly

Apply...

1. Explain what limits the power of a price-making monopoly to raise prices.

    _____

    _____

    _____

    _____

2. Why will a business in a perfectly competitive industry choose not to charge a price either higher or lower than the market price?

    _____

    _____

    _____

    _____

    _____

to be continued

 **Apply...**

continued

3. Explain the connection between pricing power and elasticity of demand. Then use the connections between elasticity of demand and total revenue to explain why businesses want pricing power.

    _____

    _____

    _____

    _____

    _____

    _____

Market Structure

 Identify three main characteristics of market structure and explain their influence, with elasticity of demand, on a business's pricing power.

The markets for newly invented products (photocopiers in 1959, Apple's iPhone in 2007) and wheat are extreme cases. Most businesses are in between the extremes of all-powerful price makers and passive price takers. What factors common to all markets affect businesses' pricing power? The details of market structure — the characteristics that affect competition and a business's pricing power — provide the answer. **Market structure** has three main characteristics: available substitutes, number of competitors, and barriers preventing new competitors from entering the market. Let's look at each of these before re-examining the concept that sums up a business's pricing power — elasticity of demand.

"What's a Market" Depends on What's a Substitute

A market is not a place or a thing, it's a process — the interaction between buyers and sellers. A market brings together buyers and sellers of a *particular* product or service. *Particular* is an important word.

Broad Markets, More Substitutes, Less Pricing Power   How we define a market depends on how we define a *particular* product or service. In 2007, the iPhone was unique because of Apple's touchscreen software and distinctive design. There were other products combining cell phones, music players, and web browsers — the RIM BlackBerry and the Palm Treo. If we shift from a narrow definition of the market for iPhones to a broader definition of the market for smartphones — mobile cell/music/web devices — then Apple was no longer the single seller, and buyers had a wider set of choices. There are always substitutes. The more broadly we define a market the more substitutes there are, the more competitors there are, and the less pricing power businesses have.

Narrow Markets, Fewer Substitutes, More Pricing Power   The reverse is also true. The more narrowly we define a market, the fewer substitutes there are, the fewer competitors there are, and the more pricing power businesses have. For the broadly defined wheat market, our farmer has thousands of competitors, and consumers can choose among thousands of identical bushels of wheat. But the definition of the market gets narrower if the "buy and eat local" movement (eat only foods grown within 200 kilometres of where you live) becomes fashionable. Then farmers within a 200-kilometre radius of each city have far fewer competitors, and "buy local" consumers in those cities have fewer substitutes — meaning more inelastic demand. Local farmers gain market power, and we expect higher prices for locally grown wheat.

One more example for the coffee addicts out there. Do you have a favourite brand: Tim Hortons, Second Cup, or Starbucks? If you are a die-hard Tims addict, then you don't consider other brands as substitutes, and there is a limited number of sellers you'll buy from (probably only one or two Tims in your neighbourhood). But if all you want is hot caffeine, there are many substitutes and many sellers with less price power.

Product Differentiation, Fewer Substitutes, More Pricing Power
Businesses or sellers are always trying to develop brand loyalty among customers, because when customers rule out other substitutes, the seller has fewer competitors and greater ability to raise prices. Any attempt by a business to distinguish its product or service from those of competitors is called **product differentiation**. If the wheat farmer tried raising prices to (non-local) customers, his sales would fall to zero. But Tim Hortons can charge a higher price than 7-Eleven for coffee, and Apple can charge a higher price than generic phone manufacturers like Huawei. The more a seller can convince potential buyers that there are fewer substitutes out there, the more likely the seller will be a price maker rather than a price taker.

Product differentiation may come from actual product differences (smartphones may have different features, styles, pricing plans) or from advertising that attempts to convince you that one coffee brand is better, even though the coffee tastes pretty much the same.

Counting Competitors

Once you define your market and identify which products or services are substitutes, the second characteristic affecting competition and pricing power is the number of other businesses selling similar products or services. For all market structures, the general rule is *the fewer competitors, the more pricing power; the more competitors, the less pricing power*.

Counting your competitors is not always as easy as it seems. Some markets are mostly local. If you are a business selling piercings, dry cleaning, or fruits and vegetables, most of your customers and competitors are in a limited geographical area around you. You can easily identify them.

But other markets are not bound by geography, and counting competitors is hard. Wahid, in Chapter 7, located his web design business in the design district of the city because that's where most of his city customers expect to find design services. It's also where most of Wahid's local competitors are. But the Internet, digital technologies, video conferencing, and inexpensive airfares have exploded the geographical boundaries of competition.

Good and Bad News for Businesses   This explosion of competition is good and bad for businesses. The good news for Wahid is that he can extend his market, sell his services anywhere in the world, and increase his sales. The bad news is that design companies anywhere in the world can compete for Wahid's customers, which limits his pricing power. If you are selling design services, books, or movies, your competitors are not just local businesses, but also Chapters, Amazon, and sellers anywhere in the world connected through eBay or Kijiji or other websites. Counting competitors is hard!

Good News for Consumers   For consumers, the Internet's explosion of competition is generally good news — more choices and lower prices. When consumers can easily compare restaurants or hotels on Yelp! or Trip Advisor, businesses must keep prices close to those of competitors, reducing business pricing power.

Barriers to Entry

Competitors may be actual businesses already selling in your market, or potential sellers looking to enter your market because they are attracted to your high economic profits. When Xerox was earning profits at rates of 1000 percent per year, you can bet other businesses were very interested in figuring out how to start producing photocopy machines and getting a piece of that hugely profitable action. This is the green-light scenario from Chapter 7.

As new businesses enter a market, supply increases (market supply curve shifts rightward) and prices and economic profits fall. For a monopoly to continue earning economic profits, it must find ways to keep out potential competitors. Economists call ways to keep out competitors **barriers to entry**. There are two main types of barriers — legal barriers and economic barriers.

Legal Barriers to Entry   New inventions, like Xerox's photocopy machine or Apple's iPhone, or new production methods can be protected against competition by legal patents. A **patent** gives an inventor the exclusive right to supply a new product or service, or to license it to other businesses in exchange for royalty payments for 20 years in Canada. Apple took out more than 200 patents on the iPhone before the product appeared. Similarly, a legal **copyright** gives exclusive rights to the creator of a literary, musical, dramatic, or artistic work. Patents and copyrights give inventors property rights over their products, one of the rules of the game that is necessary for markets to work well.

So, governments keep new competitors out of a market by passing laws giving a business the exclusive right to supply a product or service. Why, I hope you are wondering, would the government restrict competition and help guarantee economic profits for certain businesses and artists? Patents and copyrights are necessary to create incentives encouraging the research, development, and creation of inventions and art that improve our standard of living and quality of life.

Imagine what might happen if patents and copyrights did not exist. Pharmaceutical companies can spend decades and invest tens of millions of dollars developing and producing new lifesaving drugs, like antibiotics, or costly drugs that end up failing. Without patents, competitors could buy the successful drugs, analyze their chemical composition, and create comparable drugs to sell at a much lower price. Competition would drive drug prices down to the cost of production, and the inventing company would never recover the research and development investment. As a business, why would you ever again spend money on research and development?

Patents and copyrights attempt to balance businesses' and artists' need for "incentives to invent" with consumers' desires for reasonably priced products and services. Once businesses and artists have a reasonable chance to recover their investments and earn economic profits, patents and copyrights expire. The entry of competitors forces down prices to where more consumers benefit. After patents expire, generic versions of drugs appear at much lower cost. For example, you can now buy no-name ibuprofen for much less money than Advil, which had the original, now-expired patent on the formula for ibuprophen.

Economics Barriers to Entry A business may be able to keep competitors out and economic profits high simply by being big. For most products, short-run average total cost (when some inputs are fixed and some are variable) — the total cost per unit of output — decreases as the business produces larger quantities of output. Long-run average costs (when all inputs are variable) also often decrease as business builds larger factories producing larger quantities of output. Economists describe this benefit of being big as **economies of scale** (lower long-run average costs at increased quantities of output — see Chapter 7 for more details about cost concepts). If a big business is already supplying most of a market, a new competitor trying to enter starts with lower sales and higher average total cost. The new business simply can't compete on price. Average total cost (both in the short run and long run) is the most important cost concept for understanding economic barriers to entry.

Competition and Elasticity of Demand

The three characteristics of market structure — available substitutes, number of businesses, and barriers to entry — make up the competitive environment for a business and determine its market power — its ability to be a price maker rather than a price taker. Market power determines where price settles between the maximum consumers are willing to pay and the minimum businesses are willing to accept (covering all opportunity costs of production). All three characteristics of market structure relate to elasticity of demand, which gives us a shortcut for understanding market power.

High Pricing Power with Inelastic Demand Businesses with the highest pricing power have the most inelastic demand. In 1959, Xerox had enormous power to set a high price for its photocopy machines. Like the extreme case of inelastic demand for insulin by diabetics, a rise in price caused almost no decrease in quantity demanded, because few good substitutes were available. Xerox was the only seller, and patents created barriers to the entry of new businesses.

With fewer substitutes, consumers have less choice and are in a weaker bargaining position. Businesses have more market power to be able to raise prices (be more of a price maker) and still keep selling. Product differentiation can create the same pricing power and decrease the elasticity of demand. If a business can develop brand loyalty, it makes demand for its product more inelastic.

Low Pricing Power with Elastic Demand Businesses with the lowest pricing power tend to have the most elastic demand. Take the extreme case of the demand for wheat. No farmer in perfect competition can raise his price without losing all sales because there are many perfect substitutes. There are many competing businesses and no barriers to entry.

With more substitutes, consumers have more choice and are in a stronger bargaining position. Businesses have no power to raise prices. With perfect substitutes there is no product differentiation or brand loyalty, so the demand for every supplier's particular bushel of wheat is perfectly elastic.

In general, the higher the pricing power, the more inelastic demand is. The lower the pricing power, the more elastic demand is.

Figure 3 gives you the different characteristics of the full range of market structures. These groupings of market structure are often used in media reporting of economic events, and we will use them again in Chapter 11 to talk about government policies to deal with abuses of competition and monopoly.

Figure 3   Market Structure and Pricing Power

Market Structure Characteristic	Monopoly	Oligopoly	Monopolistic Competition	Perfect Competition
Pricing Power	Price Maker (maximum pricing power)	Price Maker (much pricing power)	Price Maker (limited pricing power)	Price Taker (no pricing power)
Product Substitutes	No Close Substitutes	Differentiated Substitutes	Differentiated Substitutes	Many Perfect Substitutes
Number of Sellers	1	Few	Many	Great Many
Barriers to Entry	High	Medium	None	None
Elasticity of Demand	Inelastic	Inelastic	Elastic	Elastic

 Practice…

6. Which is *not* a main characteristic of market structure?

   a. number of competitors

   b. number of customers

   c. extent of product differentiation

   d. barriers preventing new entry

7. Monopolies can exist even though economic profits are supposed to attract entry from new businesses if there are

   a. economies of scale.

   b. legal barriers preventing new businesses from entering.

   c. economic barriers preventing new businesses from entering.

   d. all of the above.

8. Patents and copyrights increase market power by

   a. increasing the number of buyers.

   b. increasing the number of sellers.

   c. preventing other businesses from competing.

   d. encouraging other businesses to compete.

9. Economies of scale mean that as a business sells more output,

   a. long-run average cost decreases.

   b. long-run average cost increases

   c. monopoly power increases.

   d. it hires more workers.

10. Which combination of market structure characteristics is *correct*?

   a. broad markets, fewer substitutes, more pricing power

   b. broad markets, more substitutes, more pricing power

   c. narrow markets, fewer substitutes, more pricing power

   d. narrow markets, more substitutes, less pricing power

 **Apply...**

4. Why do governments around the world offer the monopoly protection of patents and copyrights?

   _____

   _____

   _____

   _____

   _____

   _____

5. Even after patents expire, brand-name drugs like Advil and Tylenol sell for more than chemically identical no-name generic drugs. Describe two strategies that the companies that produce the brand names can employ to keep existing customers and gain new ones. How can they get consumers to pay more for their brand names than for no-name generics?

   _____

   _____

   _____

   _____

   _____

   _____

   _____

   _____

6. You are thinking of opening a gardening business during the summer — you will cut, weed, rake, and water lawns. What market structure would you be competing in? Describe your pricing strategy using the term "elasticity of demand."

   _____

   _____

   _____

   _____

   _____

   _____

   _____

   _____

   _____

How Do Businesses Compete?

 Explain how businesses compete, and why the process of creative destruction improves productivity and living standards.

Competition in business takes many forms, but it is always an active attempt to increase profits and gain the market power of monopoly.

To Compete Is a Verb

Cutting Costs   Cutting costs is a key competitive weapon. If your business can reduce waste, find lower-cost raw materials, or develop new technologies that save money, you gain competitive options. With its ruthless efficiency, size, and buying power, Walmart is famous for forcing its suppliers to "cut to the bone" — to cut the prices of products they provide to Walmart to the lowest point possible. By cutting costs, a business can earn higher profits while matching competitors' prices, or by profitably cutting prices to attract customers away from competitors. Attracting customers is especially effective when demand is price elastic.

Improving Quality and Product Innovation   Instead of competing on price, a business may compete by providing a higher-quality product or by offering better service or warranty protection. Getting a post-secondary education differentiates your quality from high school graduates and earns you more pricing power in labour markets.

Improved quality also takes the form of new products. "To compete" may mean developing innovative new products like the photocopy machine or the iPhone. Innovation creates a product or service not available to your competition. These actions differentiate your product or service from those of your competitors, earning you some pricing power and inelasticity of demand.

Advertising and Brand Loyalty Advertising   Advertising can expand a business's market and establish brand loyalty that gives pricing power. Does your tablet have "Intel Inside"? Would you ever wear a pair of Gap jeans instead of Tommy Hilfiger? Advertising not only can make demand more inelastic, but also can increase the demand for your product or service by stealing customers from competitors, or by finding new consumers who didn't know about your product or service.

Eliminating Competition   Businesses also compete by buying out or merging with competitors to reduce substitutes and gain economies of scale. In 2012 Leon's Furniture bought out its rival The Brick to reduce Canadian competition. The buyout also gave the combined businesses economies of scale by creating a single national distribution network and online shopping service. Eliminating the competition reduces the number of available substitutes and increases a business's pricing power.

Building Barriers to Entry   Businesses can also gain market power by building barriers to entry. Have you ever wondered why there seems to be a Starbucks on every corner in some neighbourhoods? Is there really enough coffee business to go around? Don't more sales at one Starbucks come from fewer sales at the Starbucks down the block? Maybe. But the Starbucks business strategy is to take as many good locations as possible to prevent competitors from setting up at those locations. Densely spaced locations serve as a barrier to entry for other coffee competitors — there's just nowhere for them to open.

Here's another surprising example of a barrier to entry. The market for laundry detergent seems very competitive, with many, many substitute products — Tide, Ivory, Gain, Downy, Cheer. But all these products are made by the same company, Procter & Gamble (P&G). What about Wisk and All? Both made by Unilever. While the detergent market appears to be highly competitive, it is in fact an oligopoly, with just a few major players producing all the different products.

Why does P&G make so many competing brands? The variety serves as a barrier to entry to new businesses. If P&G made only one brand, a new supplier could target its advertising against a single competitive product and get noticed. But with five P&G products, each with advertising and brand loyalty, the chances of success for a new detergent are much lower, so most businesses don't even try.

What is common to all these competitive actions is the active attempt to beat your rivals using every possible tactic to increase your profits.

The Invisible Hand, Like Gravity, Is Unforgiving

Individual competitive actions by businesses spread quickly throughout a market, unless there are barriers like patents. Businesses that don't keep up with the competition suffer economic losses and eventually go bankrupt or out of business. Only businesses that stay competitive survive.

Economic Freedom   One of the great ironies of the market economy is that it provides all of us with extraordinary economic freedom — freedom to make business decisions, to invest and spend our money as we please, to choose our occupations, to pursue our own self-interest. These freedoms are greater than in any other economic system in history. But because we all, whether as businesses or individuals, play the role of sellers who depend on the market to earn a living, we must play by the market's competitive rules. Not every choice is really available to us all the time.

Competitive Pressure   The competitive pressure of the market limits the choices we can make if we want to succeed as a seller. For example, Wahid may believe advertising for his web design business is a waste of money. But if all his competitors advertise, and his sales suffer, he will be forced to advertise. As a caring boss, Paola may want to pay her piercing employees generous wages. But if her competitors pay less and can undercut her piercing prices and take all her customers, she must pay lower wages, cut other costs, or risk going out of business. After the successful introduction of Apple's iPhone, imagine the "choice" that competitors had about whether or not to innovate and attempt to match the iPhone's features — no choice at all. And even if you don't expect to run a business but dream of being a writer or an artist, if you can't sell your work you'll continue to be a restaurant server who does some art in your spare time. The market economy gives us tremendous freedom of choice, but the pressure of competition is relentless.

Matching competitors' actions usually means matching price cuts on existing products or services. Once a business takes a competitive action or tactic that generates economic profits, the forces of competition pull those profits back down to earth. Just like gravity pulls everything down to the ground, competitive forces are always pulling prices down toward the level of perfect competition, where businesses earn only normal profits. The only resistance to the downward pull of competitive prices comes from the pricing power your business develops because of product differentiation or barriers to entry. If prices are not forced down by the actions of competitors within your market, economic profits will attract new competitors, and the increased supply will pull down prices and profits. The market, like gravity, constantly puts downward pressure on prices.

Back to Long-Run Equilibrium   The price toward which competition continually pulls businesses is the **long-run market equilibrium** price of Chapter 7, which balances quantity demanded and quantity supplied, while businesses earn just normal profits. This equilibrium price coordinates the smart choices of consumers and businesses. No consumer is kicking himself for paying too much, and each business is earning the average rate of profits being earned in any other market (adjusted for risk and other market structure differences).

Paradoxically, the competitive actions businesses take pursuing the economic profits of monopoly pull each market back to a long-run equilibrium, where most businesses and products and prices are similar, prices just cover all opportunity costs of production, and businesses earn only normal profits, as in perfect competition. Competition is the force behind Adam Smith's invisible hand, channelling business self-interest — the dream of monopoly profits — to yield the unintended consequence of the production of all the products and services consumers want at the lowest possible costs.

Competition as Creative Destruction

When markets work well, businesses supply the products and services that consumers most want, and do so efficiently, at lowest cost. Not surprisingly, business leaders and wealthy individuals who benefit from markets make this claim all of the time. Even Karl Marx (1818–1883), the famous communist thinker and revolutionary, was a great admirer of the productivity of the market economy!

Why Marx Admired Capitalism   Marx was a severe critic of the market economy due to the inequalities in wealth he observed. He called it the capitalist system, referring to the capitalists who ran it as "the bourgeoisie" (the ruling class) and the workers he observed being exploited as "the proletariat" (wage labourers). At the same time, though, he recognized the market's great strength. In his call to revolution in *The Communist Manifesto* (1848, co-authored with Friedrich Engels), Marx wrote that "The bourgeoisie, during its rule of scarce one hundred years, has created more massive and more colossal productive forces than have all preceding generations together."

What makes market economies so enormously productive? Why are we so much better off than our great-grandparents? What accounts for these continual increases in our ability to produce products and services and the impressive increases in standards of living (whether those increases are spread equitably or inequitably across the population)? The answers lie in the same competitive forces of Adam Smith's invisible hand that channel the restless energy of profit-seeking self-interest into the public good.

The competitive actions that businesses take do much more than pull prices back to competitive levels, pull economic profits back to zero, and bring demand and supply into equilibrium. Over a longer period of time, these competitive innovations make businesses more productive and improve living standards and product choices for consumers.

Schumpeter's Creative Destruction   Joseph Schumpeter (1883–1950) was a brilliant economist who recognized that competition drove the ever-changing and ever-more-productive market economy. Business's competitive actions "incessantly revolutionize the economic structure from within, incessantly destroying the old one, incessantly creating a new one. This process of **creative destruction** is the essential fact about capitalism." (Is that not a great phrase — creative destruction?)

Competitive innovations not only generate economic profits for the winners, but also destroy the losers while making the world better for consumers. Computers made typewriters and carbon paper obsolete — have you ever used a typewriter at all, let alone to make carbon copies? DVDs destroyed VHS tapes, digital downloads and mobile music players destroyed CDs and DVDs, LED lights are eliminating incandescent bulbs, robotic assembly lines replaced the jobs of craftspeople who used to make cars and clothing and bread. All these innovations were introduced in the competitive quest for monopoly profits, but ended up improving living standards while destroying the less productive or less desirable products and services and production methods. The resources that used to make now obsolete products and services moved into new, more productive industries.

This incessant process of change is behind many of the controversial competitive trends we see today. Jobs in Canada are being destroyed as corporations move manufacturing to Asia and "off-shore" their coding and call-centre jobs to India. The outcome is more efficient businesses, with cheaper products and services for most of us (understanding that a win for consumers as a whole can still have individual losers — sellers and workers in the destroyed markets).

The innovations of the Canadian business RIM (BlackBerry) revolutionized business communication, making it faster and more efficient, while earning handsome profits for shareholders. But BlackBerry's success destroyed jobs among competitors, reduced business profits in competing forms of communication, and eliminated jobs for secretaries who used to handle business correspondence. Then BlackBerry itself was attacked by those same continuous forces of creative destruction.

The inherent and incessant change and growth of the market economy comes from unleashing the power of self-interest in all humans, but channelling it through competition and the invisible hand to improve living standards. This strength of a market economy is also a weakness. Sometimes the quest for monopoly power is so excessive and successful that it is not in the public interest. When competition fails, governments step in with competition laws, which we will examine in Chapter 11. Constant change can also contribute to "boom and bust" cycles of economic activity, which are the focus of much of macroeconomics.

But before we get to any of that, we will look more closely at how businesses in any market structure make smart choices of the precise combination of price and quantity that yields maximum profits.

Practice...

11. Business competition takes many forms, but the goal of most businesses is to act like
    a. a competitive business.
    b. the invisible hand.
    c. a monopoly.
    d. oligopolists.

12. When one business discovers a successful technique,
    a. other businesses avoid the same technique.
    b. the government should take over this business.
    c. businesses in other industries will go bankrupt.
    d. other businesses in the industry try to copy it.

13. Which is usually *not* a goal of advertising?
    a. making your demand less elastic
    b. making your demand more elastic
    c. stealing customers from your competitors
    d. increasing demand for your product

14. Businesses compete by
    a. decreasing quantity supplied.
    b. reducing barriers to entry.
    c. raising prices.
    d. cutting costs.

15. When Starbucks replaces its workers with cost-saving robot baristas, the process is called
    a. creative destruction.
    b. destructive creationism.
    c. extra-bold roasting.
    d. natural selection.

 **Apply...**

7. In 2015, the photography retailer Blacks Camera closed all 59 of its stores. Blacks used to be the largest, most powerful photography business in Canada. Explain what happened, who wins, and who loses from the Blacks shutdown.

_____
_____
_____
_____
_____
_____
_____

8. Explain why Karl Marx was a great admirer of the productivity of capitalism and its potential to raise living standards by "producing the goods" (if the "goods" were more equally distributed among families).

_____
_____
_____
_____
_____
_____
_____
_____
_____
_____

9. Markets combine freedom of choice with tremendous competitive pressure to supply products and services that markets value. This combination is connected to the age-old philosophical question about whether humans have free will, or whether our choices are all determined by other forces in society. Argue that your choice of "what you want to be when you grow up" is an example of free will. Then argue that the freedom of your choice is an illusion and that your choice is determined by economic forces in society.

Your instructor may use this question for a class discussion.

Pricing for Profits

 Explain the roles of marginal revenue and marginal cost for smart business decisions about price and quantity, and state the rule that all price-taking and price-making businesses use to earn maximum profits in all market structures.

Imagine you run a business and have some pricing power. How do you find the combination of price and quantity that gives you maximum profits? There are so many variables to consider. On the demand side, how much are your customers willing to pay, and how much will your sales decrease if you raise prices? On the supply side, what are your costs, and are they increasing, decreasing, or constant as you increase quantity? And what about the competition — what substitutes are available, how many other businesses are you competing against, and what barriers are keeping out new competitors?

Rule for Maximum Profits

Making a smart business choice about price and quantity sounds complicated. Do you need to hire an economist? Actually, you don't — business owners make these decisions on their own all the time simply by following one rule. It's simple enough to state in one sentence, and it yields smart choices no matter how much or how little pricing power a business has.

> Estimate marginal revenues and marginal costs,
> then set the highest price that allows you to sell the highest quantity
> for which marginal revenue is greater than marginal cost.

The important terms in this rule are *marginal revenue* and *marginal cost*.

Let's look at a simple business decision to get a feel for the roles of marginal revenue and marginal cost.

Suppose Paola's Parlour for Piercing and Nails is open weekdays from 11 a.m. to 7 p.m. Some of Paola's customers tell her it would be more convenient for them if the shop stayed open later, until 10 p.m. Is it smart for Paola to stay open later?

Marginal Revenue   How would you make that decision? Well, a smart business decision will increase Paola's profits, and profits increase when revenues are greater than costs. To determine if Paola increases her profits by staying open later, you need to know her *additional revenues* and her *additional costs*. Additional revenues are how much additional money she will take in selling piercings and nail sets during those three extra hours. Economists call additional revenues **marginal revenue**. Marginal revenue can be calculated as the change in total revenue — revenue from additional sales between 7 p.m. and 10 p.m. — or as the revenue from selling one more unit of a product or service.

Marginal Cost   Be careful about estimating additional costs. The additional three hours of wages Paola must pay her employees clearly count, as do costs of additional studs, nail polish, and extra electricity from operating lights and equipment. These are all variable costs. The additional costs Paola must pay as a result of staying open later are **marginal costs** — changes in her variable costs. Fixed costs, like rent or insurance, do not change with the decision to stay open later. Fixed costs do not change with changes in the quantity of output a business produces. Fixed costs do not affect smart decisions — only marginal costs do.

Choose When Marginal Revenues Are Greater Than Marginal Costs
If Paola's estimated marginal revenues are greater than her marginal costs, her profits increase by staying open later. It's a smart decision and she and her customers will be happy. But if her estimated marginal costs are greater than her marginal revenues, her profits decrease. If marginal costs are greater than marginal revenues, she should continue to close at 7 p.m., even though it means a few disappointed evening customers.

Whether it's extending hours, introducing a new product or service, opening a new location, launching an advertising campaign, or hiring new employees (more on this in Chapter 13) — any of these decisions are smart as long as estimated marginal revenues are greater than marginal costs. Businesses always compare marginal revenues and marginal costs in making smart decisions.

With that simple snapshot, let's look in more detail at marginal revenues and marginal costs.

Marginal Revenue

Marginal revenue depends on market structure — how competitive your industry is, and whether your business is a price taker or a price maker.

Let's return to our farmer selling wheat in a market structure of perfect competition. The market price of a bushel of wheat is $4 and he is a price taker. As one of many small farmers, he can sell as much as he can produce at that $4 price. He can't charge a higher price, or he will lose all of his customers. And he has no reason to charge a lower price if he can get $4 per bushel.

Last year, he planted and harvested 10 000 bushels of wheat and sold his crop for $40 000. That $40 000 was his total revenue — price × quantity. This year he plants more wheat, harvests 11 000 bushels, and sells his crop at $4 a bushel for $44 000. His total revenue increased from $40 000 to $44 000.

The farmer's decision to plant more wheat is like Paola's decision to keep her shop open later. Both decisions increase total revenue.

Marginal revenue can be defined and calculated in two ways: change in total revenue and revenue from selling one more unit.

Change in Total Revenue   The farmer's total revenue increases by $4000, from $40 000 to $44 000. This is the marginal revenue from the farmer's decision to plant more wheat. Marginal revenue is the change in total revenue.

Revenue from Selling One More Unit   Marginal revenue can also be defined and calculated as the additional revenue from selling one more unit of your product or service. The farmer gets additional revenue of $4000 from selling an additional 1000 bushels of wheat. So his additional revenue per bushel is $4000 divided by 1000 bushels — $4 per bushel.

Marginal Revenue Equals Price for Price Takers   The calculation of marginal revenue per unit is obvious when a business is a price taker in perfect competition. The wheat farmer's decision to produce more wheat has no effect on the market because as a small producer — one of thousands of suppliers — his increase in supply does not affect market supply or market price. Each small business in perfect competition can sell as many units as it can produce at the market price, so the marginal revenue for each additional unit sold is the price.

The demand curve facing an individual business in perfect competition looks like Figure 4 on the next page. And since marginal revenue equals price, this demand curve is also a marginal revenue curve.

Figure 4 Demand and Marginal Revenue for Price Takers

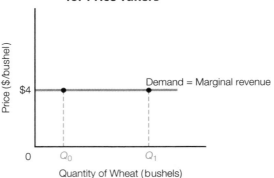

To read Figure 4 as a demand curve, start at the price and go over and down to the quantity. At the market price of $4 per bushel, the market will demand any quantity that you can produce (for example, Q_0 or Q_1). You don't have to lower your price to sell more in perfect competition.

This demand curve is also a marginal revenue curve. You read a marginal revenue curve the same way you read a marginal benefit curve or marginal cost curve. Start at the quantity, and go up and over to the marginal revenue. Whether the farmer is selling his 10th bushel (suppose Q_0 = 10) or his 10 000th bushel (suppose Q_1 = 10 000), going up and over to the price axis, the marginal revenue is $4. Each bushel brings the farmer a marginal revenue equal to the price of a bushel of wheat.

What seems so obvious for price takers turns out *not* to be true for price makers. Not all demand curves double as marginal revenue curves. We will discuss marginal revenue for price makers in Chapter 10.

Marginal Cost

The rule for maximum profits is:

> Estimate marginal revenues and marginal costs,
> then set the highest price that allows you to sell the highest quantity
> for which marginal revenue is greater than marginal cost.

So far we've discussed marginal revenue. What about marginal cost?

Different businesses have different marginal cost patterns. To learn more about marginal cost, we have to shift our focus to the supply side, which depends on costs. Let's look at the two most likely patterns of what happens to marginal cost as quantity increases — increasing marginal cost and constant marginal cost.

Figure 5 shows increasing (a) and constant (b) marginal costs.

Increasing Marginal Cost Paola's shop is busy, with all her employees either piercing or nail painting. If a busload of tourists shows up all wanting piercings, what happens to Paola's marginal costs as she tries to increase piercing output?

Figure 5 Increasing and Constant Marginal Costs

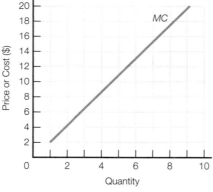

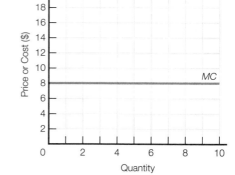

a) Increasing Marginal Cost   b) Constant Marginal Cost

There is not enough time to call in additional employees, so the only way for Paola to supply more piercings is to shift employees away from nail painting. Chapter 2 illustrated that as she switches employees from nail painting to piercing her marginal opportunity costs increase. She switches her worst nail painters first and doesn't lose much, but eventually she has to switch her best nail painters and loses more nail revenues. Of course, she is earning more revenues on the piercing side to offset the reduced revenues on the nail side. Her ultimate choice, as we will see in Chapter 10, depends on a comparison of marginal revenues and marginal costs. But for now, we are just looking at the cost side, and Paola has increasing marginal costs as she increases her output of piercings.

Diminishing Marginal Productivity   The wheat farmer in perfect competition provides a different example of increasing marginal costs. As in the Chapter 7 description, as the farmer adds more labour to fixed amounts of land and other inputs, the marginal product of each additional labourer decreases because of diminishing marginal productivity. When increases in output lead to **diminishing marginal productivity**, marginal costs increase.

Most businesses operating close to capacity have increasing marginal costs as they try to increase output. Increasing output can mean adding more employees, or more employee hours, often at more expensive overtime rates. In some businesses, like oil drilling, to increase output they must shift to more expensive sources of inputs, like going from easily drilled oil wells to more difficult and costly oil sands extraction. There are businesses in all market structures — perfect competition, monopolistic competition, oligopoly, and monopoly — that have increasing marginal costs. Their marginal cost curves look like Figure 5a, sloping up to the right. As quantity increases, marginal cost also increases.

Constant Marginal Cost   If Paola's shop is not very busy when the busload of piercing-seeking tourists arrives, what happens to her marginal costs?

If Paola is already paying her employees for being at work, those wages are a sunk cost. What are Paola's additional costs in increasing her output of piercings? Remember, fixed costs like rent and insurance do not change with increases in output. Paola's additional costs, or the marginal cost of one more piercing, is just the cost of the stud and the additional electricity used by the piercing gun. That is a small, constant amount for each additional piercing.

Most businesses that are *not* operating near capacity have constant marginal costs as they increase output. If the wheat farmer has unused land and equipment, each additional labourer can use those inputs to produce as much wheat as each previous labourer, for a constant cost per bushel. If a plane is not full, what is the marginal cost of adding one more passenger? A very small amount — the cost of snacks served (if any, these days!), and the tiny increase in fuel consumption for the extra weight of the passenger and luggage. All other costs of flying this extra passenger (salaries, airport landing fees, advertising, cost of buying new airplanes) are fixed costs — they do not change with one additional ticket. The same goes for the constant marginal cost of a seat in a movie theatre.

Many price makers in the market structures of monopolistic competition, oligopoly, and monopoly have constant marginal costs. Their marginal cost curves look like the horizontal line in Figure 5b — as quantity increases, marginal cost stays constant.

In making a smart business decision, you need to identify if your business has increasing marginal costs or constant marginal costs. But no matter whether your marginal costs are increasing or constant, the same rule applies for pricing for maximum profits.

Estimate marginal revenues and marginal costs,
then set the highest price that allows you to sell the highest quantity
for which marginal revenue is greater than marginal cost.

Chapter 9 applies the rule for profit maximization to price takers in perfect competition, and Chapter 10 applies the rule to price makers in the less-than-perfect-competition market structures of monopoly, oligopoly, and monopolistic competition.

 # Practice...

16. It is a smart business decision to increase output as long as marginal revenue is more than

    a. zero.

    b. price.

    c. average total cost.

    d. marginal cost.

17. The marginal revenue from selling the 4th seat on an airplane is the difference between the

    a. costs for the 3rd and 4th seats.

    b. prices charged for the 3rd and 4th seats.

    c. total revenue gained from the 3rd and 4th seats.

    d. marginal revenue gained from the 3rd and 4th seats.

18. The marginal revenue curve for a price-taking business in perfect competition

    a. is a horizontal line.

    b. is the same as the business's demand curve.

    c. intercepts the vertical axis at the market price of the product.

    d. is all of the above.

19. Businesses operating near capacity have

    1 increasing marginal costs.

    2 constant marginal costs.

    3 upward-sloping marginal cost curves.

    4 horizontal marginal cost curves.

    a. 1 and 3

    b. 1 and 4

    c. 2 and 3

    d. 2 and 4

20. A business probably has constant marginal costs if

    a. workers are messaging constantly instead of working.

    b. customers are angry that wait times at the checkout are ridiculously long.

    c. it is paying workers increased overtime-pay rates

    d. it sells Christmas trees and it is the Christmas season.

 **Apply...**

10. The Vanherk family has a pig farm in a small town near Stratford, Ontario. The family currently charges the market price because the pig market is extremely competitive. Explain why the Vanherk family has no ability or incentive to raise or lower its pig prices.

_____

_____

_____

_____

11. Explain how each of these decisions will be a smart choice by comparing estimated marginal revenues with marginal costs. For each decision, do you think marginal costs will be constant or increasing?

   a. launching an advertising campaign

_____

_____

_____

_____

   b. hiring a new employee

_____

_____

_____

_____

   c. extending business hours

_____

_____

_____

_____

12. What if, when the busload of piercing-seeking tourists arrives at Paola's busy shop, she has employees on standby (each with her own tools) who she could bring in very quickly, and who would be paid their regular hourly wage? What difference, if any, would that make to Paola's marginal cost of increasing piercing output?

_____

_____

_____

_____

_____

KNOW...

Learning Objectives

1. Businesses aim for **monopoly's** economic profits and **market power** as a **price maker**. Competitors usually push businesses toward the normal profits of a **price taker** in **perfect competition**. Market power depends on **market structure**. The four main market structures are **monopoly, oligopoly, monopolistic competition**, and **perfect competition.**

2. Pricing power depends on the competitiveness of a business's **market structure** — available substitutes, number of competitors, barriers to the entry of new competitors — and on elasticity of demand. Pricing power increases with more narrowly defined markets, fewer substitutes, product differentiation, and fewer competitors. Pricing power also increases with more **barriers to entry** — through **patents** and **copyrights** or **economies of scale**.

3. Business **competition** is an active attempt to increase profits and gain the pricing power of monopoly. This process of **creative destruction** drives competitors who do not respond out of business, while unintentionally improving productivity and living standards for all.

4. The rule for profit maximization for all price-making and price-taking businesses is "Estimate marginal revenues and marginal costs, then set the highest price that allows you to sell the highest quantity for which marginal revenue is greater than marginal cost." **Marginal revenue** depends on market structure, and **marginal cost** can be either increasing (from **diminishing marginal productivity**) or constant (for businesses not operating near capacity).

Key Terms

barriers to entry: legal or economic barriers preventing new competitors from entering a market

competition: active attempt to increase profits and gain the market power of monopoly

copyright (and **patent):** exclusive property rights to sell or license creations, protecting against competition

creative destruction: competitive business innovations generate economic profits for winners, improve living standards for all, but destroy less productive or less desirable products and production methods

diminishing marginal productivity: as you add more of a variable input to fixed inputs, the marginal product of the variable input eventually diminishes

economies of scale: lower long-run average costs at increased quantities of output

long-run market equilibrium: quantity demanded equals quantity supplied, economic profits are zero, no tendency for change

marginal cost: additional opportunity cost of increasing quantity supplied, changes with circumstances

marginal revenue: additional revenue from more sales or from selling one more unit of output

market power: business's ability to set prices

market structure: the characteristics that affect a business's pricing power — available substitutes, number of competitors, and barriers to entry

monopolistic competition: many small businesses make similar, but slightly differentiated products or services

monopoly: only seller of a product or service; no close substitutes available

oligopoly: a few big sellers control most of the market

patent (and copyright): exclusive property rights to sell or license creations, protecting against competition.

perfect competition: many sellers producing identical products or services

price maker: monopoly with maximum power to set prices

price taker: business with zero power to set prices

product differentiation: attempt to distinguish a product or service from those of competitors

Answers to Practice

1. **d** Definition.
2. **b** Even price makers must live by the law of demand.
3. **d** The demand curve is horizontal at the market price, which the individual business must take.
4. **c** The bad news for a business in perfect competition is that it is a price taker; the good news is that the market demands whatever quantity it produces without lowering price.
5. **a** All businesses are price takers. Zero pricing power.
6. **b** Customers not one of the three characteristics of market structure.
7. **d** All are barriers to entry.
8. **c** Patents and copyrights are barrier to entry.
9. **a** The definition of economies of scale is lower *long-run* average costs at increased quantities of output, but businesses can also have lower short-run average total costs at increased quantities of output.
10. **c** The market for designer blue jeans is narrower than the entire blue jean market. Designer businesses have more pricing power with consumers who won't consider generic blue jeans as substitutes.
11. **c** All businesses dream of being a price maker like a monopoly, and dread the state of perfect competition where they have no pricing power.
12. **d** Businesses must at least match — if not better — the actions of other competitors in a market in order to survive.
13. **b** More elastic demand means *less* pricing power.
14. **d** Other competitive actions are improving quality, advertising, eliminating competition, and building entry barriers.

15. **a** Creative destruction improves living standards for all, but destroys less productive production methods.

16. **d** Rule for profit maximization.

17. **c** Marginal revenue is the change in total revenue. If the price, for example, of all seats was $200, then answers **b** and **d** both equal zero, when the marginal revenue is actually $200.

18. **d** See Figure 4 on page 210.

19. **a** Increasing marginal cost from diminishing marginal productivity means increasing output increases marginal cost.

20. **a** Unused labour time indicates unused capacity.

9 Perfect Competition

LEARNING OBJECTIVES

L01 Explain why marginal revenue equals price for price-taking businesses in perfect competition.

L02 Demonstrate how the marginal cost curve determines the supply curve for businesses in perfect competition.

L03 Explain the three possible short-run economic profit scenarios in perfect competition.

L04 Explain economic losses and profits as signals for businesses to exit or enter perfectly competitive industries, which changes supply and achieves economic efficiency.

LEARN...

All businesses dream of gaining monopoly's price-making power and economic profits. But businesses have nightmares about competitive forces that push toward perfect competition's price taking and normal profits.

By combining the cost-curve information from Chapter 7 with the market-structure information from Chapter 8, a business in perfect competition can make smarter decisions. How do businesses decide what quantity to supply? Where does the upward-sloping supply curve come from? How do marginal costs affect other business costs? Exactly how do economic profits direct the invisible hand?

Marginal revenue and marginal cost are the most important concepts for answering these questions.

Although perfectly competitive markets are not common in the real world, there are three important reasons to examine them. First, some markets closely approximate perfectly competitive markets. The analysis in this chapter gives direct and useful insights into the behaviour of these markets. Second, perfect competition allows us to isolate the effects of competitive forces that are at work in *all* markets, even in those that do not match the assumptions of perfect competition. Third, the perfectly competitive model is a useful standard for evaluating the relative efficiency of different market structures in later chapters.

Marginal Revenue and Price

 LO1 Explain why marginal revenue equals price for price-taking businesses in perfect competition.

The market structure of **perfect competition** has

- many small businesses.
- identical products.
- no barriers to entry.
- zero pricing power.

Many sellers produce identical (or standardized) products or services. With no barriers to entry, it is easy for businesses to enter the industry if there are economic profits, and easy to exit the industry if there are economic losses. As a result, all businesses are price takers.

The wheat industry is a good example of the market structure of perfect competition. Each business is a price taker, but can sell as much output as it can produce at the market price. Figure 1a shows the market demand and supply curves for the wheat industry. At the intersection of demand and supply, the equilibrium, market-clearing price for wheat is $4 per bushel.

Figure 1 **Perfect Competition Industry and Individual Business Demand and Price**

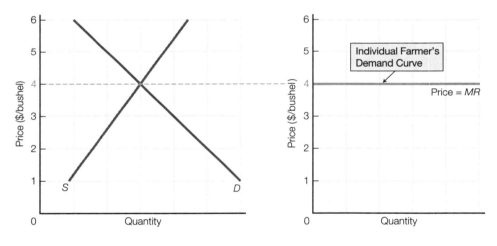

a) Wheat Industry   b) Individual Wheat Farmer

The demand curve facing an individual wheat farmer in Figure 1b is the horizontal line at the market price of $4 per bushel. No buyer will pay even a penny more than $4 because she can easily get the identical product elsewhere for $4. Because the small farmer can sell as much wheat as he can grow at the price of $4, there is no need to lower price to sell more. **Marginal revenue** equals price. This horizontal demand curve is also a marginal revenue curve for the farmer.

The market structure of perfect competition has a simple relationship between marginal revenue and price: They are the same. That's why this section is so short! (Pages 209-210 in Chapter 8 explain in more detail why marginal revenue equals price for a business in perfect competition.)

Practice...

1. Which is *not* a characteristic of perfect competition?

   a. downward-sloping industry demand curve

   b. horizontal demand curve facing each individual business

   c. slightly differentiated products

   d. each business decides its quantity of output

2. A business facing a perfectly elastic demand curve for its product

   a. is not a price taker.

   b. wants to lower its price to increase sales.

   c. wants to raise its price to increase total revenue.

   d. has a marginal revenue curve equal to the price of the product.

Three points on the demand curve for a perfectly competitive business are

Price	Quantity
$4	8
$4	9
$4	10

Use this information to answer questions 3 and 4.

3. If the business sells 8 units of output, its total revenue is

   a. $4.

   b. $32.

   c. $36.

   d. $40.

4. If the business increases output from 8 units to 9 units, marginal revenue is

   a. $4.

   b. $32.

   c. $36.

   d. $40.

5. The demand curve for an individual business in perfect competition is

   a. perfectly elastic.

   b. perfectly inelastic.

   c. also the business's marginal cost curve.

   d. also the business's total revenue curve.

 **Apply...**

1. Explain the difference between the shape of the demand curve facing a perfectly competitive business and the shape of the demand curve facing a monopoly. What explains the differences in shape?

2. Even though perfect competition is not common in the real world, list three justifications for spending time on understanding perfectly competitive market structures. Your instructor may use this question for class discussion.

3. Identify an industry other than wheat that fits the description of perfect competition. Explain your choice.

Marginal Cost Curve Determines the Individual Business Supply Curve

 Demonstrate how the marginal cost curve determines the supply curve for businesses in perfect competition.

Every price-taking business in perfect competition must accept the market price. Without any pricing power, the only business decision is what quantity of output to produce.

Using just the **marginal cost** curve and the **average total cost curve** from Chapter 7, we can explain the wheat farmer's quantity decision, the upward-sloping supply curve, and how profits direct the invisible hand.

To make a smart choice, our wheat farmer, like any business in any market structure, follows the rule for profits.

> Estimate marginal revenues and marginal costs,
> then set the highest price that allows you to sell the highest quantity
> for which marginal revenue is greater than marginal cost.

Marginal revenue equals the market price of $4 per bushel of wheat. Marginal costs appear on the marginal cost curve. The farmer's only decision is to find the highest quantity for which marginal revenue is greater than marginal cost.

Figure 2   Smart Quantity Choice for Economic Profits with Different Prices

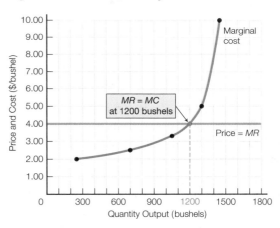

a) Smart Quantity Choice for Economic Profits when Price = $4

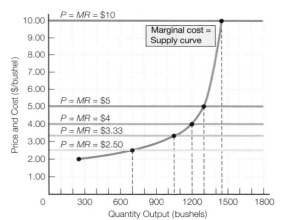

b) Smart Quantity Choice for Economic Profits with Different Prices

Maximum Economic Profits Where $MR = MC$

Applying the rule for profits to Figure 2a, the farmer's smart choice for the quantity of output is 1200 bushels of wheat. The horizontal marginal revenue curve and the upward-sloping marginal cost curve intersect at the quantity 1200 bushels. If the farmer produces any less, marginal revenue is greater than marginal cost for each bushel, so the farmer misses out on profits. If the farmer produces more than 1200 bushels, marginal cost is greater than marginal revenue. The farmer loses money on every bushel above 1200. So 1200 bushels is the smart choice of quantity for maximum profits.

Figure 2b on the previous page shows the farmer's smart quantity decision for different prices that might be set in the wheat market. If the market price is $2.50, the marginal revenue and marginal cost curves intersect at 700 bushels, which is the quantity supplied yielding maximum profits at that price. At a market price of $5, the marginal revenue and marginal cost curves intersect at 1300 bushels, which is the quantity supplied yielding maximum profits at that price. Using this simple graph, the wheat farmer can easily choose the quantity of wheat to supply at any given price to earn maximum profit.

Marginal Cost Curve Determines the Supply Curve The **law of supply** states that if the price of a product or service rises, the quantity supplied increases. An increase in price increases quantity supplied as you move up along the supply curve.

You have just traced the supply curve of the individual farmer! Look at Figure 3, which pairs different market prices with the quantity supplied by the farmer at each price.

Figure 3   Individual Wheat Farmer's Supply of Wheat

Price (S per bushel)	Quantity Supplied (bushels per year)
$ 2.50	700
$ 3.33	1050
$ 4.00	1200
$ 5.00	1300
$10.00	1450

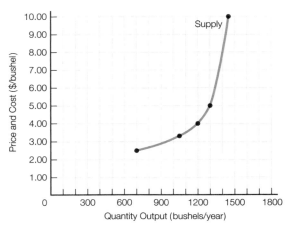

A supply curve shows, for any price, what the business's quantity supplied will be. For each price, there is a quantity supplied that is best for the farmer — the quantity that results in maximum profits. In general, the marginal cost curve is the supply curve for a business in perfect competition.

The marginal cost curve is a supply curve "in general" because businesses will not supply at prices that are so low they don't even cover variable costs. In the graph for Figure 3, notice that the farmer does not supply any wheat below a market price of approximately $2. The supply curve does not go down to a zero price.

(Your textbook or instructor may include the average variable cost curve on similar diagrams. In perfect competition, the minimum price a business will accept is at the intersection of the marginal cost curve and average variable cost curve. That point of intersection is also called the **shutdown point***. I have purposefully omitted the average variable cost curve to make it easier to focus on the most important parts of supply decisions — marginal cost and average total cost.)*

Market Supply Curve The market supply curve comes from adding up all individual business's supply curves. For any price, the market supply curve shows the total quantity supplied from all businesses in the industry. If there are 1000 identical wheat farmers, the market supply curve for wheat is shown in Figure 4.

Figure 4   Market Supply of Wheat with 1000 Farmers

Price (\$ per bushel)	Quantity Supplied (bushels per year)
\$ 2.50	700 000
\$ 3.33	1 050 000
\$ 4.00	1 200 000
\$ 5.00	1 300 000
\$10.00	1 450 000

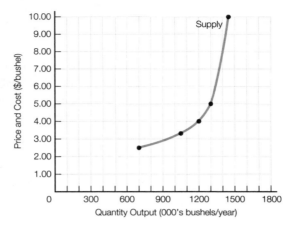

The market supply curve also slopes upward to the right — as price increases, quantity supplied increases — since all identical businesses face **diminishing marginal productivity**. Diminishing marginal productivity — the source of increasing marginal costs as output increases — is the most important force determining the upward slope of individual business and market supply curves in perfect competition.

Add diminishing marginal productivity to the list of reasons you have learned for how higher prices create incentives for increased quantity supplied:

- Higher prices are necessary to cover increasing marginal costs that arise because inputs are not equally productive in all activities.

- Higher prices can bring higher profits, whether marginal costs are increasing or constant.

- Higher prices are necessary to cover increasing marginal costs that arise from diminishing marginal productivity.

The rule for profits explains the smart decisions about quantity supplied along a supply curve for a wheat farmer in perfect competition. The law of supply works as long as other factors besides price do not change.

The next section of this chapter uses the average total cost curve and economic profits to explore changes in supply — shifts of the supply curve — when one of those other factors does change.

Practice...

6. In perfect competition, each business
   a. chooses price but not quantity of output.
   b. chooses quantity of output but not price.
   c. chooses both price and quantity of output.
   d. cannot choose either price or quantity of output.

7. If a perfectly competitive business follows the rule for profits, we know that
   a. $MR = MC$.
   b. Price = MC.
   c. Price = MR.
   d. all of the above are true.

8. The supply curve for a business in perfect competition is generally its
   a. marginal product curve.
   b. marginal revenue curve.
   c. marginal cost curve.
   d. average total cost curve.

9. A perfectly competitive industry has 100 identical businesses. When the price is $50, one business's quantity supplied is 7 units and market supply is
   a. 350 units.
   b. 700 units.
   c. 5000 units.
   d. impossible to calculate without more information.

10. In perfect competition, the market supply curve
    a. comes from adding up the quantity supplied by all businesses at each price.
    b. comes from adding up the price charged by all businesses at each quantity.
    c. is vertical at the total quantity of output produced by all businesses.
    d. is horizontal at the market-clearing price.

 **Apply...**

4. Explain why the marginal cost curve is also the supply curve for businesses in perfect competition.

   _____

   _____

   _____

   _____

   _____

   _____

   _____

   _____

5. If the market price of wheat falls from $5 to $4 per bushel in Figure 2 on page 221, calculate the change in the farmer's quantity-supplied decision. Explain why the farmer makes that change.

   _____

   _____

   _____

   _____

   _____

   _____

   _____

   _____

   _____

   _____

6. Give three different explanations for how higher prices create incentives for increased quantity supplied.

   _____

   _____

   _____

   _____

   _____

   _____

   _____

   _____

   _____

   _____

   _____

   _____

Short-Run Equilibrium

 Explain the three possible short-run economic profit scenarios in perfect competition.

There is another smart choice for a business in perfect competition — whether to stay in its current industry or move to a different industry.

As discussed in Chapter 2, a change in the number of businesses is one of the six factors that can change supply, shifting the supply curve. When businesses exit or enter an industry, the industry supply curve shifts. To make the smart decision to go or to stay, the business needs to know about its economic losses or profits. That's where the average total cost curve — which includes normal profits — comes in.

Three Short-Run Economic Profit Scenarios

Figures 5 to 7 show three different short-run economic profit scenarios. These scenarios are similar to those Wahid's Web Wonders business faced in Chapter 7. All businesses want maximum economic profits, which equal total revenues minus total costs. The graphs have information that allows you to see economic profits, even though total revenues and total costs don't appear directly.

From Economic Profits to Economic Profits per Unit   To connect the graphs to economic profits, follow these few steps.

$$\text{Economic Profits} = \underset{(\text{Price } \times \text{ Quantity})}{\text{Total Revenue}} - \text{Total Costs}$$

If we divide by the number of units (Q), we get

$$\frac{\text{Economic Profits}}{Q} = \frac{\text{Total Revenue}}{Q} - \frac{\text{Total Costs}}{Q}$$

So we end up with

$$\underset{\text{per unit}}{\text{Economic Profits}} = \text{Price} - \text{ATC}$$

This formula for economic profits per unit allows us to calculate economic profits (or losses) in each scenario.

Scenario One — Economic Losses
In Figure 5, the market price is $2.50 per bushel. The rule for maximum profits says the farmer's smart quantity supplied choice is 700 bushels. At 700 bushels, the price of $2.50 equals the farmer's marginal costs, so the price is enough to pay the farmer's marginal cost. But there is not enough left over to pay all the other costs, including normal profits. At 700

Figure 5   Scenario One — Economic Losses

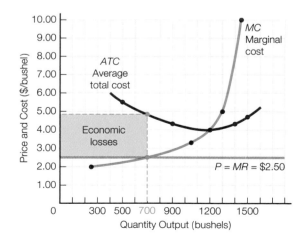

bushels, the farmer's average total cost (*ATC*) is about $4.90, which includes all fixed costs (including normal profits) and variable costs.

The formula for economic profit per unit is

$$\text{Price} - ATC = \$2.50 - \$4.90 = -\$2.40 \text{ (economic loss)}$$

You can see the $2.40 economic loss per bushel as the vertical distance on the red rectangle labelled *Economic losses*. The horizontal distance on the red rectangle measures the number of bushels produced (700). Total economic losses is the area (height × width) of the red rectangle, which is $2.40 economic loss per bushel times 700 bushels = –$1896.

This quantity of 700 bushels is a short-run equilibrium output for the farmer, because he is making the smartest choice he can with the given price, his fixed inputs, and variable inputs. But the farmer is not happy — he is kicking himself. This is not a long-run equilibrium because the price does not cover all opportunity costs of production. There are economics losses — a red light. Smart businesses exit the industry, and move their time, money, and inputs to where there is a promise of economic profits.

Scenario Two —
Breakeven Point

In Figure 6, the market price is $4 per bushel. The farmer's smart quantity-supplied choice is 1200 bushels. At 1200 bushels, average total cost (*ATC*) is also $4, because the *P = MR* curve intersects both the *MC* curve and the *ATC* curve at $4. The $4 market price just covers the farmer's average total costs, which include all costs, including normal profits. The farmer

Figure 6   Scenario Two — Breakeven Point

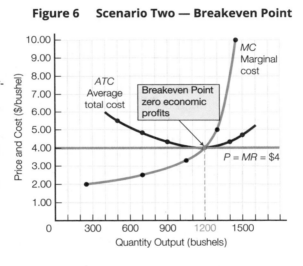

is making normal profits, but no more. His economic profits are zero.

Economic profit per unit is

$$\text{Price} - ATC = \$4 - \$4 = \$0 \text{ (zero economic profits)}$$

This is the **breakeven point** for the farmer. He is doing as well as the best alternative uses of his time and money. His profits are normal profits only — the same as average profits in other industries. This quantity of 1200 bushels is a short-run equilibrium output for the farmer because he is making the smartest choice he can with his fixed inputs and variable inputs. It is also a long-run equilibrium because economic profits are zero, and there is no incentive for the farmer to change industries.

Scenario Three — Economic Profits

In Figure 7, the market price is $10 per bushel. The farmer's smart quantity-supplied choice is 1450 bushels. At 1450 bushels, the farmer's average total cost (*ATC*) is about $4.50. The $10 market price not only covers the farmer's marginal costs, it more than covers his average total costs, which include all costs including normal profits.

Figure 7   Scenario Three — Economic Profits

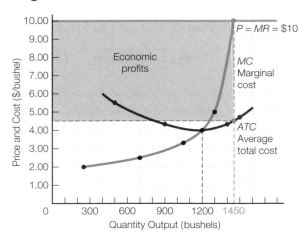

The formula for economic profit per unit is

$$\text{Price} - ATC = \$10.00 - \$4.50 = \$5.50 \text{ (economic profit)}$$

You can see the $5.50 economic profit per bushel as the vertical distance on the green rectangle labelled *Economic profits*. The horizontal distance on the green rectangle measures the number of bushels produced (1450). Total economic profits on all bushels produced is the area (height × width) of the green rectangle, which is $5.50 economic profit per bushel × 1450 bushels = $7975.

This quantity of 1450 bushels is a short-run equilibrium output for the farmer, because he is making the smartest choice he can with his fixed inputs and variable inputs. Even though the farmer is happy with this outcome, it is not a long-run equilibrium. Economic profits are a signal that consumers are willing to pay a price greater than businesses' opportunity costs of production. This green light directs the farmer to invest more time and money in the industry. It is also a signal for other businesses to enter.

For each of these short-run scenarios, the next section looks at what happens in the long run.

Practice...

11. A business in perfect competition will earn economic profits when

   a. marginal revenue is greater than average total cost.

   b. marginal revenue is less than average total cost.

   c. marginal revenue equals average total cost.

   d. price equals average total cost.

12. If a profit-maximizing business in perfect competition is earning economic profits, it must be producing a quantity of output where

   a. price is greater than marginal cost.

   b. price is greater than marginal revenue.

   c. marginal cost is greater than average total cost.

   d. marginal cost is less than marginal revenue.

13. When economic profits are zero in a perfectly competitive industry,

   a. the product will not be produced in the short run.

   b. the product will not be produced in the long run.

   c. revenues are not covering implicit costs.

   d. none of the above are true.

This graph shows the cost curves and possible marginal revenue curves of a business in a perfectly competitive industry. Use this graph to answer questions 14 and 15.

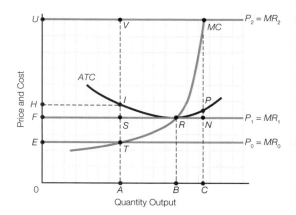

14. If the market price is P_2, in short-run equilibrium the business

   a. has economic losses.

   b. has economic profits.

   c. breaks even.

   d. exits the industry.

15. If the market price is P_0, a business following the rule for profits has short-run economic

   a. profits of area *HITE*.

   b. losses of area *HITE*.

   c. losses of area *FSTE*.

   d. profits of area *HISF*.

 **Apply...**

7. Which of the three scenarios would cause businesses to enter an industry? Explain why that increase in the number of businesses in an industry causes the market supply curve to shift rightward.

   _____
   _____
   _____
   _____
   _____
   _____
   _____

8. In Figure 6 on page 227, explain why the breakeven point is a market price of $4 per bushel and an output of 1200 bushels.

   _____
   _____
   _____
   _____
   _____

9. A business in a perfectly competitive industry has this cost information.

Output (Q)	Average Total Cost	Marginal Cost
12	25.0	
		11
13	23.9	
		13
14	23.1	
		15
15	22.6	
		17
16	22.3	
		19
17	22.1	
		21
18	22.0	
		23
19	22.1	
		25
20	22.2	

Apply...

a. What is the business's breakeven price? How do you know?

_____
_____
_____
_____
_____

b. If the market price is P = $16, what quantity of output will the business produce?

_____
_____
_____
_____
_____

c. What are economic profits or losses at the output in part **b**?

_____
_____
_____
_____
_____

Long-Run Equilibrium and Efficiency after Exit and Entry

 LO4 Explain economic losses and profits as signals for businesses to exit or enter perfectly competitive industries, which changes supply and achieves economic efficiency.

In microeconomics, the **short run** is a planning period for businesses when the quantities of some inputs are fixed, while the quantities of other inputs are variable. In **short–run market equilibrium**, quantity demanded equals quantity supplied, but economic losses or profits lead to changes in supply.

The **long run** is a planning period for businesses when the quantities of all inputs are variable. In **long-run market equilibrium**, quantity demanded equals quantity supplied, economic profits are zero, and there is no tendency for change.

Long-Run Economic Profit Adjustments

For each of the three possible short-run economic profit scenarios facing the wheat farmer in perfect competition, Figure 8 shows what happens in the long run.

Figure 8   Short-Run and Long-Run Equilibrium in the Wheat Industry

a) Economic Losses
b) Breakeven Zero Economic Profits
c) Economic Profits

Scenario One — Long Run Adjustments to Economic Losses   Figure 8a (similar to Chapter 7's Figure 4a on page 171 tells the story of economic losses and exit. The market supply curve for wheat associated with the short-run equilibrium price (P_S) of $2.50 per bushel is S_0. With economic losses at the $2.50 price, businesses exit the wheat industry, shifting the market supply curve leftward toward S_1. The market price rises, businesses keep exiting, and supply keeps shifting leftward until reaching S_1. Once at supply curve S_1, the new $4 market price is high enough to just cover all opportunity costs of production. The $4 per bushel price of wheat is a long-run equilibrium price (P_L). Businesses no longer have any incentive to move or shift supply.

Scenario Two — Breakeven Point Is Long-Run Equilibrium   Figure 8b shows the wheat industry's market demand and supply curve when the price is $4 per bushel. This is both a short-run equilibrium price and a long-run equilibrium price. With zero economic profits, businesses stay where they are. No one is kicking herself. There is no incentive for businesses to exit or enter the wheat industry.

Zero economic profits are a yellow light signalling proceed with caution. Yellow is an "equilibrium" signal — no reason to change. This industry has average, or normal, profits. No economic profits, but no economic losses either.

Scenario Three — Long-Run Adjustments to Economic Losses Figure 8c (similar to Chapter 7's Figure 4b on page 171) tells the story of economic profits and entry. The market supply curve for wheat associated with the short-run equilibrium price (P_S) of $10 per bushel is S_0. With economic profits available, businesses enter the wheat industry, shifting the market supply curve rightward toward S_1. The market price falls, businesses keep entering, and supply keeps shifting rightward until reaching S_1. Once at supply curve S_1, the new $4 market price has fallen enough to just cover all opportunity costs of production. That $4 per bushel price of wheat is a long run equilibrium price (P_L). Businesses no longer have any incentive to move or shift supply.

Long-Run Supply

In each of the three scenarios above, the market always returns to the same long-run equilibrium price (P_L). Always returning to the same long-run equilibrium price after changes in supply or demand is only one of three possible patterns.

The **long-run supply curve** shows the prices at which a purely competitive industry supplies quantities in the long run. Figure 9 shows three possible patterns for the long-run supply curve — for a constant-cost industry, an increasing-cost industry, and a decreasing-cost industry.

Figure 9   Long-Run Supply Curve

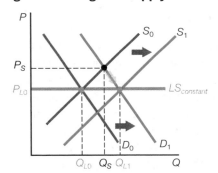

a) Constant Cost Industry

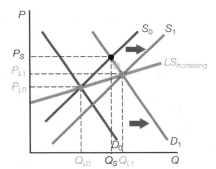

b) Increasing Cost Industry

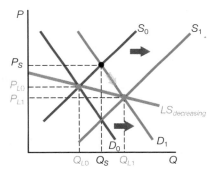

c) Decreasing Cost Industry

Constant-Cost Industry   In a constant-cost industry, the entry of new businesses has no effect on input prices and costs of production. Look at Figure 9a. The industry is initially in long-run equilibrium at price P_{L0} and quantity Q_{L0}, with zero economic profits. There is an increase in demand, from demand curve D_0 to D_1. The new short-run equilibrium price is P_S. This is a short-run price because there are economic profits since P_S is higher than P_{L0}. The economic profits are a signal for new businesses to enter. As the supply curve shifts rightward from S_0 to S_1, price falls as we move down along demand curve D_1. The new long-run equilibrium price returns to P_{L0}, at the intersection of D_1 and S_1. Connecting the points of long-run equilibrium gives the horizontal long-run supply curve $LS_{constant}$. Because the entry of new businesses has no effect on input prices and costs, the long-run equilibrium price is constant.

Increasing-Cost Industry   In an increasing-cost industry, the entry of new businesses raises input prices and costs of production. Look at Figure 9b. The industry is initially in long-run equilibrium at price P_{L0} and quantity Q_{L0}, with zero economic profits. There is an increase in demand, from demand curve D_0 to D_1. The new short-run equilibrium price is P_S. This is a short-run price because there are economic profits since P_S is higher than P_{L0}. The economic profits are a signal for new businesses to enter. As the supply curve shifts rightward from S_0 to S_1, price falls as we move down along demand curve D_1. The new long-run equilibrium price P_{L1} — at the intersection of D_1 and S_1 — is *higher* than the original long-run equilibrium price P_{L0}. Connecting the points of long-run equilibrium gives the upward-sloping long-run supply curve $LS_{increasing}$. Because the entry of new businesses raises input prices and costs, the new long-run equilibrium price (with zero economic profits) must be higher to cover increasing costs.

Decreasing-Cost Industry   In a decreasing-cost industry, the entry of new businesses lowers input prices and costs of production. Look at Figure 9c on the previous page. The industry is initially in long-run equilibrium at price P_{L0} and quantity Q_{L0}, with zero economic profits. There is an increase in demand, from demand curve D_0 to D_1. The new short-run equilibrium price is Ps. This is a short-run price because there are economic profits since P_S is higher than P_{L0}. The economic profits are a signal for new businesses to enter. As the supply curve shifts rightward from S_0 to S_1, price falls as we move down along demand curve D_1. The new long-run equilibrium price P_{L1} — at the intersection of D_1 and S_1 — is *lower* than the original long-run equilibrium price P_{L0}. Connecting the points of long-run equilibrium gives the downward-sloping long-run supply curve $LS_{decreasing}$. Because the entry of new businesses has lowered input prices and costs, the new long-run equilibrium price (with zero economic profits) must be lower to just cover the decreasing costs.

Efficiency of Perfect Competition and Price Takers

The market structure of perfect competition gives more complete explanations of an individual business's costs, economic profits, and quantity-supplied decisions. We have examined those decisions in the short run, when some inputs are fixed, and in the long run when all inputs are variable. In the short run, **diminishing marginal productivity** is the force behind increasing marginal costs, shaping the upward-sloping marginal cost curve, the individual business supply curve, and the market supply curve. **Returns to scale** (pages 183-184) are the key for understanding long-run costs and the shape of the long-run average cost curve.

The detailed cost information makes it easier to see different economic loss and profit scenarios, which serve as signals for businesses to exit or enter industries. Economic losses and profits cause changes in supply, which change prices and quantities, moving an industry from a short-run equilibrium to a long-run equilibrium with zero economic profits.

Figure 10 shows long-run equilibrium in a perfectly competitive wheat market.

Figure 10   Long-Run Equilibrium in Perfect Competition

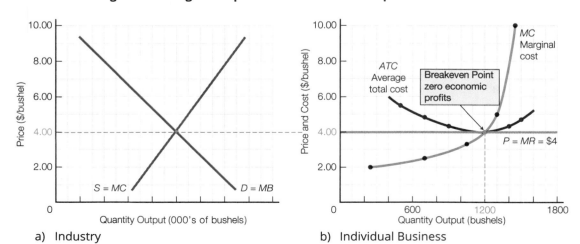

a) Industry

b) Individual Business

Figure 10a shows the industry demand and supply curves. The market demand curve is the sum of all of the individual consumers' demand curves, and the market supply curve is the sum of all of the individual businesses' marginal cost curves. The demand curve is also a **marginal benefit** curve; the supply curve is also a **marginal cost** curve. At the equilibrium price where the curves intersect — $4 per bushel — marginal benefit equals marginal cost. This is one of the conditions for economic efficiency. Look back at Figure 10 in Chapter 3, page 74. When a market is producing the quantity where marginal benefit equals marginal cost, total surplus (consumer surplus plus producer surplus) is at a maximum.

Figure 10b carries over the $4 price to show the horizontal demand (and marginal revenue) curve facing the individual farmer. Each self-interested, individual business applies the rule for maximum profits:

Estimate marginal revenues and marginal costs,
then set the highest price that allows you to sell the highest quantity
for which marginal revenue is greater than marginal cost.

In this perfectly competitive market, the individual farmer is a price taker, so the only decision to make is the quantity of output to produce. Apply the rule that profit-maximizing output is where the horizontal, green marginal revenue curve intersects the upward-sloping, red marginal cost curve, at 1200 bushels of wheat. For all bushels of wheat between zero and 1200, marginal revenue is greater than marginal cost.

This is a long-run equilibrium because each business is producing at the breakeven point, where economic profits are zero and average total costs are at a minimum. Because average total costs include normal profits, the farmer is just covering all opportunity costs of production, including normal profits. Each business is producing efficiently, at the lowest possible average total cost. This is another desirable, efficient outcome of perfect competition.

The final desirable outcome comes from the role of short-run economic losses and profits, signalling the invisible hand to direct business owners' self-interest to unintentionally produce the miracle of markets — the products and services that consumers most value in long-run equilibrium. These are the competitive forces that operate in all market structures, although not always as effectively as in perfect competition.

In the next chapter, we look at market structures that are less competitive than perfect competition — monopoly, oligopoly, and monopolistic competition. While the same rule for profit-maximizing decisions applies, the efficiency of the outcomes fall short of perfect competition.

 **Practice...**

16. A perfectly competitive industry is in short-run market equilibrium with price below average total cost. Which is *not* a prediction of what happens in long-run market equilibrium?
    a. Price rises.
    b. Industry output increases.
    c. Economic profits will be zero.
    d. Businesses exit the industry.

17. If businesses enter a perfectly competitive industry, the
    a. economic profits of remaining businesses decrease.
    b. economic profits of remaining businesses stay the same.
    c. industry output decreases.
    d. market supply curve shifts leftward.

18. Businesses stop exiting an industry only when
    a. marginal revenue equals price.
    b. marginal revenue equals marginal cost.
    c. all remaining businesses have zero normal profits.
    d. all remaining businesses have zero economic profits.

19. The long-run supply curve for a perfectly competitive industry will be upward sloping for a(n)
    a. constant-cost industry.
    b. decreasing-cost industry.
    c. increasing-cost industry.
    d. increasing returns to scale industry.

20. An economic outcome is efficient if
    a. marginal benefit equals marginal cost.
    b. businesses produce at lowest average total cost.
    c. economic profits are zero.
    d. all of the above are true.

 Apply...

10. A business in a perfectly competitive industry has the same cost information as in Apply question 9 on page 230.

Output (Q)	Average Total Cost	Marginal Cost
12	25.0	
		11
13	23.9	
		13
14	23.1	
		15
15	22.6	
		17
16	22.3	
		19
17	22.1	
		21
18	22.0	
		23
19	22.1	
		25
20	22.2	

a. What is the long-run equilibrium price in the industry? How do you know?

_____

_____

_____

b. What is this business's long-run equilibrium quantity of output?

_____

_____

_____

c. Using cost and revenue numbers for the output in part **b**, explain why that output is a long-run equilibrium output.

_____

_____

_____

_____

_____

to be continued

continued

11. The paper-clip industry is a perfectly competitive, constant-cost industry, and is initially in long-run equilibrium. Then the demand for paper clips decreases because people are using tablets and less paper. Using one graph for the paper-clip industry and one graph for an individual business like Figure 10 on page 234, tell the story of what will happen to market price, economic profits or losses, and the adjustment to a new long-run equilibrium.

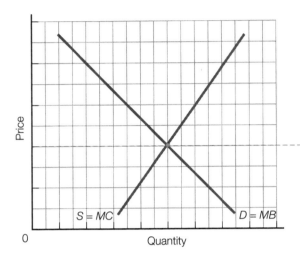

a) Industry

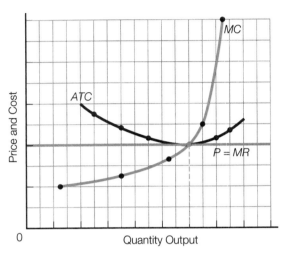

b) Individual Business

_____

_____

_____

_____

_____

_____

_____

_____

_____

KNOW...

Learning Objectives

1. The demand curve for an individual price-taking business in **perfect competition** is also a **marginal revenue** curve — a horizontal line at the market price. Because each small business can sell as much at it produces at the given market price, there is no need to lower the price to sell more.

2. The **marginal cost** curve determines the supply curve for businesses in perfect competition. Using the rule for profits, each business chooses a quantity of output where price = marginal revenue = marginal cost.

3. In **short-run market equilibrium**, each business chooses the quantity of output where marginal revenue equals marginal cost. The business may have economic losses, economic profits, or zero economic profits. Economic loss or profit per unit is price minus average total cost. Economic losses and economic profits are signals for businesses to exit or enter an industry, shifting industry supply leftward or rightward.

4. Short-run economic losses or profits are signals for businesses to exit or enter an industry. Those changes in supply return the industry to **long-run market equilibrium**, where economic profits are zero and average total costs are at a minimum. The **long-run supply curve** shows the prices at which a purely competitive industry supplies quantities in the long run, connecting positions of long-run equilibrium as demand and output increase. The long-run supply curve is horizontal for a **constant-cost industry**, upward-sloping for an **increasing-cost industry**, and downward-sloping for a **decreasing-cost industry**. The long-run market equilibrium outcome is efficient — marginal benefit equals marginal cost, economic profits are zero, and average total costs are at a minimum.

Key Terms

average total cost: total cost divided by quantity of output

breakeven point: business just earning normal profits — no economic profits, no economic losses; at the intersection of the marginal cost curve and the average total cost curve

constant-cost industry: entry of new businesses has no effect on input prices and costs of production; long-run supply curve is horizontal

decreasing-cost industry: entry of new businesses lowers input prices and costs of production; long-run supply curve is downward sloping

diminishing marginal productivity: as you add more of a variable input to fixed inputs, the marginal product of the variable input eventually diminishes

increasing-cost industry: entry of new businesses raises input prices and costs of production; long-run supply curve is upward sloping

law of supply: if the price of a product or services rises, quantity supplied increases, other things remaining the same

long run: in microeconomics, a planning period for businesses where the quantities of all inputs are variable

long-run market equilibrium: quantity demanded equals quantity supplied, economic profits are zero, no tendency for change

long-run supply curve: shows the prices at which a purely competitive industry supplies quantities in the long run; connects positions of long-run equilibrium as demand and output increase

marginal benefit: additional benefit from a choice, changing with circumstances

marginal cost: additional opportunity cost of increasing quantity supplied, changing with circumstances

marginal revenue: additional revenue from more sales or from selling one more unit of output

perfect competition: market structure with many sellers producing identical products or services, no barriers to entry, and zero pricing power

returns to scale: changes in output when all inputs change by the same percentage

shutdown point: minimum price a business in perfect competition will accept to continue supplying; at the intersection of the marginal cost curve and average variable cost curve

short run: in microeconomics, a planning period for businesses where the quantities of some inputs are fixed, while the quantities of other inputs are variable

short-run market equilibrium: quantity demanded equals quantity supplied, but economic losses or profits lead to changes in supply

Answers to Practice

1. **c** All businesses produce identical products in perfect competition.

2. **d** MR = price because the business does not have to lower price to sell more.

3. **b** Total revenue = price × quantity = $4 × 8 = $32.

4. **a** Marginal revenue = price = $4. Marginal revenue also equals the change in total revenue from 8 to 9 units. $36 − $32 = $4.

5. **a** Horizontal line at market price; also the business's marginal revenue curve.

6. **b** Businesses are price takers in perfect competition.

7. **d** Quantity at intersection of MR and MC curves.

8. **c** For any given market price, business chooses the quantity where the horizontal $P = MR$ curve intersects the upward-sloping MC curve.

9. **b** At the market price of $50, each of the 100 businesses produces 7 units, for a total of 7 × 100 = 700 units.

10. **a** For any price, the market supply curve shows the total quantity supplied from all businesses in the industry.

11. **a** MR equals price. ATC includes normal profits. Since $P > ATC$, price covers all opportunity costs of production, leaving extra room for economic profits.

12. **c** A quantity to the right of (greater than) the breakeven quantity.

13. **d** Product is produced, revenues cover all opportunity costs of production, including implicit costs, and no tendency for change.

14. **b** Rule for profits say choose the quantity where $MR = MC$. At that quantity, Price (= MR) is greater than ATC.

15. **b** Business produces quantity A. Average total cost per unit is I, while price per unit is T. Since ATC is greater than price, loss per unit is distance IT, and number of units is distance TE.

16. **b** With economic losses, businesses exit the industry, so industry supply decreases.

17. **a** Supply shifts rightward, industry output increases, and falling prices decrease economic profits.

18. **d** Zero economic profits in long-run equilibrium. In perfect competition, price always equals marginal revenue for price takers, and businesses choose the quantity where marginal revenue equals marginal cost in the short run and long run.

19. **c** In an increasing-cost industry, the entry of new businesses raises input prices and costs, so a new long-run equilibrium price is higher. When there are increasing returns to scale (**d**), this affects the downward slope of the long-run average cost curve (*LRAC*), not the long-run supply curve.

20. **d** This is the long-run outcome of perfect competition. See Figure 10 on page 234.

10 Pricing for Profits in Imperfect Competition

LEARNING OBJECTIVES

LO1 Explain why marginal revenue is less than price for a price-making business following the one-price rule.

LO2 Use the rule for maximum profits to explain the quantity and price decisions of a business with pricing power, and show the importance of marginal revenue and marginal cost.

LO3 Define price discrimination and explain how it leads to higher profits by taking advantage of differences in elasticity of demand.

LO4 Explain why maximum profits bring efficiency for perfect competition and inefficiency for market structures with price-making power. Compare the benefits and costs of market structures.

LEARN ...

The profit-maximizing rule for perfect competition also applies to businesses in less competitive market structures — monopoly, oligopoly, and monopolistic competition. But there is a difference. Businesses in these market structures of "imperfect competition" have some pricing power — they are price makers rather than the price takers of perfect competition. When applying the rule for maximum profits, price makers have two decisions to make — what quantity to produce and what price to set.

This chapter focuses on decisions about quantity and price common to all imperfect competition market structures. There are also differences among monopolists, oligopolists, and monopolistic competitors that your textbook or instructor may discuss. Those differences, including barriers to entry, advertising, and short-run versus long-run economic profits, are not included here. Chapter 11 will look more closely at another form of monopoly called natural monopoly, and at some additional strategic complications of oligopoly pricing.

Price-making businesses use the rule for maximum profits and their pricing power to create economic profits, to innovate, and to produce a desirable variety of products and services that perfect competition lacks. But every choice has an opportunity cost, and you will also learn about the inefficiency of market structures of imperfect competition.

Marginal Revenue, Price, and Marginal Cost for Price Makers

L01 Explain why marginal revenue is less than price for a price-making business following the one-price rule.

The business rule for maximum profits applies to all market structures, including those with less-than-perfect, or imperfect, competition — monopoly, oligopoly, and monopolistic competition.

> Estimate marginal revenues and marginal costs,
> then set the highest price that allows you to sell the highest quantity
> for which marginal revenue is greater than marginal cost.

Oligopoly pricing has some additional strategic complications that we will discuss in Chapter 11, but the rule for maximum profits applies to all businesses with pricing power. Price-taking businesses in perfect competition can only choose their profit-maximizing quantity. Price-making businesses *choose both quantity and price*.

Marginal revenue and marginal cost are still the key concepts for smart, profit-maximizing choices. Price-taking businesses do not have to lower price to sell additional output, so marginal revenue equals price. Their marginal revenue curve is a horizontal line at the given market price. That perfectly elastic marginal revenue curve is also the demand curve facing a business in perfect competition. Because each business is small, it can sell as much as it can produce at the market price.

Marginal revenue looks very different for a business with pricing power.

One-Price Rule

You walk into Tim Hortons, order a medium double-double, and pay the usual $2. How would you feel if the next customer ordered the same coffee and were charged only $1?

Most products and services have one price, not a different price for each customer. Why is that? First, it's not a good idea to make your customers angry and resentful. Second, competitive economic forces tend to equalize prices. Tims customers like you, who paid $2, would save money by not buying at the counter, but instead by offering to buy coffee from the low-price customers for less than $2. Low-price customers would make easy money by reselling their coffees for more than $1 to customers like you. Self-interest and competition coffee drinkers would push the price toward a single price.

Most products that are easily resold tend to have a single price. But as you will see later in the chapter, sometimes businesses *can* charge different customers different prices for the same product or service to increase profits. For now, we will stick to examples where a business has to charge all customers the same price for the same product or service. The one-price rule has a big impact on a business's marginal revenue.

Marginal Revenue for Price Makers

What happens if a business in perfect competition tries to charge more than the given market price? It loses all customers because there are identical substitutes easily available at the market price. What about businesses with pricing power? Price makers — whether monopolies, oligopolies, or small monopolistic competitors like Paola's Parlour for Piercing and Nails — can raise prices without losing all of their sales to competitors. Barriers to entry, brand loyalty, or advertising all can create pricing power. But price makers still face the law of demand. They will sell less if they raise their prices. And *to sell more, they must lower their prices.* The demand curve for price makers is downward-sloping.

Calculating Marginal Revenue for Price Makers   This is where the one-price rule becomes important. As long as a product can be resold and a business does not want to anger its customers, to sell more, price makers must lower the price on *all units*, not just on new sales. The result is that *for price makers, marginal revenue per unit is less than price.* Let's look at a simple example with made-up numbers.

Figure 1   Demand and Marginal Revenue for Price Makers with One-Price Rule

Row	Price ($)	Quantity Demanded	Total Revenue (price x quantity)	Marginal Revenue (change in total revenue)
A	$20	0	$ 0	
				$18
B	$18	1	$18	
				$14
C	$16	2	$32	
				$10
D	$14	3	$42	
				$ 6
E	$12	4	$48	
				$ 2
F	$10	5	$50	

Figure 1 shows how many piercings Paola expects her customers to demand at different prices, and her revenues. (We will add costs shortly.) These numbers are for each hour her parlour is open. The second column shows the different prices Paola is *thinking* about setting for a single piercing. The third column shows how many piercings she estimates her customers will demand at each price. The fourth column calculates her total revenues (price multiplied by quantity). If Paola charges $20 (row *A*), she will have no customers and no revenues. If instead she sets a price of $18 (row *B*), she will sell one piercing and get total revenues of $18 ($18 × 1). If she sets a price of $16 (row *C*), she will sell two piercings and get total revenues of $32 ($16 × 2). Paola must lower her price to sell more piercings — that is the law of demand.

To understand marginal revenue — the last column in Figure 1 — let's compare two prices that Paola is considering in rows *B* and *C*. In planning her price-making strategy, if she wants to increase her sales from one to two piercings, she must drop the price from $18 to $16. If she does so, total revenues increase from $18 to $32. So what is Paola's additional, or marginal, revenue from selling the second piercing? It is the change in total revenue from $18 for one piercing to $32 for two piercings, or $14 ($32 − $18). The $14 appears *between* rows *B* and *C* because marginal revenue is the change in moving *between* the total revenues of rows *B* and *C*.

Are you surprised by the $14? If Paola sells the second piercing in row *C* for $16, why is her marginal revenue only $14, and not the $16 price?

The answer lies in the one-price rule. To sell the second piercing at the lower price of $16, Paola must also drop the price of the first piercing from $18 to $16. So *while Paola gets an additional $16 from the second piercing, she has to subtract the $2 less she gets on the first piercing: $16 − $2 = $14.* That is why Paola's marginal revenue from selling the second piercing is only $14, not $16.

Time Machine Explanation for Why Marginal Revenue Is Less Than Price

Still not clear? This is where a time machine is helpful. Paola, like most business owners, has to make a price-making decision *before* sales start. Customers want to know the prices when they walk into the store.

Suppose she chooses the row *B* price of $18 for a piercing. After one hour, she has sold one piercing, for total revenue of $18. Now take the time machine back to before Paola decides on a price. This time, she chooses the row *C* price of $16. After one hour, she has sold two piercings for a total revenue of $32. Both piercings had to sell for the same price of $16 because of the one-price rule. One more trip back in the time machine. Paola chooses the row *D* price of $14. After one hour, she has sold three piercings for a total revenue of $42.

The marginal revenue *between* the decisions of an $18 price in row *B* and a $16 price in row *C* is $14 ($32 – $18). The marginal revenue between the decisions of a $16 price in row *C* and a $14 price in row *D* is $10 ($42 – $32). Does that make more sense — not the time machine, but the calculations of marginal revenue as the change in total revenue *between* pricing decisions?

In reality, there is no time machine, and Paola only gets to choose one price, and must sell all piercings at that price. Think about the pricing decision as being *planned* — on paper, or in discussions, before the selling begins. Which time-machine scenario price will be most profitable for Paola?

Marginal Revenue Curve for Price Makers   Figure 2 graphs the information from Figure 1. Points *A – F* on the demand curve correspond to rows *A – F* in the table. This is a typical downward-sloping shaped demand curve for any price-making business. To keep the table of numbers from getting too long, I omitted the points on the demand curve below *F*.

Figure 2   Demand and Marginal Revenue for Price Makers

Row	Price ($)	Quantity Demanded	Total Revenue (price x quantity)	Marginal Revenue (change in total revenue)
A	$20	0	$ 0	
				$18
B	$18	1	$18	
				$14
C	$16	2	$32	
				$10
D	$14	3	$42	
				$ 6
E	$12	4	$48	
				$ 2
F	$10	5	$50	

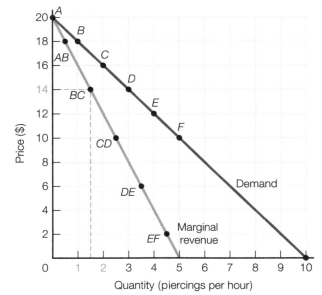

What's new on the graph is the marginal revenue curve (actually a straight line). The points on the marginal revenue curve come from the marginal revenue column in the table of numbers.

You draw a marginal revenue curve the same way you read it — start at the quantity and go up and over to the marginal revenue. But we calculate marginal revenue between quantities. For example, *between* rows B and C, quantity demanded goes from one to two piercings. Since we are moving between quantity 1 and quantity 2, we split the difference and use the quantity 1½ to plot the value for marginal revenue — point BC on the marginal revenue curve. All other points on the marginal revenue curve are plotted the same way, halfway *between* the quantities used for the marginal revenue calculations.

Notice that *the marginal revenue curve for price makers is not the same as the demand curve*. For any quantity, marginal revenue is less than price for price makers.

How to Draw a Marginal Revenue Curve   There is an easy trick for drawing the marginal revenue curve for any straight-line demand curve. The point where the marginal revenue curve touches the vertical price axis is the same as for the demand curve. In Figure 2, that is at the price of $20. The point where the marginal revenue curve touches the horizontal quantity axis is always *half* the output of where the demand curve touches the horizontal quantity axis. In Figure 2, that marginal revenue quantity is 5 units, while the demand curve quantity is 10 units. Connecting those two end points of the marginal revenue curve gives the straight-line marginal revenue curve. The marginal revenue curve is a downward-sloping straight line whose slope is twice as steep as the slope of the corresponding demand curve.

What about Total Revenue?   Marginal revenue is one key concept in the recipe for maximum profits — choose when marginal revenues are greater than marginal costs. But even as marginal revenue is falling, total revenue is still increasing. Look again at the table. Total revenue increases from $0 in row A, to $18, to $32, . . . to $50 in row F. For the same rows, marginal revenue is falling from $18, to $14, . . . to $2. Even though marginal revenue is falling, as long as it is greater than zero, it is adding to total revenue.

As the growth in your height slowed down in your late teens, each year you grew a little less. But as long as you kept growing, you kept getting taller. Your marginal growth (additional growth per year) was falling, but your total height kept increasing.

You might think that a price-making business would keep cutting its price to increase total revenue. But you would be wrong. There is a reason why the concepts in the rule for maximum profits are *marginal* revenue and *marginal* cost. Smart choices are made at the margin — Key 2 of the Three Keys to Smart Choices. But before I can explain why marginal revenue is more important than total revenue, we must first add the marginal cost concept.

Marginal Cost

As you learned in Chapter 8 (pages 210-211), different businesses have different marginal cost patterns. The most common patterns of what happens to marginal cost as quantity increases are shown in Figure 3 on the next page — increasing marginal cost and constant marginal cost.

Figure 3   Increasing and Constant Marginal Costs

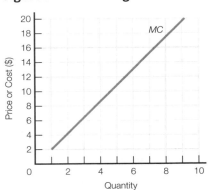

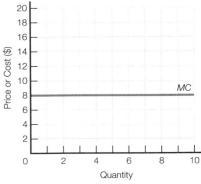

a) Increasing Marginal Cost   b) Constant Marginal Cost

Businesses have increasing marginal costs — the upward sloping line in Figure 3a — where there is diminishing marginal productivity or they are operating close to capacity. Businesses not operating near capacity often have constant marginal costs. Many price makers in the market structures of monopoly, oligopoly, and monopolistic competition have constant marginal costs. Their marginal cost curves look like the horizontal line in Figure 3b — as quantity increases, marginal cost stays constant.

In most of the examples that follow, we will use constant marginal costs, with one example of increasing marginal costs. Remember, the rule for profit-maximizing choices is the same for any pattern of marginal costs.

 # Practice...

1. Which statement about price and marginal revenue is *true*?

    a. Marginal revenue equals price for monopolists.

    b. Marginal revenue equals price for businesses in perfect competition.

    c. Marginal revenue is greater than price for monopolists.

    d. Marginal revenue is greater than price for businesses in perfect competition.

2. The marginal revenue curve for a price-making business

    a. is horizontal.

    b. intercepts the price axis at the market price of the product.

    c. is more steeply sloped than the business's demand curve.

    d. intercepts the quantity axis at double the output of where the demand curve intercepts the quantity axis.

3. Self-interest and competition will most likely push the price toward a single price for

    a. Broadway show tickets.

    b. snowboarding lessons.

    c. haircuts.

    d. coffee.

4. At $100 a room, The No-Tell Motel rented 3 rooms. They dropped the price to $90 and rented 4 rooms. Marginal revenue for the 4th room is

    a. $60.

    b. $10.

    c. $90.

    d. $100.

5. In order to increase sales from 7 units to 8 units, a one-price oligopolist must lower the price from $7 per unit to $6. What is the marginal revenue in this range?

    a. $48

    b. $6

    c. $1

    d. – $1

Apply...

1. Ori the ice-cream truck driver knows he can sell 50 single-scoop ice-cream cones on a hot, sunny day if his price is $3 each. His brother, who used to be in the ice-cream business, tells him he can probably sell 80 single-scoop ice-cream cones if he lowers his price on all cones to $2. What is Ori's marginal revenue if he lowers the price to $2?

_____

_____

_____

_____

_____

_____

2. The connection between marginal revenue and price depends on a business's competitive environment. Why are marginal revenue and price the same for a business that is a price taker in perfect competition? Why is marginal revenue less than price for a business that is a price maker?

_____

_____

_____

_____

_____

_____

_____

_____

3. Here is a demand curve facing a one-price business in monopolistic competition. Seven points along the demand curve are labelled A – G.

Row	Price ($)	Quantity Demanded	Total Revenue (price x quantity)	Marginal Revenue
A				
B				
C				
D				
E				
F				
G				

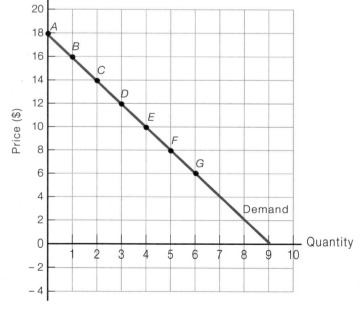

to be continued

Apply...

continued

a. In the blank table on the previous page, fill in the columns for Price and Quantity Demanded.

b. For each row in the table (*A — G*) calculate Total Revenue.

c. Fill in the column for Marginal Revenue.

d. On the graph, plot six points on the marginal revenue curve, and connect them to draw the marginal revenue curve.

e. What is the quantity where the marginal revenue curve intersects the quantity axis? What is the slope of the marginal revenue curve? What is the slope of the demand curve?

f. What happens to marginal revenue if the business increases output from 5 to 6 units? Would this ever be a smart choice?

Quantity and Price Decisions for Price Makers

 Use the rule for maximum profits to explain the quantity and price decisions of a business with pricing power, and show the importance of marginal revenue and marginal cost.

The rule for maximum profits is

Estimate marginal revenues and marginal costs,
then set the highest price that allows you to sell the highest quantity
for which marginal revenue is greater than marginal cost.

Once a business estimates marginal revenues and marginal costs, a smart entrepreneur must make two related decisions about quantity and price:

- Find the highest quantity for which marginal revenue is greater than marginal cost.

- Set the highest price that still allows you to sell that quantity.

It is easiest to apply the rule if we make the quantity decision first, and follow it with the price-setting decision.

Applying Rule for Profits in Numbers

Let's continue using the simple numbers from Figure 1. Figure 4 reproduces those numbers, showing how many piercings Paola estimates her customers will demand at different prices, and the revenues she will collect. Like any business with pricing power, Paola must lower her price to sell more. Because the one-price rule applies, that means Paola's marginal revenue falls with each increase in piercings sold, and marginal revenue falls faster than the falling price — compare columns 2 (Price) and 5 (Marginal Revenue).

Figure 4   Paola's Marginal Revenues and Marginal Costs for Piercings

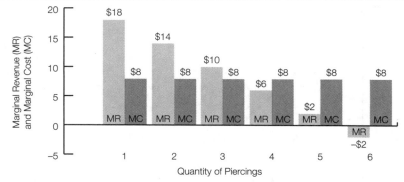

Column						
1	2	3	4	5	6	7
Row	Price	Quantity Demanded	Total Revenue	Marginal Revenue	Marginal Cost	Change in Total Profit
A	$20	0	$ 0			$ 0
				$18	$8	
B	$18	1	$18			+ $10
				$14	$8	
C	$16	2	$32			+ $ 6
				$10	$8	
D	$14	3	$42			+ $ 2
				$ 6	$8	
E	$12	4	$48			– $ 2
				$ 2	$8	
F	$10	5	$50			– $ 6
				–$ 2	$8	
G	$ 8	6	$48			– $10

Marginal revenue is listed *between* quantities of output (for example, between quantity 1 in row *B* and quantity 2 in row *C*) because marginal revenue is the change in moving *between* the total revenues from selling different quantities ($18 for 1 unit in row *B* and $32 for 2 units in row *C*).

Marginal cost may be increasing or constant. Let's start with constant Column 6, Marginal Cost, shows Paola's marginal cost for each additional piercing is constant at $8, no matter what the quantity. This is the case when Paola is not operating near capacity, and is already paying her employees for being at work. The only additional costs for a piercing are the costs of the stud and the additional electricity used by the piercing gun. Paola estimates those marginal costs are $8 per piercing. Like marginal revenue, marginal cost is listed *between* quantities because it is the additional cost in moving *between* different quantities of output.

Quantity Decision   What is Paola's smart quantity decision? How many piercings should she produce to get maximum profits? The rule says, "Find the highest quantity for which marginal revenue is greater than marginal cost." Let's look at the quantities one by one, starting with the first piercing (row *B*).

If Paola produces one piercing, marginal revenue is $18 and marginal cost is $8. That is clearly a smart decision because marginal revenue is greater than marginal cost. The last column in Figure 4 shows the net impact on Paola's total profits from producing that first piercing. Total profits go up by $10, which is the amount by which marginal revenue ($18) exceeds marginal cost ($8).

Moving to row *C*, if Paola increases output to two piercings, her marginal revenue is $14 and her marginal cost is $8. Total profits increase by a further $6, so this is still a smart decision. Moving to row *D*, if Paola continues to increase output to three piercings, total profits increase by a further $2 — still smart.

Things change with row *E*. If Paola increases output to four piercings, her marginal revenue is $6, which is less than her marginal cost of $8. Total profits *decrease by $2* if Paola produces the fourth piercing. Not a smart decision. Things get even worse if Paola produces a fifth or sixth piercing. After three piercings, profits fall as additional costs are greater than additional revenues.

Price-Making Decision Once you have all the information for the quantity decision, the price-making decision is easy. Like any business, Paola wants to set the highest possible price that allows her to sell her target quantity of three piercings. Look at row *D* in Figure 4 on the previous page. The highest price Paola can charge and still sell three piercings is $14.

Rule for Profits in Graphs

Figure 5 combines the demand and marginal revenue curves from Figure 2 with the constant marginal cost curve from Figure 3b.

Figure 5   Marginal Revenue and Marginal Cost

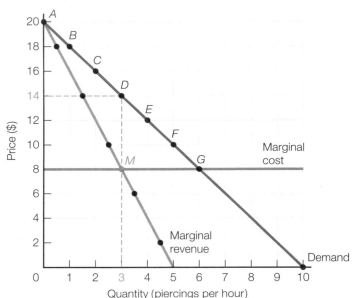

The graph shows how to apply the two related decisions about quantity and price in the rule for profits.

Quantity Decision To make the quantity decision first, look for where the marginal revenue and marginal cost curves intersect (point *M*). Go down from point *M* to read the number on the quantity axis — three piercings. Three is the highest quantity for which marginal revenue is greater than marginal cost. For all quantities less than three, marginal revenue is greater than marginal cost. Producing any of these quantities is a smart choice. For all quantities greater than three, marginal cost is greater than marginal revenue. Any quantity greater than three is *not* a smart choice. Three piercings is the dividing line between quantities that increase profits (up to three) and quantities that decrease profits (over three).

Price-Making Decision To set the highest price that still sells the highest quantity, start with three piercings on the quantity axis and go up to the demand curve (point *D*) and over to the price axis to find the price to charge — $14.

Where Marginal Revenue and Marginal Cost Intersect The point (*M*) where the marginal revenue curve intersects the marginal cost curve is the key to the graphical version of the rule for profits. Reading down from point *M* gives you the quantity (3) for maximum profits. Reading up from point *M* to the demand curve and over gives you the highest price the business can charge for those three units ($14).

Based on the rule for maximum profits, the monopolist supplies a single combination of quantity and price. Businesses in perfect competition have a supply curve that shows what quantity will be supplied for any price. A *price maker does not have a supply curve*. Paola has a single supply point. In Figure 5, point *D*, the combination of 3 units and a price of $14 per unit, is Paola's supply.

Pricing for Maximum Economic Profits

When Paola applies the rule for maximum profits, her smart business decision is to produce three piercings and to set her price at $14. How do we know *this* combination of price and quantity yields maximum *economic profits*? Businesses are ultimately interested in economic profits — revenues minus all opportunity costs (explicit costs plus normal profits). We looked at marginal revenues and marginal costs, and how Paola's decisions *change* total profits, but what about Paola's obvious fixed costs, like rent and insurance? Fixed costs do not change with the quantity of output produced. And what about the normal profits Paola must earn if she is to do as well as in any other business? The success of the rule for profits is judged by whether *economic profits* are greatest, when all costs are included.

Figure 6 reproduces all the information on revenues and costs from Figures 1 and 4 and adds two more columns. The Total Costs column adds Paola's fixed costs to the sum of all of her marginal costs. To keep the numbers very simple, assume that the portion of her fixed costs for piercings is $10. That number includes the normal profits she must earn on her investment to be doing as well as in any other line of business. The Economic Profits column subtracts Total Costs (which include fixed costs and normal profits) from Total Revenues.

Figure 6 Paola's Calculation of Economic Profits for Piercings

							Column	
1	2	3	4	5	6	7	8	9
Row	Price	Quantity Demanded	Total Revenue	Marginal Revenue	Marginal Cost	Change in Total Profits	Total Costs (Fixed Costs + Sum of Marginal Costs)	Economic Profits (Total Revenue − Total Costs)
A	$20	0	$ 0			$ 0	$10 (Fixed Costs)	− $10 (Losses)
				$18	$8			
B	$18	1	$18			+ $10	$18	$ 0
				$14	$8			
C	$16	2	$32			+ $ 6	$26	$ 6
				$10	$8			
D	$14	3	$42			+ $ 2	$34	$ 8
				$ 6	$8			
E	$12	4	$48			− $ 2	$42	$ 6
				$ 2	$8			
F	$10	5	$50			− $ 6	$50	$ 0
				− $ 2	$8			
G	$ 8	6	$48			− $10	$58	− $ 8 (Losses)

In row *A*, if Paola has no revenues and still has fixed costs of $10, her economic profits are a loss of $10. In row *B*, if Paola sells one piercing for $18, total revenues are $18 and total costs are $18 ($10 fixed costs plus $8 marginal cost for one piercing), so economic profits are $0. In row *C*, if Paola sells two piercings for $16 each, total revenues are $32, total costs are $26 ($10 fixed costs plus $8 marginal cost for the first piercing and $8 marginal cost for the second piercing), so economic profits are $6.

According to the rule, row *D* has maximum profits. If Paola sells three piercings for $14 each, total revenues are $42 and total costs are $34, so economic profits are $8. What if Paola — thinking that more seems better — increases her output more?

Look at row *E* to see why that would be a mistake. If Paola sells four piercings for $12 each, total revenues are $48 and total costs are $42, so economic profits are $6. That is *less than* the smart choice of three piercings at a price of $14. Economic profits get even worse for five or six piercings.

It is important to understand the difference between the related columns Change in Total Profits and Economic Profits. Change in Total Profits tells you *by how much profits change* as a result of a decision, while Economic Profits are the *final outcomes* — what your business actually earns. Smart business decisions are based on economic profits.

Back to the Three Keys to Smart Choices

The rule for maximum profits is

Estimate marginal revenues and marginal costs,
then set the highest price that allows you to sell the highest quantity
for which marginal revenue is greater than marginal cost.

I hope this rule for pricing for profits reminds you of the Three Keys to Smart Choices model.

3 KEYS TO SMART CHOICES

1 CHOOSE ONLY WHEN ADDITIONAL BENEFITS ARE GREATER THAN ADDITIONAL OPPORTUNITY COSTS.

2 COUNT ONLY **ADDITIONAL** BENEFITS AND **ADDITIONAL** OPPORTUNITY COSTS.

3 BE SURE TO COUNT **ALL** ADDITIONAL BENEFITS AND COSTS, INCLUDING **IMPLICIT COSTS** AND **EXTERNALITIES.**

The rule for pricing for profits is much like Keys 1, 2, and 3. Paola's business "benefits" are her economic profits. A smart, profit-maximizing business decision is producing only when *marginal* revenues (*additional* benefits) are greater than *marginal* costs (*additional* opportunity costs). Differences in fixed costs (including *implicit costs* from Key 3) will not change Paola's decision.

Key 2 says focus only on *marginal* revenues (*additional* benefits) and *marginal* costs (*additional* costs). In Figure 6 on the previous page, if Paola focuses instead on maximum *total* revenues, which are $50 for five piercings, her economic profits are zero — not a smart decision. If Paola focuses on minimum *total* costs, which are $10 in Figure 6 for producing no piercings at all, her economic profits are a loss of $10 — again, not smart.

By producing the highest quantity for which marginal revenue is greater than marginal cost — three piercings — and then setting the highest possible price that allows her to sell all three piercings, Paola maximizes her economic profits ($8) and makes a smart choice.

The rule for pricing for profits works for any business that has to follow the one-price rule. But what happens if businesses can set different prices for different customers for the very same product or service? That's the topic of the next section.

Practice...

6. With each additional unit of output sold by a monopolist under the one-price rule,

    a. total revenue falls.

    b. marginal revenue falls by less than price.

    c. marginal revenue falls by the same amount as price.

    d. marginal revenue falls by more than price.

7. To maximize profits, a price maker chooses outputs where

    a. marginal revenue is greater than marginal cost.

    b. marginal cost is greater than marginal revenue.

    c. price is less than marginal revenue.

    d. price is less than marginal cost.

8. A price-making business must follow the one-price rule and faces the following demand schedule: at prices of $7, $6, $5, and $4, quantity demanded is 300, 400, 500, and 600 units respectively. If the business's marginal cost is constant at $50, it maximizes profits by producing

    a. 600 units and charging a price of $4.

    b. 500 units and charging a price of $5.

    c. 400 units and charging a price of $6.

    d. 300 units and charging a price of $7.

9. Use this graph to answer the question below,

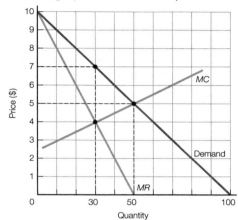

To maximize profits, this price-making business produces a quantity of _____ and charges a price of _____.

    a. 50; 7

    b. 50; 5

    c. 30; 7

    d. 30; 4

10. Four price makers are talking at an expensive restaurant. Which of their statements below is a correct rule for maximum profits?

    a. "We don't increase output unless we know that the larger output will raise total revenue."

    b. "I think cost minimization is the key to maximum profits."

    c. "We try to make the most of our equipment by producing at maximum capacity."

    d. "I don't keep close track of total profits, but I don't approve any business deal unless it increases my revenue more than it increases my costs."

 **Apply...**

4. You have been working too many hours at your part-time job (which pays $15 per hour), and your economics marks are suffering. Your father wants you to do better in school but recognizes your desire for cash, so he offers you this deal. For every 1-percent increase in your mark on the next test, he will pay you $6. You estimate that one additional hour of studying will raise your mark 5 percent; a second hour of studying will raise your mark 4 percent; a third hour, 3 percent; and a fourth hour, 2 percent. If all you are trying to do is make the most money, how many hours should you study?

_____

_____

_____

_____

_____

5. Suppose Paola's marginal revenues and fixed costs are the same as on Figure 6 page 253, but her marginal costs are increasing: $1 for the first piercing, $2 for the second, $3 for the third, $4 for the fourth, $5 for the fifth, and $6 for the sixth piercing. Fill in this table to figure out what quantity and price Paola chooses if she makes a smart decision. Explain your answer.

Row	Price	QD	TR	MR	MC	Total Costs	Total Profits
A							
B							
C							
D							
E							
F							
G							

_____

_____

_____

_____

_____

_____

6. Sami's Samosas is the only samosa seller in Thunder Bay, Ontario. The graph below shows the market demand curve for samosas, and Sami's marginal cost curve.

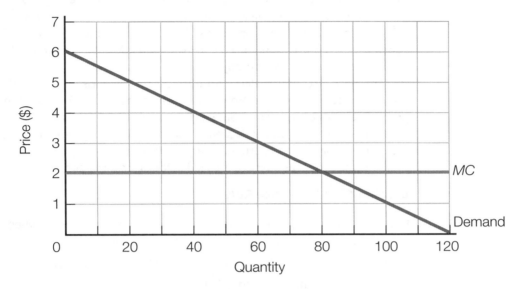

a. Draw Sami's marginal revenue curve. Explain how you knew where to draw it.

_____

_____

_____

_____

_____

_____

b. If Sami follows the rule for maximum profits, what quantity will she produce? What price will she charge?

_____

_____

_____

_____

_____

_____

Price Discrimination for Higher Profits

 Define price discrimination and explain how it leads to higher profits by taking advantage of differences in elasticity of demand.

If businesses price for profits, why do they give some customers discounts for the same product or service? Seniors and children pay less for movies, even though the cost to the movie theatre of one more bum in one more seat (the marginal cost) is the same, regardless of age. For the same airline ticket from Vancouver to Montreal, you pay much less if you book at least two weeks in advance and stay over a Saturday.

Are these discounts really smart business pricing decisions, or are the businesses being charitable? How can a business be pricing for maximum profits if it is not charging the same high price to all customers? These differential prices are definitely smart and not at all charitable — they actually increase a business's total profits. Charging different customers different prices for the same product or service is called **price discrimination**.

Breaking the One-Price Rule

Price discrimination breaks the one-price rule, and is possible only when a business can

- prevent low-price buyers from reselling to high-price buyers.
- control resentment among high-price buyers.

It's easy to resell a physical product like an iPad or a camera or a textbook — think kijiji or eBay. So it's not accidental that most examples of price discrimination involve services (getting pierced, viewing a movie, flying on an airline, using phone minutes) that cannot be easily resold. Ticket takers at movie theatres will not let in a 20-year-old holding a senior or child ticket. Airlines were checking ID long before the post-9/11 security concerns — you always had to prove you were the person named on the ticket.

How do businesses control resentment among the high-price buyers? It's all in the marketing, and the key word is *discount*. Businesses describe the higher price as the "regular" price, and the lower price as the "discounted" price. They could just as easily call the lower price the regular price, and the higher price a "premium" price. You don't need to be a marketing genius to understand why businesses choose the word *discount*!

Discriminate (Cleverly) by Elasticity

So why charge lower prices to some customers? The answer goes back to elasticity of demand. In Chapter 4 we asked whether it is a smart choice for a business to hold a sale and cut prices. For revenues (price × quantity), it is a smart choice as long as the increase in quantity more than makes up for the decrease in price. Remember: "You make it up in volume." That happens when demand is elastic. Even a small fall in price produces a large, responsive (elastic) increase in quantity demanded. Customers with elastic demands have a lower willingness to pay and respond well to discounts.

But if demand is inelastic — a change in price produces only a small, unresponsive (inelastic) change in quantity demanded — then the smart choice is to raise the price to increase revenues. The higher price more than makes up for the small decrease in quantity. Customers with inelastic demands have a higher willingness to pay and they won't all disappear if you raise prices.

So if you can break the one-price rule and set more than one price for your service, it is smart to set a lower price for customers with elastic demands, and a higher price for customers with inelastic demands.

How do you identify customers with different elasticities of demand and get them to voluntarily pay different prices? This is where price discrimination schemes are so clever. No customers will volunteer their *high* willingness to pay if they know you will then charge them a higher price. That would be as foolish as going to a car dealership dressed in a tuxedo and announcing how desperately you want the car whose price you are about to negotiate. The clever business strategy is to set conditions that divide customers into groups roughly dividing elastic demanders and inelastic demanders, and then charging the elastic demanders a lower price and the inelastic demanders a higher price. How do businesses accomplish what sounds like another complicated rule for pricing for profits?

Price Discrimination at the Movies   Let's start with movies. Seniors often have fixed incomes and are less willing or able to pay $15 for a movie. And parents, who pay for most of the children's tickets are less willing to pay for a child (especially if they have more than one!) than for themselves. This group (seniors and children) has, generally, more elastic demand. A lower price leads to a relatively large increase in quantity demanded, increasing total revenues. For other adults, especially the prime age group of 18- to 35-year-old moviegoers, movies are an important part of social life, and they are more willing and able to pay for a movie. You don't need to offer them a discount to get them into the seats. Society accepts these price differences, as it seems fair that people who are less able to pay get a lower price.

Price Discrimination on Airplanes   The secret for successful price discrimination for airlines is to distinguish business customers from non-business customers, and set higher prices for the business customers (oops, I mean give discounted prices to non-business customers).

How do the airlines get away with that, since no customer will voluntarily tell you she is a business traveller if she knows you will charge a higher price? Airlines set restrictions (buy weeks in advance and stay over a Saturday) on the cheaper tickets, which makes them unattractive to business travellers but pose few problems for holiday travellers. Businesspeople often have to travel at the last minute — if the client is demanding, you usually have to go. Most business travellers, especially if they have families, do not want to be away for the weekend. Businesses are also willing to pay more for tickets because they are a legitimate cost that can be charged back to the customer. For all these reasons, the airline restrictions identify the travellers whose demand is more inelastic, and who are more willing and able to pay.

On the other hand, if you are planning a holiday, buying an airline ticket in advance is no big deal. You have to ask your boss for the days off in advance anyway. You want to stay over the weekend because it adds days to your holiday beyond the workweek. And holiday travellers are very price sensitive. If an airline ticket is too expensive, they might take a driving vacation instead. Discounted tickets mean far more holiday trips, and higher revenues from non-business customers whose demand is more elastic and who are less willing and able to pay.

Rules for Price Discrimination   The basic rules for using price discrimination to increase profits are

- prevent resale of the product or service.
- charge a lower price to the elastic demand group (lower willingness to pay).
- charge a higher price to the inelastic demand group (higher willingness to pay).
- control resentment among higher-price buyers.

Price discrimination is a way of lowering the price to attract additional customers who are more sensitive to price (elastic demanders) without lowering the price to everyone else (inelastic demanders).

Dynamic Pricing   Price-discrimination strategies are not limited to only two groups. **Dynamic pricing** is price discrimination that continuously adjusts for many variables affecting willingness to pay. It has been made possible by technological advances including software algorithms that analyze past data, predict future demand, and adjust prices to match. It also has become socially acceptable, avoiding resentment among consumers. Uber surge pricing, differential pricing on weekend meals at popular restaurants, and differential pricing on popular Broadway shows are examples of dynamic pricing that increases total revenue for businesses.

Putting It All Together

All businesses have to live by the law of demand — a rise in price causes a decrease in quantity demanded. Smart businesses choose their price points depending on *how much* consumers' quantity demanded responds to a change in price — in other words, on price elasticity of demand.

This chapter combines that information about price elasticity of demand (which affects marginal revenue) with cost information (marginal cost) to find the rule for pricing to get maximum economic profits. For businesses with price-setting power, price discrimination fine-tunes that rule, letting them get around the law of one price, prevent resale, and control resentment to set different price points for different subgroups of consumers.

Practice...

11. A successful price-discriminating business must be able to

    a. prevent consumer resale.

    b. differentiate consumers with elastic demand and charge them higher prices.

    c. differentiate consumers with inelastic demand and charge them lower prices.

    d. do all of the above.

12. The passenger next to you who paid more than you did for her airline ticket is probably

    a. smarter than you.

    b. older than you.

    c. travelling for business.

    d. all of the above.

13. What happens if the SkyDome, where the Blue Jays play baseball, introduces discounts for seniors and students?

    a. Fewer seniors will buy tickets.

    b. The Blue Jays will win a few more games.

    c. The cost of providing a seat increases.

    d. Revenues increase.

14. Price discrimination is only profitable if a business

    a. creates barriers to entry.

    b. identifies consumers with different price elasticities of demand.

    c. identifies consumers with different cross elasticities of demand.

    d. identifies consumers with different income elasticities of demand.

15. With price discrimination, customers who are _____ pay the highest price.

    a. most able to substitute

    b. least willing to pay

    c. most price sensitive

    d. least price sensitive

Apply...

7. What are the requirements for a business to be able to successfully price discriminate? Why do stores offer discounts to customers who have coupons, instead of just lowering the price for everyone?

_____

_____

_____

_____

8. Price discrimination can be profitable for a monopoly when different consumer groups have different willingness to pay for the product. The smart price-discriminating monopolist treats the groups as different markets. The rule for maximum profits for a price-discriminating monopoly is to find the quantity of output where *marginal revenue in each market = marginal cost*. Then, in each market, charge the maximum price the consumer group is willing to pay for that quantity (on each demand curve).

   Barney's Bistro has two kinds of customers for lunch: stockbrokers and retired senior citizens. The demand for lunches for the two groups are in the table below.

Price	Stockbrokers			Senior Citizens		
	QD	TR	MR	QD	TR	MR
$8	0			0		
$7	1			0		
$6	2			0		
$5	3			1		
$4	4			2		
$3	5			3		
$2	6			4		
$1	7			5		
$0	8			6		

   Barney decides to price discriminate between the groups by treating each demand separately and charging the price that maximizes profit in each of the two submarkets.
   Marginal cost and average total cost are equal and constant at $2 per lunch.

   a. Complete the table by calculating the total and marginal revenue for stockbroker demand, and then the total and marginal revenue for senior citizen demand.

Apply...

b. What is the profit-maximizing quantity and price for stockbrokers? Explain.

_____

_____

_____

c. What is the profit-maximizing quantity and price for senior citizens? Explain.

_____

_____

_____

d. What is Barney's total economic profit?

_____

_____

_____

e. Show that the total economic profit in part **d** is the maximum by comparing it with total economic profit if instead Barney served

    i.   1 more lunch _each_ to stockbrokers and senior citizens, or

_____

_____

_____

_____

_____

    ii. 1 less lunch _each_ to stockbrokers and senior citizens.

_____

_____

_____

_____

_____

9. Explain the difference between dynamic pricing and price discrimination. State your opinion on the fairness of these pricing strategies. Should businesses be allowed to use them? Explain your answer. Your instructor may use this as a discussion question.

_____

_____

_____

_____

_____

Market Structure and Efficiency

 Explain why maximum profits bring efficiency for perfect competition and inefficiency for market structures with price-making power. Compare the benefits and costs of market structures.

For maximum economic profits, the rule for any business in any market structure is **set the highest price that allows you to sell the highest quantity for which marginal revenue is greater than marginal cost**. Smart businesses produce all quantities up to where marginal revenue equals marginal cost, and then charge the highest possible price that allows them to sell all output.

But is what's good for business profits good for the economy as a whole? If all businesses follow the rule for profits, does that produce an efficient outcome? The answers to these questions depend on market structure.

Let's apply the Chapter 3 concepts of consumer surplus and producer surplus (pages 72–75) to the marginal revenue and marginal cost information. The relationship between marginal revenue and price is different for different market structures. For price-taking businesses in perfect competition, marginal revenue equals price. For all other market structures where businesses have some price-making power, marginal revenue is less than price. These differences create different outcomes for the economy as a whole.

In all market structures, marginal cost may be increasing or constant as output increases. To simplify our efficiency comparisons and discover what's best for the economy as a whole, we will look only at examples of increasing marginal cost for all market structures. (The results would be similar with constant marginal costs.)

Efficiency of Perfect Competition and Price Takers

In perfect competition, many small sellers produce identical products. Each business is a price taker, but can sell as much output as it can produce at the market price. The price just covers all marginal opportunity costs of production. A business does not have to lower price to sell more quantity, so price equals marginal revenue. Each identical business is following the rule for profits, producing the quantity where marginal revenue equals marginal cost. Due to perfect competition, the maximum profits to be earned are just normal profits. Let's check the efficiency of this outcome.

Perfect Competition Is Efficient The market demand and supply curves for perfect competition are shown in Figure 7a, (which is similar to Figure 11 on page 74 of Chapter 3). The demand curve is the sum of all of the individual consumers' demand curves, and the supply curve is the sum of all of the individual businesses' marginal cost curves. The demand curve is also a marginal benefit curve; the supply curve is also a marginal cost curve. The equilibrium price where the curves intersect — in this case $60 — equals both the marginal benefit and the marginal cost of the 600th unit. For all quantities up to 600 units, marginal benefit is greater than marginal cost. Consumer surplus equals the shaded green area under the marginal benefit (demand) curve, but above the market price. Producer surplus equals the shaded blue area below the market price, but above the marginal cost (supply) curve. Total surplus (consumer surplus plus producer surplus) is maximum for perfect competition. This is an efficient market outcome, coordinating the smart choices of consumers and businesses.

Figure 7   Efficiency of Price Takers and Inefficiency of Price Makers

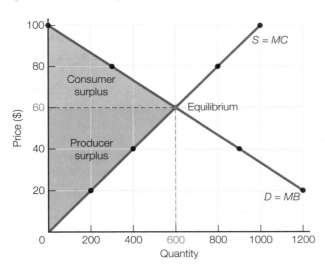

a) Efficiency of Perfect Competition

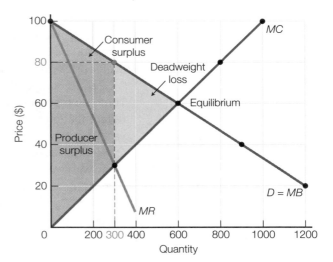

b) Inefficiency of Market Structure with Price Makers

Inefficiency of Market Structures with Price Makers

For the same demand curve and supply curves in Figure 7a, imagine the market is now supplied by one monopolist instead of many small businesses. The demand curve is now the demand curve facing the monopolist. The monopolist has price-making power, and must lower price to sell more. Because of the one-price rule, marginal revenue is less than price. To apply the rule for maximum profits, we must draw the marginal revenue curve in Figure 7b. The supply curve is now the monopolist's marginal cost curve, which is the same as the sum of all of the previous businesses' increasing marginal cost curves.

Price-Making Power Is Inefficient   Using the recipe for profits, the monopolist finds the quantity where the marginal revenue and marginal cost curves intersect, which is 300. The highest possible price for selling 300 units is $80. Compare the price and quantity of monopoly with perfect competition. The monopolist restricts output from 600 units to 300 units, and raises price from $40 to $80. With the same inputs, the monopolist is producing less and charging a higher price — clearly inefficient for the economy as a whole!

We can also judge efficiency by comparing the consumer and producer surpluses of the monopolist with those of perfect competition. Compared to Figure 7a, the monopolist's consumer surplus in Figure 7b has shrunk to the green triangular area below the demand curve but above the price line of $80. The monopolist captures some of the lost consumer surplus as producer surplus.

The shaded grey area is **deadweight loss** (see page 75) — potential consumer and producer surplus from the units between 300 and 600 that the monopolist does not produce. Deadweight loss reduces the total surplus for this price-making monopolist — consumer surplus plus producer surplus — to less than for perfect competition. Deadweight loss signals an inefficient market outcome.

Price-making power allows businesses to restrict output and raise prices to maximize their profits, but creates deadweight loss. The outcome for the economy as a whole is not as good as the efficient outcome of price-taking perfect competition.

Are Inefficient Price Makers All Bad?

The market structure of perfect competition is more efficient than any market structure with price makers — monopoly, oligopoly, or monopolistic competition. But there are reasons besides efficiency that might lead us to prefer price-making market structures.

Perfect competition has identical businesses producing identical products. There is no product differentiation. That would get boring very fast. Product differentiation creates price-making power and inefficiency, but the gains in variety may be worth the losses in efficiency.

New products are also inconsistent with perfect competition. New products come with some price-making power for their innovators. While, over time, competitors develop similar products — Apple's iPhone was followed pretty quickly by Samsung and other Android smartphones — new products are not usually created by price-taking businesses in perfect competition.

The economic profits of price makers, while inefficient, can finance innovation — research and development, new products, new cost-cutting techniques, new management structures, new low-cost sources of labour overseas. These competitive acts of **creative destruction** generate economic profits for the winners, while improving living standards for all.

Market structures with price-making power are inefficient, but have other benefits. In the next chapter we will look at some government policies aimed at fixing those inefficiencies and their outcomes.

 # Practice...

16. Which is true for businesses in perfect competition, monopolistic competition, and for single-price monopoly?

    a. many substitute products available

    b. zero economic profits in the long run

    c. maximum profits from producing all quantities where marginal revenue is greater than marginal cost

    d. barriers to entry

17. Industries with perfect competition have

    a. maximum total surplus.

    b. deadweight loss.

    c. the benefits of creative destruction.

    d. product variety.

18. Industries with price-making power have

    a. deadweight loss.

    b. the benefits of creative destruction.

    c. marginal revenue equals marginal cost at quantity with maximum total profits.

    d. all of the above.

19. Compared to a perfectly competitive industry, an industry with price-making power

    a. increases output, raises price, and earns higher profits.

    b. increases output, raises price, and earns normal profits.

    c. restricts output, raises price, and earns higher profits.

    d. restricts output, raises price, and earns normal profits.

20. When businesses follow the rule for maximum profits, the outcome is

    a. always efficient.

    b. efficient for price-taking market structures and inefficient for price-making market structures.

    c. efficient for price-making market structures and inefficient for price-taking market structures.

    d. also best for the economy.

Apply...

10. Use Figure 7 on page 265 to answer these questions.

   a. What is the difference in the quantity and price outcomes for market structures with price makers compared to perfect competition?

_____

_____

_____

   b. Use only the concepts of marginal benefit and marginal cost (not consumer or producer surplus) to explain why consumers are worse off in the market structure with price makers.

_____

_____

_____

_____

_____

11. Here are the demand and marginal cost curves for a price maker.

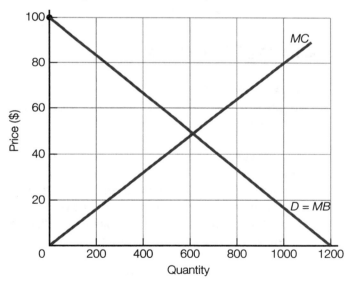

   a. What are the profit-maximizing output and price?

_____

_____

_____

   b. Identify the areas of consumer surplus, producer surplus, and deadweight loss.

_____

_____

to be continued

Apply...

continued

12. Is the statement that "efficient price-taking businesses are better for society than inefficient price-making businesses" positive or normative? Do you agree with the claim? What arguments would you make to support your position?

_____

_____

_____

_____

_____

_____

KNOW...

Learning Objectives

1. Marginal revenue equals price for price takers and is less than price for price makers. Because of the one-price rule, to sell more output, price makers must lower the price on all units, not just on new sales.

2. A smart business decision for maximum economic profits involves both quantity and price decisions. The quantity decision is to produce all quantities for which marginal revenue is greater than marginal cost. The price decision is to set the highest possible price that allows you to sell that quantity. The key to maximum profits is to focus on marginal revenues and marginal costs, not on total revenues and total costs.

3. **Price discrimination** is a business strategy that divides customers into groups. Businesses increase profits by lowering the price to attract additional price-sensitive customers (elastic demanders), without lowering the price to others (inelastic demanders). **Dynamic pricing** is a form of price discrimination that continuously adjusts for many variables affecting willingness to pay.

4. Maximum profits bring efficiency for perfect competition, but inefficiency for market structures with price-making power. Relative to perfect competition, price-making market structures restrict output, raise prices, decrease total surplus, and increase **deadweight loss**. The inefficiencies of price-making market structures must be weighed against the benefits of product diversity and innovation financed by economic profits.

Key Terms

creative destruction: competitive business innovations generate economic profits for winners, improve living standards for all, but destroy less productive or less desirable products and production methods

deadweight loss: the decrease in total surplus compared to an economically efficient outcome

dynamic pricing: price discrimination that continuously adjusts for many variables affecting willingness to pay

price discrimination: charging different customers different prices for the same product or service

Answers to Practice

1. **b** Because they are small, businesses in perfect competition can increase sales without lowering the (market-set) price.

2. **c** Always below the demand curve and more steeply sloped because it intercepts the quantity axis at *half* the output of the demand curve.

3. **d** Easily resold and less differentiated than services listed in other choices.

4. **a** Total Revenue changes from $300 to $360, for additional revenue of $60.

5. **d** The change in total revenue from $49 to $48 is – $1.

6. **d** To sell more, must lower price on all units sold.

7. **a** Rule for profits — sell the highest quantity for which marginal revenue is greater than marginal cost. Price will be greater than marginal revenue and marginal cost for a price maker.

8. **a** Marginal revenue moving from 300 to 400 units is $300 ($2100 to $2400), greater than marginal cost of $50. From 400 to 500 units, marginal revenue is $100 ($2400 to $2500), greater than marginal cost of $50. From 500 to 600 units, marginal revenue is – $100 ($2500 to $2400), less than marginal cost of $50.

9. **c** Quantity where *MR* = *MC*. Highest price for selling 30 units is $7, on the demand curve.

10. **d** Increase output if additional revenue is greater than additional cost.

11. **a** Prevent resale; charge higher prices to inelastic demand consumers and lower prices to elastic demand consumers.

12. **c** Demand for business travel is more inelastic.

13. **d** Because more seniors and students buy tickets and other fans pay more.

14. **b** Charge high price to those with price inelastic demand and low price to those with price elastic demand.

15. **d** Least price sensitive means most inelastic demand.

16. **c** Rule for profits applies to all market structures.

17. **a** No deadweight loss, or innovation, or product variety.

18. **d** Same rule for profits; inefficient but with benefits of creative destruction.

19. **c** Restricts output to intersection of *MR* and *MC*, then sets highest price to still sell that quantity.

20. **b** Maximum total surplus for perfect competition and deadweight loss for other market structures.

11 Market Failure and Competition Policy

LEARNING OBJECTIVES

L01 Define market failure and explain the challenge for policymakers of a natural monopoly.

L02 Explain how strategic interaction between competitors complicates business decisions, creating two smart choices.

L03 Explain how governments use laws and regulations to promote competition, discourage cartels, and protect the public from dangerous business practices.

L04 Differentiate between the public-interest view and the capture view of government regulation.

LEARN...

Are you happy with your local cable TV company's prices and service? Did you know that the Canadian Radio-television and Telecommunications Commission (CRTC) willingly gives your cable company a legal monopoly on providing services in your neighbourhood?

Why would the CRTC prevent competition? Why not just allow the competitive market to operate? Markets usually work to provide the products and services we value most. Adam Smith's invisible hand can channel smart choices for you into smart choices for all. But sometimes markets fail to produce outcomes that are in society's best interests. The next three chapters will explore market failures that result in problems, such as natural monopolies (like cable TV), cartels (like the Organization of Oil Exporting Countries — OPEC), pollution (Chapter 12), and poverty and inequalities (Chapter 13). When markets fail, governments often step in to correct the failures. Regulations, Crown corporations, and competition laws are all attempts by governments to produce more efficient and desirable outcomes for society.

While well-intentioned, these government policies sometimes do more harm than good, making the outcome less efficient and less desirable. Like rent controls, government regulations can have negative, unintended consequences. We call those consequences government failure rather than market failure. Sometimes policies designed to protect the public work well, but sometimes government policies end up promoting the special interests of the businesses being regulated.

This chapter examines the trade-offs from government policies to deal with market failures. Understanding these trade-offs will help you make better choices as a citizen voting for politicians supporting regulation policies you approve — and may even reduce your frustration with your cable company!

Market Failure and Natural Monopoly

 L01 Define market failure and explain the challenge for policymakers of a natural monopoly.

Imagine a world where many cable TV companies compete for your business. Sounds like a consumer's dream come true, doesn't it? Competitors provide choices, which consumers value. And just like the downward pull of gravity, competitive forces pull prices down toward levels of perfect competition, where businesses cover all opportunity costs but earn only normal profits. While the dream of cable competitors sounds wonderful, be careful what you wish for. What would happen if your dream came true?

The largest cost, by far, for cable companies is the network of thousands of kilometres of fibre-optic cable running under the streets or paralleling electricity wires above ground. Once the network is in place and the company has paid for programming, the marginal cost of supplying a signal to an additional subscriber is almost zero — the cost of flipping a switch. While the fixed costs of the network are high, the marginal and variable costs of adding subscribers are very low. The result is that *average total costs keep decreasing as the high fixed costs are spread over a larger number of subscribers*.

Right now in your neighbourhood, there is only one such cable network because the CRTC has granted a local monopoly to Rogers, Eastlink, Shaw, or whichever company is your provider. If there were competition in the cable TV industry, every entering competitor would have to dig or string a complete network. And every time you or a neighbour decided to switch providers, there would be digging or rewiring to hook you up to the other cable system. Besides those higher variable costs, each cable company would end up with fewer subscribers over which to spread costs. Average total costs would be higher for all. Competition forces prices down to levels just covering average total costs and normal profits. But if average total costs are higher with multiple competing cable companies, prices will be higher compared to a single cable company.

Natural Monopoly

The cable TV business, like water and electricity utilities, has lower average costs as the scale of output increases, both in the short run and the long run. In the microeconomic **short run** (when some inputs are fixed and other inputs are variable), as output increases, **average total cost** can decrease as fixed costs are spread over a larger quantity of output. In the microeconomic **long run** (when all inputs are variable), **economies of scale** refers to decreasing long-run average costs, as businesses build larger and larger plants. The percentage increase in a business's output is greater than the percentage increase in inputs, lowering long-run average costs.

The common use of the phrase "economies of scale" often suggests that bigger is better — larger businesses have lower average costs, whether in the short run or the long run. Economists call these kinds of businesses **natural monopolies**. To achieve lowest average (total) costs, economies of scale allow only a single seller.

Even if competitors were allowed in the cable TV industry, eventually the company with the greatest economies of scale would underprice the smaller companies — forcing them out of business or into takeovers or mergers. The competitive forces that force down prices would result in a single seller with a monopoly's price-making power! This type of monopoly seems inevitable, like a force of nature. But is it really?

Market Failure

Sometimes the market's competitive forces fail to bring prices down to just cover all opportunity costs of production, and do not push costs down to minimum average total costs. **Market failure** happens when market outcomes are inefficient or inequitable. Instead of producing the miracle of markets, markets fail and produce outcomes that are not in society's best interests.

Efficiency and Equity Again   We can evaluate the inefficiency of market failure: Does the market outcome have lowest average total cost, or maximum total surplus (consumer surplus plus producer surplus on pages 72–75)? But even an efficient market outcome — where products and services produced at lowest cost go to those most willing and able to pay — may not be fair or equitable (pages 129–132).

Inequality and "society's best interests" are harder to evaluate than efficiency because they involve normative judgments. Evaluating the equity of market outcomes involves answering questions like, "Do you believe that markets should meet the equity standards of equal outcomes or equal opportunities?" And, "If there is a trade-off between efficiency and equity, which one should the government, acting in 'society's best interests,' try and achieve?"

Government faces many challenges designing policies to try to correct market failures.

The Government Policy Challenge

The only way to achieve the efficiency of lowest-cost production in businesses with economies of scale is to have a single large business supply the entire market. Size matters. But that private business, for example your local cable provider, will act like any other profit-maximizing monopoly. While its costs may be low, no competitors are forcing it to pass on those cost savings to consumers through lower prices. The monopolist with economies of scale follows the same rule for profits as any other business with pricing power: Estimate marginal revenues and marginal costs, then set the highest price that allows it to sell the highest quantity for which marginal revenue is greater than marginal cost. Compared to the competitive outcome, the monopolist restricts output and raise prices, setting the price well above average total costs to earn the highest possible economic profits.

This is the challenge facing government policymakers:

How do you gain the low-cost efficiencies of economies of scale, but avoid the inefficiencies of monopoly's restricted output and higher price?

The two major policies that governments around the world use to deal with this challenge are public ownership and regulation.

Public Ownership: Crown Corporations   In Canada, public ownership of businesses with economies of scale takes the form of Crown corporations. Crown corporations are created by the federal or provincial governments, which own 100 percent of the corporation's assets. **Crown corporations** can be created, or government can buy out the assets of private businesses. There are Crown corporations in electricity, water, and gas, as well as in industries that don't have economies of scale but are seen as publicly important for other economic, political, or social reasons (culture, alcohol, lotteries, agriculture, fisheries). Examples of Crown corporations in Canada include BC Hydro, Canada Post, Canadian Broadcasting Corporation (CBC), GO Transit, and VIA Rail Canada.

While Crown corporations such as utilities (water, gas, electricity) achieve economies of scale, they are not a perfect solution to the policy challenge. The disadvantages come from the lack of competitive pressure. Incentives are weak for reducing costs, increasing efficiency, or exploring innovative new technologies. And there are the usual risks of a large, bureaucratic organization — waste, lack of performance incentives, and too many rules.

Regulated Private Monopoly   The other government response to the policy challenge of economies of scale is to allow a single private business, but have the government regulate it. This is what the CRTC does in regulating the cable TV industry. Each cable provider is given a monopoly for its assigned neighbourhoods, but the price it can charge subscribers is regulated by the government.

In principle, government regulators try to set prices that just cover average total costs, including normal profits. In practice, regulators do not directly observe costs, and can't tell how hard the business is trying to keep costs low, so they use a technique called **rate of return regulation**. The regulated monopoly is allowed to charge a price that earns it the normal rate of return, or normal profits — the average rate of profits in other industries.

Rate of return regulation is not a perfect solution to the policy challenge either. The "normal rate of return" policy creates an incentive for managers of the regulated businesses to exaggerate their reported costs, since they are guaranteed a normal rate of return on all costs. "Costs" may include luxury consumption for management, such as a private box at the Air Canada Centre (justified in the name of entertaining clients), limousines, company jets, international travel, entertainment, and so on.

In the final section of this chapter, we will look again at the advantages and disadvantages of unregulated monopolies and at government alternatives for dealing with the challenges of natural monopolies.

What's So Natural about Natural Monopoly?

The term *natural monopoly* implies there is something inevitable about these technologies that will always produce a monopoly, like a law of nature that never changes. Natural monopolies arise when the technology has economies of scale that require a single supplier. But technologies change. Before 1990, the only way to place a long-distance call from Canada to Europe was through the single undersea cable that linked the continents. Phone companies had a natural monopoly. But the development of new technologies changed the industry to a more competitive market structure. Advances in fibre optics and VoIP (Voice over Internet Protocol) technologies mean that phone company cables can carry television signals, and cable companies can provide phone services. Satellites are another technology for delivering phone and television signals. So what had been a regulated monopoly changed. Natural monopolies are only as natural as the current technology.

Practice...

1. A natural monopoly has
    a. low fixed cost and low marginal cost.
    b. low fixed cost and high marginal cost.
    c. high fixed cost and low marginal cost.
    d. high fixed cost and high marginal cost.

2. Which is *least* likely to be a natural monopoly?
    a. electric utility
    b. taxi service
    c. water and sewer service
    d. cable TV service

3. Market failure can happen when there are
    a. inequalities.
    b. economies of scale.
    c. inefficiencies.
    d. all of the above.

4. The challenge facing government policymakers is how to
    a. gain the low-cost efficiencies of economies of scale, but avoid the inefficiencies of monopoly's restricted output and higher price.
    b. avoid the low-cost efficiencies of economies of scale, but gain the efficiencies of monopoly's increased output and lower price.
    c. gain the low-cost efficiencies of economies of scale, and gain the efficiencies of monopoly's increased output and lower price.
    d. avoid the inefficiencies of economies of scale, and avoid the inefficiencies of monopoly's restricted output and higher price.

5. An industry with high _____ probably has economies of scale.
    a. average total costs
    b. marginal costs
    c. opportunity costs
    d. fixed costs

Apply...

1. In your own words, explain the challenge facing government policymakers in dealing with natural monopolies.

    _____

    _____

    _____

    _____

2. The telecommunications regulatory body in Canada — the Canadian Radio-television and Telecommunications Commission (CRTC) — supports the move toward greater competition but retains control over telecommunications prices.

    a. Until the late 1990s, prices of telecommunication services were set by the CRTC at levels that covered total costs. Explain why linking prices with costs reduces supplier incentives to develop cost-saving technology.

        _____

        _____

        _____

        _____

        _____

        _____

    b. The telecommunications industry has a slow rate of entry of new competitors into local residential service. Some argue that if prices were allowed to rise, more competitors would enter. Explain why price regulation holds back the progress toward a more competitive industry.

        _____

        _____

        _____

        _____

        _____

        _____

3. Identify one Crown corporation or regulated private monopoly you buy services from. Find out from its website everything you can about its costs and the regulations under which it operates. Do you think its services could be improved? Explain your answer.

    _____

    _____

    _____

    _____

    _____

    _____

Prisoners' Dilemma and Conspiracies

 Explain how strategic interaction between competitors complicates business decisions, creating two smart choices.

Almost every Thursday before a long weekend, prices seem to rise simultaneously at gasoline stations across Canadian cities. By Saturday or Sunday a few stations cut their prices, and within a few days, prices fall everywhere. This odd pricing behaviour repeats in regular cycles.

Gasoline Price Wars and Conspiracies

Gasoline price swings often cause motorists to complain so much that governments form committees to investigate if the oil companies are conspiring unfairly to raise prices. The investigations usually do not find clear evidence of conspiracy (although gas-station owners in Quebec were convicted in 2012 of conspiring to fix gasoline prices).

Both simultaneous gasoline price rises and gas price wars result from strategic, competitive decisions by the stations and the oil companies that own them. Gas prices fluctuate wildly on long weekends not because of changes in the cost of oil used to produce gasoline, but because of a tension that exists between stations trying to agree to keep prices high, but being tempted to cheat on the agreement in order to sell more gas. Let me explain using the unlikely example of police interrogation tactics.

The Prisoners' Dilemma: Game Theory and Strategic Behaviour

Strategic competitive decisions, like gas pricing, can be better understood using **game theory**. Game theory began as an abstract mathematical tool developed in the 1940s by John von Neumann and Oskar Morgenstern. It was extended by John Nash, a Princeton professor who won the Nobel Prize in Economics in 1994 and was the subject of the 2001 movie *A Beautiful Mind*. The beauty of game theory is its simplicity in helping us understand any strategic situation where the players of the game have to make decisions while worrying about what their rivals will do. Game theory is used by economists and political scientists to understand the OPEC oil cartel, nuclear arms races between countries, and even gasoline price wars.

The simplest example of game theory is called the **prisoners' dilemma**, which describes a scenario you have seen on countless TV detective shows. Two criminals, let's say Bonnie and Clyde, are caught in the act of robbing a bank. They know the police have the evidence to convict them of bank robbery. The police suspect the pair murdered a bank teller in a previous robbery, but don't have the evidence to prove murder.

The detective in charge has a plan to get Bonnie or Clyde to confess to the murder. He places the prisoners in separate rooms, with no ability to communicate with each other. He then sets up rewards (reduced jail time) for cooperating with the police by confessing, and penalties (more jail time) for denying the murder charge if the other prisoner confesses. The detective's plan is to build up mistrust between Bonnie and Clyde, and to get each one to worry the other will confess.

Payoffs Depend on the Other's Choice   The rewards and penalties are illustrated in Figure 1. Let me explain how to "read" the figure. The two players are Bonnie and Clyde. Each has a single strategic choice — either to confess to the murder, or to deny the murder. The payoff to each choice depends on the other prisoner's choice. Bonnie's payoffs are in beige; Clyde's payoffs are in dark orange. Look at payoff box A. If Bonnie and Clyde both confess to the murder, they each get 10 years in prison for both crimes — armed bank robbery and murder. Look at payoff box B. If Bonnie confesses but Clyde denies, Bonnie gets rewarded with only a 5-year sentence for both crimes, while Clyde gets hit with the maximum 25-year sentence. Payoff box C is the reverse of B. If Clyde confesses but Bonnie denies, Clyde gets the lower 5-year sentence and Bonnie gets 25 years. And if both deny the murder, they can be convicted only of bank robbery and get 7 years each (box D).

Figure 1   The Prisoners' Dilemma of Bonnie and Clyde

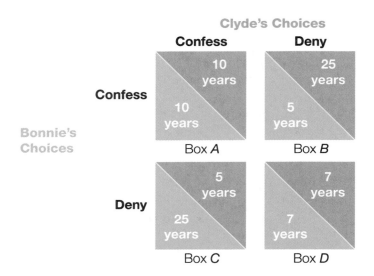

Nash Equilibrium   What choices are Bonnie and Clyde likely to make? We need to figure out Bonnie's best choice given Clyde's choice, and Clyde's best choice given Bonnie's choice. This is called a **Nash equilibrium** (after John Nash), and tells us the outcome of the game.

Let's start with Bonnie (payoffs in beige). If Clyde confesses, Bonnie's best choice is to confess, because 10 years in jail (box A) is better than 25 years (box C). If Clyde denies, Bonnie's best choice again is to confess, because 5 years in jail (box B) is better than 7 years (box D). No matter what choice Clyde makes, the detective has set up the outcomes so Bonnie's best choice is to confess.

What about Clyde (payoffs in orange)? If Bonnie confesses, Clyde's best choice is to confess, because 10 years in jail (box A) is better than 25 years (box B). If Bonnie denies, Clyde's best choice again is to confess, because 5 years in jail (box C) is better than 7 years (box D). No matter what choice Bonnie makes, the detective has set up the outcomes so Clyde's best choice is to confess.

So both Bonnie and Clyde confess, each gets a 10-year jail sentence, and the detective gets promoted. This outcome (except for the promotion) is the Nash equilibrium of the game.

The "dilemma" part of the prisoners' dilemma comes from the fact that each prisoner is motivated to confess, when each would be better off if they could trust each other to deny (7 years instead of 10 years). Game theory exposes a complication to our rule for smart choices — choose only when additional benefits are greater than additional opportunity costs. There seem to be *two* smart choices for the prisoners, hence the dilemma. The smart choice is to *confess if you don't trust the other*. But the other smart choice is to *deny if you can trust the other*. Smart choices are complicated by considering what your rivals will do, and whether or not you can trust them.

Game Theory and Gas Prices   What does all this have to do with gas prices? Everything! Gas-station owners face the same dilemma. Their strategic choice is not to deny or confess, but to cooperate with an implicit agreement to keep prices high, or to cheat on the agreement and cut prices. There is no need for a clever detective to set the incentives of the game. Self-interest, the quest for profits, and competition do the trick.

If station owners can trust each other to raise prices before the weekend and cooperate with the agreement to keep them high (like box *D* in the prisoners' dilemma, where both prisoners deny and get their best outcome), profits are maximized for all. But each owner has an incentive to cheat on this agreement (confess), hoping that if his is the only station to lower prices just a little, he will sell far more gasoline at what is still a relatively high price. But once cheating begins, trust breaks down and all owners are driven to the Nash equilibrium outcome, where everyone cheats (like box *A*, where both prisoners confess). Prices fall and profits are reduced. Eventually, reduced profits lead owners to take a chance on trusting each other again, since they figure it couldn't be worse than the existing low prices and profits. All stations raise their prices, and the cycle of pricing behaviour begins again. But hopefully, now that you know some game theory, the pricing behaviour doesn't seem quite so odd — the instability of price and profit outcomes is explained by the cycle of trust and no trust.

Trust or No Trust?   The important insight of game theory is the tension between the Nash equilibrium outcome (where the best choice for players who can't trust each other is to confess or cheat) and the fact that both players could make themselves better off if they could trust each other (and deny or cooperate). With the complication of trust, there are now two smart choices. Keeping gas prices simultaneously high is one smart choice based on trust. Gas price wars, another smart choice, break out when there is no trust.

The possibility of two smart choices complicates pricing decisions, especially for the market structure of oligopoly, where there only a few big players. The small number of businesses makes cooperation more likely, but the question of trusting or not trusting your "cooperating" partner remains. We will look at oligopoly pricing games in the Apply questions and in the next section.

Practice...

6. In the prisoners' dilemma with Bonnie and Clyde, each prisoner will be best off if

    a. both prisoners confess.

    b. both prisoners deny.

    c. Bonnie denies and Clyde confesses.

    d. Clyde denies and Bonnie confesses.

7. John Nash, who extended the ideas of game theory, was the subject of what Academy Award-winning movie?

    a. *Beauty and the Beast*

    b. *A Beautiful Economist*

    c. *A Beautiful Body*

    d. *A Beautiful Mind*

8. There is a Nash equilibrium when

    a. both players have no reason to change their choices once seeing their opponent's choice.

    b. player one cooperates and player two cheats.

    c. player one cheats and player two cooperates.

    d. each player has a strategy.

9. Cheating on cartel agreements occurs because each member has an incentive to

    a. restrict its output to maximize profits.

    b. restrict the number of members in the cartel.

    c. lower its price to sell more than the agreed quantity.

    d. raise its price to maximize profits.

The table below gives the payoffs in economic profits for Companies A and B when each has two strategies: (1) charge a low price, or (2) charge a high price.

		Company B	
		Lower Prices	Higher Prices
Company A	Lower Prices	A: $2 \\ B: $5	A: $20 \\ B: - $10
	Higher Prices	A: - $10 \\ B: $25	A: $10 \\ B: $20

10. In Nash equilibrium, Company A makes economic profits of

    a. $2.

    b. $5.

    c. $10.

    d. $20.

Apply...

4. What is a Nash equilibrium?

   _____

   _____

   _____

5. The most fun way to understand the abstract, mathematical techniques of game theory is to watch the bar scene (Governing Dynamics — Ignore the Blonde) from _A Beautiful Mind_ (https://tinyurl.com/flextext-beautiful-mind). This film about John Nash won the 2001 Oscar for Best Picture.

   Game theory is about strategic interaction. The "game" in the movie clip is how each of the four guys in the bar can get lucky and go home with the girl of his choice. Your instructor can use this clip to start a discussion about identifying players, strategies, and outcomes in the game.

   _____

   _____

   _____

   _____

   _____

   _____

6. A small Ontario town has two bakeries — Always Fresh and Never Stale. Transportation costs are high relative to the price of bread, so the bakeries do not get any out-of-town competition. The local bread industry is an oligopoly with only two businesses, called a duopoly (from the Greek words _duo_ [meaning "two"] and _poly_ [meaning "seller"]). Always Fresh and Never Stale have the same costs, and each currently makes an annual profit of $2000.

   Suppose that a new advertising service, Philomena's Flyers, starts up. If one bakery advertises in Philomena's Flyers, its annual profits increase to $5000, while the other bakery loses $2000. If both advertise, each makes a zero profit. If neither advertises, each bakery continues to make an annual profit of $2000.

   a. Represent this duopoly as a game by identifying the players' strategies and possible outcomes.

   b. Construct the payoff matrix.

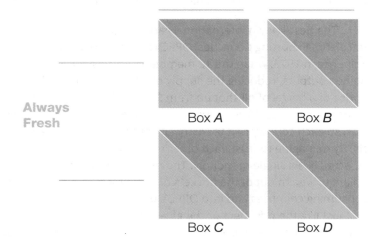

Never Stale

Always Fresh

Box _A_   Box _B_

Box _C_   Box _D_

to be continued

Apply...

continued

    c.   What is the Nash equilibrium outcome? Explain.

_____

_____

_____

_____

_____

_____

Cartels, Collusion, Cheating, Competition Law, *Caveat Emptor*

L03   Explain how governments use laws and regulations to promote competition, discourage cartels, and protect the public from dangerous business practices.

Economists, consumers, and governments have long worried about businesses secretly cooperating to improve profits by fixing prices, restricting output, or sacrificing safety to cut costs.

Cartels and Collusion

Cooperate is a polite, friendly sounding word. The other words generally used to describe businesses that cooperate are *collusion* by a *cartel*. The dictionary definition of **collusion** is "secret or illegal cooperation or conspiracy, especially in order to cheat or deceive others." A **cartel** is an association of manufacturers or suppliers formed to maintain high prices and restrict competition.

OPEC   The best-known international cartel today is OPEC — the Organization of Petroleum Exporting Countries. OPEC formed in 1961 and gained world prominence in 1973, when the 12 member countries agreed to restrict their combined outputs, reducing the supply of oil and driving up the world price. The price of a barrel of oil shot up from $3 to $12 over just four months — a 300 percent increase! The collusive agreement set individual production quotas, so each country had to restrict its output below its previous production levels. By managing to trust each other to stick to the quotas in the agreement, OPEC acted like a single monopoly. The rise in oil prices transferred billions of dollars of wealth out of the pockets of consumers and businesses in oil-consuming countries and into OPEC's pockets.

    But just like the prisoners or the gas-station owners, OPEC members had — and continue to have — an ever-present temptation to cheat on their agreement.

Over time, energy conservation efforts and new oil suppliers (attracted by the economic profits and not being part of OPEC) caused prices to fall. The recession of 1981–1983, which reduced economic activity and decreased demand for oil, caused a more dramatic fall in price. OPEC members began to cheat and increase output, causing oil prices to fall further. Since that time, OPEC swings between periods of trust and high oil prices, and periods of mistrust, cheating, and lower oil prices. Just as game theory predicts!

There is great temptation for businesses to form cartels because the payoffs to collusion are high. Cartels generally transfer money from consumers to business profits. Collusive agreements to fix prices are a clear and knowing conspiracy against consumers. To put it bluntly, consumers get robbed. An Australian government official said it well: "Cartels are theft — usually by well-dressed thieves." Recently, Loblaws admitted to colluding with other grocery companies in Canada to artificially keep bread prices high for more than fourteen years!

Competition Law

The OPEC cartel does not break the law, but only because there is no international law prohibiting cartels. But almost every country has national laws prohibiting collusion among businesses to fix prices and restrict competition.

In the late 1800s, there were Canadian cartels in many industries, from biscuits to coal to coffins to fire insurance. These cartels (called *combines* or *trusts* at the time) attracted consumer and government concern. Parliament passed the first *Anti-Combines Act* (also called anti-trust) in 1889, making it illegal for businesses to combine to form monopolies or near-monopolies. The Act also forbade collusion among businesses to raise prices or restrict supplies to customers, or to do anything that would "unduly lessen" competition.

Most industrialized countries passed similar laws as part of the legal rules of the game (along with **property rights** and the enforcement of contracts) governing economic activity and markets. Such laws make it illegal for businesses to communicate about fixing prices, and prevent cartels from signing legal contracts to enforce cooperation. Anti-combines laws drive price-fixing agreements underground, making it harder for colluding businesses to see each other's actions, to trust each other, and to enforce their collusion. These laws, like the detective putting prisoners in separate rooms, prevent communication and cooperation among companies. The goal is to encourage each business to compete and act only in its individual self-interest in order to get invisible-hand outcomes that are better for consumers and society as a whole.

The Competition Act   Today's anti-combines law is called the *Competition Act*, passed by Parliament in 1986. Its purpose is "to maintain and encourage competition in Canada in order to promote the efficiency and adaptability of the Canadian economy."

This purpose sounds clear, but it is often hard to distinguish competitive business behaviour from collusive behaviour. Competition takes many forms, but it is (as we saw in Chapter 8) always an active attempt to increase profits and gain the market power of monopoly. When businesses buy or merge with other competitors in their markets, they increase their profits and pricing power by eliminating competitors and substitute products.

But if the merger also provides economies of scale that lower costs or allow the business to better compete internationally, the merger promotes "efficiency and adaptability."

The *Competition Act* distinguishes two kinds of anti-competitive offences with different legal penalties.

- *Criminal offences* include price fixing, bid rigging, and false or misleading advertising. Trials are held by the courts, and penalties include prison sentences and fines.

- *Civil offences* are less serious, and include mergers, abusing a business's dominant market position, and other actions that lessen competition. Charges are heard by a quasi-judicial Competition Tribunal composed of federal judges and business experts. Penalties include fines and legal prohibitions of mergers and anti-competitive business practices.

Criminal Offences   Canada, along with Australia, Britain, France, Germany, Ireland, Japan, and the United States, uses prison time to penalize business executives convicted of price fixing. When large, sophisticated businesses make secret agreements to fix prices, they are conspiring against consumers. These underground agreements are highly profitable and hard to discover, so tough penalties like prison terms help discourage collusive agreements.

The *Competition Act* raises the expected costs (prison time) to businesses of price-fixing compared to the expected benefits (profits). Fines do the same, but a fine alone that is large enough to discourage price fixing could financially ruin a business, reduce competition, and unintentionally penalize innocent players like suppliers to the company (who might lose sales) and workers (who might lose their jobs).

The threat of prison terms also helps governments uncover secret cartels. Like the detective in the Bonnie and Clyde case, government officials can offer deals — reduced sentences or amnesty — to whistle-blowers who reveal the cartel agreement. This sets up a Nash equilibrium similar to the prisoners' dilemma because each conspirator can make herself better off by confessing to the agreement and escaping punishment. The tougher the prison penalties, the greater the incentive to be the first to confess.

Civil Offences   Civil, or non-criminal, offences like mergers are reviewed by a Competition Tribunal. The Tribunal first determines if the merger will lessen competition in that market. The Tribunal then also must determine if the merger will create any increased efficiencies. The decision must weigh the costs of the merger (decreased competition) with the benefits (increased efficiencies). Does this sound familiar? It is Key 1 of the Three Keys to Smart Choices! The Competition Tribunal prohibits the merger if expected costs are greater than expected benefits, and allows the merger if expected benefits are greater than expected costs.

ADDITIONAL BENEFITS VS. OPPORTUNITY COSTS

Regulatory Agencies in Canada

In recent years in Canada, hundreds of dogs and cats died from eating tainted pet food that contained the poison polyvinyl. Mattel and Hasbro recalled thousands of toys because they contained lead paint that was potentially poisonous for children. And inexpensive toothpastes imported from China contained a toxic ingredient that was cheaper than the proper ingredient. It was discovered only when the few unfortunate people who were the first to use the toothpaste died.

In pursuing lower costs, competitive advantage, and higher profits, private businesses may use cheaper, even dangerous, materials and compromise workers' and consumers' health and safety. The same economic forces behind the invisible hand may produce deadly results when used by reckless and unethical businesses and individuals.

Competition ensures that, *eventually,* as word gets around, consumers will stop buying from businesses that produce harmful products and turn to safe competitors. But few citizens want to be the laboratory mice who serve as the signal to future consumers to beware, so they call on their elected representatives in government to do something. That usually takes the form of regulating the questionable industry.

Let the Buyer Beware?   *Should* the government play the role of regulator for products and services? If so, how effective will that regulation be? The debate over this question goes back centuries, to the beginning of trade. You can tell the debate is ancient because the phrase used to describe it — *caveat emptor* — is from Latin. **Caveat emptor** means "Let the buyer beware."

One answer to the question is that it is the responsibility of consumers, not government, to monitor the quality of what they buy. Far too many products and services exist for government to be able to monitor them all. Even if the government were capable of such an enormous task, the required bureaucracy would cost far more than the benefits of screening out the minority of products that are dangerous (additional costs of regulation greater than additional benefits — Key 1 for smart choices).

Another answer is that there are certain products — nuclear power, medicines, poisonous insecticides, and so on — that the average consumer is simply not capable of evaluating. Similarly, there are professional services — from doctors, lawyers, accountants, tradespeople — for which most of us will not know whether individual professionals are doing a good job or whether they are only pretending to do a good job. As a consumer, you don't want to be the one to be deceived, especially if the deception costs you your health, your fortune, or even your life (additional benefits of regulation greater than additional costs).

Forms of Regulation   There is no single right answer to the regulation question. As a result, some products and services are regulated, and many others are not. There are three major forms of government regulation in Canada.

Federal and provincial *government departments* regulate certain industries or roles. For example, the Department of Labour enforces regulations designed to prevent businesses from compromising worker safety when trying to keep costs down.

Governments appoint independent *agencies and boards*, usually called commissions, to regulate another type of industry. Examples include the CRTC, the Public Service Commission, the Canadian Dairy Commission, the Nova Scotia Board of Public Utility Commissioners, the Canadian Wheat Board, and the Atomic Energy Control Board. Senior government bureaucrats at these agencies and boards are usually experts in the industry, and often are recruited from the regulated businesses. The guiding principles the government legislation provides — that businesses act "in the public interest," or allow only "just and reasonable rates" — are sufficiently vague that regulators have considerable freedom in setting and enforcing regulations.

Because professions like medicine or law or trades involve specialized training, they can be knowledgeably regulated only by a member of that profession or trade. Governments give *professional associations*, like the Canadian Medical Association, the Canadian Bar Association, and the International Brotherhood of Electrical Workers, the authority to regulate themselves. The associations decide who is qualified to practice, and discipline members who don't live up to their professional standards.

But there is a fine line between ensuring quality service and ensuring the self-interest of the profession. For example, rules that guarantee a certain type of training for doctors or engineers also prevent professionals who have trained in different countries from practicing here. This restricts the supply of doctors, lawyers, engineers, and tradespeople, which restricts competition and raises the price consumers pay for these services.

All of these regulations are intended to serve the public interest. But do they? The guiding principles are vague, and there are close relationships between the regulatory bodies and the industries they regulate. It is also possible that the regulators serve the interests of businesses in the industry at the public's expense — the subject of the final section of this chapter.

 **Practice…**

11. According to game theory,
    a. businesses within cartels are tempted to cheat.
    b. businesses within cartels have incentives to cooperate.
    c. prison penalties help governments uncover secret cartels.
    d. all of the above are true.

12. What outcome of mergers is viewed as *undesirable* under *Canada's Competition Act*?
    a. lower costs
    b. economies of scale
    c. decreased competition
    d. increased international competitiveness

13. Anti-combines (or anti-trust) laws attempt to
    a. support prices.
    b. prevent monopoly practices.
    c. establish Crown corporations.
    d. regulate monopolies.

14. Criminal offences in the *Competition Act* include
    a. price fixing.
    b. bid rigging.
    c. false advertising.
    d. all of the above.

15. The *unintended consequence* of governments appointing professional associations like the International Brotherhood of Electrical Workers may be to
    a. restrict the supply of electricians and keep their incomes high.
    b. discipline members who don't meet professional standards.
    c. certify who is qualified to practice.
    d. certify the quality of electrical services.

 **Apply...**

7. Adam Smith is often described as a supporter of free markets and opposed to government intervention. But consider this quote from Smith's *Wealth of Nations*: "People of the same trade seldom get together, even for merriment and diversion, but the conversation ends in a conspiracy against the public, or in some contrivance to raise prices." What do you think of Smith's quote? Do you think Smith would support a role for government like enforcing the *Competition Act*? Your instructor may use these questions for a class discussion.

    _____

    _____

    _____

    _____

    _____

    _____

    _____

8. Do you agree with the principle of *caveat emptor*? Explain your answer, providing details from both sides of the argument.

    _____

    _____

    _____

    _____

    _____

    _____

    _____

9. Outline the two kinds of anti-competitive offences in the 1986 *Competition Act*, and explain the basic difference between them. In the media, find an example of a recent story where the *Competition Act* is being applied to an industry, and explain what kind of offence is involved.

    _____

    _____

    _____

    _____

    _____

    _____

    _____

Market Failure or Government Failure?

 Differentiate between the public-interest view and the capture view of government regulation.

In most situations, market outcomes serve society's best interest — the public interest. Thanks to the competitive pressures of the invisible hand, markets provide the products and services we value most, do so efficiently, and at the lowest possible cost. But markets can fail when there are natural monopolies with economies of scale, when there is monopolistic collusion among competitors, and when there is unethical behaviour among profit-seeking businesses. When markets fail, consumers call on governments for action, believing that government regulation will improve the outcome. Consumers as citizens speak up to say, "Government should regulate industries where there is market failure."

Public Interest and Capture Views of Regulation

The word *should* signals that the statement "Government *should* regulate industries where there is market failure" is normative. Normative statements involve value judgments or opinions — as opposed to positive statements, which can be evaluated as true or false by checking the facts.

Even the most careful economic thinking cannot answer the normative question, "*Should* government regulate industries where there is market failure?" That answer will be different for different individuals, and depends on the values they hold. Economic thinking *is* helpful in answering a related *positive* question — "When will government action improve market failure outcomes, and when will government action produce an outcome that is actually worse than market failure?"

Public-Interest View of Government Regulation   When government actions improve on market (failure) outcomes, they contribute to the public interest. Economists call this the **public-interest view** of government regulation. According to this view, government regulations act to eliminate waste, achieve efficiency, and promote the public interest, just like the invisible hand of markets usually does when markets work well.

Capture View of Government Regulation   When government actions turn out to be worse than the market (failure) outcomes, it is often because industry interests turn the regulatory process to their own advantage. Economists call this the **capture view** of government regulation. The regulators have been "captured" by the industry they are supposed to regulate. The regulations are set and enforced in ways that promote the interests of businesses in the industry instead of promoting the public interest.

Which view of government regulation is correct? The available evidence is mixed — some supports the public-interest view and some supports the capture view. Let's look at a few examples of the evidence. And since the evidence is not always available or clear, it is also useful to look at the explanations behind the two views.

Evidence

Regulated natural monopolies tend to earn higher rates of return than the average rate of profits in the economy. For example, the regulated cable TV industry earns more than a 10-percent rate of return per year, almost double the economy average. The fact that the rate of return is greater than the economy average supports the capture view. On the other hand, the public-interest view gets some support as long as the 10-percent rate of return is less than what a private monopolist would earn running the industry. We don't know what the private returns would be, since there are no private cable TV businesses operating outside of the regulations.

Do Crown corporations operate as efficiently as private businesses? Research studies have tried to answer this question by comparing two similar businesses, where one is run publicly and one privately. Comparisons include a Canadian public railway (Canadian National — CN) with a private railway (Canadian Pacific — CP), and an Australian public domestic airline (Trans Australia Airlines — TAA) with a private domestic airline (Ansett Australia). The studies found that costs for the Crown corporations were significantly higher than for the private businesses. For example, CN's costs were 14-percent higher than CP's costs. But it is not clear if the results of these studies can be generalized and used to judge other industries.

Another way to evaluate the competing views of government regulation is to look at what happens to regulated industries when they are deregulated — when government regulations are removed. If the public-interest view is true, we expect prices and profits to rise after deregulation. If the capture view is true, we expect prices and profits to fall. The airline and trucking industries used to be heavily regulated by Transport Canada, and long-distance phone industries (among others) were regulated by the CRTC. In the 1980s, many governments around the world removed regulations and allowed businesses to compete in the marketplace.

Mixed Results   The evidence is mixed over all industries, but for the airline, trucking, and long-distance industries, prices fell and outputs increased after deregulation. This supports the capture view, suggesting that the regulated industries were operating like a cartel, restricting output and raising prices.

Much of the strongest evidence supporting the capture view comes from the Canadian agricultural sector. The National Farm Products Council (NFPC) regulates the production of eggs, chickens, and turkeys, much like a cartel, establishing production quotas for each producer and setting prices. These regulations are justified in terms of promoting "efficient, competitive Canadian agriculture," "a stable supply of poultry and eggs for Canadian consumers," and "stable farm incomes." One study estimated that the regulated prices of the NFPC transferred over $100 million a year from Canadian consumers to 4600 individual chicken producers, in much the same way that OPEC transfers money from consumers and businesses in oil-consuming countries into OPEC's pockets. Similar evidence from the Canadian dairy industry supports the capture view.

The evidence on the effectiveness of the Canadian *Competition Act* is much more uniform. Most economists agree that legislation has served the public interest well.

For many regulated industries, there simply isn't conclusive evidence that allows us to evaluate whether the public-interest view or the capture view more accurately describes the outcomes. For that reason, it is also helpful to understand the explanations behind each view, so you can at least think a bit more carefully about whatever information is available.

Explanations

There is a straightforward explanation behind the public-interest view of government regulation. Government regulators have the public's interest in mind, and make decisions on the basis of what is best for society.

The explanation behind the capture view of government regulation is more complicated. The capture view seems to imply that government regulators collude with those in the industry being regulated, and conspire against the public interest. The actual explanation is not so sinister. It is basically a cost–benefit explanation applied to politics.

According to the capture view, even if government regulators begin with the public interest in mind, the decisions they end up making are influenced by the lack of competitive incentives, vague regulation guidelines, and necessarily close relations between the regulators and the industry being regulated.

Political Pressures   It's not just the regulators who are influenced. Regulations that favour industry interests over the public interest are passed and supported by elected politicians who can be influenced by lobbying, campaign contributions, and political pressure to act in the interests of businesses, labour organizations, or other special interest groups. When the Canadian Dairy Commission is considering a rise in the regulated price of cheese, think about the potential political reactions. If you are a consumer, how important is the extra 25 cents per kilogram that you will have to pay? If you even hear about the price rise, will it cause you to change your vote for your Member of Parliament or make a large campaign contribution to make sure your interests are represented? Not likely.

But if you are one of the average B.C. dairy farmers with net assets of $5.6 million and average net cash income of $155 000, that 25 cents per kilogram means tens of thousands of dollars every year, and even more in terms of the value of your assets. As a producer in the industry, you have a very, very strong incentive to be politically active when regulations are discussed.

The political pressures from the unequal distribution of costs and benefits tempt politicians to support regulations that favour producers. The tiny cost to many consumers creates only weak political pressure to lower prices. The huge benefits for the relatively few producers in the regulated industry make it worth their while to apply enormous political pressure (votes, political actions, campaign contributions) to "capture" the interests of the politicians to raise prices.

Those same unequal costs and benefits lead "captured" politicians to support regulations, like those in the dairy industry, that enforce cartel-style collusion within the industry; keep out new (and lower-cost) potential competitors; and monitor prices to avoid cheating on quotas. All these regulations are passed in the name of protecting quality or safety or promoting a "stable supply" in the public interest. But the businesses in the industry benefit the most.

Trade-Offs: Market Failure or Government Failure?

We began this chapter by identifying a key market-failure challenge facing government policymakers: How do you gain the low-cost efficiencies of economies of scale, but avoid the inefficiencies of monopoly's restricted output and higher price? The policy responses to that challenge include regulated natural monopolies, Crown corporations, and competition laws to discourage collusion and cartels.

All these government attempts to deal with market failure involve trade-offs. It's important for you, as a citizen who elects the politicians who create these policies, to understand the trade-offs. As you know only too well, every choice, even a policy choice to leave the market alone, has an opportunity cost. This chapter exposes those opportunity costs so that you can make smart political choices based on the values you hold.

What are the trade-offs? First, you want to compare any choice with the next best alternative. It is not useful to compare a market failure outcome with an ideal but unattainable government policy outcome. Keep it real!

When comparing a market-failure outcome with a government-regulation outcome, weigh the costs and benefits of the actual outcomes. That means evaluating whether the government outcome is better or worse than the market failure outcome. If the public-interest view applies to that industry, the government outcome may be superior to the market failure outcome.

Government Failure?   If the capture view applies, it is more difficult to tell. It may be a case of comparing market failure with what economists call **government failure**. Government failure occurs when regulations fail to serve the public interest. Even when aiming for the public interest, government policymakers sometimes lack timely and accurate information for making smart policy decisions. Add in the complexity of the economy, and government policymakers can make "honest mistakes" when trying to solve complex problems. Policymakers can also be influenced to support the industry being regulated.

- Sometimes the market outcome, even with monopoly power, is better than the government regulation outcome if there is significant government failure.

- Sometimes the government outcome, especially with public-interest regulations, is better than the market outcome if there is significant market failure.

In comparing industry outcomes, we can often make positive statements about which is better for consumers in terms of efficiency, and lowest costs of production, prices, and rates of return.

But there are other aspects of the outcomes that are not so easy to compare. What is the value of public safety? How much is it worth to you to know that you will not be poisoned by the toothpaste you buy, or that nuclear power plants are operated safely, or that your doctor is well-trained? If governments step in and regulate those industries, and the prices of the products or services goes up, is that a worthwhile trade-off? That is a normative question — it depends on how you value low prices relative to the risk of the occasional dangerous product (one nuclear accident sure can ruin your day) or the wrong medical advice.

Economic thinking cannot make those normative choices for you. As a citizen, your views on regulation will depend on the relative values you place on many outcomes, including efficiency, equity, low prices for consumers, public safety, and quality control. Economic thinking can help answer the related *positive* question, "When will government action improve market failure outcomes, and when will government action fail and actually produce an outcome that is worse than market failure?" The answer to that positive question depends on available evidence. Which failure is worse — market failure or government failure? No option is perfect; each has an opportunity cost. Pick your poison.

Practice...

16. Which statement(s) about government regulation is/are *true*?

    a. The public interest view suggests government actions improve market failure outcomes.

    b. The capture view suggests government actions produce government failure.

    c. Government failure can be worse than market failure if regulators work for the regulated industry instead of consumers.

    d. All of the above.

17. If a new government regulator successfully gets competitive behaviour from a natural monopolist, we do *not* expect to see

    a. normal profits.

    b. higher prices.

    c. lower costs.

    d. higher output.

18. If the public-interest view of regulation is correct, we will see

    a. prices rise when an industry is deregulated.

    b. prices fall when an industry is deregulated.

    c. profits decrease when an industry is deregulated.

    d. profits increase when an industry is regulated.

19. If the capture view of regulation is correct, we will see

    a. profits decrease when an industry is deregulated.

    b. profits increase when an industry is deregulated.

    c. costs increase when an industry is deregulated.

    d. costs decrease when an industry is regulated.

20. Economic thinking can be helpful in answering the question(s):

    a. "When will government action improve market failure outcomes?"

    b. "When will government action fail?"

    c. "When will government action produce an outcome that is worse than market failure?"

    d. All of the above.

Apply...

10. Explain the public-interest and capture views of government regulation.

    _____

    _____

    _____

    _____

    _____

    _____

11. If a previously regulated industry is deregulated, and we observe that prices rise and output decreases, which view of government regulation does that evidence support? Explain why.

    _____

    _____

    _____

    _____

    _____

    _____

12. Chapter 5 noted that a conservative politician on the political right might value efficiency more than equity, while a left-leaning politician might value equity more than efficiency. Which of the two views on government regulation — public-interest or capture — do you think a conservative politician is more likely to hold? Which view is a left-leaning politician more likely to hold? Explain your answers.

    _____

    _____

    _____

    _____

    _____

    _____

    _____

    _____

    _____

KNOW...

Learning Objectives

1. **Natural monopolies** are a **market-failure** challenge for policymakers — gain the low-cost efficiencies of **economies of scale**, but avoid the inefficiencies of monopoly's restricted output and higher price.

2. Strategic interaction among competitors complicates business decisions, creating two smart choices — one based on trust and the other based on lack of trust. **Game theory** is a mathematical tool for understanding how players make strategic decisions, taking into account what they expect rivals to do. The **prisoners' dilemma** is a game with two players who must each make a strategic choice, where results depend on the other player's choice. The outcome is a **Nash equilibrium**, where each player makes her own best choice given the choice of the other.

3. Governments use laws and regulations to try to promote competition, discourage **collusion** and **cartels**, and protect the public from dangerous business practices. Canada's *Competition Act* distinguishes criminal offences (price fixing, bid rigging, false or misleading advertising) from civil offences (mergers, abusing a dominant market position, and lessening competition).

4. The **public-interest view** of government regulation suggests government actions improve market-failure outcomes, while the **capture view** suggests government actions benefit the regulated industry at the expense of consumers, producing **government failure**.

Key Terms

average total cost: total cost per unit of output

capture view: government regulation benefits regulated businesses, not public interest

cartel: association of suppliers formed to maintain high prices and restrict competition

caveat emptor **("let the buyer beware"):** the buyer alone is responsible for checking quality of products before buying

collusion: conspiracy to cheat or deceive others

Crown corporations: publicly owned businesses in Canada

economies of scale: percentage increase in a business's output is greater than the percentage increase in inputs; decreasing long-run average costs

game theory: mathematical tool for understanding how players make decisions, taking into account what they expect rivals to do

government failure: when regulations fail to serve the public interest

long run: in microeconomics, a planning period for businesses where the quantities of all inputs are variable

market failure: when market outcomes are inefficient or inequitable

Nash equilibrium: outcome of a game in which each player makes her or his own best choice given the choice of the other player

natural monopoly: economies of scale allow only single seller to achieve lowest average (total) cost

prisoners' dilemma: a game with two players who must each make a strategic choice, where results depend on other player's choice

property rights: legally enforceable guarantees of ownership of physical, financial, and intellectual property

public-interest view: government regulation eliminates waste, achieves efficiency, promotes public interest

rate of return regulation: sets a price allowing the regulated monopoly to just cover average total costs, including normal profits

short run: in microeconomics, a planning period for businesses where the quantities of some inputs are fixed, while the quantities of other inputs are variable

Answers to Practice

1. **c** So only a single seller can reach lowest average total cost.

2. **b** Only example without high fixed cost.

3. **d** Definition of market failure.

4. **a** Must allow only a single seller to get efficiency, but prevent the profit-maximizing restricted output and high price of monopoly.

5. **d** Spreading high fixed costs over a large quantity of output decreases short-run average total costs and long-run average cost.

6. **b** If the prisoners can trust each other.

7. **d** 2001 Oscar for Best Picture.

8. **a** Each player makes his own best choice given the choice of the other player.

9. **c** Cartels agree to keep prices high. But each member has an incentive to lower its price to sell more, or to increase quantity, which has the effect of lowering the market price.

10. **a** Nash equilibrium is both players cheat and lower prices. A's payoff to the Lower/Lower quadrant is $2.

11. **d** Tension between cheating and cooperating.

12. **c** But benefits of economies of scale or increased international competitiveness might be greater than costs of decreased competition.

13. **b** Prevent collusion and price-fixing.

14. **d** Punished by prison time and fines.

15. **a** Other answers are intended consequences.

16. **d** See descriptions of capture and public-interest views.

17. **b** Successful regulation supports public-interest view and leads to lower prices, increased output, and normal profits.

18. **a** Regulation previously kept prices low to benefit consumers.

19. **a** Regulated industry had higher profits because captured regulators support industry, not consumers.

20. **d** All are positive questions.

12

Externalities

LEARNING OBJECTIVES

LO1 Describe how externalities cause market failure, so smart private choices differ from smart social choices.

LO2 Explain the rule for coordinating private choices with smart social choices when there are negative externalities.

LO3 Identify how government policies for polluters can internalize externalities to create smart social choices.

LO4 Explain how positive externalities create the free-rider problem of public goods and cause markets to fail.

LO5 Identify how government subsidies can internalize positive externalities to create smart social choices.

LEARN...

Everyone seems to be an environmentalist today, and for good reason. We clearly understand environmental problems like pollution and global warming. But acceptable solutions are less clear. I'll bet money that you — and most people — would answer "yes" if I asked, "Do you want a world without pollution?" Well, we could have a world without pollution — all we have to do is eliminate all internal combustion engines and most other power sources, reduce our standard of living, and go back to living in caves. When described this way, most people do not want a world without pollution. While the environmental benefits are appealing, the opportunity costs (in reduced standard of living) are enormous. All choices, including environmentally sound choices, have opportunity costs.

So how do we, individually and collectively, make smart choices about how much pollution to tolerate? The concept of *externalities* brings clarity to making smart choices about pollution. When exhaust from your car causes lung problems for non-drivers, the cost of treating those medical problems is a *negative externality* you don't consider in your decision to drive. *Positive externalities* exist when others benefit from your actions without paying. If most people get flu shots, even those who don't get shots benefit from the reduced likelihood of catching the flu.

Markets fail when externalities exist, producing too many of the things we don't want (like pollution and traffic jams) and too few of the things we do want (like vaccinations and good public transit). This chapter shows you, as a voter, how to identify the costs and benefits of smart policy choices for dealing with externality-based market failures.

Market Failure with Externalities

 L01 Describe how externalities cause market failure, so smart private choices differ from smart social choices.

If markets work well producing the "goods" (products and services) we want, why does market coordination of economic activity also produce "bads" like pollution and traffic jams? The answer, in a word, is externalities. **Externalities** cause market failure by disconnecting smart choices for individuals from smart choices for society as a whole.

How Much Does Driving Really Cost?

You are ready to buy a car after years of riding buses, and are crunching the numbers to see if you can afford it. Your private additional costs include monthly payments, insurance, gas, repairs, and maybe parking. If you can afford it, and if the additional benefits of driving versus taking transit make you willing to pay those costs, then buying a car is a smart choice for you.

Your decision is based mostly on Key 1 of the Three Keys to Smart Choices: Choose only when additional benefits are greater than additional *opportunity costs*. Key 2 enters with the emphasis on *additional* benefits and costs.

There are also social costs you don't have to consider when choosing your car. The exhaust from your driving will contribute to air pollution and to global warming. By adding one more car to the roads, you will (marginally) worsen traffic jams and increase other drivers' commute times. Your choice creates real costs to others, *but you don't have to directly pay for them*.

Negative Externalities   Economists call these additional social costs **negative externalities,** or **external costs**. They are costs to society from your private choice that affect others, but that you do not pay. External costs affect people external to the original activity — people not involved in the exchange between you and the car dealer.

This brings us at last to Key 3 for smart choices (which we haven't discussed except for implicit costs in Chapter 7), which emphasizes the word *all*: Be sure to count *all* additional benefits and additional opportunity costs, including *implicit costs* and *externalities*.

IMPLICIT
COSTS &
EXTERNALITIES

When there are negative externalities, opportunity costs include both private costs and external costs. The costs to society — social costs — are greater than just private costs.

Social Costs = Private (Opportunity) Costs + External (Opportunity) Costs

Economists also refer to negative externalities as "spillover effects."

The Invisible Hand Fails   Based only on your private costs, buying the car may be a smart choice for you. But adding in the external costs, it may not be a smart choice for society. When there are negative externalities, smart private choices (using Keys 1 and 2) are different from smart social choices (Keys 1, 2, and 3). There is **market failure** — the outcome is inefficient and not in society's best interests. The invisible hand fails to coordinate smart individual choices with smart social choices.

If we had to pay the external costs as well as the usual private costs of our choices, then we would buy fewer cars and produce less coal-generated electricity. But because we generally do not pay external costs, consumers buy, and businesses produce, too many products and services with negative externalities.

Positive and Negative Externalities

Externalities come in two flavours — negative and positive. Negative externalities involve external costs; positive externalities involve external benefits. Key 3 says to be sure to count *all* additional benefits as well as additional opportunity costs.

Positive externalities happen on the benefits side. Think about your decision to go to college or university. Your additional private benefits include your significantly higher lifetime income compared to high school graduates, and the satisfaction from acquiring more knowledge. You obviously estimated that those additional private benefits were greater than your additional opportunity costs of attending school.

There are also social benefits you probably did not consider when choosing to go to school. With the skills you gain, employers will not have to spend as much money and time training you. Educated citizens, who can make informed political choices and participate in public debate and election campaigns, also improve the functioning of our democracy, which benefits all citizens. Evidence shows that citizens with more education are less likely to commit crimes or depend on social assistance payments. Your smart decision saves industry and the government money as well as aiding our democratic institutions.

Positive Externalities   These additional social benefits are **positive externalities** or **external benefits**. They are benefits to society from your private choice that affect others, but that others do not pay (you) for. External benefits go to people external to the original activity — others not involved in the exchange between you and your school.

When there are positive externalities, benefits include both private benefits and external benefits. So, when positive externalities are added in, social benefits are greater than private benefits.

$$\text{Social Benefits} = \text{Private Benefits} + \text{External Benefits}$$

Public transit is another example of a positive externality. If you decide not to buy the car and continue to take public transit, your private benefits include the ability to get around inexpensively, without car expenses. But by keeping one more car off the roads, you unintentionally reduce pollution for everyone, reduce traffic jams, and decrease other drivers' commute times. Do you get any thanks or reward from others who benefit from your choice? No.

Free Riders   Economists call people who benefit from the positive externalities of other people's actions without paying *free riders*. Based only on your private benefits and costs, choosing school over work may be a smart choice for you. But many workers would switch their choices to school *if only they were paid for the external benefits of that choice*. Taking public transit may be a smart choice for you. But many drivers would switch to public transit *if only they were paid for the external benefits of that choice*. When there are positive externalities, smart private choices (using Keys 1 and 2) are different from smart social choices (Keys 1, 2, and 3). External benefits allow others to "free ride" on our private choices. There is market failure — the outcome is inefficient and not in society's best interests.

If there were a way to force the free riders to pay students and transit riders for the benefits the free riders receive, there would be more education and more public transit. But free riders do not have incentives to pay us for the external benefits that our choices produce, so consumers buy, and businesses produce, too few products and services with positive externalities.

No Ownership, No Incentives, No Coordinated Choices

What is it about externalities, both negative and positive, that causes market failure and problems for Adam Smith's invisible hand? The answer is *lack of clear property rights*. **Property rights** — government's legal protection of property and enforcement of contracts — are a necessary part of the "rules of the game" for markets to work. Without property rights, you have no incentive to produce for exchange because customers could take your work for free. Property rights give us the incentive to make smart choices because we have to pay for costs and because we are legally entitled to receive benefits and rewards for producing products and services.

Tragedy of the Commons   Lack of clear property rights causes a problem with the dramatic name "the tragedy of the commons." In medieval England, commons were lands held in common by all the villagers, rather than privately by the nobles. If no rules determined how many animals each villager could pasture on the commons, then too many animals could eat all the grass and destroy the pasture. The "tragedy of the commons" is the overuse and depletion of a resource. It is the destruction of a common good. The tragedy of the commons includes the free-rider problem and the negative externality problem.

An example of the tragedy of the commons is the depletion of the east-coast cod fishery in Canada. There are no property rights to fish swimming in international waters, and the use of sophisticated, massive fishing ships from many countries led to overfishing and the depletion of the fish stocks. A ban on cod fishing in the North Atlantic in 1992 prevented the total destruction of the fishery, but it is not clear if the fish population will ever recover to previous levels.

No Incentives   If you don't pay a cost or receive a payment because no property rights exist, you don't consider those costs or payments in your choices. External costs are someone else's problem, and external benefits are someone else's gain. Quite reasonably, you ignore them all.

Wrong Prices   Those missing costs and payments affect prices, which are the incentives we respond to when making smart choices. When there are negative externalities, prices are too low because of missing costs. Prices do not cover all opportunity costs of production, including social costs. When there are positive externalities, prices are too high because of missing benefits and payments. And in the case of common resources, there are no prices at all. The invisible hand helps markets coordinate private smart choices to be smart choices for society as a whole *when prices adjust to reflect all costs and all benefits*. Without ownership and property rights, externalities arise, and prices don't accurately reflect all social costs and benefits. Markets fail because the invisible hand is handcuffed.

Practice...

1. Which statement is *false*?

    a. There is too much pollution in the world.

    b. There are too many cars on the road during rush hour.

    c. There are too many people getting vaccinations.

    d. There are too many people smoking.

2. Education creates a positive externality because each course you take

    a. helps you earn money once you graduate.

    b. costs you money.

    c. imposes external costs on other people.

    d. creates external benefits for other people.

3. A noisy party that irritates the neighbours is an example of

    a. a negative externality.

    b. a positive externality.

    c. the free-rider problem.

    d. the decline of civilization.

4. Levels of acid rain caused by air pollution are

    a. more than efficient levels due to external benefits.

    b. more than efficient levels due to external costs.

    c. less than efficient levels due to external benefits.

    d. less than efficient levels due to external costs.

5. The tragedy of the commons is

    a. a name from the common east-coast fishery.

    b. a positive externality problem.

    c. a play by Shakespeare.

    d. the overuse of a free resource.

Apply...

1. Talking in large lecture halls is a problem, both for instructors who can't concentrate and attentive students who can't hear. Can you explain this problem in terms of externalities? Why is this problem hard to solve?

   _____

   _____

   _____

   _____

   _____

2. What is the *tragedy of the commons* problem, and why does it occur? Apply your explanation to the example of ocean fisheries.

   _____

   _____

   _____

   _____

   _____

3. Two prairie pioneers, Jethro and Hortense, have fields next to each other. Because they get along so well and always work out any problems that arise, they have not bothered to put up a fence. Then one day Jethro buys a new pig, Babe. Babe sometimes wanders into Hortense's field and eats her corn. If Babe would only stay on Jethro's farm, he would eat valueless garbage. Suppose that Babe eats $500 worth of Hortense's corn per year (a negative externality imposed on Hortense) and that to build a fence between the farms costs $300. No property rights to keep animals off the fields have been established yet.

   a. If the property right is given to Jethro so Babe can continue to wander, will Hortense build a fence? Explain.

   _____

   _____

   _____

   b. If, instead, the property right is given to Hortense, so that she can charge Jethro for the corn Babe eats, will Jethro build a fence? Explain.

   _____

   _____

   _____

   c. Does it matter who gets the property right?

   _____

   _____

   _____

   _____

What Is an Efficient Amount of Pollution?

 L02 Explain the rule for coordinating private choices with smart social choices when there are negative externalities.

Economists argue that a smart society should choose an "efficient" amount of pollution. This position angers many environmentalists who claim that *any* pollution is too much — zero pollution is their goal.

The Price (Opportunity Cost) of Pollution

A world that has eliminated pollution sounds good in principle, but most of us are unwilling to pay the price — the opportunity cost — of a dramatically lower standard of living. Small reductions in pollution like eliminating lead from gasoline and paint, or conserving energy to reduce output from coal-fired electrical plants, don't cost much. But to get to zero pollution, the opportunity cost is huge — eliminating all cars and airplanes; outlawing all power except solar, wind, and hydroelectric power; and shutting down most factories. Economists conclude that some level of pollution is "efficient" — there is a smart choice that balances the costs of a lower standard of living against the benefits of lower pollution.

Efficient Combinations of Output and Pollution

The rule for an efficient combination of output and pollution is a simple refinement of Key 1 that accounts for all costs, including negative externalities. For any product or service (output) whose production also creates a negative externality, the rule for smart choices is:

Choose the Quantity of Output Where
Marginal Social Cost = Marginal Social Benefit
(MSC) = (MSB)

There are two new concepts in the rule — **marginal social cost** and **marginal social benefit** — that are related to the definitions of social cost and social benefit on pages 298-299.

Marginal Social Cost   When there are negative externalities, social costs are greater than private costs. When we focus on additional costs and benefits, that relationship is

Marginal Social Cost = Marginal Private Cost + Marginal External Cost
(MSC)   Directly Received by   Imposed on Others
             Consumers (MC)

A pulp mill's decisions about quantities to produce and prices to charge depends on the opportunity costs the mill pays directly — labour, wood, power, and so on. The mill's smokestacks also emit sulphur dioxide — causing acid rain, air pollution, and contributing to global warming. The marginal external cost per tonne of pulp produced is the price of preventing or cleaning up the damage from the pollution. Marginal social cost (*MSC*) is the sum of the marginal private cost (*MC*) and the marginal external cost.

Marginal Social Benefit   When there are positive externalities, social benefits are greater than private benefits.

Marginal Social Benefit = Marginal Private Benefit + Marginal External Benefit
(MSB)   Directly Received by   Enjoyed by Others
             Consumers (MB)

Your post-secondary education gives you private benefits like increased lifetime income. There are also external benefits to employers and government. The marginal external benefit is the value of the reduced average training costs and reduced government expenditures. In our example, the pulp mill does not produce positive externalities, so *marginal social benefit* is the same as *marginal private benefit*. It is the value of the pulp bought and sold in markets.

Pulp Industry Challenge   Figure 1 provides some simple, made-up numbers for the daily output of all the mills producing for the pulp market. The left three columns show market demand, and the right three columns show market supply. The first column on both the demand and supply sides is *Output*, the different quantities of pulp the businesses might produce. The rule for making a smart choice focuses first on the *quantity to produce and the associated levels of pollution*. That's why the first column on both the demand and supply sides is quantity, instead of price.

Figure 1   Demand, Supply, and Negative Externalities in the Pulp Market

Demand			Supply		
Output (tonnes/day)	Marginal Private Benefit (*MB*)	Marginal Social Benefit (*MSB*)	Output (tonnes/day)	Marginal Private Cost (*MC*)	Marginal Social Cost (*MSC*)
1	$140	$140	1	$50	$ 80
2	$120	$120	2	$60	$ 90
3	$100	$100	3	$70	$100
4	$ 80	$ 80	4	$80	$110
5	$ 60	$ 60	5	$90	$120

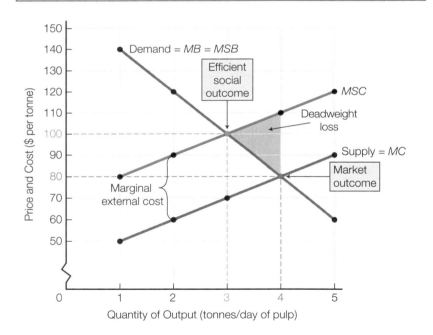

Demand   The *Marginal Private Benefit* (*MB*) column, shows, for each quantity, the maximum price buyers are willing and able to pay. The private marginal benefit of the first tonne of pulp is $140, but that marginal benefit diminishes for each successive tonne. The downward-sloping marginal private benefit curve graphs these numbers. Remember, you read a marginal benefit curve up and over — from quantity up to the marginal benefit curve and over to the maximum price people are willing and able to pay.

You can also read the first two columns of numbers as a demand curve. Think of column 2 as *the price buyers are willing and able to pay* for the different quantities of pulp in column 1. When the price is $140 per tonne, quantity demanded is only 1 tonne. As the price falls, quantity demanded increases. The marginal private benefit curve is also a demand curve.

The *Marginal Social Benefit* column is the same as *Marginal Private Benefit* because there are no positive externalities. So the downward-sloping curve in Figure 1 has three identities — it is a *marginal private benefit* curve, a demand curve, and a *marginal social benefit* curve. Hence the label Demand = *MB* = *MSB*.

Supply   Supply curves can also be read two ways — as a marginal cost curve and as a supply curve. The *Marginal Private Cost* (*MC*) column shows the costs the pulp mills actually pay for additional labour, wood, power, and other inputs for each additional tonne of pulp. Marginal costs increase as output increases. The upward-sloping *marginal private cost* curve graphs these numbers. You read a marginal cost curve, just like a marginal benefit curve, up and over.

You can also read columns 4 and 5 as a supply curve. *Marginal private cost* is the minimum price the business will accept to supply that additional quantity — price must cover all marginal opportunity costs of production. As price rises, quantity supplied increases. The *marginal private cost* curve is also a supply curve, hence the label Supply = *MC*.

Marginal Social Cost Again   The pattern of numbers so far for demand and supply is similar to Chapter 3, where the invisible hand works well. The big difference is in the last column, *Marginal Social Cost* (*MSC*). Let's say each tonne of pulp generates $30 of external costs — the costs of either preventing or cleaning up the damage from the pollution associated with that tonne of pulp. The pulp mills do not pay these external costs. But these costs to society must be added to the marginal private costs to calculate marginal social cost. The upward-sloping *marginal social cost* curve combines quantities supplied with marginal social costs. Marginal social cost is $30 higher per tonne than marginal private cost, due to the external costs of pollution.

Putting It All Together   Figure 1 on the previous page tells the story, both in numbers and graphs, of what the market outcome will be, and what the smart social choice should be. Let's focus on the story in the graph.

For the private decisions of consumers and businesses, the market outcome is at the intersection of the *marginal private benefit* curve and the *marginal private cost* curve. Pulp sells for $80 per tonne and 4 tonnes are sold and bought. These numbers are highlighted in red.

The smart social choice is at the intersection of the *marginal social benefit* curve and the *marginal social cost* curve. The smart social outcome has pulp selling for $100 per tonne and 3 tonnes are sold and bought. These numbers are highlighted in green.

Understanding the Smart Social Choice   The rule for a smart social choice is to choose the quantity of output where marginal social cost equals marginal social benefit. The graph explains why this rule works. For any quantity of pulp, starting with tonne 1, go up to the marginal social cost curve and marginal social benefit curve. Marginal social benefit is greater than marginal social cost for every quantity up to 3 tonnes. For any quantity greater than that, marginal social benefit is less than marginal social cost. Society should produce 3 tonnes of pulp, accepting the associated "efficient" amount of pollution.

Compared to the market outcome, the smart choice for society means producing less of a product with a negative externality (3 tonnes of pulp instead of the market's 4 tonnes) and charging a higher price ($100 per tonne instead of $80 per tonne). Markets tend to overproduce products and services with negative externalities, and the price charged is too low because it does not incorporate the external costs.

Inefficiency of Overproduction   For all output between 3 and 4 tonnes of pulp, the marginal social cost is greater than the marginal social benefit. The grey **deadweight loss** triangle represents the loss in **total surplus** (consumer surplus plus producer surplus) compared to an efficient market outcome. The loss in efficiency from the overproduction of products and services with negative externalities is similar to Figure 11b on page 74.

 Practice...

6. The opportunity cost of reducing pollution includes the costs of
    a. taking shorter showers.
    b. taking public transit rather than driving.
    c. shutting down factories.
    d. all of the above.

7. If there is a negative externality and no positive externality, marginal private cost
    a. *equals* marginal social cost, and marginal private benefit *equals* marginal social benefit.
    b. *is less than* marginal social cost, and marginal private benefit *is less than* marginal social benefit.
    c. *is less than* marginal social cost, and marginal private benefit *equals* marginal social benefit.
    d. *equals* marginal social cost, and marginal private benefit *is less than* marginal social benefit.

8. If there is a negative externality and a positive externality, marginal private cost
    a. *equals* marginal social cost, and marginal private benefit *equals* marginal social benefit.
    b. *is less than* marginal social cost, and marginal private benefit *is less than* marginal social benefit.
    c. *is less than* marginal social cost, and marginal private benefit *equals* marginal social benefit.
    d. *equals* marginal social cost, and marginal private benefit is *less than* marginal social benefit.

Use this graph to answer questions 9 and 10.

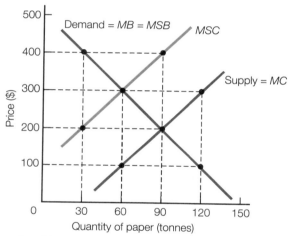

9. The equilibrium market outcome in the paper market is a quantity of
    a. 90 tonnes and a price of $200.
    b. 90 tonnes and a price of $400.
    c. 60 tonnes and a price of $100.
    d. 60 tonnes and a price of $300.

10. At the equilibrium market output of the paper market, the marginal social cost of producing a tonne of paper is
    a. less than the marginal benefit to consumers.
    b. greater than the marginal benefit to consumers.
    c. less than the marginal private cost of production.
    d. equal to the marginal benefit to consumers.

 **Apply...**

4. Your roommate is an environmentalist who is horrified with the economic concept of an "efficient" level of pollution. She argues that since everyone agrees pollution is "bad," society must work toward eliminating all pollution. How can you, as an economics student, convince her that it is *not* in society's best interests to eliminate all pollution?

_____

_____

_____

_____

_____

_____

_____

5. A few years ago, the Toronto Transit Commission (TTC) proposed taxing car drivers and using the money to pay for more public transit. Outraged drivers argued that they should not have to pay for public transit they don't use. Use this information to answer the following questions.

a. What is the rule for a smart choice for any product or service that generates an externality? Define all terms in the rule.

_____

_____

_____

_____

_____

_____

b. Using the concept of a negative externality, explain how the tax on drivers to pay for public transit is a smart social choice. Begin your explanation with "Car drivers supply transportation services . . ."

_____

_____

_____

_____

_____

_____

_____

_____

to be continued

 **Apply...**

continued

6. This table shows private and social costs and benefits of producing chemical fertilizer.
   Use this information to answer the questions below.

Market for Chemical Fertilizer				
Quantity of Output	Marginal Private Benefit (*MB*)	Marginal Social Benefit (*MSB*)	Marginal Private Cost (*MC*)	Marginal Social Cost (*MSC*)
1	$70	$70	$10	$30
2	$60	$60	$20	$40
3	$50	$50	$30	$50
4	$40	$40	$40	$60
5	$30	$30	$50	$70
6	$20	$20	$60	$80

a. What is the market-clearing equilibrium quantity? What is the market-clearing equilibrium price?
   Explain how you chose those numbers.

b. What is the socially best quantity? What is the socially best price?
   Explain how you chose those numbers.

c. What kind of externality does the chemical fertilizer market have?
   What is the external benefit or cost per unit?

d. Explain the relationship between the equilibrium quantity and price, and the socially best quantity and price.

Internalize the Externality to Liberate the Invisible Hand

 Identify how government policies for polluters can internalize externalities to create smart social choices.

Without clear property rights to the environment, individuals and businesses do not have to pay for the external costs their choices create. In fact, businesses usually save money and improve profits by ignoring external costs like pollution, soil contamination, and global warming. Businesses have incentives to take actions that make society worse off. And without having to pay for personal contributions to global warming, individuals are more likely to buy a car instead of taking public transit.

When markets work well, self-interest leads us to make smart choices that are also good for everyone else, and markets produce the products and services we most desire at the lowest possible cost. With negative externalities, markets fail and self-interest leads to social problems like environmental damage.

What can restore the power of the invisible hand?

Government Support for the Invisible Hand

Roads are a commonly shared space, just like the environment. If there were no traffic laws — no rules of the road — self-interested drivers would not have to stop at intersections, signal turns, or obey speed limits. There would be traffic chaos. Government traffic laws improve the functioning of roadways to the benefit of all drivers.

Government also has a crucial role to play in correcting the market failures caused by negative externalities.

Create Property Rights   Government can effectively create social property rights to the environment by making it illegal to pollute. With pollution laws, those who pollute pay criminal penalties (jail time) or financial penalties (fines or taxes).

The principle for any government policy is to set the environmental rules of the game to align smart private choices with smart social choices. That means everyone voluntarily chooses the quantity of output where *marginal social benefit* equals *marginal social cost*.

Carbon Taxes and Cap-and-Trade System for Emissions

Two environmental policies that lead individuals and businesses to choose the quantities of outputs (and associated levels of pollution) that are best for society are

- carbon taxes.
- a cap-and-trade system for emissions.

Both policies force polluters to pay the cost of preventing or cleaning up the external damage they cause.

Carbon Taxes   Noxious emissions cause negative externalities, such as carbon dioxide increasing global warming, sulphur dioxide causing acid rain, or harmful chemicals causing health problems. **Emissions taxes** are designed to pay for the external cost of preventing or cleaning up the damage from emissions. A **carbon tax**, paid by anyone using carbon-based fossil fuels (like oil, gas, or coal) is the best-known example of an emissions tax.

How does a government carbon tax affect the choices of the pulp mills in our previous example? A smart carbon tax is set equal to the marginal external cost of the damage associated with a tonne of pulp. If that marginal external cost is $30 per tonne, the tax should be $30 per tonne.

Figure 2 reproduces the numbers in Figure 1, with one change. The last column is now labelled *Marginal Private Cost + Tax*, showing the costs the mill must now pay for each additional tonne of pulp it produces. For the first tonne, the mill pays $50 in marginal private costs for inputs like labour, wood, and power, and the $30 emissions tax to the government, for a total of $80.

Figure 2   Pulp Market with $30/Tonne Emissions Tax

Demand			Supply		
Output (tonnes/day)	Marginal Private Benefit (MB)	Marginal Social Benefit (MSB)	Output (tonnes/day)	Marginal Private Cost (MC)	Marginal Private Cost + Tax
1	$140	$140	1	$50	$ 80
2	$120	$120	2	$60	$ 90
3	$100	$100	3	$70	$100
4	$ 80	$ 80	4	$80	$110
5	$ 60	$ 60	5	$90	$120

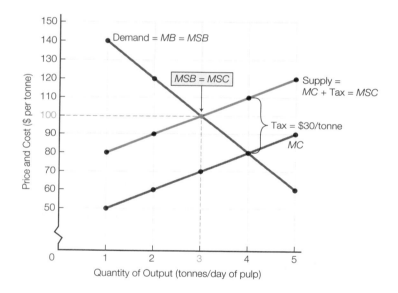

Given the new tax, what is the equilibrium output and price for the pulp industry? Look at the graph in Figure 2. The only difference from Figure 1 is that the red marginal social cost curve is now also the supply curve, including private marginal costs and the emissions tax. Businesses now choose to produce at the intersection of the demand and supply curves, where marginal social benefit equals marginal social cost. The efficient price and quantity for the pulp market is $100 per tonne and 3 tonnes per day. These numbers, highlighted in green, are also the equilibrium price and quantity. The pollution associated with 3 tonnes of pulp per day is the "efficient" amount of pollution.

By forcing producers to pay the external marginal cost of the negative externalities, emissions taxes get producers to voluntarily choose the socially best combination of output and price and associated level of pollution. Economists say that the emissions tax **internalizes the externality**. Remember that phrase. The tax transforms the external cost into a cost the producer must pay to the government.

Cap-and-Trade System for Emissions   A smart social choice of an efficient amount of pollution involves a combination of output, price, and associated levels of pollution. While emissions taxes increase the price of output to reflect internal and external costs, cap-and-trade policies focus on the *quantity of emissions*.

In a **cap-and-trade** system for emissions, the government establishes property rights to the environment and restricts the emission of pollutants. The system sets a limit, or cap, on the quantity of emissions that businesses can release. Businesses must have permits to pollute, which the government auctions off to the highest bidders. The total quantity of emissions allowed by the permits is set equal to the government target for emissions.

A market for emissions permits is established, where businesses can buy and sell (that is, trade) permits. Businesses that reduce their emissions can sell permits they don't need to other businesses. Those other businesses are willing to pay the costs of additional pollution permits because the products or services they produce are sufficiently valuable that consumers will pay higher prices. The cap-and-trade system gives businesses a choice of reducing pollution themselves or buying pollution permits.

In theory, the price of an emissions permit reflects the marginal external cost of the pollution produced. As this becomes a private cost to the business buying the permits, a smart cap-and-trade system internalizes the externality, just like an emissions tax, and leads to the socially best choice of output, prices, and pollution. Although the initial focus of the cap-and-trade system is on the quantity of emissions, the additional costs businesses pay for emissions permits eventually turns into higher prices for consumers.

Licence to Pollute?   A common objection to the cap-and-trade system is that it allows businesses to "buy a licence to pollute" — and we are told pollution is always bad. But once we give up on the idea of a world with zero pollution because the associated standard of living is unacceptably low, there will be some pollution. To achieve the efficient amount of pollution, pollution must have a price that reflects the marginal external cost of the damage done. Pollution that is "priced" or "licensed" gives individuals and businesses incentives to make choices that are smart for society.

What's the Difference?   Does it make any difference which policy a government uses — a carbon tax or a cap-and-trade system?

There is a difference in who pays initially. With a carbon tax, anyone using energy, whether consumers filling up gas tanks or businesses buying energy for their factories, pays the tax up front. With a cap-and-trade system, businesses pay initially for emissions permits. But consumers pay eventually as the additional cost is passed on in higher prices for products and services.

A carbon tax makes the cost of a negative externality directly obvious to consumers and businesses. The costs of emissions permits in a cap-and-trade system are far less obvious to the final consumer. This hidden quality makes cap-and-trade systems more popular with politicians, who want to be seen to be supporting the environment, but don't want to be blamed for higher prices!

A cap-and-trade system sets a quantity limit for emissions, allowing targets to be set and progress toward those targets to be clearly measured. A carbon tax sets an estimated price on the costs of negative externalities, but the quantity of total emissions depends on the interaction of all the choices made by individuals and businesses. Quantities of emissions are more uncertain with a carbon tax.

Both government policies to internalize the externalities of pollution — a carbon tax and a cap-and-trade system — have three shared benefits:

- As carbon-based energy becomes more expensive, less carbon-based energy will be consumed. The law of demand applies — when something gets more expensive, people economize on its use and look for substitutes.

- Carbon taxes and emissions-permit auctions raise revenues that can be used by government to repair the environmental damage, or for other environmentally friendly initiatives.

- Higher carbon-based energy prices make solar, wind, and hydro power more competitive, and encourage businesses to search for alternative (cheaper) energy sources.

Green Trade-Offs of Efficiency versus Equity

Smart government policies raise the prices of products and services to include indirect external costs to the environment on top of direct costs of production. That helps restore the power of the invisible hand to coordinate smart private and social choices.

As prices rise, quantity demanded decreases because fewer people are willing and able to buy at the higher prices. As government policies raise gasoline and other energy prices, fewer people can afford to buy. This is part of the trade-off between achieving less pollution at the cost of a lower standard of living.

Those hurt most by higher energy prices are often those least able to afford them. There is a trade-off between efficiency and equity. Policies that are smart in yielding an "efficient" amount of pollution may also be inequitable by hurting lower-income consumers more than higher-income consumers. There is no "magic-bullet policy" that can significantly reduce pollution without also reducing living standards, especially of those who are poorest, or those in energy-sensitive industries like trucking, air travel, or automobile production.

Practice...

11. Smart cap-and-trade systems
    a. externalize the internality.
    b. internalize the externality.
    c. externalize the majority.
    d. internalize the minority.

12. Without government action, a profit-maximizing perfectly competitive business producing a product with an external cost produces a quantity where price
    a. is greater than marginal private cost.
    b. is less than marginal revenue.
    c. is less than marginal private cost.
    d. equals marginal private cost.

13. Carbon taxes are *not* equitable if
    a. lower-income consumers are affected more.
    b. lower-income consumers get a tax break.
    c. lower-income consumers get a subsidy.
    d. higher-income consumers are affected more.

Use this graph to answer questions 14 and 15.

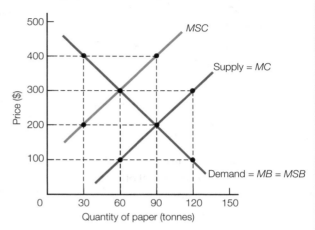

14. To get the socially best outcome in the paper market, the government should impose an emissions tax on each tonne of paper of
    a. $400.
    b. $300.
    c. $200.
    d. $100.

15. After the government imposes a smart emissions tax, the socially best outcome for the paper market is a quantity of
    a. 90 tonnes and a price of $200.
    b. 90 tonnes and a price of $400.
    c. 60 tonnes and a price of $100.
    d. 60 tonnes and a price of $300.

Apply...

7. This graph shows an industry that produces a product with an *external cost*.

    a. Label each of the 3 curves on the graph.

    b. On the graph, show the

    - point representing the market outcome and label it *MO*.

    - point representing the efficient social outcome and label it *ESO*.

    - amount of the external cost per unit.

    - deadweight loss.

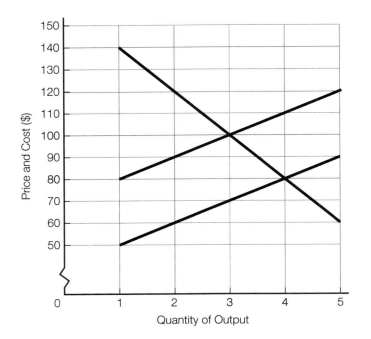

    c. Externalities create market failure and inefficiency. As a result:

    (Fill in the blanks — order of i) or ii) does not matter.)

    i) Markets _____ products and services with _____externalities.

    ii) Markets _____ products and services with _____externalities.

8. Cap-and-trade systems and carbon taxes are both policy solutions for negative externalities.

    a. Explain the differences between a cap-and-trade system and a carbon tax for dealing with the problem of negative externalities. Be sure to use the words *price* and *quantity* in your explanation.

    _____

    _____

    _____

    b. What is common to both policy solutions — what is the shared principle behind properly designed cap-and-trade systems and carbon taxes?

    _____

    _____

    _____

    c. Which policy do most politicians tend to favour? Explain why.

    _____

    _____

    _____

 Apply...

9. Some environmental groups try to expose businesses that pollute by posting information and photos on public websites while buying only from environmentally friendly "green" businesses. Explain how this strategy may "internalize the externality" for the polluters, even without government action.

_____

_____

_____

_____

_____

_____

Public Goods and Free Riders

LO4 Explain how positive externalities create the free-rider problem of public goods and cause markets to fail.

Internet scams offering to make you rich are everywhere — emails alert you to forgotten prize winnings, foreign lottery payoffs, and oppressed billionaires who direly need your assistance. If you ever get a message promising you riches from a fabulous lighthouse investment opportunity, I can promise you it's a scam. Here's why.

The Free-Rider Problem

Think about the business case for lighthouses. They provide an extremely valuable service. They prevent ships from running aground or sinking, thereby saving millions of dollars every year in lost or damaged cargo and ships. Sounds like a service that ship owners would gladly pay for.

But think about a cost-conscious ship-owner's decision to buy lighthouse services. The service is valuable, but once the lighthouse is operating, the ship owner can get the "service" for free! No one can be excluded from seeing a lighthouse signal beacon. Why be a fool and pay — let other foolish ship owners pay to start up the lighthouse, and then free ride on the light. All ship owners will eventually figure out this free-riding strategy, so any private lighthouse business will end in bankruptcy.

Public Goods Lighthouses are a classic example of a **public good**. Public goods can be consumed simultaneously by everyone; no one can be excluded. National defence is another example. Once a country has a standing army in place, everyone benefits and no one can be excluded. Even though public goods provide valuable services, markets will not produce them because no business can make a profit from them. Public goods like lighthouses and national armed forces are extreme cases of positive externalities.

Positive externalities are not as "in-your-face" a problem as negative externalities. The problem with negative externalities is clear — markets produce too many "bads," like acid rain, global warming, and traffic jams. The more subtle problem is why markets don't produce more "goods" with positive externalities like education, public transit, and vaccinations. This is the **free-rider problem** — markets tend to underproduce products and services with positive externalities, and the price charged to buyers is too high and to sellers is too low.

Efficient Combinations of Output and External Benefits

The rule for finding an efficient combination of output and external benefits is the same as for an efficient combination of output and pollution. The rule for smart choices is

Choose the Quantity of Output Where
Marginal Social Cost $=$ Marginal Social Benefit
$(MSC) = (MSB)$

Let's use the example of *privately* provided post-secondary education. Schools produce "educational services" that are sold to students. The schools pay for instructors, buildings, computer systems, energy, and other inputs. These are marginal private costs. Assume the schools are "green" and do not produce any pollution or other external costs. *Marginal social cost (MSC) equals marginal private cost (MC)*.

When there are positive externalities, social benefits are greater than private benefits:

Marginal Social Benefit $=$ Marginal Private Benefit $+$ Marginal External Benefit
(MSB) — Directly Received by Consumers (MB) — Enjoyed by Others

The main private benefit to students of post-secondary education is increased lifetime income. The marginal external benefit is the value, per student educated per year, of the reduced training costs and reduced government expenditures.

Figure 3 provides some simple, made-up numbers for the yearly output of all schools in the private post-secondary education market. The left three columns show market demand, and the right three columns show market supply. The first column on both the demand and supply sides is *Output*, showing the different quantities of educational services (measured in students educated per year) the schools might choose to produce.

Figure 3 Demand, Supply, and Positive Externalities in a Private Post-Secondary Education Market

Demand			Supply		
Output (students/year)	Marginal Private Benefit (MB)	Marginal Social Benefit (MSB)	Output (students/year)	Marginal Private Cost (MC)	Marginal Social Cost (MSC)
100	$7 000	$10 000	100	$4 000	$4 000
200	$6 000	$9 000	200	$4 500	$4 500
300	$5 000	$8 000	300	$5 000	$5 000
400	$4 000	$7 000	400	$5 500	$5 500
500	$3 000	$6 000	500	$6 000	$6 000
600	$2 000	$5 000	600	$6 500	$6 500
700	$1 000	$4 000	700	$7 000	$7 000

Figure 3 *(Continued)*

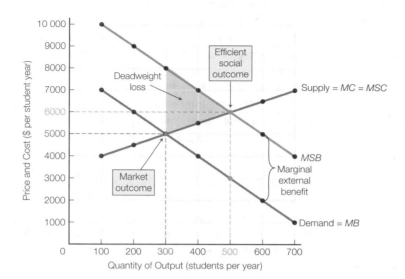

Demand   The *Marginal Private Benefit* (*MB*) column shows, for each quantity, the maximum price students (the buyers) are willing and able to pay. The private marginal benefit of the first 100 student-years of education (output = 100) is $7000, but that marginal benefit diminishes for each successive year. The downward-sloping blue marginal private benefit curve graphs these numbers. When the price is $7000 per student-year, quantity demanded is only from 100 students. As the price falls, quantity demanded increases. So the *marginal private benefit* curve is also a demand curve.

Marginal Social Benefit   Compared to a market where the invisible hand works well, the *Marginal Social Benefit* (*MSB*) column shows the important difference in the numbers. Each 100 student-years of education generates $3000 in external benefits — the cost savings to employers and governments in training and assistance payments. Employers and government do not have to pay (they get a free ride) for the benefits, but these benefits must be added to *marginal private benefits* to calculate *marginal social benefits*. The downward-sloping green *MSB* curve shows marginal social benefit for any quantity demanded. For any quantity of educational services, marginal social benefit is $3000 higher per 100 student-years than the *marginal private benefit*.

Supply   Supply curves can be read two ways — as a marginal cost curve and as a supply curve. The *Marginal Private Cost* (*MC*) column shows the costs the schools actually pay for instructors, buildings, computer systems, energy, and other inputs for each additional 100 students per year. Marginal costs increase as output increases. The upward-sloping marginal private cost curve graphs these numbers.

You can also read columns 4 and 5 as a supply curve. *Marginal private cost* is the minimum price the schools will accept to supply that additional quantity — price must cover all marginal opportunity costs of production. As the price rises, the quantity supplied increases. The *marginal private cost* curve is also a supply curve, hence the label Supply = *MC*.

The *Marginal Social Cost* (*MSC*) column is the same as marginal private cost because there are no negative externalities. So the upward-sloping blue curve in Figure 3 has three identities — it is a marginal private cost curve, a supply curve, and a marginal social cost curve. Hence the label Supply = *MC* = *MSC*.

Putting It All Together   Figure 3 on the previous page tells the story, both in numbers and graphs, of what the market outcome will be, and what the smart social choice should be. Let's focus on the story in the graph.

For the private decisions of students and schools, the market outcome is at the intersection of the *marginal private benefit* curve and the *marginal private cost* curve. Educational services sell for $5000 per year and 300 student-years are sold and bought. These numbers are highlighted in red.

The smart social choice is at the intersection of the *marginal social benefit* curve and the *marginal social cost* curve. The smart social outcome has educational services selling for $6000 per year, and 500 student-years are sold and bought. These numbers are highlighted in green.

Understanding the Smart Social Choice   The rule for a smart social choice is to choose the quantity of output where marginal social cost equals marginal social benefit. The graph explains why this rule works. For any quantity of education services up to 500 student-years, marginal social benefit is greater than marginal social cost. For any quantity greater than that, marginal social benefit is less than marginal social cost.

Compared to the market outcome, the smart social choice is to produce more of products with positive externalities (500 student-years of education instead of the market's 300 student-years).

Inefficiency of Underproduction   For all output between 300 and 500 student-years of education, marginal social benefit is greater than the marginal social cost, yet the market does not produce those quantities. The grey **deadweight loss** triangle represents the loss in **total surplus** (consumer surplus plus producer surplus) compared to an efficient market outcome. The loss in efficiency from the underproduction of products and services with negative externalities is similar to Figure 11a on page 74.

Is There a Smart Social Price?   There is no equilibrium price that provides incentives to coordinate demand and supply for 500 student-years of output. To be willing to buy (demand) the smart social quantity of 500 student-years of education, students will pay only $3000 per year — the value of their marginal private benefits only, because students are not compensated for external benefits to others. But to supply the smart social quantity of 500 student-years, schools need to receive $6000 per student-year. Market failure occurs because externalities drive a wedge between individuals' smart choices and the smart choice for society as a whole.

Markets tend to underproduce products and services with positive externalities. The market-clearing price is too high for buyers to be willing to buy the socially best quantity of output, and too low for sellers to be willing to supply that socially best quantity. Neither buyers nor sellers are being paid for the external benefits their exchange creates. Can a government policy solve this problem?

 **Practice...**

16. Free riding occurs when there are
    a. positive externalities.
    b. negative externalities.
    c. horses.
    d. unicorns.

17. The production of too few products or services with positive externalities is an example of
    a. government failure.
    b. market failure.
    c. external costs.
    d. collusion.

18. Most people will *not* pay privately for security guards because the
    a. marginal social benefits are less than the marginal social cost.
    b. marginal private benefits are greater than the marginal social cost.
    c. marginal private benefits are less than the marginal private cost.
    d. marginal social benefits equal the marginal social cost.

19. Wealthy superstars hire private security guards because the
    a. marginal social benefits are less than the marginal social cost.
    b. marginal private benefits are greater than the marginal private cost.
    c. marginal private benefits are less than the marginal private cost.
    d. marginal social benefits are greater than the marginal social cost.

20. In a market economy, public goods are always
    a. publicly provided.
    b. underused.
    c. overproduced.
    d. underproduced.

 **Apply…**

10. Smart students often don't like group projects. Explain why, using the concept of free riding.

_____

_____

_____

_____

11. This graph shows an industry that produces a product with a positive externality.

    a. Label each of the 3 curves on the graph.

    b. On the graph, show the

    • point representing the market outcome and label it *MO*.

    • point representing the efficient social outcome and label it *ESO*.

    • amount of the external benefit per unit.

    • deadweight loss.

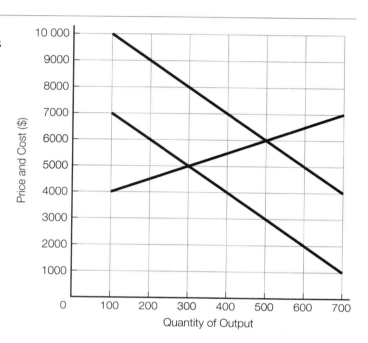

12. This table shows private and social costs and benefits of producing education in Hicksville. Use this information to answer the questions below.

Market for Education in Hicksville				
Quantity of Students	Marginal Private Benefit (*MB*)	Marginal Social Benefit (*MSB*)	Marginal Private Cost (*MC*)	Marginal Social Cost (*MSC*)
100	$500	$800	$200	$200
200	$400	$700	$250	$250
300	$300	$600	$300	$300
400	$200	$500	$350	$350
500	$100	$400	$400	$400
600	$0	$300	$450	$450

    a. What is the private market-clearing equilibrium quantity of students? What is the private market-clearing equilibrium price? Explain how you chose those numbers.

_____

_____

_____

Apply...

b. What is the socially best quantity of students? Explain how you chose that quantity.

_____

_____

_____

_____

Subsidies for the Public Good

LO5 Identify how government subsidies can internalize positive externalities to create smart social choices.

Markets fail when there are positive externalities. Prices do not reflect the external benefits associated with producing products and services we desire. Because of the free-rider problem, smart individual choices leave society with too few products and services with positive externalities. If there is a way to "internalize the (positive) externalities," everyone could end up better off.

Adam Smith's Vote for Government

Government has as much, if not more, of a role to play correcting market failures from positive externalities as from negative externalities. Adam Smith, the father of the invisible hand, recognized this back in 1776 when he explicitly gave government the responsibility for providing valuable public goods that markets would not supply. There is a reason why lighthouses are operated by governments. In Adam Smith's words, "the profit could never repay the expense" to a private supplier.

The key principle for government policy is to remove the wedge that positive externalities drive between prices for buyers and sellers, so that self-interested individuals and businesses choose the socially best outcomes. The two main policy tools to accomplish this are

- subsidies.
- public provision.

Subsidies

How can private individuals and businesses whose choices create positive externalities be compensated for the benefits that go to others outside the original exchange? Governments can do that, and internalize externalities, by granting **subsidies**, or payments, equal to the value of the positive externality. Subsidies are the opposite of taxes. Instead of government adding a cost on individuals or businesses equal to the damage done by their negative externalities, subsidies reward those whose choices create positive externalities for others.

External benefits are widely spread over many others, so government can act on behalf of all, taxing the general public to raise revenues to pay the subsidies to those whose actual choices generate positive externalities.

A smart subsidy equals the marginal external benefit — in our example, the savings to others associated with a student-year of education. The marginal external benefit is $3000 per student-year, so that is the subsidy. To get a smart social outcome, the government can pay the subsidy to either the demanders or suppliers.

Subsidy to Suppliers What happens when the government pays the subsidy to the schools? Figure 4 reproduces the numbers in Figure 3, with one change. The last column is now labelled *Marginal Private Cost – Subsidy*. This column lists the costs schools pay for each additional student-year of education *after subtracting the subsidy* received from the government. For each of the first 100 student-years, the schools pay $4000 in *marginal private costs* for inputs, but they now receive a payment of $3000. So the net *marginal private cost*, with the subsidy, is $1000. For all other quantities of output, the numbers in the last column equal the *marginal private cost* minus the subsidy of $3000 per student-year.

Figure 4   Post-Secondary Education Market with $3000 Subsidy to Schools

Demand			Supply		
Output (students/ year)	Marginal Private Benefit (*MB*)	Marginal Social Benefit (*MSB*)	Output (students/ year)	Marginal Private Cost (*MC*)	Marginal Private Cost – Subsidy
100	$7 000	$10 000	100	$4 000	$1 000
200	$6 000	$ 9 000	200	$4 500	$1 500
300	$5 000	$ 8 000	300	$5 000	$2 000
400	$4 000	$ 7 000	400	$5 500	$2 500
500	$3 000	$ 6 000	500	$6 000	$3 000
600	$2 000	$ 5 000	600	$6 500	$3 500
700	$1 000	$ 4 000	700	$7 000	$4 000

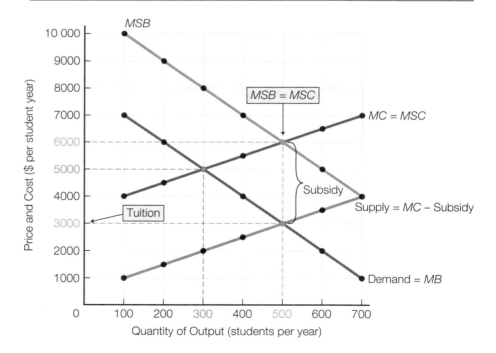

The new subsidy changes the rules of the game by affecting the private costs of schools. What does the subsidy do to the equilibrium output and price for the post-secondary education? Look at the graph in Figure 4. The only difference from Figure 3 is the new red supply curve labelled *MC – Subsidy*. Because subsidies to suppliers lower total input costs, there is an increase in supply. The vertical distance between the original supply curve (*MC*) and the new supply curve (*MC – Subsidy*) is the amount of the subsidy — $3000 per student-year of education.

This new supply curve, which takes marginal private costs and subtracts the subsidy, intersects the unchanged private demand curve (Demand = *MB*) at the efficient outcome of 500 student-years and a price of $3000 per student-year (in green). At the quantity of 500 student-years, the marginal social benefit is $6000 per student-year.

With the subsidy, both student-demanders and school-suppliers choose the socially efficient quantity of educational services. Students pay the $3000 price equal to their private benefits, and schools receive that $3000 plus the $3000 subsidy from government. That total of $6000 going to the schools covers their marginal opportunity costs.

Subsidies Remove the Wedge By paying the schools for the marginal external benefits, government subsidies get students and schools to voluntarily choose the socially best combination of output and price and the associated level of external benefits. The subsidies remove the wedge that positive externalities drive between prices for buyers and sellers, so that self-interested individuals and businesses choose the outcomes that are also best for society.

Paying subsidies to the students instead of the schools also achieves an efficient social outcome. See Apply question 13 at the end of this section.

Public Provision

Instead of paying subsidies to private suppliers or demanders, governments may choose to directly provide a product or service with positive externalities. Education from kindergarten to grade 12 falls into this category, as well as most public infrastructure like roads, bridges, streetlights, public transit, and lighthouses. Economists call this **public provision**. Governments provide these services when positive externalities are widespread and important for citizens, and/or when it is difficult to collect revenues from users.

With public provision, governments can run the business itself (most primary and secondary schools) or contract out the actual operations (hiring private contractors to build roads and bridges). Public provision is based on the same principle as subsidies — set policies that get everyone to voluntarily choose the quantity of output where *marginal social benefit equals marginal social cost*.

In Canada, post-secondary education is the responsibility of provincial governments, and there are almost no private institutions. College and university education services are funded by a combination of public provision and subsidies. Tuition covers less than 25 percent of the cost of delivering post-secondary education. Most costs are paid by government subsidies to colleges and universities because of the large positive externalities from post-secondary education.

Paying for Externalities Government pays for public provision using tax revenues. If the external benefits are widespread, as they are for education, governments may use general tax revenues or property tax revenues to finance public provision. In the case of roads, governments often use a tax on gasoline to finance construction and upkeep of city streets, on the principle that motorists benefit most from having good roads.

Liberating the Invisible Hand   When there are externalities — negative or positive — markets fail. Smart private choices (using Keys 1 and 2) are different from smart social choices (Keys 1, 2, and 3). Because private individuals or businesses don't pay for external costs and don't get paid for external benefits, they do not have incentives to make choices that are good for society, and the invisible hand fails to coordinate individual choices to balance social benefits with social costs.

Smart government policies that internalize the externality through taxes, emission controls, subsidies, and public provision are essential for liberating the invisible hand to allow markets to produce more of the "goods" we desire and fewer of the "bads."

 # Practice...

21. Smart subsidies for public goods equal the amount of the marginal

    a. msocial cost.

    b. social benefit.

    c. external benefit.

    d. external cost.

22. Seneca College offers free anti-virus software to all staff and students. This is an example of

    a. corporate generosity.

    b. irrational decision-making.

    c. bureaucratic inefficiency.

    d. public provision of a public good.

23. A subsidy to a private supplier of a product with a positive externality shifts the

    a. marginal private cost curve up by the amount of the subsidy.

    b. marginal private cost curve down by the amount of the subsidy.

    c. marginal private benefit curve up by the amount of the subsidy.

    d. marginal private benefit curve down by the amount of the subsidy.

24. Subsidies are

    a. the opposite of taxes.

    b. paid by governments.

    c. rewards for those creating positive externalities.

    d. all of the above.

25. The quantity of a public good produced by private markets

    a. is less than the efficient quantity.

    b. equals the efficient quantity.

    c. is greater than the efficient quantity.

    d. maximizes marginal external benefit.

 Apply...

13. What if the government gave the $3000 subsidy from Figure 4 on page 322 directly to students instead of to schools? Construct a table like Figure 3, and discover whether the students' private choices would still be the same as the smart choice for society. [*Hint*: The *Marginal Private Benefit* column shows willingness to pay. Create a new column showing willingness to pay with the subsidy (*Marginal Private Benefit + Subsidy*).]

Output (students/year)	Marginal Private Benefit (MB)	Marginal Private Benefit + Subsidy	Marginal Private Cost (MC)	Marginal Social Cost (MSC)
100				
200				
300				
400				
500				
600				
700				

14. This table shows private and social costs and benefits of producing an unknown product. Use this information to answer the questions below.

Quantity of Output	Marginal Private Benefit (MB)	Marginal Social Benefit (MSB)	Marginal Private Cost (MC)	Marginal Social Cost (MSC)
30	$600	$750	$150	$150
40	$500	$650	$200	$200
50	$400	$550	$250	$250
60	$300	$450	$300	$300
70	$200	$350	$350	$350
80	$100	$250	$400	$400
90	$ 0	$150	$450	$450

a. What is the market-clearing equilibrium quantity? What is the market-clearing equilibrium price? Explain how you chose those numbers.

b. What is the socially best quantity? Explain how you chose that quantity.

c. What kind of externality does this market have? What is the external benefit or cost per unit?

d. For the socially best quantity in **b**, what is the price consumers are willing to pay? What is the minimum price suppliers need to be willing to supply that quantity?

to be continued

Apply...

continued

15. Some European countries have free tuition for post-secondary education. If you were a member of parliament defending this policy (knowing that any money needed to provide "free" education had to be raised by new taxes), what arguments would you make? If you defended the Canadian system, where students must pay some tuition, what arguments would you make? Your instructor may use this question for a class discussion.

_____

_____

_____

_____

_____

_____

_____

_____

_____

_____

KNOW...

Learning Objectives

1. When **externalities** exist, prices don't reflect all social costs and benefits; markets fail to coordinate private smart choices with social smart choices. With **market failure**, markets produce too many products and services with negative externalities, and too few with positive externalities.

2. For an efficient market outcome when there are externalities, choose the quantity of output where **marginal social cost** equals **marginal social benefit**. When there are **negative externalities**, "efficient pollution" balances the additional environmental benefits of lower pollution with the additional opportunity costs of reduced living standards.

3. If polluters are forced by government to pay the marginal external costs of their pollution, this **internalizes the externalities** into private choices, creating smart social choices. Government can remedy market failure from externalities by creating social property rights to the environment, making polluting illegal, and penalizing polluters. **Emission taxes**, like **carbon taxes**, set the price of emissions, and the market adjusts the quantities. **A cap-and-trade system** sets allowable quantities for emissions, and the market adjusts the price.

4. With **positive externalities**, buyers and sellers are not paid for the external benefits their exchange creates. The market-clearing equilibrium price is too high for buyers to be willing to buy the socially best quantity of output, and too low for sellers to be willing to supply. Because of the **free-rider problem**, markets underproduce products and services with positive externalities. **Public goods** — which provide external benefits consumed simultaneously by everyone and no one can be excluded — are an extreme example of positive externalities.

5. When there are positive externalities, government **subsidies** can get everyone to voluntarily choose the socially best quantity of output where marginal social benefit equals marginal social cost. Another policy is **public provision** of products or services with positive externalities, financed by tax revenue.

Key Terms

cap-and-trade system: limits the quantity of emissions businesses can release into the environment

carbon tax: emissions tax on carbon-based fossil fuels

deadweight loss: decrease in total surplus compared to an economically efficient outcome

emissions tax: tax to pay for external costs of emissions

external benefits (positive externalities): benefits to society from your private choices that affect others, but that others do not pay you for

external costs (negative externalities): costs to society from your private choices that affect others, but that you do not pay

externalities: costs or benefits that affect others external to a choice or trade

free-rider problem: markets underproduce products and services with positive externalities

internalize the externality: transform external costs into costs the producer must pay privately to the government

marginal social benefit (*MSB*): marginal private benefit plus marginal external benefit

marginal social cost (*MSC*): marginal private cost plus marginal external cost

market failure: when markets produce outcomes that are inefficient or inequitable

negative externalities (external costs): costs to society from your private choices that affect others, but that you do not pay

positive externalities (external benefits): benefits to society from your private choices that affect others, but that others do not pay you for

property rights: legally enforceable guarantees of ownership of physical, financial, and intellectual property

public goods: provide external benefits consumed simultaneously by everyone; no one can be excluded

public provision: government provision of products or services with positive externalities, financed by tax revenue

subsidy: payment to those who create positive externalities

total surplus: consumer surplus plus producer surplus

Answers to Practice

1. **c** Markets underproduce services like vaccinations with positive externalities.

2. **d** Employers and governments do not have to pay you for their reduced costs. **a** and **b** are private benefits and costs from your choice.

3. **a** External cost that affects others not at the party, but that partygoers do not pay.

4. **b** Overproduction with a negative externality.

5. **d** Overuse and depletion of a free resource that no one can be excluded from because of missing property rights. East-coast fishery is an example.

6. **d** Opportunity costs of reduced living standards.

7. **c** Use rule for smart social choices.

8. **b** Use rule for smart social choices.

9. **a** Where MC intersects MB.

10. **b** At quantity of 90, reading up and over, MSC is 400 and MB is 200.

11. **b** General policy rule for achieving the socially best outcome.

12. **d** Private market outcome where MC (supply) intersects MB (demand). For a perfectly competitive business, price equals marginal cost. Price is less than marginal social cost.

13. **a** The higher price of energy may be harder to afford for consumers with lower incomes than higher incomes.

14. **c** Equal to the vertical distance between MC and MSC.

15. **d** Where MSC intersects MSB.

16. **a** Free riding causes markets to underproduce products and services with positive externalities.

17. **b** Markets fail to produce the socially best outcome when there are positive (or negative) externalities.

18. **c** Without much need for security, marginal private benefits are low.

19. **b** Security guards do not have negative externalities, so marginal private cost equals marginal social cost. For superstars, marginal private benefits are greater than marginal private (and social) costs.

20. **d** Governments can choose not to provide public goods.

21. **c** Smart subsidy internalizes the positive externality.

22. **d** Like vaccines, anti-virus software has positive externalities.

23. **b** See Figure 4 on page 322.

24. **d** Definition.

25. **a** Markets underproduce products and services with positive externalities.

13 Inputs, Incomes, and Inequality

LEARNING OBJECTIVES

L01 Describe four types of income and how they are determined in input markets.

L02 Explain the importance of marginal revenue product for labour income and for smart business hiring decisions.

L03 Explain how to calculate present value and how it informs smart capital investment choices.

L04 Describe economic rent, and explain its importance for determining land and superstar income.

L05 Explain the sources of poverty and describe trade-offs in policies to help the poor.

LEARN...

Whatever you want out of life — riches, love, adventure, to make the world a better place — economics, and the Three Keys to Smart Choices, will help you get it. But no matter how smart your choices, how much you earn largely determines whether you reach your material goals for life.

Markets provide the products and services we want to buy, as well as jobs and investment opportunities for us to earn money. In output markets, consumers are the demanders and businesses are the suppliers. This chapter shifts focus to input markets: markets for labour, capital, and other inputs used to produce outputs. In input markets, businesses are the demanders, and consumers (or households) are the suppliers. What you are worth, in a market economy, is what the market is willing to pay for your inputs. Your income depends on your inputs and productivity, and in this chapter you will learn what you can do to improve both.

Output markets can fail due to economies of scale, monopoly, or externalities. Input markets can also fail in different ways, resulting in poverty and inequality. Input markets for labour and capital can work well to coordinate smart choices of consumers and businesses, ensuring businesses have the inputs they need to produce the products and services consumers want. Adam Smith's invisible hand of competition applies to input markets too. But even when businesses get the inputs they need, the resulting distributions of income and wealth may not be equitable. Government policies can help remedy inequality and poverty, but even smart policies to help the poor have opportunity costs that should be evaluated.

Incomes Are Prices and Quantities in Input Markets

L01 Describe four types of income and how they are determined in input markets.

The circular flow of economic life (reproduced in Figure 1) appeared in Chapter 1 as the simplest "big picture" of how economists think about economic choices.

Figure 1   Circular Flow of Economic Life

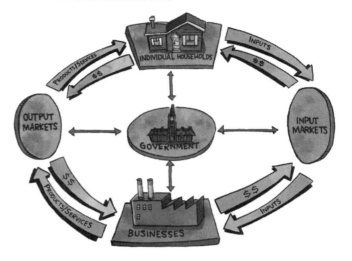

Finding Your Way Around the Circle

All the complexity of the economy is reduced to three sets of players — households, businesses, and governments. Households and businesses interact in two sets of markets — input markets (where businesses buy from households the inputs they need to produce products and services) and output markets (where businesses sell their products and services to households). Governments set the rules of the game and can choose to interact, or not, in almost any aspect of the economy. When markets work well, self-interest and the invisible hand of competition coordinate the smart choices of households and businesses in both sets of markets.

We now come back to the circular flow, but are switching sides to focus on input markets, where households are the sellers and businesses are the buyers.

Input Markets   Good models like Figure 1 focus on the most important information. Let's follow the circle, beginning at the top. Individuals in households sell or rent out their labour (ability to work), capital, land, and entrepreneurial abilities to businesses. In exchange, businesses pay households wages, interest, rent, and other money rewards. These exchanges, or trades, happen in input markets, where households are the sellers and businesses are the buyers.

Output Markets   Businesses use those inputs to produce products and services to sell to households. In exchange, households use the money they have earned in input markets to pay businesses for these purchases. These exchanges, or trades, happen in output markets, where households are the buyers and businesses are the sellers.

At the end of the trip around the circle, households have the products and services they need to live, and businesses end up with the money. That sets the stage for the next trip around the circle, where businesses again buy inputs from individuals in households, produce outputs that households buy — and the flow goes on.

Inputs and Income

What does this circular flow have to do with the income you earn? Everything! Incomes are determined by prices and quantities in input markets. Figure 2 summarizes the four types of inputs that households supply in input markets, and the forms of income that households receive from businesses for using those inputs. (**Inputs** are also called **factors of production**, and input markets are also called markets for factors of production.)

Labour   If you earn $15 per hour at Mr. Sub and work 20 hours per week, your income for the week is $300. To calculate income, you normally multiply the price you receive for your input times the quantity of the input that you sell. In the labour market, that price is the wage rate you receive, and the quantity is the number of hours you work.

Figure 2   Inputs and Incomes

Input	Income
Labour	Wages
Capital ($)	Interest
Land (and other resources)	Rent
Entrepreneurship	Profits (normal and economic profits)

Capital   If you loan $5000 for a year to a business (your own or someone else's), at an interest rate of 8 percent (0.08) per year, your income is $400 per year from the input market for capital. The interest rate is the price of capital (capital here means money for investment purposes) and the quantity is the number of dollars you loan. If instead you put that money in a savings account and earn interest, the total amount of interest earned is likewise income to you.

Land   If you own 10 hectares of land that you rent out to a farmer for $500 per hectare per month, your income is $5000 per month from the input market for land.

Income Is a Flow, Wealth Is a Stock

When we calculate income as price × quantity for whatever the input — labour, capital, land, or other resources — the resulting number is meaningful *only when there is a time dimension attached*. If someone tells you that her income is $50 000, what does that mean? It makes a big difference if it is $50 000 a year, or $50 000 a month, or $50 000 an hour! When a measurement — like income — makes sense only when there is a time dimension attached, economists call it a **flow**. A flow is measured as an *amount per unit of time*.

On the other hand, your wealth — the total value of all the assets you own — is a **stock**. It is an *amount at a moment in time* — like a photo. When you read reports about Bill Gates being the richest person in the world (estimated wealth in 2017 of $86 billion), the rankings are based on wealth, which is measured as an amount at a moment in time. Your wealth is the total value of all the things you own.

Income is what you earn; wealth is what you own.

One Concept for Each Income   We will talk more about income and wealth — and who earns and owns what — in the final section of this chapter. Before that, we will explore the most important concept determining each type of input's income — marginal revenue product for labour, present value for capital, and economic rent for land and other resources.

Entrepreneurs' Income Is Different

Entrepreneurs' income is the one type that does not fit the price × quantity formula. Individuals in households supply entrepreneurial talent or services to businesses (often their own). Those services, which involve the entrepreneur's time, are often accompanied by an investment of his or her own money too. The reward, or "payment," for this entrepreneurial input into production usually takes the form of *profits*.

Entrepreneurs are smart to offer their services only when they expect to make at least normal profits. **Normal profits** are what an entrepreneur could have earned in the best alternative use of his time and money.

But entrepreneurs are really after **economic profits**: profits over and above normal profits. What sets economic profits apart from all other types of income is that economic profits — the reward for innovation and risk-taking — are a residual. They are what is left over from revenues after all opportunity costs of production (including normal profits) have been paid for.

 # Practice...

1. Wealth differs from income because

    a. income is a stock; wealth is a flow.

    b. wealth is derived from income.

    c. income is what you earn; wealth is what you own.

    d. income is what you own; wealth is what you earn.

2. Which statement is *false*?

    a. Wealth is income received from supplying labour.

    b. Rent is income received from supplying land.

    c. Normal profits are income received from supplying entrepreneurial abilities.

    d. Interest is income received from supplying capital.

3. Economic profits are

    a. equal to revenue after taxes.

    b. equal to wages plus interest plus rent.

    c. equal to the owner's best alternative use of her time and money.

    d. the owner's residual claim on the income of the business.

4. Which statement measures a *flow*?

    a. Today there are 2 metres of snow on the ground.

    b. This week Joanne earned $400.

    c. Joanne has $5000 in her bank account.

    d. Joanne is almost 2 metres tall.

5. Input incomes are wages for labour, rent for land,

    a. normal profits for capital, and economic profits for entrepreneurship.

    b. interest for capital, and profits for entrepreneurship.

    c. profits for capital, and interest for money.

    d. dividends for capital, and interest for money.

 **Apply…**

1. Households and businesses interact in two sets of markets: input markets and output markets.

   a. Explain the difference in how households and businesses interact in the two markets.

   _____

   _____

   _____

   _____

   b. Give an example of each type of market interaction.

   _____

   _____

   _____

   _____

2. Incomes are determined in input markets.

   a. What is the general formula for calculating the income of labour, capital, or land inputs?

   _____

   _____

   _____

   _____

   b. How is entrepreneur's income different from other forms of income?
      What are the components of entrepreneur's income?

   _____

   _____

   _____

   _____

3. If you have $10 000 in a savings account, and no other assets, what is your income from capital
   if the interest rate is 8 percent per year? What is your wealth at the end of the first year?
   Which answers are flows, and which are stocks?

   _____

   _____

   _____

   _____

   _____

   _____

Labour and Marginal Revenue Product

 Explain the importance of marginal revenue product for labour income and for smart business hiring decisions.

Income depends on prices and quantities. But what do prices and quantities depend on? The answer here is the same as it was in Chapter 3. Prices (and quantities) come from the interaction of demand and supply. But now we are looking at demand and supply in input markets instead of output markets. Businesses are now the demanders, and households are the suppliers. The resulting prices and quantities determine the income of that input.

Back to the Future of Wahid's Web Wonders Business

Labour markets are the most important input markets. The prices are wage rates, and the quantities tell us how many people are employed. There is a different labour market with its own wage rate and quantity of labour employed for each type of labour — markets for retail sales, construction, accountants, auto mechanics, chefs, and so on.

Let's look at the labour market for web designers, and go back to the Chapter 7 example of Wahid's Web Wonders. Wahid's business is booming, and he needs to hire additional web designers to increase his output of webpages. As long as he keeps his webpage prices competitive, there seems to be no limit to how much he can expand his output and sales. How many new designers should he hire? To answer that question, for Wahid or any business, we need to know more about supply and demand in labour markets.

Show Me the Money (Again): Supply of Labour

In an Apply question in Chapter 2, your boss calls you in a panic on Sunday night and wants you to work as many hours as possible in the week ahead. As she increases the wage she is willing to pay you from $15 per hour to double time to triple time, the number of hours you are willing to work increases. In general, a rise in price (the wage rate) increases quantity supplied — the **law of supply**.

Paying Increasing Marginal Opportunity Costs As you shift your time from alternative uses to work, the marginal cost of your time increases. You first give up the least valuable time, and continue giving up increasingly valuable time as the wage you are offered rises. The market wage is determined when supply decisions of all households are combined with demand decisions of all businesses in a labour market.

To hire any input, including labour, a business must pay a price that matches the best opportunity cost of the input owner. Wahid is competing with other design businesses to hire workers. So he must pay at least what other businesses are paying web designers. Suppose the usual market wage for web designers is $50 per hour.

Wahid knows what additional workers will cost, but what will they do for him?

Derived Demand for Labour

Businesses' demand for workers is not quite the same as consumers' demand for doughnuts. When you buy a tasty doughnut, you own it, you eat (consume) it, it's gone, and you are no longer hungry. When businesses buy labour, they don't own the labourer — that would be slavery. Businesses don't generally hire you because you taste good or look good (well, except for the modelling business). Businesses demand labour for the services the labourers provide. Workers help produce outputs that can be sold to earn revenues and (hopefully) profits for the business. The demand for labour is a **derived demand**, because businesses are not interested in the labour for its own sake (like a doughnut), but for the output and profits the business owner can derive from hiring labour.

Wahid is a demander, or buyer, in the labour market because he wants to employ web designers to produce webpages to sell to customers to earn revenues and profits. How does Wahid make a smart choice about the quantity of web designers to hire?

Smart Business Choices in Hiring Labour

The first two keys to smart choices are also key to Wahid's decision about hiring web designers.

1 CHOOSE ONLY WHEN ADDITIONAL BENEFITS ARE GREATER THAN ADDITIONAL OPPORTUNITY COSTS.

2 COUNT ONLY ADDITIONAL BENEFITS AND ADDITIONAL OPPORTUNITY COSTS.

Additional Costs and Additional Benefits

The cost, or supply-of-labour, side of the cost–benefit comparison is easy. What is the additional opportunity cost of a web designer to Wahid? It is the $50 per hour he must pay to attract a designer away from the designer's best alternative employment. The marginal cost of each additional designer is $50 per hour.

The *additional benefits* are derived from the additional output of webpages the designer can produce, and the revenues and profits from selling those additional webpages.

Figure 3 contains the information Wahid needs to decide how many web designers to hire. Column 1 lists the quantity of designers Wahid is considering hiring, from zero to five. In column 2, **marginal product** measures the additional *productivity* of this designer (labourer) — how much additional product (measured in webpages per hour) his or her work adds to output.

Figure 3   Labour Hiring Decision for Wahid's Web Wonders Business

Column			
1	2	3	4
Quantity of Labour (designers)	Marginal Product (MP) (additional webpages per hour)	Price (P_{output}) (per webpage)	Marginal Revenue Product ($MRP = MP \times P_{output}$) (additional revenue per designer hour)
0			
	6	$15	$90
1			
	5	$15	$75
2			
	4	$15	$60
3			
	3	$15	$45
4			
	2	$15	$30
5			

Diminishing Marginal Productivity The first designer has a marginal product of six webpages per hour, but subsequent designers each have lower marginal products. Economists call this **diminishing marginal productivity**, and it occurs in most businesses that have some fixed inputs. As you add more of a variable input to fixed inputs, the marginal product of the variable input eventually diminishes.

Wahid has limited office space, only one printer, and a part-time technical support person. Plus, there is only one Wahid to supervise all the designers. As the office starts to get more crowded, there are problems sharing the printer, designers have to wait longer for technical support for computer problems, and each receives less supervision. Each additional designer stresses the sharing of these fixed inputs a bit more, causing the decreasing marginal productivity.

Column 3 on the previous page lists the market price (always $15) that Wahid can sell each additional webpage for in the output market for web design services. Wahid's output market is close to perfect competition (Chapter 9), so he has little pricing power. That's the bad news. The good news as a small competitor is that Wahid can increase his output and sales without having to lower his $15 price per webpage. For Wahid's webpages, price equals marginal revenue.

Marginal Revenue Product Column 4 contains the most important concept for Wahid's smart hiring choice. **Marginal revenue product** is calculated by multiplying marginal product (column 2) times price of output (column 3). The first designer produces six additional webpages per hour, each selling for $15. Hiring that first designer adds $90 of revenue per hour. Just like marginal products, marginal revenue products diminish as Wahid's business adds more designers.

Rule for Profits for Hiring Inputs With the information about additional costs of hiring a web designer ($50 per hour), and additional benefits in the form of marginal revenue products, what is Wahid's smart choice? The simple rule for maximum profits is:

Hire additional inputs when
marginal revenue product is greater than marginal cost.

Figure 4 shows the numbers from Figure 3 in a graph. In Figure 4a, the marginal revenue product per hour for each designer is represented by a green (for revenue) bar, and the wage rate for each additional hour of designer labour is the red (for cost) line at $50 per hour.

Figure 4 Marginal Revenue Product and the Hiring Decision

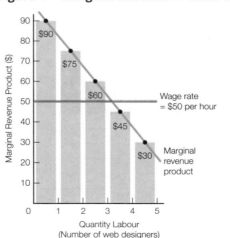

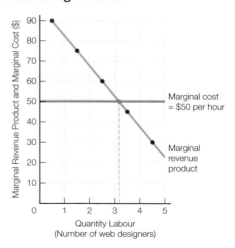

a) Marginal Revenue Product and the Wage Rate

b) Marginal Revenue Product Curve and Marginal Cost Curve

Use Figure 4a to evaluate Wahid's choices, designer by designer. If he hires the first web designer, Wahid's revenues go up by $90 per hour, while his costs go up by only $50 per hour. This is clearly a smart choice that adds to profits, since additional revenues are greater than additional costs. Hiring the second and third web designers each adds more to revenues than to costs. But if Wahid hires a fourth or fifth designer, costs go up by more than revenues.

Figure 4b presents the same information about marginal revenue product and the wage, but graphed as a marginal revenue product curve and a marginal cost curve. Like all marginal values, marginal revenue product is plotted halfway between quantities of labour, because it measures the additional revenue per hour moving between designers. The downward slope of the green marginal revenue product curve is due to diminishing marginal productivity. Because each additional designer costs the same $50 per hour, the marginal cost curve is the horizontal red line at the wage rate of $50 per hour.

Up to three designers, marginal revenue product is greater than marginal cost, adding to total profits. Beyond three designers, marginal cost is greater than marginal revenue product, reducing total profits. Not smart. Wahid should hire three designers.

Marginal Productivity and Income

Your boss wants you (your labour) for your productivity, and there is a close connection between how much you are paid in wages and what you contribute to the productivity, revenues, and profits of your employer — your marginal revenue productivity.

 # Practice…

6. The additional benefits from hiring an additional web designer are derived from the additional

   a. output of webpages she produces.

   b. revenues from selling her additional webpages.

   c. profits from selling her additional webpages.

   d. all of the above.

7. Marginal revenue product equals price of output

   a. divided by marginal product.

   b. minus marginal product.

   c. multiplied by marginal product.

   d. plus marginal product.

8. Germaine is paid $40 an hour. Her hourly marginal product is 20 units of output. The business must sell output at a price per unit that is at least

   a. $2.

   b. $40.

   c. $80.

   d. $800

9. The demand for labour is a

   a. determined demand.

   b. desperate demand.

   c. derived demand.

   d. kinked demand.

10. A profit-maximizing business hires labour in a competitive labour market. If the marginal revenue product of labour is greater than the wage rate, the business should

    a. decrease the quantity of labour hired.

    b. increase the quantity of labour hired.

    c. decrease the wage rate.

    d. increase the wage rate.

Apply...

4. Suppose Susur Lee, the world-famous Canadian chef, is trying to determine how many assistant cooks to hire.

   a. Use the cliché "too many cooks in the kitchen" to describe the concept of diminishing marginal revenue product.

   _____

   _____

   _____

   _____

   b. The table below describes the number of meals the restaurant could produce per hour, depending on how many cooks are hired. The price of a meal at the restaurant is $20. Because of his fame, Susur Lee can sell as many $20 meals as he chooses to produce. Fill in the 12 grey boxes.

Quantity Labour (cooks)	Total Quantity Output (meals/hour)	Marginal Product (MP) (additional meals/hour)	Total Revenue ($)	Marginal Revenue Product (MRP)
			Price of Meal = $20	
0	0		$ 0	
1	12			
2	22			
3	30			
4	38			

   c. Explain two different methods you could use to calculate marginal revenue products in the last column of the table.

   _____

   _____

   _____

   _____

   _____

   d. What is the general rule for a smart choice in hiring inputs to production? If the cost of a cook is $210 per hour, how many cooks should be hired? Explain how you got your answer.

   _____

   _____

   _____

   _____

   _____

 **Apply...**

5. Explain why the marginal revenue product of labour curve is the same as a business's demand curve for labour.

_____

_____

_____

_____

_____

_____

_____

6. In the example in Figure 3 on page 335, what happens to Wahid's hiring decision if the price for which he could sell webpages rises from $15 to $20 per page? Falls from $15 to $10? Explain your answers.

_____

_____

_____

_____

_____

_____

_____

Interest on Capital and Present Value

 Explain how to calculate present value and how it informs smart capital investment choices.

Most income depends on the wage or salary you earn for your labour, but I hope you will accumulate some savings to invest to also earn income in the form of interest. If you invest your "capital" of $5000 in a savings account that pays 4-percent interest per year, the calculation of your interest income uses the simple *price × quantity* formula, where the price of capital is the interest rate and the quantity is the number of dollars. At the end of the year, you earn $0.04 \times \$5000 = \$200$ in interest income.

Comparing the Present and Future

Most investment calculations are not so simple because the payoffs from today's investments extend far into the future. When businesses build new factories that last decades, or invest in expensive machine tools that improve productivity and output for years to come, how do they decide whether those are smart investment choices? If someone offers to sell you a small apartment building with six tenants who pay a total of $9000 in rent per month, how much should you pay today for that building?

These long-lived investments produce a stream of revenues over many years, yet the business or investor is faced with a single purchase price in the present. How do we apply Key 1 for smart choices, "Choose only when additional benefits are greater than additional opportunity costs," when the benefits are spread out over the future and the cost is in the present? How do you simplify that future stream of revenues to a single number today you can compare with the cost today to make a smart choice?

The key concept for that simplification is called **present value.** Let's work through some examples to help you to make sense of it.

> The present value of a future amount of money is the amount that,
> if invested today,
> will grow as large as the future amount, taking account of earned interest.

From Present to Future

Even if you don't yet understand the definition of present value, you can see that interest rates play an important role. One of the reasons present value is confusing is that it reverses the way we usually think about time, money, and interest rates. Present value uses interest rates to convert a future value of money to a value in the present — today. Usually, we think about an amount of money we have in the present — today — and how much it will be worth in the future after earning interest. Let's start with the more usual move from present to future.

Suppose you have $1000 today, and your bank is offering a special interest rate of 12 percent on savings accounts. How much will your $1000 be worth in the future, after one year? You calculate the interest you will earn, which is 0.12 × $1000 = $120. Add that interest to your original $1000 and you will have $1120 at the end of the year. That number, $1120, is the answer to the question, "What is the future value of $1000 in the present?" To calculate the future value of money today, we take account of earned interest.

From Future to Present

Now, let's answer the reverse question — "What is the present value of that future $1120?" You already know the answer from the example above! If the interest rate is 12 percent, the present value is $1000. The definition says:

The present value of a future amount of money ($1120) is the amount ($1000) that, if invested today, will grow as large as the future amount, taking account of earned interest ($120).

But what if you want to do a future-to-present calculation, and don't know the present-to-future numbers? There is a formula to calculate the present value of any future amount of money.

Suppose Wahid is thinking about buying a colour laser printer for producing sharper-looking printed reports for customers. The printer costs $1000 and wears out entirely after one year. During that time, Wahid estimates that, because of the beautiful-looking reports, customers will pay him an additional $1100 in revenues. This sounds like a good investment according to Key 1, since $1100 in additional revenues is greater than $1000 in additional costs.

But that comparison of revenues and costs does not account for the role of time and interest. If Wahid's bank offers the same 12-percent interest rate on savings accounts, then the printer investment does not look so good. If Wahid invested $1000 today in the savings account instead of the printer, at the end of the year he would have $1120 guaranteed (0.12 × $1000 = $120 in interest, added to the $1000) instead of his expected $1100 in additional revenues from the printer.

Implicit Costs   Key 3 comes back here, "Be sure to count all additional benefits and additional costs, including implicit costs and externalities," especially Chapter 7's *implicit costs of forgone interest*. The $1100 value for future income does not take into account implicit costs — the interest Wahid could have earned if he had saved the $1000 cost of the printer in the present and then collected the interest after a year.

IMPLICIT COSTS & EXTERNALITIES

Present value takes that interest into account, and allows us to reduce, or discount, Wahid's stream of future income into a number he can compare with the $1000 cost to see if buying the new printer is a smart choice.

Even though I haven't finished explaining present value, here is the formula for making the calculation that Wahid — and any investor — will use:

$$\text{Present Value} = \frac{\text{Amount of Money Available in } n \text{ Years}}{(1 + \text{Interest Rate})^n}$$

In the formula, n stands for the number of years the investment pays revenues. If a machine is expected to last 10 years, $n = 10$. This formula is scary looking but, for our simple example where $n = 1$, it is not so scary.

For Wahid's example, where $n = 1$ year and an interest rate of 12 percent (0.12), the formula becomes

$$\text{Present Value} = \frac{\$1100}{(1 + 0.12)} = \frac{\$1100}{1.12}$$

$$\text{Present Value} = \$982.14$$

This is the answer to the question, "What is the present value of $1100 in the future?" Going back to the definition of present value, $982.14 is the amount of money that, if invested today, will grow to be as large as $1100, taking account of earned interest.

So how does this tell us whether Wahid is making a smart investment choice? The modification of Keys 1, 2, and 3 for investment decisions comes down to this:

Invest when the present value of the stream of future earnings
is greater than the price of the investment.

For Wahid, the present value of $982.14 is *less than* the price of the investment ($1000), so it is not a smart choice. Wahid would make more money if he put his $1000 in the bank ($120 instead of $100).

What happens to the choice when the interest rate changes? If the interest rate falls to 5 percent (0.05), while everything else about the investment stays the same, the present value calculation becomes

$$\text{Present Value} = \frac{\$1100}{(1 + 0.05)} = \frac{\$1100}{1.05}$$

$$\text{Present Value} = \$1047.62$$

Now the present value of $1047.62 is *greater than* the price of the investment ($1000), so it becomes a smart choice. You can check the wisdom of this choice by calculating what Wahid would earn in the bank if he invested his $1000 for one year at 5-percent interest. This is the simpler present-to-future question: What is the future value of $1000 in the present? At the end of the year he would have $1050 from the bank, which is less than the $1100 he would have from investing in the laser colour printer. (To keep things simple, I am assuming Wahid believes there is a 100-percent probability he will get the $1100, so there is no need to add the complication of risk compensation.)

Intuition behind Present Value   Don't be concerned about other complications of the formula for investments with longer payoffs (when *n* is greater than 1), or uneven amounts of money available in different years. That's what accountants, calculators, and accounting software are for. Your instructor may give you explanations of the complicated present value forumula.

What is most important is the *idea* of present value that underlies all those calculations. Understanding present value calculations is essential for any business owner or investor. The intuition behind present value is that $1 in the future is not worth as much as $1 today because if you had the dollar invested today you could earn interest on it. That's why, to calculate the value today of a stream of future revenues, you can't simply add up those future revenues. They are not worth as much as the same sum today because they don't take into account the interest that you could have earned if you had invested that sum today.

Discounting   Accountants (and economists) would say you have to **discount** the future revenues to adjust for forgone interest. In the simple savings example, your revenues of $1120 at the end of the year in the bank are discounted to be worth only $1000 in the present, taking into account forgone interest. Wahid's revenues of $1100 next year from the printer are discounted to be worth only $982.14 in the present, taking into account forgone interest.

The concept of present value gives you, and any investor, a method to simplify the future stream of revenues from an investment to a single number today. Present value converts a flow of future revenues into a stock concept, into a value at a moment in time — today — that you can compare with cost today to make a smart choice. And, to repeat, the recipe for a smart investment choice is:

Invest when the present value of the stream of future earnings
is greater than the price of the investment.

 Practice…

11. An investment choice is smart when the
    a. future stream of revenues is greater than the price of the investment.
    b. future stream of revenues is less than the price of the investment.
    c. present value of the future stream of revenues is greater than the price of the investment.
    d. present value of the future stream of revenues is less than the price of the investment.

12. When interest rates fall, the
    a. present value of future money increases.
    b. present value of future money decreases.
    c. future value of money today increases.
    d. future value of money today is unchanged.

13. The present value of a future amount of money is
    a. a stock concept.
    b. less than the future amount because future revenues are discounted to adjust for forgone interest.
    c. the amount that, if invested today, will grow as large as the future amount, taking account of earned interest.
    d. all of the above.

Practice...

14. The interest rate is 20 percent. $100 invested today for one year has a future value of
    a. $5.
    b. $20.
    c. $120.
    d. $200.

15. When the interest rate is 20 percent, $60 paid at the end of the year has a present value of
    a. $72.
    b. $50.
    c. $12.
    d. $5.

Apply...

7. What is the comparison problem that the concept of present value helps solve?

_____

_____

_____

_____

8. A man named Alberto, dressed in a pin-striped suit and wearing Dolce & Gabbana sunglasses, shows up at Wahid's Web Wonders office and makes the following business proposition:

"I've got the best webpage development software on the market. It's guaranteed to boost your revenues by $3000 by the end of the year. I'll lease it to you for the year for $2800, cash up front."

What is the present value of the investment if the interest rate is 10 percent? Is it a smart investment? Why or why not?

_____

_____

_____

_____

_____

9. Suppose someone offers you a bond that will pay you $2000 at the end of a year. If the interest rate is 7 percent (0.07), what is the most you would be willing to pay for the bond today? Why?

_____

_____

_____

_____

_____

_____

Land, Economic Rent, and Superstars

 Describe economic rent, and explain its importance for determining land and superstar income.

What does the rent you pay your landlord have in common with Sidney Crosby's (the hockey superstar) income? More than you think.

Economic Rent

Economists have a concept called **economic rent**, which is a form of income that is paid to any input in relatively inelastic supply. Elasticity is about responsiveness, and inelastic supply means that the quantity supplied is *un*responsive to a rise in price. As the price rises, the quantity supplied hardly increases at all.

Land is a classic example of an input in inelastic supply. Consider a block of land at the corner of Burrard and Alberni streets in downtown Vancouver. No matter how high rents go for that piece of land, it won't cause more land to grow at that corner. The retail shops on this block pay very high rents to the landowners, and the shops also charge very high prices for the products and services they sell to the consumers who shop in this neighbourhood.

How do we explain these high prices — both the high rents paid to landlords and the high prices of products and services sold in the shops? The usual answer for an economist is that prices (and quantities) come from the interaction of demand and supply. For inputs like land in inelastic supply, the answer is different — prices are effectively determined by demand only.

For most outputs and inputs, the law of supply applies. A rise in price increases quantity supplied. If the price rises high enough to generate economic profits, more businesses enter the industry (increase in supply), and price falls until businesses just earn normal profits. The invisible hand adjusts quantities so that demand and supply balance, and the market provides the products and services we value most along with the inputs necessary to produce those outputs.

With land and other inputs in inelastic supply, there is no supply response. If demand increases, the input price rises but there is no increase in quantity supplied. Even with economic profits, there can be no increase in supply. If demand for the input decreases, the input price falls but there is no decrease in quantity supplied. Lack of responsiveness does strange things to the relationship between high rents and high prices for products and services sold in the high-rent shops.

High Input Prices Cause High Output Prices   For most products and services, high input prices cause high output prices. If businesses have to pay higher prices for inputs like energy or labour or raw materials, they usually pass on those higher costs to consumers in the form of higher output prices. If I asked you to explain the high prices of products and services in the shops in downtown Vancouver, you, and most people, would probably say, "The high prices for products and services are caused by the high rents the shopkeepers have to pay to landlords." But you would be dead wrong.

High Output Prices Cause High Input Prices   When an input like land is in inelastic supply, it goes to the highest bidder (demander). Why would shopkeepers be willing to pay such high rents, when they know cheaper rents are available elsewhere in the city? They know that in real estate, the three most important factors are location, location, and location. A good location generates high customer traffic, and this location brings in many high-income, free-spending customers. Smart shopkeepers know they can charge these customers high prices for products and services, so the shopkeepers bid up the rents.

For inputs like land in inelastic supply, high output prices cause high input prices (economic rents). The shopkeepers have to earn normal profits, or they wouldn't continue at that location. But it is the landlords, the owners of the input in inelastic supply, who really do well. The price, or rent, paid for the land is not proportional to the productivity of land as an input, as is the case for labour. Rents are demand driven, determined by "what the market will bear." Owners of inelastically supplied inputs are like mini-monopolists with barriers to entry. Their economic rents, like economic profits, stay high because no new competitors can enter. You can't build two buildings on one piece of land.

Is Sidney Crosby a Landlord?

What does this have to do with Sidney Crosby, and the income he and other superstars earn? Sidney Crosby, Cristiano Ronaldo, Taylor Swift, and landlords actually have much in common — they all own inputs that are in relatively inelastic supply.

When salaries go up for professional athletes and entertainers, there is a large, elastic response in the quantity supplied of people with average talent. But superstars have rare talent that is not easily reproduced. Fans will pay plenty to see superstars, but very little for average talent. That means much of superstars' income takes the form of economic rent, rather than wages paid for their marginal productivity. Superstars, like landlords, are like mini-monopolists with barriers to entry. Their talents go to the highest bidders, and their incomes are largely demand determined, just like the rent on land.

Are Superstar Salaries to Blame for High Ticket Prices?

In 2012, Sidney Crosby signed a 12-year, US$104.4-million contract with the Pittsburgh Penguins, earning an average of $8.7 million per year. He also has tens of millions of dollars in product endorsement income from Gatorade, Nike, and other companies. Fans love to complain about astronomical superstar incomes. Fans often believe that high player salaries are to blame for the high ticket prices that make NHL games unaffordable for your average fan.

But fans are making the same mistake you made if you explained high retail prices in trendy Vancouver shops as being caused by the high rents the shopkeepers have to pay landlords.

Why are NHL owners willing to bid against each other to sign Sidney Crosby and other superstars to high-priced contracts? The owners know that fans will pay a lot of money to see real talent on the ice, and those fans who can't afford to go to the games in person will flock to screens to watch. That means owners can sell the broadcast rights to the games for even more money. Fan willingness to pay so much to watch superstar hockey players causes high ticket prices; tickets are priced to "what the market will bear." In turn, high ticket prices (and broadcast revenues) are the reason why owners bid against each other and drive up superstar salaries.

The salary cap in the NHL is designed not to prevent players from being too greedy but to limit the bids owners could make for players, to ensure some of the economic rents earned by scarce superstars end up with the owners instead of the players. Since incomes of inputs in inelastic supply are entirely demand determined, the salary cap limits the demand by owners and thereby limits (believe it or not) superstar salaries, leaving more of the ticket and broadcast revenues for the owners.

Economic rent is an important concept for understanding not only incomes from land and real estate, but also incomes of superstars and the economics of industries like professional sports, music, and entertainment.

Practice...

16. Economic rent is

    a. paid only for the use of land.

    b. paid only for the use of capital.

    c. determined only by supply.

    d. income paid to any input in relatively inelastic supply.

17. Rents are determined by

    a. demand.

    b. input prices.

    c. the price of capital.

    d. all of the above.

18. For inputs in inelastic supply, such as land or superstar talent,

    a. there is no supply response to higher prices.

    b. the price paid for the input is *not* proportional to its productivity.

    c. input prices are explained by output prices.

    d. all of the above are true.

19. For inputs in elastic supply,

    a. there is no supply response to higher prices.

    b. the price paid for the input is *not* proportional to its productivity.

    c. input prices are explained by output prices.

    d. none of the above is true.

20. For most inputs other than land or superstars, input prices are

    a. determined by supply alone.

    b. determined by demand alone.

    c. determined by supply and demand.

    d. determined by output prices.

Apply...

10. For most products and services, what is the relationship between input prices and output prices? For inputs in inelastic supply, what is the relationship between input prices and output prices?

_____

_____

_____

_____

11. A rich but unknown restaurant owner wants to hire Susur Lee as a superstar chef at her new restaurant.

    a. If the owner is making a smart choice in hiring Susur Lee as an input for her restaurant, state and define the economic concept that determines how much she is willing to pay for Susur Lee's talented services.

    _____

    _____

    _____

    _____

    b. Explain the connections between input prices, output prices, and how much the restaurant owner is willing to pay Susur Lee.

    _____

    _____

    _____

    _____

12. Music groups usually go on tour to promote a new album. Given the availability of digital album downloads, what is the difference in the elasticity of supply of albums versus the elasticity of supply of concert performances? Where are (talented) musicians more likely to earn economic rents?

_____

_____

_____

_____

_____

_____

_____

Inequality and Poverty

 L05 Explain the sources of poverty and describe trade-offs in policies to help the poor.

In all your hopes and dreams about what you want out of life, do you ever dream of being poor? So why do over 3 million Canadians (almost 1 in 10 individuals) live in poverty in the midst of a market economy that supposedly does such a good job of efficiently providing the products and services we desire?

Connected through the circular flow, we all depend on markets to provide outputs supporting our standard of living, and to provide jobs and investment opportunities to earn money to buy those outputs. The income you earn depends on the quantities of inputs you own — labour, capital, land, and entrepreneurship — and the prices you can sell them for in input markets. Poverty results from those same quantities and prices — but from *not* owning enough of a labour skill or asset that the market values, or from *not* getting a high enough price for what you do own.

In this last section, we look at data on who is rich, who is poor, and how equally or unequally incomes and wealth are distributed among the population. We will briefly explain why incomes vary, what might be done to help the poor, and the trade-offs in so doing.

The interconnectedness of the circular flow is important in thinking about these questions. What you are worth depends on the prices the market places on what you own, which are derived from the prices the market places on the outputs that can be produced using your inputs. What you, or any human being, *should be* worth, and whether governments *should* help those who are poor, are normative questions that economics does not answer but that you must answer as a citizen evaluating policy choices or charitable commitments.

Measuring (In)Equality of Income and Wealth

Statistics Canada (www.statcan.gc.ca) collects data on all aspects of the Canadian economy, including income and wealth. The most recent comprehensive data were collected for 2016. These numbers, which are organized by households, not individuals, give an idea of how your household's income and wealth compare to that of other Canadian families.

Income   Figure 5 displays data for average household disposable income in 2016. **Disposable income** consists of income (after taxes and government transfer payments) from selling on markets the inputs we described — wages from labour, investment income from capital and other resources, and entrepreneurial income from self-employment.

Statistics Canada arranges all households in order, from lowest to highest earning, and then divides the population into five equal groups called quintiles. The lowest quintile is the 20 percent of all households earning the lowest incomes. The highest quintile is the 20 percent of all households earning the highest incomes.

Figure 5   Average 2016 Canadian Disposable Income, by Household Quintiles

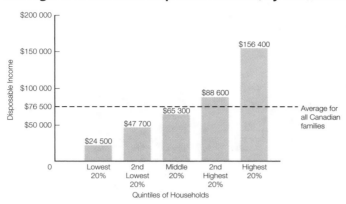

Source: Adapted from Statistics Canada, Table 378-0152

The average disposable income for all Canadian families in 2016 was $76 500. But that average comes from combining very different incomes. As you can see, average disposable income was only $24 500 for the poorest 20 percent of families, $65 300 for the middle 20 percent, and $156 400 for the richest 20 percent of families.

One way statisticians measure inequality is by calculating what percentage of total disposable income is earned by each quintile. When you add the percentages for all five quintiles, it sums to 100 percent. If income were distributed perfectly equally, each 20 percent of households would earn 20 percent of total disposable income. Figure 6 shows what those calculations look like for 2016.

Figure 6   Percentage of 2016 Total Canadian Disposable Income, by Household Quintiles

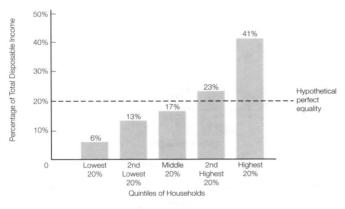

Source: Adapted from Statistics Canada, Table 378-0152

The poorest 20 percent of households earned 6 percent of total disposable income in Canada, the middle 20 percent earned 17 percent of total disposable income, and the richest 20 percent earned 41 percent of total disposable income.

Wealth   Income is what you *earn*, while wealth is what you *own*. **Wealth** is the net value of all your assets, minus any liabilities of what you owe (student loans, outstanding credit card balances, other debts).

After ranking households in order from lowest to highest wealth, Statistics Canada then divides the population into five equal quintiles. Figure 7 on the next page measures the percentage of total wealth in Canada owned by each quintile of Canadian households in 2016.

Figure 7   Average 2016 Canadian Wealth, by Household Quintiles

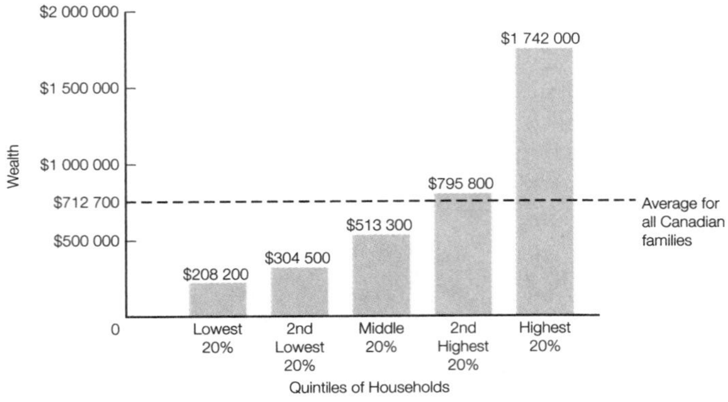

Source: Adapted from Statistics Canada, Table 378-0150

The average wealth for all Canadian households in 2016 was $712 700. But that average hides even greater differences than for disposable income. Average wealth was $208 800 for the poorest 20 percent of households, $513 300 for the middle 20 percent, and $1 742 000 for the richest 20 percent of households. The median wealth (50 percent of households had less, 50 percent of households had more) was $295 100, much lower than the average wealth.

Wealth inequality is also measured by calculating what percentage of total wealth is owned by each quintile. Figure 8 shows those calculations for 2016.

Figure 8   Percentage of 2016 Total Canadian Wealth, by Household Quintiles

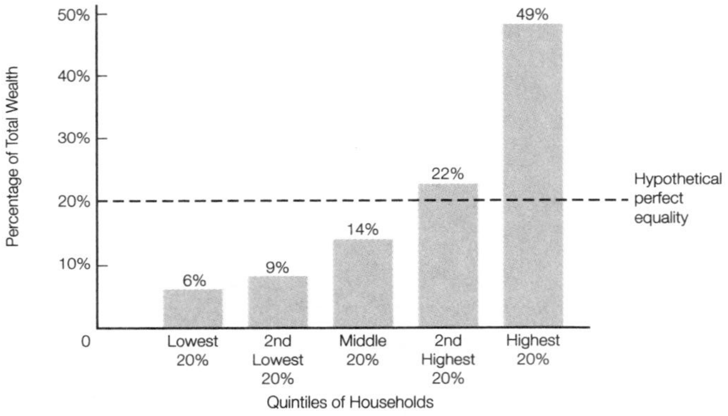

Source: Adapted from Statistics Canada, Table 378-0150

The poorest 20 percent of households owned 6 percent of total wealth in Canada, the middle 20 percent owned 14 percent of total wealth , and the richest 20 percent owned 49 percent of total wealth. Wealth is much more unequally distributed than income in Canada.

Other Wealth Issues   Besides these dramatic differences in quantities of wealth, there are also differences in the kinds of assets owned. Wealth owned by the bottom half of households consists largely of the value of their automobiles, and some savings. For the wealthy, assets consist largely of equities, bonds, real estate, life insurance, and pension plans.

There is also a connection between wealth and income. The capital and land assets you own as wealth also produce a flow of income in the form of interest, dividend, and rent payments. For households in the higher range of the income distribution of Figures 5 and 6, more of their income consists of investment income — making money from their money, thus increasing their wealth. For households in the lower ranges, most of their income consists of labour income.

Why Are You (Not) Rich?

Besides wealth, what accounts for inequalities in income? What factors are connected with being poor and being rich? Let's start by defining what it means to be poor in terms of income.

Poverty   The income and wealth data show dramatic differences between households but do not clearly identify who is poor. There are many different definitions of poverty, and poverty is a relative concept. Families considered poor in Canada would be considered extremely wealthy in many African or Asian countries, where millions survive on less than $1000 per year. Statistics Canada defines low-income families as those who spend at least one-fifth or more of their income than the average family on the basic necessities of food, shelter, and clothing.

In 2014, 3 million people in Canada lived below the poverty line, about 9 percent of the population. 8.5 percent of all children lived below the poverty line. Of those low-income individuals, 26 percent lived in a female single-parent family, while 13 percent lived in a male single-parent family.

There are many possible explanations for poverty that go beyond the scope of this book — discrimination, cultural factors, immigration adjustments, health and disability difficulties, to list just a few. We will focus only on the key economic factor that helps explain both lower and higher incomes — human capital.

Human Capital   Most Canadians' incomes come from employment, and the price you receive in the labour market depends on your productivity. Your productivity, your value to your boss, and your income all increase with your experience, your training, and your education. Economists use the term **human capital** to capture the increased earning potential individuals acquire through work experience, on-the-job training, and education.

What Can Be Done to Help the Poor?

What can be done to address inequality and poverty? Let's look at this positive question before confronting the normative question of whether governments *should* use tax revenues to help the poor and change the market distribution (before taxes and transfers) of income. If, as a society, we want to reduce inequality and poverty, two of the most powerful policy options are 1) education and training, and 2) a progressive system of taxes and transfers. Let's look at each.

Education and Training   Poverty means not having enough income. But lack of income is only a symptom of the underlying problem — a lack of inputs that the market values. Enhancing a person's human capital addresses this underlying problem. Government support for programs that increase human capital, whether through apprenticeships, training, or education, increase a person's ability to earn income and rise above poverty lines.

Education and training also have positive externalities (Chapter 11), with benefits to employers, governments, and citizens who are not directly involved in the programs that improve human capital. Education and training are win–win policies for the poor and for society as a whole.

Progressive Taxes and Transfers   Governments can also directly reduce poverty and inequality by using the tax system to implement Robin Hood's motto — take from the rich and give to the poor.

In principle, a tax system may be progressive, regressive, or proportional. Both the federal and provincial tax systems use **progressive taxes**, meaning that as your income increases, you pay a higher percentage in tax. With **regressive taxes**, as your income increases you pay a lower percentage in tax. **Proportional taxes** — often called **flat-rate taxes** — charge the same percentage regardless of your level of income.

Both the federal and provincial governments have progressive tax systems that take more from the rich than from the poor. While tax rates vary from province to province, the combined federal and provincial income tax rates look something like this. The poorest Canadians pay no income tax at all. The tax rate on additional dollars earned (the **marginal tax rate**; see the word *additional*?) is roughly 20 percent up to $45 000, 35 percent up to $90 000, and 45 percent over $145 000. That means, for example, for every dollar you earn between $45 000 and $90 000, the government takes 35 cents and you keep 65 cents.

The progressive income tax is combined with a system of **transfer payments** that redistribute the tax revenues to those toward the bottom of the income distribution. Transfers are like negative income taxes. The main types of transfers occur through welfare programs (Canada Child Tax Benefit, Canada Assistance Plan), social security programs for seniors (Old Age Security), and Employment Insurance (for the unemployed).

As a direct result of the progressive tax and transfer systems, the distribution of disposable income after transfers and taxes in Figures 5 and 6 is much more equal than the market distribution of income before taxes and transfers.

Incentive Effects of Redistribution   The redistribution of income from the rich to the poor is not as straightforward as it appears because of incentive effects and the interconnectedness of input and output markets through the circular flow. When governments take some of your income in taxes, leaving you less, it reduces the incentives you have to provide inputs and produce outputs. A market economy is based on the coordination of self-interest — and from a self-interest point of view, taking home 65 cents on the dollar is not as good as taking home all 100 cents. Because of incentive effects, taxes do not simply redistribute an unchanged quantity of products, services, and income. If taxes cause some individuals to supply less to the market because the rewards aren't as high (that's the law of supply), then input owners earn less and output markets will produce fewer products and services. To sum up the incentive effect in a phrase, "A more equally shared pie may result in a smaller pie."

Economists disagree about just how significant the incentive effect is, but unlike the largely win–win nature of education and training policies, this is a trade-off that must be considered when government is thinking about implementing tax and transfer policies.

What Should Be Done to Help the Poor?

There are policies for reducing poverty and inequality. But *should* governments use tax revenues for that purpose? This normative question is not as cold-hearted as it might sound. True, most religions throughout history have treated helping the poor as a moral obligation. Basic human compassion inclines us to help others in need, and the Golden Rule — do unto others as you would have them do unto you — even suggests an element of self-interest in charity. But every choice involves trade-offs. To know whether government policies to reduce poverty and inequality are smart choices, we must once again apply Key 1. Are additional benefits greater than additional costs?

Comparing costs and benefits is relatively easy for personal choices, where you alone pay the costs and reap the benefits. But policies to help the poor are different, as the costs and benefits apply to different people. How you feel about Robin Hood's motto depends considerably on whether you are being taken from or given to. And a personal choice to be charitable is different from a social choice by a government (even a democratically elected government) to implement a progressive tax and transfer system that takes from some to give to others.

One of the policy trade-offs that arises from the analogy "a more equally shared pie may result in a smaller pie" is the classic efficiency versus equity trade-off from Chapter 5. When we say markets are efficient in producing the products and services we value the most, with the least waste, we mean outputs go to those most *willing and able to pay*. An efficient market outcome may include people who are unable to pay for basic necessities like shelter or food or medical care. An efficient market outcome is not necessarily fair or equitable.

Suppose the incentive effect of a progressive tax and transfer policy is large, and a more equal income distribution and reduced poverty come at the expense of slightly lower standards of living for everyone else in Canada. What is the smart policy choice? Economics alone does not provide the answer. The answer, which will be different for different people, depends on the value you place personally on efficiency versus equity. If you value efficiency far more than equity, you may not be willing to sacrifice lower standards of living for all to benefit those who are most in need. If you value equity more than efficiency, the policies will seem desirable and the trade-offs acceptable.

What Is Equity?   These differing valuations of efficiency and equity are also combined with differing views about equity. You are not likely to hear abstract philosophical debates about the meaning of equity, but you will hear politicians opposing or supporting tax and transfer policies — and you have to decide for whom to vote.

The two most common definitions of equity (see Chapter 5 page 131) emphasize *equal opportunities* or *equal outcomes*.

A conservative politician on the right of the political spectrum might oppose progressive taxes and transfers because she believes the efficiency of markets is more important for generating the economic prosperity that will ultimately help the poor. She might also believe that markets are already equitable because they provide everyone with equal opportunities (and fully expects that each person's accomplishments in life and income will differ with differences in talents, initiative, and luck). From her perspective, inequality and poverty are the result of either personal choices, failures, or misfortunes. They are not systemic "market failures" that require government intervention to correct. Personal charity is a more appropriate response for personal misfortune.

A left-leaning politician might favour progressive taxes and transfers because he believes equal outcomes are more important than efficiency. He is concerned with improving the equality of incomes, and does not believe poor children have the same opportunities as rich children. Inherited wealth stacks the rules of the game in favour of children who are born into wealth, and he believes the misfortune (only from an income perspective) of being born into a family with a single, female parent should not condemn such children to a lifetime of poverty. He thinks all individuals are worthy of having the basic necessities, and takes issue with the market principle that what you are worth is simply what the market is willing to pay for the inputs you provide. From his perspective, poverty and inequality are market failures, failures of a market system that responsible, democratic governments should correct.

You cannot decide that one politician is right and the other is wrong just on the basis of facts, or by using the Three Keys to Smart Choices. What you can — and, as a citizen, must decide — is which politician's values best match your own.

Practice...

21. Human capital

    a. is equally distributed across individuals.

    b. allows people to be bought and sold like machines.

    c. is created by education.

    d. is illegal in Canada.

22. Economists believe that poverty is caused by

    a. stupidity.

    b. not owning marketable labour skills or assets.

    c. not knowing the right people.

    d. laziness.

23. Economists suggest that due to incentive effects, a more equally shared pie might be

    a. smaller.

    b. larger.

    c. apple.

    d. more efficient.

24. If the marginal tax rate increases as income increases, the income tax is

    a. progressive.

    b. proportional.

    c. negative.

    d. regressive.

25. What is the relationship between economic efficiency and economic equity?

    a. Income is equitably distributed in market economies without government action.

    b. More equality is generally more efficient.

    c. Redistribution of income reduces economic equality and increases economic efficiency.

    d. There is a trade-off between equality and efficiency.

 **Apply...**

13. Explain the differences between income and wealth.

   _____
   _____
   _____
   _____
   _____

14. What are the two main policy options for reducing poverty and inequality? What other policies can you think of to address other causes of poverty?

   _____
   _____
   _____
   _____
   _____
   _____
   _____
   _____

15. James Heckman is a Nobel Prize–winning economist who argues passionately that governments *should* pay for early childhood education (ECE). But his passion is more than a normative value judgment. Here is his argument.

   > "Traditionally, equity and efficiency are viewed as competing goals. . . .
   > What is remarkable is that there are some policies that both are fair —
   > i.e., promote equity — and promote economic efficiency. Investing in
   > the early years of disadvantaged children's lives is one such policy."

   Watch this video (https://tinyurl.com/Flextext-Heckman) or read this print article (https://tinyurl.com/Flextext-Heckmann-print). Your instructor may have a class discussion, identifying the details of Heckman's arguments, and debating the trade-off between efficiency and equity.

   _____
   _____
   _____
   _____
   _____
   _____

KNOW...

Learning Objectives

1. Incomes are determined by prices and quantities in **input** markets (markets for **factors of production**), where households supply to businesses labour, capital, and land in exchange for wages, interest, and rent. Entrepreneurial inputs seek **economic profits**, which are a different form of income — a residual after all opportunity costs of production (including **normal profits**) have been paid. Incomes are a **flow**, wealth is a **stock**.

2. For maximum profits, businesses hire additional labour when **marginal revenue product** is greater than marginal cost. Because of **diminishing marginal productivity**, a business's marginal revenue product curve is downward sloping, and also serves as its **derived demand** curve for labour. In competitive labour markets, the marginal cost of labour equals the wage rate.

3. **Present value** tells you what money earned in the future is worth today. Future revenues are **discounted** to adjust for forgone interest. Present value compares the price you pay for today's investment against the investment's future revenues. For a smart choice, the present value of the investment's future revenues is greater than the investment's price today.

4. **Economic rent** is income for any input in inelastic supply — for example land or superstar talent — that is determined by demand alone. For most products and services, high input prices cause high output prices. But for inputs in inelastic supply, high output prices cause high input prices.

5. Government policies to address the market's unequal distributions of income and wealth involve trade-offs between efficiency and equality. For economists, poverty stems from a lack of **human capital** — the increased earning potential individuals acquire through work experience, on-the-job training, and education. Policies to address inequality and poverty include education and training, and **progressive taxes** and **transfers**. There are unintended incentive effects from redistribution, so a more equally shared pie may result in a smaller pie, with a trade-off between equity and efficiency.

Key Terms

derived demand: demand for output and profits businesses can derive from hiring labour

diminishing marginal productivity: as you add more of a variable input to fixed inputs, the marginal product of the variable input eventually diminishes

discount: reduction of future revenues for forgone interest

disposable income: income after taxes and government transfer payments

economic profits: revenues minus all opportunity costs (explicit costs plus implicit costs)

economic rent: income paid to any input in relatively inelastic supply

factors of production: the inputs of labour, capital, land, and entrepreneurship

flat-rate (proportional) taxes: tax rate the same regardless of income

flow: amount per unit of time

human capital: increased earning potential from work experience, on-the-job training, education

inputs: productive resources — labour, natural resources, capital equipment, and entrepreneural ability — used to produce products and services

law of supply: if the price of a product or services rises, quantity supplied increases, other things remaining the same

marginal product: additional output from hiring one more unit of labour

marginal revenue product: additional revenue from selling output produced by additional labourer

marginal tax rate: rate on additional dollar of income

normal profits: compensation for business owner's time and money; sum of implicit costs; what business owner must earn to do as well as best alternative use of time and money; average profits in other industries

present value: amount that, if invested today, will grow as large as the future amount, taking account of earned interest

progressive taxes: tax rate increases as income increases

proportional (flat-rate) taxes: tax rate the same regardless of income

regressive taxes: tax rate decreases as income increases

stock: fixed amount at a moment in time

transfer payments: payments by government to households

wealth: net value of assets you own minus liabilities of what you owe

Answers to Practice

1. **c** Income is a flow, wealth is a stock.
2. **a** Wages are income from labour.
3. **d** Definition. **c** describes normal profits.
4. **b** Notice time dimension of $400 *per week*.
5. **b** See Figure 2 on page 331.
6. **d** All are related to marginal revenue product.
7. **c** Additional units of output multiplied by the price of output.
8. **a** Since *MC* = $40, *MRP* must be at least $40. 20 units × $2 per unit = $40.
9. **c** Demand for the output and profits businesses can derive from hiring labour.
10. **b** Continue hiring as long as *MRP* > wage rate. Business has no control over wage rate.

11. **c** Rule for smart investment choice.

12. **a** Interest rate is in denominator of present value formula.
When denominator gets smaller, value of formula gets larger.

13. **d** Definitions.

14. **c** $100 today plus $20 interest = future value of $120.

15. **b** $60 ÷ (1 + 0.2) = $50.

16. **d** Definition.

17. **a** Because supply is relatively inelastic and does not change.

18. **d** Income earned is a monopoly rent; not proportional to marginal
revenue product.

19. **d** Opposite of **a**, **b**, and **c** true for most inputs in elastic supply.

20. **c** For most inputs in elastic supply, input prices determine output prices,
and input prices change with changes in supply and in demand.

21. **c** Increased earning potential for work experience, on-the-job training,
and education.

22. **b** Poverty comes from a lack of inputs that the market values.

23. **a** If taxes cause input owners to supply less, then output markets produce
fewer products and services.

24. **a** Definition of progressive tax.

25. **d** Government taxes and transfers make income distribution more equal.
Opposite of **b** and **c** true.

Notes

Notes